5/16
always, over
very best,
Lisa!

Marilyn R. Dugler

Robert Alm

HANDBOOK OF RESEARCH ON ENTREPRENEURS' ENGAGEMENT IN PHILANTHROPY

Dedication

Spouses and families always forgo our time and attention when a book is going through its birthing throes. No less this volume. We thank especially our spouses:

Sandra (David Renz)
Barbara Phipps (Bob Strom)
Bob (Marilyn Taylor)

In the end, they are our personal entrepreneur philanthropists – putting up with us, supporting us, and cheering us on as we strive to make our contributions to our professional world.

Handbook of Research on Entrepreneurs' Engagement in Philanthropy

Edited by

Marilyn L. Taylor

Arvin Gottlieb/Missouri Chair in Strategic Management, Henry W. Bloch School of Management, University of Missouri – Kansas City, USA

Robert J. Strom

Director of Research, Ewing Marion Kauffman Foundation, USA

David O. Renz

Beth K. Smith/Missouri Chair in Nonprofit Leadership; Director, Midwest Center for Nonprofit Leadership, Henry W. Bloch School of Management, University of Missouri – Kansas City, USA

Edward Elgar
Cheltenham, UK • Northampton, MA, USA

Published by
Edward Elgar Publishing Limited
The Lypiatts
15 Lansdown Road
Cheltenham
Glos GL50 2JA
UK

Edward Elgar Publishing, Inc.
William Pratt House
9 Dewey Court
Northampton
Massachusetts 01060
USA

A catalogue record for this book
is available from the British Library

Library of Congress Control Number: 2014937190

This book is available electronically in the ElgarOnline.com
Business Subject Collection, E-ISBN 978 1 78347 101 0

ISBN 978 1 78347 100 3

Typeset by Servis Filmsetting Ltd, Stockport, Cheshire
Printed and bound in Great Britain by T.J. International Ltd, Padstow

Contents

Contributors

Peter M. Anyansi is currently the Director for the Center for Entrepreneurship Studies and the Dean of Student Affairs at Renaissance University, Nigeria. He serves as a lecturer in entrepreneurship development and organizational behavior. Mr Anyansi served as the founding National Director for Students in Free Enterprise (SIFE), Nigeria and escorted Nigerian National Champions to SIFE world competitions to such countries as Germany, Spain, France and Canada from 2002 to 2005. He operated his own business, Pete-Masi Enterprises, from 1980 to 2000. Mr Anyansi obtained his Diploma in Civil Engineering at the College of Technology (now Institute of Management and Technology Enugu) and an MSc in Business Administration from LaSalle University Louisiana, USA. He is a member of several university organizations and sits on the board of many non-governmental organizations in Nigeria.

Chi Anyansi-Archibong received her PhD in Strategic Management, with minors in International Management and Entrepreneurship, from the University of Kansas, USA. She is currently a professor at North Carolina A&T State University, USA. She is actively engaged in educational development programs at national and international levels. Dr Anyansi-Archibong is the author of four research and business case books; over 133 refereed journal and proceedings articles and cases; 15 grant proposals and reports; and numerous teaching materials such as 'experiential exercises' and skills development materials in both her discipline and related subject areas. She has appeared as invited speaker at national and international conferences and holds diverse leadership roles in professional organizations and the university. She is a reviewer for several text book publishers, professional organizations and journals. She also serves on several nonprofit organizations' boards.

David B. Audretsch is a Distinguished Professor and Ameritech Chair of Economic Development at Indiana University, USA, where he also serves as Director of the Institute for Development Strategies. He also is an Honorary Professor of Industrial Economics and Entrepreneurship at the WHU-Otto Beisheim School of Management in Germany. Additionally, he serves as an Honorary Professor at the Friedrich Schiller University of Jena, Germany, and is a Research Fellow of the Centre for Economic Policy Research, UK. Audretsch's research has focused on links between entrepreneurship, government policy, innovation, economic development and global competitiveness. His recent books include *Entrepreneurship and Economic Growth* (Oxford University Press, 2006), and *The Entrepreneurial Society* (Oxford University Press, 2007). He is co-founder and co-editor of *Small Business Economics: An Entrepreneurship Journal.* He was awarded the 2001 Global Award for Entrepreneurship Research by the Swedish Foundation for Small Business Research.

Xiaoming Bai is a doctoral candidate in human resource management, School of Business, Nanjing University, China. He works with Professor Shuming Zhao in the area of human resource management, entrepreneurship and leadership development. He has published a paper on labor conflicts management which was co-authored with Professor Zhao.

William J. Baumol is Professor Emeritus of Economics in the Stern School of Business at New York University, USA. He is also Senior Economist and Professor Emeritus in the Department of Economics at Princeton University, USA. Professor Baumol is a past President of the American Economic Association and is a member of the US National Academy of Sciences, the American Philosophical Society, the Accademia Nazionale Dei Lincei (Italy), and the British Academy. He is the author of more than 80 books and 500 articles published in professional journals.

Candida G. Brush is Professor of Entrepreneurship and Chair of the Entrepreneurship Division at Babson College, USA where she holds the Franklin W. Olin Chair in Entrepreneurship, and serves as Research Director of the Arthur M. Blank Center. She was awarded an honorary doctorate from Jonkoping University, Jonkoping, Sweden in 2010 and is a visiting adjunct at the University of Nordland, Norway. Brush is a founding member of the Diana Project International, and winner of the 2007 International Award for Entrepreneurship and Small Business Research, the foremost global award for entrepreneurship research, recognizing scholars who produce scientific work of outstanding quality and importance. Her research investigates growth-oriented women entrepreneurs, angel investing and strategies of emerging ventures. She has authored nine books, 120 journal articles and other publications. She serves as an editor for *Entrepreneurship Theory and Practice*, is an angel investor, and also a board member for several companies and organizations.

Emmett D. Carson is an internationally recognized thought leader in the field of philanthropy on issues of social justice, public accountability and African-American giving. As founding chief executive officer (CEO) of

Silicon Valley Community Foundation, he led the unprecedented merger that created the Foundation, an institution that is now over $3.5 billion. Dr Carson oversees its work to help families and corporations achieve their local, national and global philanthropic interests.

Nancy M. Carter leads Catalyst's groundbreaking research on issues related to women's advancement in business and the professions. Prior to joining Catalyst, she was Leverhulme Visiting Professor at the London Business School, UK. She has worked professionally in advertising and marketing research and collaborates with government and private sector initiatives promoting women's advancement. She has published widely on gender, strategy and entrepreneurship. Her most recent research reported in the *Harvard Business Review* tracks the career advancement of high-potential men and women around the world. She co-founded the Diana Project and with her colleagues is the recipient of the 2007 International Award for Entrepreneurship and Small Business Research, the foremost global award for entrepreneurship research, recognizing scholars who produce scientific work of outstanding quality and importance. Her research on women and minority entrepreneurs has been funded by the National Science Foundation (USA), US Small Business Administration, National Business Women's Council (USA), and Ewing Marion Kauffman Foundation.

Theresa T. Coates is an Assistant Professor of Business at Limestone College, USA. She teaches in the areas of strategy, entrepreneurship and new business development. Dr Coates has extensive consulting experience in several areas, in particular new venture planning for numerous large firms such as Analog Devices, GE Plastics and McGraw Hill. Her research areas include emerging technologies, competence development, virtual teams and innovation management. She has authored numerous business case studies and several articles on entrepreneurial and innovation strategy. Dr Coates completed her MBA at the University of Minnesota, USA and her doctorate at Rensselaer Polytechnic Institute, USA.

Vickie Cox Edmondson is Professor of Management at Morehouse College, USA. She served as the Executive Director for the Follow Me Foundation from 1998 to 2009. Dr Cox Edmondson received a BA from Spelman College, USA, an MBA from Mercer University, USA, and a PhD in strategic management from the University of Georgia, USA. Prior to joining Morehouse, she taught the strategic management course at the University of Alabama at Birmingham, USA for 15 years. Dr Cox Edmondson has written and co-authored academic and trade articles in the areas of strategic management, entrepreneurship, as well as articles about race and diversity issues in organizations, organizational change and employee voice.

Maryann P. Feldman is the Heninger Distinguished Professor in the Department of Public Policy at the University of North Carolina at Chapel Hill, USA. Her research and teaching interests focus on the areas of innovation, the commercialization of academic research and the factors that promote technological change and economic growth. A large part of Dr Feldman's work concerns the geography of innovation – investigating the reasons why innovation clusters spatially and the mechanisms that support and sustain industrial clusters. Her recent work explores emerging industries, entrepreneurship and the process of regional transformation. This was the topic of the edited book, *Cluster Genesis: The Origins of Technology-Based Economic Development*.

Elizabeth J. Gatewood is Associate Director of the Center for Enterprise Research and Education and directed Wake Forest University's Kauffman Campus Initiative, a program focused on multidisciplinary entrepreneurship education. In addition to directing academic entrepreneurship units at Wake Forest University, USA and Indiana University, USA, she directed the Small Business Development Center (SBDC) Network for southeast Texas, providing consulting and training to entrepreneurs and small and medium-sized enterprises (SMEs). She was the 2013 recipient of the Max S. Wortman, Jr Lifetime Achievement Award for Entrepreneurship by the United States Association of Small Business and Entrepreneurship. She has been Principal Investigator of grants from the National Science Foundation, Small Business Administration, Department of Commerce, Department of Defense, and other US institutions totaling over $30 million. She is a co-founder of the Diana Project, a multi-country network of researchers examining women's entrepreneurship, which won the International Award for Entrepreneurship and Small Business Research, the foremost global award for entrepreneurship research, recognizing scholars who produce scientific work of outstanding quality and importance. She serves on the board of Delta Apparel, Inc. (NYSE:DLA).

Alexandra Graddy-Reed is a doctoral student in the department of public policy at the University of North Carolina at Chapel Hill, USA. Her field is public economics and policy with research interests in philanthropy and nonprofits, innovation and economic development. Alex's current research is focused on the private provision of public goods through for-profit and nonprofit sources. She received her undergraduate degree in comparative public policy from Hendrix College, USA.

Patricia G. Greene is the Paul T. Babson Chair in Entrepreneurial Studies at Babson College, USA where her current assignment is to serve as the national academic director for the Goldman Sachs 10 000 Small Businesses initiative and advisor to the 10 000 Women program. As such, she is able to practice two of her favorite activities: designing entrepreneurship programs and educating entrepreneurship educators. Dr Greene is a founding member of the Diana Project, the 2007 winners of the SFS-NUTEK Award for work on women's entrepreneurship. Greene has also been recognized as a Top 100 Small Business Influencers by Small Business Trends and Smallbiztechnology.com, and as the 2012 recipient of the John E. Hughes Award for Entrepreneurial Advocacy from the US Association of Small Business and Entrepreneurship. She is a federal appointee to the national advisory board for the US Small Business Administration's Small Business Development Centers program.

Myra Hart is a founding member of the Diana Project and served as the MBA Class of 1961 Professor of Entrepreneurship at Harvard Business School, USA from 1995 to 2007. During her dozen years at HBS, Hart taught MBA, executive and alumni courses, co-chaired the Models of Success initiative, and directed two major case writing initiatives that introduced more women protagonists and broader definitions of success into the curriculum. She was twice awarded Harvard Business School's Greenhill Award for faculty leadership and also received the Apgar Award for innovative teaching and course development. Prior to joining Harvard in 1995, Hart was on the founding team of Staples the Office Superstore, serving as Vice-President of Growth and Development from launch through initial public offering (IPO). She currently serves on the board of directors of public companies and as an advisor to several entrepreneurial ventures.

Joshua R. Hinger is a graduate student at Indiana University, USA, where he is completing a dual master's degree program with the School of Public and Environmental Affairs (SPEA) and the Department of Central Eurasian Studies. He works closely with Distinguished Professor David Audretsch at the Institute of Development Strategies and SPEA's Overseas Education Program office. He is a three-time recipient of the Foreign Language Area Studies (FLAS) Fellowship, and SPEA's International Engagement Fellowship. His research focus is on links between entrepreneurship, economic development and taxation. In particular, he is interested in illicit entrepreneurship, government policy and economic development in the Central Asian context, as well as the role of linguistics in management and corporate governance. His most recent work includes a systematic literature review of the field of language in management to be presented at the Academy of Management, USA in 2014.

Rhonda Holman is Vice President Grants Administration at the Health Care Foundation of Greater Kansas City, USA. Previously she was a senior associate at the Ewing Marion Kauffman Foundation. She completed her MBA at Rockhurst University, USA and has continued advanced graduate studies in Public Administration Bloch School at the University of Missouri – Kansas City, USA. Her research interests focus on minority entrepreneurship and the community benefits fostered by minority-owned businesses and their owners.

Frank Hoy is the Paul R. Beswick Professor of Innovation & Entrepreneurship at Worcester Polytechnic Institute, USA where he also serves as Director of the Collaborative for Entrepreneurship and Innovation. He was Dean of the College of Business Administration at the University of Texas (UTEP), USA from 1991 to 2001 and founded and directed UTEP's Entrepreneurship Center. Previously he was the Carl R. Zwerner Professor of Family-Owned Businesses at Georgia State University, USA. Dr Hoy's research concentrations are family business, entrepreneurship and economic development, franchising, and technology entrepreneurship. He is a past editor of *Entrepreneurship Theory and Practice*. His most recently co-authored books are *Entrepreneurial Family Firms* (2010) and *Small Business Management* (2014). Hoy received the Max S. Wortman Lifetime Achievement Award from the United States Association for Small Business and Entrepreneurship in 2014. He received his PhD in Management from Texas A&M University, USA.

Kellie Liket is currently completing her Economics PhD in social impact measurement at the School of Economics, Rotterdam University, the Netherlands. She is affiliated with the Erasmus Centre for Strategic Philanthropy (ECSP). Her PhD thesis will be published in April 2014. After completing her BA in Economics and Psychology, she acquired a MSc in Business Psychology and Development Economics from the London School of Economics, UK. Her research has a dual focus: to assist mission-driven organizations in conducting complex and challenging social impact measurements, and to research the extent of the use and implications of information on impact flowing from these measurements on organizations and the philanthropic eco-system. She has published in numerous academic journals about nonprofit organizations and philanthropy, as well as about corporate social responsibility and corporate philanthropy. Her work has appeared in the *Journal of Business Ethics, Nonprofit and Voluntary Sector Quarterly* and the *American Journal of Evaluation*.

Lucas Meijs is Professor of Strategic Philanthropy at Rotterdam School of Management and the Erasmus Centre for Strategic Philanthropy, Erasmus

University, the Netherlands. His current research focuses on issues related to strategic philanthropy, volunteer and non-profit management, corporate community involvement, business–society partnerships, voluntary energy as a natural resource, re-embedding voluntary energy, student volunteering and involved learning (lifelong development by volunteering). He has published on this topic in a variety of nonprofit, business and public policy journals including the *Journal of Business Ethics, Nonprofit and Voluntary Sector Quarterly* and *Youth and Society*. Professor Meijs teaches a strategic philanthropy and nonprofit management course at the master's level, as well as a service learning course related to social entrepreneurship at the bachelor's level. Currently, he is one of the editors of the academic journal *Nonprofit and Voluntary Sector Quarterly*.

David O. Renz is the Beth K. Smith/Missouri Chair in Nonprofit Leadership and Director of the Midwest Center for Nonprofit Leadership in the Henry W. Bloch School of Management of the University of Missouri – Kansas City, USA. Dr Renz teaches and conducts research on nonprofit and public service leadership and, especially, governance and board effectiveness. He is especially interested in governance and management in socially entrepreneurial organizations. Dr Renz has worked with more than 120 boards, commissions and leadership networks in the past decade. He writes frequently for both the academic and practice communities and has produced more than 120 chapters, reports and articles for journals such as *Nonprofit Management and Leadership, Nonprofit Quarterly, Strategic Governance, Public Administration Review* and *Nonprofit and Voluntary Sector Quarterly*. He also is editor of the third edition of *The Jossey-Bass Handbook of Nonprofit Leadership and Management*. Dr Renz earned his PhD in Organization Studies at the University of Minnesota, USA.

Kirby Rosplock is a recognized researcher, innovator, advisor, author and speaker in the family business and family office realms. For the last decade, Dr Rosplock was director of research and development at GenSpring Family Offices. As the founder of Tamarind Partners, Inc., a research, advisory and consultancy practice that works with families, advisors and institutions connected to the family office market, Rosplock provides leading-edge insights and knowledge to the family office domain. She was the lead researcher on the Women & Wealth Study (2006), Men & Wealth Study (2007), Alignment Study (2008) and the Sustaining the Family Enterprise Study (2011). Dr Rosplock is editor of *A Thought Leader's Guide to Wealth* (2009) and author of *The Complete Family Office Handbook* (2014). She is a Fellow of the Family Firm Institute, board member of the FFI Practitioner, board member and owner of her family's fourth-generation business, and sits on numerous advisory boards including Family Enterprise USA.

Lonneke Roza is a research associate and PhD candidate at Rotterdam School of Management, the Netherlands, and affiliated with the Erasmus Centre for Strategic Philanthropy, Erasmus University, the Netherlands. Her main research areas are (corporate) philanthropy, volunteering, corporate social responsibility, corporate community involvement and nonprofit–business collaboration. After her bachelor's degree in Business Administration, she acquired a master's in Global Business and Stakeholder Management from Rotterdam School of Management. Her master's thesis topic focused on nonprofit–business collaboration, and more specifically on the effects of participation in corporate volunteering programs for the company and the participant. Her PhD project extends this interest and focusses on the program design of corporate volunteering programs for both companies as well as nonprofit organizations. She teaches, lectures and provides workshops on her topics of interest.

Paul G. Schervish is Professor of Sociology and Director of the Center on Wealth and Philanthropy at Boston College, USA. He served as Fulbright Professor of Philanthropy at University College, Cork, Ireland and was selected five times to the *NonProfit Times* 'Power and Influence Top 50'. He received the 2013 Distinguished Career Award from the Altruism, Morality, and Social Solidarity Section of the American Sociological Association. Schervish is the author of *Gospels of Wealth: How the Rich Portray Their Lives* and co-author with Keith Whitaker of *Wealth and the Will of God*. He is currently writing *Aristotle's Legacy: The Moral Biography of Wealth and the New Physics of Philanthropy*. With John Havens, he co-authored the 1998 report, *Millionaires and the Millennium*, which predicted the well-known $41 trillion wealth transfer. Findings from their 2012 revised model are reported in *The Golden Age of Philanthropy Still Beckons: National Wealth Transfer and Potential for Philanthropy*.

Leigh Stilwell is the first Chief of Donor Experience and Engagement at Silicon Valley Community Foundation, USA. In this role, she leads one of the world's largest and fastest-growing donor advisory programs serving individuals and families. Leigh oversees strategy, delivery and evaluation of world-class experiences, to inspire effective giving and connect donors with shared charitable interests living throughout the US and around the globe to leverage their philanthropy for greater impact. Leigh has extensive experience advising individuals and families of all sizes and ages on their giving, and serves on several boards, including the Bernard A. Newcomb Foundation, Good Ventures, the Dirk and Charlene Kabcenell Foundation and Startup:Education.

Robert J. Strom directs the Ewing Marion Kauffman Foundation's commissioned research, working with top scholars to advance knowledge in entrepreneurship. Prior to joining the Foundation, he was a visiting professor at the Henry W. Bloch School of Business at the University of Missouri – Kansas City, USA and vice president of the National Council on Economic Education. Strom also has been Assistant Vice-President for Public Affairs at the Federal Reserve Bank of Kansas City, President of the Missouri Council on Economic Education, a professor of economics at the University of Missouri at Columbia, and a member of the economics department at Miami University in Oxford, Ohio, all in the USA. Strom has written extensively on topics related to entrepreneurship in academic and professional publications. He is co-editor of three books on entrepreneurship and economic growth, and regularly speaks on entrepreneurship to professional and academic audiences. Strom holds a PhD in economics from the University of Cincinnati, USA.

Marilyn L. Taylor is Gottlieb-Missouri Chair in Strategic Management at the University of Missouri – Kansas City Henry W. Bloch School of Management, USA. Prior to joining UMKC, she taught at the University of Kansas (KU), USA. Dr Taylor has published numerous articles and cases as well as nine books, the most recent *Doing Case Study Research* (Sage Publications, forthcoming). Most of her cases focus on strategic issues. Her research is primarily qualitative and has most recently focused on entrepreneurs' philanthropy, the born global phenomenon, and social responsibility in China. At UMKC and KU and within academic professional associations she has served in multiple leadership roles. Taylor has been recognized for her research, teaching and mentoring, and leadership at the local, regional, national and international levels, most recently through Armenia's Center for Education, Policy Research and Economic Analysis (CEPREA) Alternative Scientific Council at Yerevan State University. She completed her MBA (with distinction) and DBA at Harvard Graduate School of Business Administration, USA.

John Tyler has been the General Counsel and Secretary for the Ewing Marion Kauffman Foundation, USA, since 1999. In that role, he operates across the spectrum and at the intersection of theory, law, strategy, execution and assessment in furthering the Foundation's core mission areas of entrepreneurship and education. Going beyond the law, John also contributes as a scholar who has published and spoken broadly on topics that include the role of foundations in society, the emerging hybrid forms, US policy regarding high-skilled immigration, and advancing university innovation. In the USA he also serves or has served on the boards of the Philanthropy Roundtable (secretary), the Philanthropic Collaborative (chair), Independent Sector's Public Policy Committee, the National Center on Philanthropy and the Law at NYU School of Law, School Board for the Diocese of Kansas City-St Joseph (president), Ronald McDonald House Charities of Greater Kansas City, and many others.

Marjelle Vermeulen has studied History of Society at the Erasmus School of History, Culture and Communication, Erasmus University, the Netherlands. During her studies, she focused mainly on the political and religious developments in early modern Europe. Currently Marjelle is a research associate at the Erasmus School of Economics (ESE). In addition, she is affiliated with the Erasmus Centre for Strategic Philanthropy (ECSP). At ESE and ECSP, Marjelle conducts research in the fields of impact measurement, corporate social responsibility and sustainability, in both the public and private sectors. She writes research reports and professional publications on her topics of interest for large (multinational) organizations and government agencies.

Shuming Zhao is Nanjing University Chair Professor and Honorary Dean of the School of Business, Nanjing University, China. He served as President of the International Association of Chinese Management Research (IACMR, Third Term) and President for Jiangsu Provincial Association of Human Resource Management. Professor Zhao is an internationally known scholar in human resource management and multinational business management. He was among the first group of scholars to introduce Western human resource management theory to China and has conducted several national studies funded by National Natural Sciences of China to advance the understanding of human resource management practices in Chinese firms. He has published more than 20 books and over 300 academic papers and articles. He received the Chancellor's Medallion from the University of Missouri-St Louis, USA in 2008 and the Management Excellency Award by Fudan Premium Fund of Management in 2010. He received a PhD in higher education and human resource management from Claremont Graduate University, USA in 1990.

Yixuan Zhao is a doctoral student in human resource management, School of Business, Nanjing University, China. She works with Professor Zhengtang Zhang in the area of human resource management, entrepreneurship and personal branding. She recently published a paper on 'A study of personal branding management and career planning for employees'.

Preface

This volume is devoted to the exploration of a heretofore mostly ignored phenomenon of entrepreneurs and their involvement in philanthropy. As editors we have the good fortune to work with an exceptional set of chapter authors who offer their multiple perspectives. We believe you will find, as we have, a delight in pursuing the various contributions and the insights they offer. Our purpose in pursuing this realm of investigation was twofold. One was to broaden and deepen our understanding of the phenomena. The second was to encourage additional systematic investigation into the phenomena. This volume both celebrates and seeks to understand the entrepreneurs' experiences, their motivations, and the dynamics of the intersection of their entrepreneurial ventures and their engagement in philanthropic activities.

Acknowledgements

As editors, we first of all want to thank the Ewing Marion Kauffman Foundation which sponsored the Fall 2013 Forum that brought the authors and manuscripts together. The Forum provided opportunity for the authors to share their multiple perspectives and research domains. It goes without saying that each of us appreciates the influence, either directly or indirectly, that Ewing Marion Kauffman has had on significant dimensions of our professional lives, initially through his company, Marion Labs, and beyond his lifetime through the investment he made in the Ewing Marion Kauffman Foundation.

We also wish to thank our support team. First, Jared Konczal, Senior Analyst in Research and Policy at the Ewing Marion Kauffman Foundation, brought considerable logistics and planning skills to the Forum. He, along with Michelle St Clair, Executive Assistant in Research and Policy at Kauffman, assured the success of the Forum. More recently Alyse Freilich's editorial skills have been a defining factor in bringing this volume to fruition. We also want to thank Alan Sturmer, Executive Editor at Edward Elgar Publishing, who saw the potential for our venture into this domain and has encouraged us in various ways to see the original vision come to fruition.

Marilyn L. Taylor, Robert J. Strom and David O. Renz

Introduction
Marilyn L. Taylor, Robert J. Strom and David O. Renz

This volume is about how and why entrepreneurs who drive success in the for-profit world become engaged in philanthropy. The topic is both simple and yet profound. It requires an understanding of entrepreneurs in their for-profit world and an understanding of the world of philanthropy. It entails an investigation into the motivations that drive entrepreneurs and philanthropists, and the social and political environments that are conducive to their success. In this brief introduction, we offer some preliminary thoughts on and definitions of entrepreneurship and philanthropy in an effort to establish the parameters of this volume, as both phenomena are difficult to define; definitions, in fact, are the subject of much debate in the scholarly literature for both domains. We also describe our independent interests in this topic and its relationship to previous work, as well as how we came together to collaborate on the project. We close with a brief overview of each of the four sections in the volume.

0.1 DEFINITIONS AND DISTINCTIONS

To date, there is relatively little academic research on the intersection of entrepreneurship and philanthropy: the journey by which entrepreneurs become engaged in philanthropy. There is an extensive body of historical research on the careers of wealthy industrialists and when and how they turned their attention to philanthropy, such as the philanthropic philosophies, behaviors and practices of wealthy business barons of the past such as Carnegie, Rockefeller, Ford and Morgan. And there is a significant and growing body of research on the philanthropy and giving patterns of the wealthy. But we differentiate the behaviors and practices of the successful entrepreneur from the larger world of the wealthy. In contrast to the wealthy who generate their wealth by investing in existing enterprises, the entrepreneur-philanthropists discussed in this volume are unique because they have generated their wealth through the creation and development of their own enterprises. As will become clear from many of the chapters of this book, this kind of experience and history are significant to the unique journeys of entrepreneurs as they become increasingly engaged in philanthropy.

This volume reflects a relatively early stage in the development of a new stream of research. At this stage in the development of a field, it is not unusual to see some significant variation and even lack of clarity in definitions. To some extent, this variation is reflected in the discussions of this *Handbook*. Given its exploratory nature, this project did not start with precise definitions, and our authors have had the latitude to employ their own definitions. Some have done so more explicitly than others. Thus, it is important to recognize the nuances implicit in the descriptions they offer. Chapter 12's author, Tyler, for example, offers a relatively general definition of entrepreneur: those who 'successfully started and/or grew a business and generated wealth for themselves and/or others'. Similarly, Schervish writes in Chapter 7 of entrepreneurs as 'self-made' people who start with modest means and achieve significant financial success. Somewhat distinctively, Zhao and his colleagues (Chapter 10) define the Chinese entrepreneurs they describe as 'founders and chairpersons of firms' who 'have a great deal of wealth and other resources and are, therefore, better equipped to take on social responsibility and promote its development in Chinese society as a whole'. This is relatively consistent with the orientation of Roza and her European colleagues. In Chapter 9 they describe the entrepreneurs they studied as so highly successful as to be, as described by Harvey et al. (2011: 428) 'world-makers'. In general, the entrepreneurs we describe in this volume are individuals who have successfully assembled the resources necessary to create for-profit organizations that have generated wealth for themselves, and probably also for others.

Of course, entrepreneurs do not cease to be entrepreneurs as they become more actively and fully engaged in philanthropy. In fact, as we try to understand the entrepreneur's journey as a philanthropist, it can be useful to consider the percentage of time the entrepreneur invests in accumulating their wealth versus the percentage of time that the entrepreneur invests in allocating their wealth through their philanthropy, and how this balance changes over time and with age.

When we describe philanthropy, we begin with a general and relatively straightforward definition such as that presented in the *Merriam-Webster Dictionary*: philanthropy is 'the practice of giving money and time to help make life better for other people' (*Merriam-Webster*, 2014). However, for all that has been researched and written about philanthropy (or perhaps because of it), those engaged in this research often define philanthropy differently and more carefully. It is increasingly common to differentiate philanthropy from charity. Charity, to many both in and out of academe, is defined as giving money and time to help others; whereas philanthropy often is defined as taking a more strategic and systemic approach toward giving money and time in a way that is designed and organized (and evaluated) to address systemic or root causes of societal ills and problems. This is not merely an academic distinction, however. As long ago as 1889, when Andrew Carnegie wrote to advocate that no man should die rich, he admonished the wealthy to be strategic and systematic in their giving lest they simply exacerbate the very problems they hope to resolve. As exemplified in many chapters of this volume, this perspective is explicitly embraced by many entrepreneurs as they decide how they wish to approach philanthropy.

For this reason, readers will find that many of the authors of the chapters in this book take care to distinguish one form of philanthropy from another, although it is important to recognize that different authors employ slightly different definitions. They explain that these label differences are important because they reflect differences among philanthropic entrepreneurs, differences in world-view and values that are integral to the paths and forms of philanthropy that these entrepreneurs are most highly motivated to pursue. Chapter 7 by Schervish, for example, discusses at length several forms of philanthropy, most of which fall in the category he describes as 'activist approaches'. Chapter 8 by Carson and Stilwell offers insights from their work with entrepreneurs that underscore the significance of the differences that Schervish describes. These entrepreneurs have less interest in (and some even have active disdain for) what many would consider traditional philanthropy, as they pursue the activist approaches such as venture philanthropy, entrepreneurial philanthropy, and more. While they sound similar, these labels reflect differences in the nature and degree of engagement of the entrepreneur-philanthropist. For example:

- Traditional or grant philanthropy usually refers to the approach characterized by the entrepreneur's investment of only financial capital, usually in the form of grants or financial gifts (Tyler refers to this approach as 'donative philanthropy' in his Chapter 12).
- Managerial philanthropy usually refers to the approach characterized by the entrepreneur's investment of only expertise or intellectual capital (and no money).
- Venture philanthropy usually refers to the approach characterized by the entrepreneur's investment of both financial and human capital (that is, the entrepreneur invests time advising the recipient organization on certain particular areas in which they have significant expertise).
- Entrepreneurial philanthropy usually refers to the approach characterized by the entrepreneur's investment of both financial and

human capital, including direct hands-on and even day-to-day work in the recipient organization.

Similarly but more broadly, Roza and colleagues, in their discussion of the European experience in Chapter 9, use the label 'philanthrepreneurs' to discuss the entrepreneurs of their research. Though unfamiliar, this label has been in some general use since November 2006, when *New York Times* reporter Stephanie Strom used the label to describe the philanthropic endeavors of what she considered a new generation of philanthropists, people such as Pierre Omidyar of eBay, Stephen Case of America Online, and Bill Gates of Microsoft. Interestingly, the people Strom highlighted in her article were not focused only on their non-profit or civil society endeavors, but she described some of them as 'driven to do good and have their profit too' (Strom, 2006).

Roza and colleagues draw on the recent work of Harvey et al. to define a philanthreprenuer as an entrepreneur who pursues big social objectives on a not-for-profit basis through active investment of their economic, cultural, social and symbolic resources (Harvey et al., 2011: 428). Noteworthy with regard to Harvey et al.'s definition is an emphasis on the role of these entrepreneurs as 'world-makers', highly successful entrepreneurs in business who 'want to extend their reach into the realm of the social as a means of personal aggrandizement' (ibid.: 432). It is not necessarily true that all of the philanthropic entrepreneurs discussed in this book are world-makers, although it no doubt is fair to say that essentially all have played defining roles in their fields and industries and, often, in their communities.

It also is important, from a definitional perspective, to take care to avoid assuming that behaviors described as philanthropic are entirely altruistic or focused on helping make life better for other people. This is particularly clear in Chapter 7, where Schervish further refines our understanding by differentiating the philanthropy of entrepreneurs into three general categories:

- Adoption philanthropy, which is philanthropic behavior intended to benefit others whom the philanthropist 'adopts' (such as support or scholarships for family members such as nieces or nephews; this includes practices that are not necessarily philanthropic in the legal sense, yet they benefit others).
- Consumption philanthropy, which is philanthropic behavior intended to accrue personal and family benefits while also benefiting others or the larger community (for example, support for museums, orchestras, and so on).

- Brokering philanthropy, which is philanthropic behavior intended to enable connections and linkages that have benefit to their networks (for example, support for higher education programs that build the capacity of the business community).

Schervish uses these categories to illustrate that the degree to which philanthropy benefits others can vary from entrepreneur to entrepreneur.

Given the young and interdisciplinary nature of this new and unique stream of inquiry, it is not surprising to find that there are so many variations in the ways we define and operationalize our terms and concepts. The authors of the chapters of this *Handbook* have made an effort to be clear in their definitions and explanations, and we encourage you to take care to recognize and appreciate the distinctions they make as you consider how their observations enrich our understanding of the phenomena they describe. We also encourage you to consider how their definitions and explanations help us more fully and effectively grow our understanding of this new field. There is much to be gained from the diversity and richness of their explanations as we continue to learn more about the many ways that entrepreneurs engage in philanthropy.

0.2 COLLABORATION

As scholars and researchers, each of us developed an academic interest in this intersection of philanthropy and entrepreneurship from different perspectives and disciplines. While we have diverse academic backgrounds, representing strategic management, economics, entrepreneurship and philanthropy, we discovered a common interest in the study of entrepreneurs' philanthropy. We found that although the popular press has paid significant attention to the philanthropic contributions that entrepreneurs make to society, there has been little academic work on this important dynamic.

Each of us, in fact, was influenced by the Ewing Marion Kauffman Foundation, a private foundation in Kansas City, Missouri created by Ewing Kauffman, a highly successful entrepreneur in the pharmaceutical industry. Marilyn Taylor first encountered Mr Kauffman early in her career when she was invited to develop a teaching case about a divestment decision within his company, a case that was known internally in the company as 'The Kalo Case' and externally as 'Marion Laboratories, Inc.'[1] This small start led to a long-term academic interest in the divestment process[2] and in Mr Kauffman's evolution from an entrepreneur who focused on creating jobs and wealth for himself and his 'associates' to a philanthropist with a profound desire to benefit his community.

Taylor's interest only deepened when she joined the Henry W. Bloch School of Management faculty at the University of Missouri – Kansas City (UMKC), USA in the mid-1990s. Also at UMKC, David Renz was pursuing a long-held academic interest in philanthropy and the management of non-profits from a public affairs and administration perspective. The two found a mutual interest in how entrepreneurs evolve and engage in philanthropy, and a particular interest in Ewing Kauffman and his impact on Kansas City in both his for-profit and non-profit work.

It was this interest that led both Taylor and Renz to collaborate with Robert Strom, an economist and Director of Research and Policy at the Kauffman Foundation. Strom had worked with UMKC for many years and was part of the large-scale effort at the Foundation to establish entrepreneurship as an academic field of study. His support for grants on research related to entrepreneurship from a variety of perspectives has led to a deeper understanding of the phenomenon and the growth of a body of work and field of scholars who continue to pursue the frontiers of knowledge in this domain.

While the three editors had long shared an interest in the topics in this volume, this specific collaboration and the stream of work that follows were inspired by two case studies series, one focusing on Ewing Kauffman and one on Mario Morino, both successful entrepreneurs whose philanthropic contributions on multiple fronts are well known. These successful entrepreneurs were passionate about giving back, both in their own lives and contributions and in urging other entrepreneurs to do the same. The comparison of the experiences of these two men appears in Chapter 13 in this volume, bringing closure to the body of work it inspired.

The work for this case study quickly revealed that there was, as yet, very little systematic investigation into entrepreneurs and their philanthropic engagements. There are, as discussed above, significant and expanding literatures on entrepreneurs, philanthropists and social entrepreneurs. But we wanted to understand the for-profit entrepreneur and varying perspectives on the entrepreneur's engagement in philanthropy. We found others with similar interests, and the possibility of collaboration to expand our understanding of the dynamics of the phenomena became real.

This volume includes academics from multiple disciplines and perspectives. Some have a long history of studying entrepreneurship and had not previously investigated the philanthropic interests of the entrepreneurs who had engaged their interests to that point. Similarly, other authors had long been focused on philanthropic efforts as expressed by non-governmental organizations (NGOs) and non-profits, but had not necessarily paid much systematic attention to the issues underlying entrepreneurship.

We were fortunate to have in our spheres colleagues who had investigated issues that were clearly related to the underlying dynamics of the topic we were interested in: entrepreneurs and how and why they engage in philanthropy. We deliberately excluded social entrepreneurs, not because they are not entrepreneurs, but because there is already a significant literature on this phenomenon. Our preference, rather, was to focus on for-profit entrepreneurs and the various aspects of why and how they emerge on philanthropic scenes.

With the encouragement of the Kauffman Foundation, this set of authors came together in the Fall of 2013 at a conference at the Kauffman Foundation that examined 'both sides of the coin'. As editors and authors we found commonalities and differences in our perspectives. The energy was palpable and the results exciting as we explored our diverse interests.

0.3 OVERVIEW OF THE SECTIONS AND CHAPTERS

The design of this book was both purposeful and emergent. We wanted to understand the phenomenon at a broad level, but also share the details of personal stories. We wanted to speak to the public interest and legal implications generally, but we also wanted to share multiple perspectives. Our main focus, because of the work each of the three of us has been engaged in throughout our careers, was in the United States.

We begin the volume with chapters that present a broad view of entrepreneurs who engage in philanthropy, discussing the meaning and social benefits of both entrepreneurship and philanthropy, considering the shared traits of the primary actors in these phenomena, suggesting policy guidelines to ensure that both phenomenon continue to flourish and advance our society, and discussing the potential impact of entrepreneurs who engage in philanthropy at the local level.

We knew, however, that the experiences of both entrepreneurship and philanthropy were similar and different across various subsets of our population. Part II of the volume offers a more narrow focus on different groups of entrepreneurs in philanthropy: women, Black Americans, multi-generation family companies, and high-tech entrepreneurs engaged in impact philanthropy. These chapters explore the particular motivations, strategies, challenges and experiences of these subgroups, with the last chapter in this part serving as a case study of high-tech entrepreneurs' philanthropic activity.

Part III extends an international perspective on the phenomenon, looking at the specific circumstances and social, historical, cultural and political underpinnings of entrepreneurs' philanthropic activity in different parts of the globe, from Europe and China to Africa and the US. Case studies in some of these chapters offer an understanding of particular entrepreneurs' journeys to philanthropy in different countries, and guidelines for policy reveal similarities and differences in the climates for entrepreneurship and philanthropy in different parts of the world.

In Part IV, a final chapter offers more in-depth case studies of two American entrepreneurs, considering the similarities and differences in their experiences, the challenges they faced, the influences that drove their behavior, and the strengths that enabled them to succeed in both realms.

We trust that this volume transmits the passion that we feel about the intersection of our domains around the focal issue for this volume. And we trust that you will find the authors' passion for the topic in the various chapters as they share their insights. If this volume generates a similar passion in you to research or practice in that dynamic intersection between the world of the entrepreneur and the world of philanthropy, we will have achieved our purpose.

NOTES

1. See Taylor (1982).
2. This interest led, ultimately, to the publication of *Divesting Business Units* in 1988. See Taylor (1988).

REFERENCES

Harvey, C., M. Maclean, J. Gordon and E. Shaw (2011), 'Andrew Carnegie and the foundations of contemporary entrepreneurial philanthropy', *Business History*, 53(3), 425–450.
Merriam-Webster Dictionary Online (2014), 'Philanthropy', available at http:/www.Merriam-webster.com/dictionary/philanthropy (accessed 15 January 2014).
Strom, S. (2006), 'What's wrong with profit?', *New York Times*, November 13.
Taylor, Marilyn (1982), 'Marion Laboratories, Inc.', *Case Research Journal*, II, 105–130.
Taylor, Marilyn L. (1988), *Divesting Business Units: Making the Decision and Making it Work*, Lexington, MA: Lexington Books/D.C. Heath & Company.

PART I

OVERALL PERSPECTIVES

We open our discussion of the entrepreneur's engagement in philanthropy with a critical examination of its foundational elements and broad achievements: the definitions of entrepreneurship and philanthropy, the shared characteristics of their primary actors, the implications of policy for their development and ongoing success, and the impact that entrepreneur-philanthropists can achieve. The chapters in this section address this intersection of entrepreneurship and philanthropy at a broad level, presenting these foundational concepts, reviewing historical developments, suggesting policy guidelines for the future, and illustrating the potential impact of entrepreneurs who engage in philanthropy.

Baumol and Strom's Chapter 1, 'Entrepreneurship and philanthropy: protecting the public interest', opens the volume with a discussion of the benefits of American entrepreneurs' freedom to choose the causes they support, as well as the potential problems in corporate philanthropic practices for both companies and society as a whole. This chapter also explores the policy implications of these ideas, including the role of US law and regulations in facilitating philanthropy and the need to encourage companies with positive spillover effects and limit companies' negative spillover effects.

Audretsch and Hinger explore the shared characteristics between entrepreneurs and philanthropists in their Chapter 2, 'From entrepreneur to philanthropist: two sides of the same coin?' They review the scholarly literature on the personal traits and resources that are conducive to individuals becoming entrepreneurs and the distinct body of work on individual-specific traits that are conducive for engagement in philanthropy, discussing the similarities and differences in these findings. They find that many of the same characteristics, circumstances and resources that facilitate entrepreneurship are also conducive to philanthropy.

Feldman and Graddy-Reed close this overview with a discussion of the potential impact of entrepreneurs on their local communities in Chapter 3, 'Local champions: entrepreneurs' transition to philanthropy and the vibrancy of place'. Noting that entrepreneurs who benefit from local resources often contribute to their communities' growth and shape their future, the authors create a typology that explores the relative impact of entrepreneurs through their strategic business decisions, investments in the region and creation of philanthropic foundations that focus on the local community.

1. Entrepreneurship and philanthropy: protecting the public interest*
William J. Baumol and Robert J. Strom

1.1 INTRODUCTION

Entrepreneurs, like all other humans, come in various forms and with various inclinations. Those who are successful are apt to end up in control of prosperous business firms and personal fortunes. Historically, many of these wealthy business owners have been very generous, funding a wide range of social causes and cultural and artistic endeavors that have vastly improved the welfare of their communities. In this chapter, we consider the implications of entrepreneurs' philanthropy and the ways they 'give back' to the communities in which they find success, using both their firms' resources and their own. We begin with private philanthropy, discussing American entrepreneurs' personal giving and the diversity of funding that US laws facilitate. Going beyond the entrepreneur's private interests, we also address the corporate interest and the hazards of corporate philanthropy. Finally, we consider the public interest as we offer some thoughts on philanthropy and spillover costs and benefits, including a discussion of firms that offer social value beyond the creation of useful products and well-paying jobs, as well as productive companies whose actions damage the general welfare, as an incidental consequence of their pursuit of business goals.

1.2 THE ROLE OF PRIVATE SUPPORT: ENCOURAGING DIVERSE IDEAS AND APPROACHES

Philanthropic spending from private wealth accumulations has a long history throughout the world. In the Middle Ages, for example, wealthy kings and nobles provided funding for the construction of cathedrals that were deemed to benefit the souls of poorer inhabitants, as well as their own. This sort of spending reached a peak under the rule of the Medici in Florence, the Renaissance popes – some of whom incidentally (but hardly accidentally) came from that family, and other wealthy and powerful

11

Italians and Spaniards of that era. The ceiling of the Sistine Chapel and the Michelangelo sculptures that continue to amaze arguably are all products of this philanthropy.

Such private giving has continued, arguably peaking toward the end of the nineteenth century in the United States, when institutions like the public library system and the Metropolitan Opera were financed in this way by the entrepreneurs who were dubbed the 'robber barons'. Andrew Carnegie, a robber baron who made his fortune in steel, believed that tax laws should be changed to require the wealthy to spend their fortunes for the public good. Suggesting that the wealthy have a moral obligation to share their wealth with their communities, he famously wrote, 'The man who dies thus rich dies disgraced' (Carnegie, 1889). Some of the most prominent legacies of Carnegie's philanthropy are the 2509 libraries he founded in the late nineteenth and early twentieth centuries in the United States, the United Kingdom, Australia and New Zealand. More than half of these libraries were built in the United States, with 67 in New York City. Carnegie believed that libraries offer all individuals, and especially immigrants like him, the opportunity to become educated and achieve success.

The extraordinary US university system also was built, in good part, by support from such private sources. As part of his effort to spend his fortune, Carnegie also endowed a few technical schools in Pittsburgh that eventually became Carnegie Mellon University. Cornelius Vanderbilt, another robber baron who built his wealth in shipping and railroads, founded Vanderbilt University with a $1 million donation he made in 1873. Similarly, Duke University received substantial funding from the Duke family, starting with Washington Duke and continuing with his sons Benjamin and James, the university's most significant benefactor. James Duke acquired his wealth through his tobacco company and a power company he started with his brother, and he focused his philanthropy on the area served by the power company. Many other schools have similar histories, and private philanthropy continues to be an enormously important part of American universities' fundraising.

Carnegie was also behind the development of the private foundation. Carnegie and other wealthy entrepreneurs like John D. Rockefeller began to establish formal institutions to manage their charitable giving at the end of the nineteenth century. Charitable foundations became more common with the advent of the income tax in 1913 and the estate tax in 1917, which prompted affluent individuals to seek tax shelters to protect their wealth. Foundations proliferated as the United States economy grew following World War II, and the Tax Reform Act of 1969 ultimately shaped the private foundation as we know it today. These organizations, created and funded by wealthy individuals who desire to use their resources to enhance the general welfare, largely do not represent a set of particular political or economic orientations. Rather, they have funded institutions, such as public libraries, and beneficial research projects in the areas of health care, economics and education. The foundation has the virtue that its control can be given over to recognized specialists in the fields funded by the foundation, rather than being controlled by individual donors. Furthermore, it may outlive the donor, allowing for charitable giving in perpetuity. The result is that charitable donations can be dedicated to activities that serve the general welfare without the appearance of serving individual entrepreneurs' (or their corporations') special interests.

The Bill and Melinda Gates Foundation, currently the world's largest private foundation, serves as just one example of continuing personal philanthropic efforts today. The Foundation initially focused on bringing the Internet to public libraries and now supports a wide range of programs to control disease, help the world's poorest populations to raise their standards of living, and improve education throughout the world. In particular, the Foundation has devoted significant resources to efforts to combat malaria and develop an HIV vaccine. They are also working to develop affordable new technologies to improve sanitation in the developing world and help farmers in impoverished countries to access heartier seeds, better tools and farming practices. Within the United States, the Foundation focuses on education – from funding research on metrics that can be used successfully to assess teaching, to helping schools implement the Common Core State Standards.

While we appreciate and applaud these philanthropic efforts and the generous donations to socially beneficial causes made by enormously wealthy individuals in the past and the present, we must clarify that this discussion is not intended to advocate a further increase in economic inequality, nor should it be interpreted as a defense of current levels of inequality. As asserted in George Bernard Shaw's *Major Barbara*, we hold that poverty is indeed the greatest crime. But so long as some members of society continue to amass great islands of wealth and, consequently, great inequality remains an unstoppable reality, it is important to consider the potential public benefits that may accompany the situation. While these benefits can be achieved in ways other than recourse to private philanthropy, so long as the private funding option remains, surely full utilization of this source is desirable.

We suggest, in fact, that the very freedom entrepreneurs have to select the causes they support and to determine their level of support has enormous benefits for all of society. While United States tax laws and other institutions certainly have had and continue to have an impact on entrepreneurs' philanthropic decisions, there is, ultimately, no legal obligation for them to donate and there are no parameters for the causes an American entrepreneur can choose to support. After payment of taxes and other obligations, successful entrepreneurs are free to spend their resources as they prefer. This approach, to be sure, does protect the caprices of those who have little interest in anything other than their own entertainment, or who are driven by what Veblen described as 'conspicuous waste' – whose purpose is to advertise wealth. American entrepreneurs have license to spend legitimate earnings on causes that may be either selfish or generous. Even those causes a philanthropic entrepreneur sees as beneficial to society may, of course, be seen by some – or even by most – as detrimental (or worse).

Historically, however, this freedom of choice seems to have resulted in more good than harm, supporting great strides in culture, art, public health and knowledge. The vast majority of philanthropic dollars have been used to make positive changes to our society, and the lack of any obligations or regulations for private philanthropic choices has ensured a diversity of private funding sources that have provided enormous benefits for the United States. It is the very diversity in the interest of the philanthropists and the multiplicity of funding sources, with different goals and criteria, which allow for a wide range of essential and socially beneficial activities.

Indeed, financial support derived largely or exclusively from any single source, whether public or private, is inevitably problematic. Experience indicates that regardless of the integrity and good intentions of such a source, the funds it provides are apt to be directed disproportionately, or even entirely, to those activities that are favored by the predilections of the funding agency. The intentions are not questionable, but the result, evidently, is constraint of creativity and the handicapping of diversity.

In fact, the dramatic shift in the geographic home of creativity in the arts from Paris to New York City in the second half of the twentieth century is, to a considerable extent, ascribable to the contrast between the European model of government support of the arts and the American philanthropic approach, in which there are a variety of funding sources, representing a wide array of preferences, to which fundraisers can turn for financial assistance.

In Europe, public funding for artistic activity had long been more readily available and more reliable than in the United States. As a result it became customary for artists in Europe to rely on generous government funding. These funds were disbursed by a single government agency, operated by a group of individuals knowledgeable of the various arts, which made the funding decisions for the entire nation's artistic activities. Inevitably, such agencies tended to favor particular schools of painting, particular types of theater, and so on. It has been reported, for example, that in some European countries, the sole-source funding agencies for the arts favor classical drama, while elsewhere, new plays exploring new directions are emphatically preferred, with funding resources distributed accordingly (and with little support given to activities that are not in accord with these preferences). These preferences were often focused upon artists and arts organizations that already had achieved public recognition and, thus, were likely to attract large audiences. In some cases, these agencies did support innovative activities in the arts, leaving more conventional groups under-funded. Thus, this method of distributing financial resources to artists via a single agency made it difficult to promote variety and experimentation in the arts.

In the United States, by contrast, fundraising became a major compo-nent of artistic activity. Financial support was often obtained from wealthy individuals who were interested in particular artistic activities, from busi-ness firms, and often from the charitable foundations that had been organ-ized at the behest of wealthy Americans. As a result, the Ford Foundation, Mellon Foundation, Sloan Foundation, Rockefeller Foundations, and many others became the prime sources of funding for the arts in America. The multiplicity and heterogeneity of these sources of arts funding in the United States ensured the availability of funds to support new art forms and artists – not only those that were well established and well connected. Because there was no government agency that painters, choreographers and playwrights could rely upon to fund new directions, these innovative groups turned to wealthy individuals and private agencies to obtain the meager resources that were indispensable for their artistic experimenta-tion. The involvement of many different private funders ensured that a wide variety of arts groups obtained funding. As a result, for example, modern dance, which eschewed the uniform conventions of ballet, got its start. Martha Graham's and Merce Cunningham's revolutionary innova-tions in choreography eventually attracted enthusiastic audiences in New York. At the same time, novel theatrical performance (that is, the birth of 'Off-Off-Broadway' theaters) found a welcoming community, and experimental theatre continued to evolve. Among the early leaders of the movement was Ellen Stuart, whose La MaMa Experimental Theatre Club received indispensable early funding from the Ford Foundation – to which she turned when other funding organizations rejected her work.

The point is that the financing sources available to the creative arts in the United States – though they could provide only limited funds and could not be relied upon to continue their support indefinitely – had one critical virtue unavailable to European arts activity: the multiplicity of funding organizations encouraged greater variety and innovation in the arts. This special feature of support for the arts in the United States argu- ably played a significant role in the explosion of creativity in New York's dance, theater and painting communities at that time.

None of this, of course, is intended as criticism of support of such causes by the public sector that has, in recent periods, been the primary source of such funds in most of Europe. On the contrary, much can be said for such funding. We maintain only that there is a great need to balance public funding with a diversity of private philanthropic efforts. Moreover, private financial support has become all the more urgent, given the unhappy recent experience of public funding throughout much of the world, as governments grapple with debt and deficits. The Great Recession that the advent of the twenty-first century introduced has demonstrated the vulnerability of financial support for many socially beneficial activities to calls for containment of government deficits and public debts. Support for higher education has been cut back in various countries, and expenditures on health care have been questioned, with particular attention drawn to the sector's disturbingly high rate of cost increases. As a result, private sources of funding are now playing an increasingly crucial role in financ- ing such activities.[1]

The subsequent move in Europe toward multiple sources of funding should be regarded as the best avenue available for exit from an unfortu- nate situation. And this change brings with it one great virtue: the facilita- tion of diversity – and perhaps even heterodoxy – in arenas that previously subsisted on support from the public sector alone. Multiple funding sources or, at the very least, consideration of multiple, different viewpoints when determining how to allocate public and private funds, ensure the diversity and heterogeneity that have been successful in the past.

1.3   CORPORATE PHILANTHROPY: SPENDING 'OTHER PEOPLE'S MONEY'

While unconstrained personal philanthropy undertaken from legitimately obtained personal financial resources has provided enormous social ben- efits in the United States, the situation becomes more complicated when entrepreneurs are no longer the sole owners of their companies. Indeed, individual entrepreneurs with no partners have complete freedom to select the causes they will support; their donations benefit their vision of a better society, and any public backlash or consequences for a firm's profits affect them alone.

However, once entrepreneurs have sold part of their businesses to investors, there are other obligations to consider. At this point, the resources entailed in corporate philanthropy do not belong to the entrepreneurs and managers. Those who advocate corporate giving for good causes are, therefore, asking entrepreneur-managers to use 'other people's money' (that is, that of their investors) to promote causes that the entrepreneurs happen to favor. While this is true for all corporate giving to recipients of philanthropy, however worthy the causes may be, it is particularly thorny for corporate political donations or donations to controversial social causes. The political preferences of entrepreneur-managers and their preconceptions can differ sharply from those of their investors or stock-holders and the community as a whole, and these donations could have an adverse effect on the firms' profits.

Organized boycotts from both the left and the right in response to corporate philanthropic decisions illustrate the potential financial conse-quences of these decisions. For example, the AT&T Foundation's support for Planned Parenthood came under fire in 1990 when the Christian Action Council, an anti-abortion group, organized a letter-writing campaign and threatened boycott of AT&T. Ultimately, the AT&T Foundation discontinued its support for Planned Parenthood (Himmelstein, 1997: 80–82; Levy, 1999: 96–98). Following this success, the Council called for a boycott of all corporations that support Planned Parenthood, maintain-ing a list of those companies that make donations to the organization, even if the donations were limited to support for educational programs. Similarly, Target Corporation's 2010 donation to Minnesota Forward, a political group that supports pro-business candidates in state races, led to a boycott from gay rights supporters when it became clear that the group backed a candidate for governor who was opposed to same-sex marriage (Mullins and Zimmerman, 2010).

Certainly, donations that are meant as acts of charity can harm the interest of investors by eliciting consumer indignation. Moreover, depend-ing on one's viewpoint, some corporate donations can be seen as damag-ing the interests of the larger community. One recent event has alerted many people to the dangers of this sort of philanthropy. In 2010, the US Supreme Court ruled in the Citizens United case that corporations are entitled to all the constitutional protections of human rights guaranteed to all citizens under the US Constitution. This decision has widely been interpreted as not entirely disinterested support for particular political candidates and their legislative programs. The clear result is that calls for 'corporate responsibility', in the form of unconstrained corporate giving, now entail potentially important issues related to politics and campaign finance.

There is, however, one noteworthy exception to our caution concerning corporate philanthropy. Support that promotes the legitimate interests of the corporate donor, even indirectly, is appropriate; even potentially beneficial to the community, the entrepreneur, and the investors or shareholders. For instance, if a company's future depends heavily on the availability of postgraduates trained in computer science or some other subject, then it is surely a matter of socially beneficial self-interest for that firm to provide funding for such educational programs and students. The same is true for a firm whose activities are carried out in a community that struggles to attract well-educated employees. In that case, funding cultural activities that will help to make the community a more desirable place to live will legitimately benefit the business and, as such, seems clearly appropriate.

In practice, most nonpolitical corporate philanthropic support is targeted to the promotion of company goals. Indeed, it may even benefit a company to support causes that are more esoteric, from the company's viewpoint – such as chamber music, if the firm then can gain business by advertising its generosity. More than one opera company in the United States, for instance, has received corporate funding that clearly seems to have been given for such public relations purposes. Surely this is a legitimate activity consistent with management's responsibilities to its stockholders.

Examples from the life of Ewing Marion Kauffman, the entrepreneur who created the Kauffman Foundation, serve as useful illustrations of this idea. Kauffman was the founder of Marion Laboratories, Inc., a pharmaceutical company that focused on coronary products. One of his early philanthropic efforts was the promotion of cardiopulmonary resuscitation (CPR) training. In the late 1970s, Marion Laboratories and the Kansas City Royals baseball team (also owned by Kauffman) worked with Kansas City to educate more than 100 000 people in the Kansas City area about CPR. This work brought Kauffman a great deal of satisfaction; his biography mentions that he received a letter almost every week about a life that was saved by someone his program trained (Morgan, 1995). The program had enormous benefits for the health of Kansas City, but it also benefited Marion Laboratories. Not only did the community's appreciation for the program lead to positive associations with the company, but also the CPR training heightened the community's awareness of cardiovascular health. Moreover, most people whose lives were saved by CPR would become patients with a need for coronary products.

Some of Kauffman's later philanthropic efforts also were related to Marion Laboratories and the Kansas City Royals. In 1983, four of the Royals' players pleaded guilty to misdemeanor cocaine charges and were suspended for the following baseball season. Kauffman, stunned by the charges, was determined to become part of a solution to the drug problem in America. Both Marion Laboratories and his private foundation committed significant resources to the research, development and implementation of a drug education and prevention program in the Kansas City public schools, called STAR ('Students Taught Awareness and Resistance'). While this program certainly benefited the public images of both Marion Laboratories and the Kansas City Royals, Kauffman was motivated by the enormous need he saw and was, in fact, concerned that the 'public might perceive it as nothing more than a public-relations ploy' (Morgan, 1995). Kauffman's philanthropic activity in these cases, like so many others, was closely related to – and supported – his business activity.

1.4   THE SPILLOVER COSTS AND BENEFITS OF PHILANTHROPY: THE APPROPRIATE SOCIAL RESPONSIBILITIES OF BUSINESS

The preceding discussion has focused on entrepreneurs' decisions in spending their personal or corporate profits to serve the public interest, but it is also important to consider philanthropy as a spillover effect of a firm's business activity. Indeed, firms may benefit society – or harm it – through the workings of their businesses. The vast majority of firms are creating social benefits simply by meeting the needs of their customers, offering innovative new products and services, or creating jobs and inspiring greater vitality in their communities. Some truly innovative products have changed the way we live and have created benefits for individuals throughout society. Many, such as the iPhone, also have served as platforms for other companies' products and applications, compounding the social benefits already generated. Some companies intentionally make these social benefits an explicit part of their business models. Restaurants, for example, may promise fresh food to their customers and pledge to donate all leftover food at the end of the day. Similarly, thrift stores make a modest profit by buying clothes cheaply and selling them for only slightly more, ensuring affordable clothing for low-income individuals and eliminating waste. Red Rabbit, a New York City-based provider of healthy school food, seeks to revolutionize school lunches, while also making a profit. Other companies may allow their employees to take time off for volunteering in their communities or match employee donations to charitable organizations.

In some cases, the government promotes businesses with greater social benefits by offering incentives for innovation. In the United States, for example, subsidies are available for cars that get better gas mileage and create less pollution, in the form of federal grants, loans and even tax credits to consumers who purchase the vehicles. Electric cars meet the needs of their customers for transportation even as they benefit customers by reducing their spending on gasoline. This reduction in fuel needs also supports the greater community by reducing dependence on oil and decreasing pollution. The United States government promoted this transportation innovation through subsidies authorized in the 2009 stimulus plan, which aimed to support companies that are beneficial for the environment and create new jobs at a time when the economy was stagnating.

It is important to recognize, however, that some companies – including those that improve the social welfare in certain respects – may also cause a wide variety of social damages. They may, for instance, pollute the atmosphere and the waterways, offer products that damage consumers' health, or engage in anticompetitive behavior, among many other harmful activities. In these cases, entrepreneurs need to be obligated to rectify their wrongs. If, for instance, a firm's activities result in the emission of significant amounts of toxic pollutants, remedial steps are necessary.

In this, however, we take the heterodox position that the decision to undertake such countermeasures cannot be left to the voluntary choice of entrepreneur-managers. Rather, the responsibility must be imposed upon them by law or by government agencies that have the means to enforce the adoption of such countermeasures. Just as the government offers subsidies to encourage socially beneficial innovation, so it may address the harmful spillover effects of corporate behavior by asking companies to limit their damage or compensate for it through taxes and penalties. Companies that pollute, for example, can be limited by regulations (enforced with penalties), taxes, and the need to purchase pollution allowances or emission rights. Similarly, the government may tax consumption and thereby indirectly affect corporate behavior. For example, the cigarette tax compensates for the risk and nuisance of second-hand smoke to nonsmokers and at least partially offsets the increased cost of health care for smokers, which is shared by all Americans.

Public policy needs to encourage this type of philanthropy because a competitive market makes it difficult for entrepreneurs to be altruistic. Entrepreneurs span the spectrum of humanity in their attributes, including matters entailing virtue or vice. Some prominent business people are deeply devoted to the public interest – for example, spending generously of their free time to work in underserved communities, helping the younger inhabitants of these communities to find and take advantage of promising future opportunities. Of course, not all of their peers have similar objectives. This hints at the key problem, which is not so much that there are at least a few entrepreneurs who conduct their business with little concern for the welfare of the community. Rather, the larger problem is the likelihood that the competitive mechanism will force the hand of even the most ethical entrepreneur-managers to follow the examples of such scoundrels.

An apropos anecdote illustrates this point. A member of top management at a firm that was responsible for substantial emissions of pollutants into nearby waterways shared the following dilemma with one of the authors:

> My daughter gives me hell at breakfast every morning and denounces me as a despoiler of the environment. She isn't wrong. But what can I do about it? If we put in the expensive plant and equipment and undertake the operating costs required for real pollution control, my company will be in trouble. Our competitors are located on the same river and are doing the same thing. If I take on the pollution control and they do not, they will be able to beat our prices and drive us out of business, and the river will remain polluted. But my daughter simply refuses to see this.

Clearly, such a unilateral attempt at virtue would merely be self-destructive, with no resulting improvement in the river's condition. However, this ethical businessman could improve the situation by contacting every congressman or appropriate members of the environmental protection agency and urging them, in turn, to adopt rules that would require both his firm and its rivals to take remedial measures. Only with such regulatory assistance could the executive do the right thing for both his firm and the environment, without endangering the health of his company.

1.5 CONCLUDING COMMENT: ADAPTING THE 'RULES OF THE GAME'

Because entrepreneurs come in all shapes and sizes and span the range of morality, preaching to them about their obligations to the general welfare is virtually certain to be pointless. Moreover, the lack of such obligations for personal philanthropy results in a welcome diversity of funding, and any such obligation for corporate philanthropy potentially does a disservice to investors. While some entrepreneurs may enhance the general welfare through their business activities, others, driven by market competition, introduce damaging effects. Some, to be sure, are likely to be moved by appeals for remediation – that is, their good intentions may be stirred. But so long as competition forces every firm in the market to avoid 'wasteful costs' (that is, costs that are not offset by the resulting profits), voluntary steps are likely to be confined to measures that promote public relations but do little to remove any social damage caused by a firm's activities. In the meantime, entrepreneurs' questionable activities – from environmental damage to deliberately deceptive investment advice – are likely to continue virtually unchecked.

Given this reality, what can be done? Entrepreneurs, as a group, seek to go where the money is, so the solution that suggests itself is adaptation of the 'rules of the game' so that entrepreneurs confidently conclude that the most effective way for them to do well is by doing good. The US patent system has long served this purpose. A redesigned tax system that uses imposts to make socially damaging activities expensive while reducing the financial burden on virtuous behavior would be another obvious instrument for this purpose. This approach also has been adopted in various other ways – notably, in the institution of a system of purchasable licenses for emissions of pollutants, with a market for those rights guiding the prices of the licenses. The idea is to enforce the social responsibilities of entrepreneurs and other members of the business community not through preaching, but rather by making it financially disadvantageous for them to act against the general welfare.

Keeping all this in mind, we propose the following guidelines, in order to ensure that philanthropy by entrepreneurs serves the public interest.

1. The earnings and wealth accumulated by successful entrepreneurs, if not in some way illegitimately obtained, should be left free to be disposed of by those who hold these resources as they prefer (after payment of taxes and other legitimate obligations). While this rule enables entrepreneurs to spend both selfishly and generously, it also ensures funding for a diversity of social causes which otherwise might go unfunded.
2. Additional support for such causes by government is also desirable. The multiplicity of private resources ensures that a wide variety of goals is preserved and the preclusion of new approaches and novel activities that happen not to be favored by, for instance, a single government funding agency is prevented.
3. Management-directed grants of corporate resources for causes they favor is discouraged, unless these donations are in the corporate interest. These donations can be particularly problematic when they support political causes, as the preferences of entrepreneur-managers and their preconceptions can differ sharply from those of their stockholders and the community as a whole. These supposed acts of charity, then, can harm the interests of investors by eliciting consumer indignation, in addition to damaging those of the larger community.
4. Entrepreneurs should not be relieved of all social obligations. Entrepreneurs who are responsible for harming the general welfare

(pollution, and so on) should be obligated to do something to rectify their wrongs, but the decision to undertake such countermeasures should never be left to the voluntary choice of entrepreneur-managers. The government must require, or at least offer incentives, to discourage firm behavior that damages the general welfare.

These social obligations cannot be left to the good intentions of entrepreneur-managers, as even the most socially minded entrepreneur-manager will be prevented by the competition of less scrupulous rivals from taking more than superficial countermeasures, particularly if containment of the problem is costly. An entrepreneur-manager whose firm encounters such problems has only one effective countermeasure available: effective regulations that preclude all firms in the industry from continuing their damaging activities.

NOTES

*   Portions of this chapter are based on William Baumol's article in *Business and Society*, published by SAGE Publications, Inc. entitled, 'On the appropriate social responsibilities of successful entrepreneurs' (February 2014).
1.   For instance, the United Kingdom was not alone in moving toward cutbacks in these arenas, but it seems to have been the first of the countries in Europe whose universities recognized the desirability, indeed necessity, of turning to private sources of support.

REFERENCES

Carnegie, Andrew (1889), 'The gospel of wealth', *North American Review*, June.
Himmelstein, Jerome L. (1997), *Looking Good and Doing Good: Corporate Philanthropy and Corporate Power*, Bloomington and Indianapolis, IN: Indiana University Press.
Levy, Reynold (1999), *Give and Take: A Candid Account of Corporate Philanthropy*, Boston, MA: Harvard Business Press.
Morgan, Anne Hodges (1995), *Prescription for Success: The Life and Values of Ewing Marion Kauffman*, Kansas City, MO: Andrews & McMeel.
Mullins, Brody and Ann Zimmerman (2010), 'Target discovers downside to political contributions', *Wall Street Journal*, August 7.

2. From entrepreneur to philanthropist: two sides of the same coin?
David B. Audretsch and Joshua R. Hinger

2.1 INTRODUCTION

At first glance, entrepreneurship and philanthropy might seem to have little in common. After all, the former is focused on creating something new, while the latter is focused on assisting someone or something that already exists. Entrepreneurship has often been associated with wealth creation while, by contrast, philanthropy is seemingly about the dispersion and redistribution of wealth. However, many of the greatest and most prominent entrepreneurs in the United States have also been among the most notable philanthropists. While striking historical examples abound, such as John D. Rockefeller III, Andrew Carnegie, Ewing Marion Kauffman and the Guggenheims, more contemporary examples have caught the attention of the entire world, such as Bill Gates, Warren Buffett, Mario Batali, Michael Bloomberg and Mark Zuckerberg. According to Gaudiani (2003: 14):

> The outstanding characteristic of American generosity is its entrepreneurial character. By this I mean a drive to build something of value through hard work and risk taking. Identifying a problem or an opportunity is the crucial starting point. But the entrepreneurial spirit drives the individual or group to take action and to do so with a sense of urgency. Over the decades, and in fact centuries, private donors in America have typically made their gifts far earlier and far more quickly than other funders and investors, such as businesses or government, usually even before the market or our legislators have realized that there is a crucial need.

As Rockefeller (1984: 93) pointed out, 'How vast indeed is the philanthropic field! It may be urged that the daily vocation of life is one thing, and the work of philanthropy quite another. I have no sympathy with this notion.' While philanthropy and entrepreneurship seem to be opposed in nature, they have fundamental similarities in the sense that they both provide a service or solve a problem for a group of targeted recipients, and they both reap benefit from their activity. Entrepreneurs typically receive financial independence and marginal monetary profits, while philanthropists receive something different. As Ewing Marion Kauffman once explained, 'The more you give, the more you get. It's just that simple. The more you give to any association in life, the more you will get in return. It's not altruistic either. I don't consider myself an altruist. It's just a simple formula . . . It works in all aspects of life' (Morgan, 1995: 319). Similarly, Henry Bloch lends some insight into the motivations for philanthropic behavior by explaining his beliefs that 'true success is not measured in what you get, but in what you give back' (Bloch, 2011: 177), and that 'a commitment to the greater good is good business' (Bloch, 2011: 170).

The purpose of this chapter is to examine whether the personal characteristics that are conducive to individuals becoming entrepreneurs are in fact the same or similar to those that are conducive to individuals engaging in philanthropy. In the second section of this chapter six broad forms of entrepreneurial research are identified, followed by a discussion of characteristics that have been identified as conducive to entrepreneurship by the scholarly literature. In the third section, individual-specific characteristics that are conducive to philanthropic activity are identified. The similarities and disparities in individual-specific characteristics conducive to entrepreneurship and philanthropy are discussed in the fourth section. Lastly a summary and conclusions are presented. In particular, this chapter finds that while certain similarities exist, entrepreneurship and philanthropy may reflect two opposing sides of the same coin.

2.2   WHAT MAKES AN ENTREPRENEUR?

Perhaps the most fundamental issue in the scholarly literature on entrepreneurship is why some people choose to become entrepreneurs, while others abstain from entrepreneurship. However, answering this question and identifying general tendencies conducive to entrepreneurship have posed a challenge to scholars, largely because the entrepreneurship literature itself is shrouded with ambiguity about what actually constitutes entrepreneurship. In fact the scholarly journals in the field of entrepreneurship are mostly focused on and give priority to advancing the theoretical understanding of entrepreneurship, which generally involves the formulation of new theoretical approaches and the subjugation of such theories to empirical scrutiny. For example, the aims and scope of the *Journal of Business Venturing* has an explicit mandate, 'to deepen our understanding of the entrepreneurial phenomenon in its myriad of forms' (Shepherd, 2013). This mission to understand the entrepreneurial phenomenon is not unique to the *Journal of Business Venturing*, but rather typical of entrepreneurship journals.

Even with such an explicit aim and scope, the exact meaning of 'understanding of the entrepreneurial phenomenon' needs to be interpreted and explained. In fact, such an interpretation and explanation is gleaned by examining the actual papers and articles published in the scholarly journals of entrepreneurship. There are five main categories of research dealing with 'understanding of the entrepreneurial phenomenon'. The first category of research examines what actually constitutes the entrepreneurial phenomenon. This type of research tends to be not only theoretical in nature but also epistemological. Such research focuses on what exactly constitutes the entrepreneurial phenomenon in its 'myriad of forms' and what distinguishes entrepreneurial activity from non-entrepreneurial activity (Aldrich and Martinez, 2010; Gaglio and Katz, 2001; Gartner, 1990). While such research provides a cornerstone for the scholarly inquiry about entrepreneurship, it is not particularly relevant for public policy.

The second category of entrepreneurship research devoted to understanding the entrepreneurial phenomenon has a focus on conditions, factors and characteristics that alternatively generate or impede that phenomenon. It is important to note that this type of entrepreneurship research corresponds to the underlying force type or level of entrepreneurship policy research. Similarly, the central focus of the underlying force influence paper is on identifying conditions, characteristics or factors that are conducive to entrepreneurship. Addressing the question of what facilitates or, alternatively, inhibits entrepreneurship is a central concern in understanding the entrepreneurial phenomenon in its myriad forms.

The third category of entrepreneurship research devoted to understanding the entrepreneurial phenomenon is focused on the impact of entrepreneurship or the outcomes emanating from entrepreneurial activity. This type of entrepreneurship research corresponds to the second level of entrepreneurship policy research, known as the underlying force and influence paper, and is commonly considered by the entrepreneurship journals. A central concern of the scholarly literature in understanding the entrepreneurial phenomenon in its myriad of forms is focused on the manners in which entrepreneurial activity impacts local economic performance. Even though such papers may never explicitly mention the word 'policy', they are relevant for policy in that they shed light on the links between the underlying phenomenon of entrepreneurship and its impact on economic performance, broadly considered.

This category of entrepreneurship research also corresponds to the policy impact type research, which examines the impact of a particular policy on an element of the underlying forces. For example, Markman et al. (2005) as well as Lockett et al. (2003) analyze the impacts of university technology transfer on entrepreneurship. Lockett et al. (2005) examine the entrepreneurial activity emanating from public research institutions, and Link and Scott (2009) analyze the impacts of the United States Small Business Innovation Research (SBIR) on entrepreneurial activity.

The fourth type of entrepreneurship research, known as the instrument recommendation paper, provides a focus on and analysis of an actual instrument, or group of instruments. Research focusing on which particular policy instruments can best be utilized to attain policy targets are of great interest to policy makers but of less concern and relevance to 'understanding entrepreneurial phenomena', which is the major focus of the entrepreneurship scholarly journals. The same holds true for the fifth type of entrepreneurship research, policy evaluation, which provides an assessment or evaluation of the impacts of particular policies on specific policy targets. Policy assessment papers fall outside the five types of research typifying the published entrepreneurship literature. Thus, such research may be less suited for the scholarly journals in entrepreneurship and more appropriate for publication as a book or policy report. Such research addresses key policy concerns that do not fall within the primary focus of the entrepreneurship scholarly journals. For example, Link (1995, 2002) evaluates the economic impact of the Research Triangle Park in North Carolina with a book as the publication outlet.

In his exhaustive survey of entrepreneurship, Parker (2010) finds that the basic theoretical building block is the conceptual framework or model of entrepreneurial choice. Thus, in trying to identify the salient characteristics of an entrepreneur, scholars have been confounded by the lack of a singular definition or concept of what actually constitutes entrepreneurship. Perhaps this is what led Aldrich (1999: 76) to conclude that 'Research on personal traits seems to have reached an empirical dead end.' Still, as Rauch and Frese (2007: 353) point out, 'Relationships between personality traits and entrepreneurial behavior are frequently addressed in entrepreneurship theory building and research.' In fact, Rauch and Frese (2007) provide an extensive review of the entrepreneurship literature in order to provide a meta-analysis on the relationship between personality characteristics and the propensity to become an entrepreneur. Their findings contrast the arguments of Begley and Boyd (1987) and Frese et al. (2000), who claim personality traits impact the creation of an enterprise differently than the subsequent management and success of the enterprise, by providing evidence that the need for achievement and generalized self-efficacy were both statistically significant predictors of enterprise creation and enterprise success.

A number of key individual-specific characteristics have been consistently identified in the entrepreneurship literature to be associated with the propensity for an individual to become an entrepreneur (Krueger and Day, 2010; Shaver, 2010; Aldrich and Martinez, 2010; Parker, 2010). The literature has generally identified specific characteristics that influence the choices of individuals in deciding to engage in entrepreneurship (McClelland, 1961; Roberts, 1991; Brandstetter, 1997; Gartner, 1990; Blanchflower and Oswald, 1998). According to the model of entrepreneurial choice, an individual weighs the benefits of becoming an entrepreneur against those benefits that could be obtained through employment within an existing firm. The greater is the gap between the benefits accrued from entrepreneurship and those earned from employment, the more likely that individual is to become an entrepreneur (Parker, 2010). Additionally, despite severe methodological criticisms, McClelland (1961) pioneered the field with his work on measurements of 'the need for achievement', or achievement motive. More recently, Zhao and Seibert (2006) link the personality characteristics of entrepreneurs to the decision to start a new business. Their findings give support to the argument that entrepreneurs do in fact differ in four out of the five personality characteristics examined from individuals who hold management positions. According to their results, entrepreneurs are unique from managers in their neuroticism, openness, agreeableness and conscientiousness; however no significant difference was found in extraversion. Similarly, Reynolds et al. (2004) use a large database, the Panel Study of Income Dynamics (PSID), to identify the role that personality characteristics play in the decision of an individual to start a new business venture. Furthermore, the role of intentions to become an entrepreneur has played a particularly important role in the entrepreneurship literature (Ucbasaran et al., 2006; Shapero and Sokol, 1982; Ajzen, 1991; Gaglio and Katz, 2001).

Gender is also an important individual-specific characteristic that has consistently been found to be influential in shaping the decision to become an entrepreneur (Minniti and Nardone, 2007). Gender, of course, is independent of the life cycle of a scientist, thus it is not applicable to the life cycle models of Levin and Stephan (1991) or Stephan and Levin (1992). The majority of the literature has generated empirical evidence suggesting that females are less likely to engage in entrepreneurship (Allen et al., 2007). For example, the female self-employment rate in the United States is around half of the male self-employment rate (Allen et al., 2007). While nearly 7 percent of females participating in the labor force are classified as self-employed, the self-employment rate for males is well over 12 percent. The Global Entrepreneurship Monitor (GEM) finds that well over one in ten females in the United States own a business (Allen et al., 2007). By contrast, just less than one in five males own a business in the United States (Allen et al., 2007).

The entrepreneurship literature has found that human capital plays a central role in the decision of individuals to become entrepreneurs. Human capital comprises the stock of knowledge and skills that resides within individuals (Becker, 1964). However, human capital is most frequently measured by the number of years of education, or alternatively the highest degree attained by an individual. A number of empirical studies in the literature have explicitly focused on the relationship between individuals' level of human capital and their propensity to become entrepreneurs or start new business ventures (Evans and Leighton, 1989; Bates, 1995; Gimeno et al., 1997; Davidsson and Honig, 2003; Siegel et al., 2007), and they find with very few exceptions that human capital is positively correlated with the propensity to become an entrepreneur. The ability of an individual to recognize the presence of specific entrepreneurial opportunities has been found to be positively correlated with the level of human capital possessed by the individual. Similarly, an individual's willingness and ability to actually implement and pursue entrepreneurial opportunities have also been found to have a positive correlation with an individual's level of human capital.

While human capital refers to the knowledge capabilities of the individual, social capital reflects the extent to which an individual can take advantage of linkages and connections to other people. Just as physical capital refers to the importance of factories and machines to generate economic value (Solow, 1956), the endogenous growth theory (Romer, 1986; Lucas, 1988) shifted the emphasis to knowledge accumulation, so that knowledge capital takes on a key role in generating economic value.

By contrast, Putnam (1993) and Coleman (1988) introduced the concept of social capital to reflect the relationships, connections and linkages of individuals to other people. Coleman (1988) explains that social capital involves 'a variety of entities with two elements in common: they all consist of some aspect of social structure, and they facilitate certain actions of actors . . . within the structure'. According to Putnam (2000: 19) social capital has a positive impact on innovation and growth. He explains:

> Whereas physical capital refers to physical objects and human capital refers to the properties of individuals, social capital refers to connections among individuals – social networks. By analogy with notions of physical capital and human capital – tools and training that enhance individual productivity – social capital refers to features of social organization, such as networks that facilitate coordination and cooperation for mutual benefits.

The scholarly literature on entrepreneurship finds a positive and significant relationship between various measures of social capital and the propensity for an individual to become an entrepreneur (Mosey and Wright, 2007; Aldrich and Martinez, 2010; Shane and Stuart, 2002; Davidsson and Honig, 2003). Aldridge and Audretsch (2011) argue that social capital should play a key role in the decision of a university scientist to become an entrepreneur. In particular, they suggest that linkages, connections to, and relationships with other scientists employed by industry, as well as connections to industrial firms, will facilitate the ability of the scientist to recognize entrepreneurial opportunities and to act on those opportunities through entrepreneurial activity. Aldridge and Audretsch (2011) provide empirical evidence suggesting that those university scientists with greater social capital have a greater propensity to become entrepreneurs.

The literature on entrepreneurship has also identified the institutional context within which an individual confronts the decision to become an entrepreneur as influencing the outcome of that entrepreneurial decision. In particular, this literature suggests that certain aspects of the institutional context have been found to encourage individuals to become entrepreneurs, while other aspects have been found to deter or impede entrepreneurship (Saxenian, 1994; Karlsson and Karlsson, 2002; Henrekson and Stenkula, 2010).

As Rauch and Frese (2007) report, what is referred to in the psychology literature as the need for achievement has been consistently found to be positively related to the likelihood that a person becomes an entrepreneur. The need for achievement characterizes the tendency of an individual to select tasks that are of moderate difficulty, to take on the responsibility associated with the outcomes of those decisions, and to solicit feedback concerning those actions and outcomes. Earlier studies (McClelland, 1961) suggested that the need for achievement is one of the most salient characteristics of entrepreneurs that differentiate them from managers and other decision makers.

Innovativeness, or the capacity to identify and create novel ways for dealing with problems and issues, is another characteristic specific to individuals that has consistently been identified as having a positive correlation with the propensity to engage in entrepreneurship (Frese, 2009). The willingness and ability to inject novelty into a situation or challenge the status quo contributes to an individual's ability to recognize, create, and act upon opportunities. Additionally, a relatively low level of risk aversion has consistently been found to be conducive to entrepreneurship (Caliendo et al., 2009; Parker, 2010; Gifford, 2010). Those individuals who are less adverse to risk are more likely to become entrepreneurs.

The capacity for an individual to complete tasks and reach goals, or what is termed self-efficacy, has also been consistently identified as having a positive relationship with propensities of an individual to become an entrepreneur. The ability of an individual to persevere when confronted by challenges and obstacles facilitates management of the uncertainties inherent in entrepreneurship. As Alvarez et al. (2010) and Alvarez and Barney (2008) point out, in contrast to risk, uncertainty refers to situations where no a priori probabilities or likelihood distributions can be assigned to specific outcomes associated with decisions.

A similar individual-specific characteristic conducive to entrepreneurship is the capacity to tolerate stress. As Rauch and Frese (2007: 359) explain:

> *Generalized self-efficacy* is important for entrepreneurs because they must be confident in their capabilities to perform various (and often unanticipated) tasks in uncertain situations . . . People with high generalized self-efficacy are likely to persevere when problems arise and search for challenges and, therefore, challenging opportunities; they also show a higher degree of personal initiative; they have higher hopes for success and, therefore, take a long-term perspective; they also actively search for information, which leads to better knowledge.

Not surprisingly, given the inherent role of uncertainty in the entrepreneurial function (Alvarez et al., 2010; Gifford, 2010; Alvarez and Barney, 2008), the capacity of an individual to tolerate stress has been consistently found to be positively related to the propensity to become an entrepreneur. A considerably different personality characteristic involves the need for an individual to be autonomous (Frese, 2009; Brandstetter, 1997). According to Rauch and Frese (2007: 359), the need for autonomy 'is associated with entrepreneurs' avoidance of restrictive environments; they prefer to make decisions independent of supervisors . . . People high in need for autonomy want to be in control, they avoid the restrictions and rules of established organizations, and thus, choose the entrepreneurial role.'

A similar individual-specific personality characteristic that is positively associated with entrepreneurship is a strong or high internal locus of control (Caliendo et al., 2009; Rauch and Frese, 2007). Those people with a greater need to feel in control are more likely to eschew working for others in the context of a hierarchical organization and are more likely to want to be their own boss (Parker, 2010).

2.3   WHAT MAKES A PHILANTHROPIST?

As Phelps (1975: 2) notes, 'The range of altruistic behavior is impressive.' Piliavin and Charng (1990: 310) turn to the scholarly literature on philanthropy and altruism to address the question, 'Is there an altruistic personality?' They find that there is compelling evidence for certain types of personality characteristics to be more associated with altruistic behavior than others. For example, characteristics such as trust and faith in people, risk-taking and gender have all been found to influence the propensity for people to behave altruistically (Piliavin and Charng, 1990).

The age of an individual has been found to be positively related to the propensity to engage in philanthropy (Bekkers and Wiepking, 2006; List, 2004). At least some evidence suggests that there are diminishing returns with respect to age (Putnam, 2000; Wunnava and Lauze, 2001). However, other studies provide empirical evidence suggesting that philanthropic giving tends to increase in people who are at least 40 years old (Andreoni, 2001). Of course, this may be linked with an individual's economic income and stability. Younger individuals lack the economic establishment to give, while retired individuals are dependent on retirement accounts with limited resources.

The relationship between income and philanthropy has been consistently found to be positive (Bekkers and Wiepking, 2007; List, 2004; Andreoni, 1988). While this positive relationship may be intuitive, Brooks (2002), among others, has found that the source of that income also plays a role in influencing philanthropic giving. In particular, Brooks (2002) presents empirical evidence suggesting that income resulting from wages and dividends tends to be associated with higher levels of philanthropic donations.

Another important individual-specific characteristic found to influence a person's propensity to engage in philanthropy is gender. While the empirical evidence linking gender to philanthropy is not without ambiguities (Bekkers and Wiepking, 2007; Cox and Deck, 2006; Andreoni and Vesterlund, 2001), studies tend to suggest that the propensity for females to engage in philanthropy is greater than that of their male counterparts (Piliavin and Charng, 1990; Mesch, 2009; Bekkers, 2004; Mesch et al., 2006; Feldman, 2007; Reed and Selbee, 2000). Research has examined the propensity for females to engage in philanthropy, as distinct from male philanthropy. As Mesch (2009: 1) points out, 'Over the past thirty years, women have emerged on the philanthropic landscape as a visible and bold presence. They are changing the face of philanthropy and are transforming society around the world.' Still, as Bekkers and Wiepking (2007: 14) report in their review of the literature on philanthropic giving, 'Findings on gender differences in giving are mixed. Most studies find no reliable differences between males and females. A group of studies find that while females are more likely to give, males give higher amounts.' However, this propensity of males to give larger amounts to charities may be linked with their generally larger degree of income (Bobbitt-Zeher, 2007). Andreoni et al. (2003) examined male and female one-person households and found no difference in the levels of philanthropic giving between the two genders.

Additionally, the literature shows that to whom the philanthropists are giving varies between males and females. Regnerus et al. (1998) found that females are more likely to give to organizations that assist the poor and homeless, while Midlarsky and Hannah (1989) found that women are more likely than men to donate to organizations that assist children with birth defects. In contrast, men were found to donate more often to professional societies, recreational organizations and women's organizations (Knoke, 1990), while Brown and Ferris (2007) found that males are more likely to give to religious organizations than their female counterparts. Recent trends in research are showing that the influence of married women on charitable giving by married couples is increasing in correlation with the increase in earnings for women (Rooney et al., 2007). Brown (2005) argues that as married women develop greater earnings, they are more likely to take an active role in decision making.

A large literature has found that levels of education have an impact on philanthropy (Bekkers and Wiepking, 2007). In particular, studies have consistently found that the higher one's level of education, the greater is the propensity to engage in philanthropy (Feldman, 2007; Brooks, 2004). There is also at least some evidence that education is not homogeneous with respect to its impact on philanthropic giving. For example, Marr et al. (2005) found that alumni from Vanderbilt University had a greater propensity to engage in philanthropic giving if they had majored in economics, mathematics or social sciences. By contrast, the Vanderbilt alumni majoring in sciences and performing arts were less likely to be involved in philanthropic donations. These findings proved to be robust, even after controlling for the levels of income. Additionally, in a study on donations to political organizations, Gimpel et al. (2006: 636) found that 'Higher education levels had a positive, statistically significant effect on Republican campaign contributions in all campaign years. However, for Democrats, as the proportion of college-educated residents increased, contribution amounts decreased, especially in recent elections.' In this same study, Gimpel et al. (2006) argues that geographic context affects motives for contributing, and that people often contribute out of a desire to feel a sense of belonging to a superior social class or to a group fighting for a cause.

Yen (2002) finds that income, age and education are all contributing factors that influence charitable giving. More specifically, the study provides evidence of a relationship between education and donations to non-religious organizations, whereas there is no relationship between education and donations to religious organizations. While a positive relationship between education and philanthropy has been found to exist, the exact reason is less certain. As Bekkers and Wiepking (2007: 8) point out, 'Why education matters for philanthropy is far from settled.'

Religion has been found to play an important role in shaping the propensity for an individual to become a philanthropist (Bekkers and Wiepking, 2007). There are at least two salient issues involving the relationship between religion and philanthropic giving. The first involves the intensity of the religious activity, typically measured in terms of frequency of institutional attendance (church, mosque, synagogue or equivalent). Studies almost invariably find that the greater the intensity of the religious activity, or the more frequent is the attendance at a religious service, the more likely an individual is to engage in philanthropic behavior (Bekkers and Wiepking, 2007; Feldman, 2007; Lunn et al., 2001; Bekkers, 2006).

However, it is not just religious intensity or frequency of attendance in a religious service that influences the propensity to be engaged as a philanthropist. The particular religious denomination also influences the propensity for someone to be a philanthropist. Empirical evidence has been found suggesting that the propensity for Protestant Christians to be philanthropic exceeds that of other religious denominations (Berger, 2006; Bekkers and Schuyt, 2005; Chaves, 2002). Similarly, Hoge and Yang (1994: 125) found that 'by all accounts Jewish contributions are higher than Catholic or Protestant'.

A somewhat different factor reflecting personal wealth is home ownership. The literature on philanthropy has consistently found a positive relationship between home ownership and the propensity for an individual to be engaged in philanthropic giving (Bekkers and Wiepking, 2006; Feldman, 2007). In a Family Expenditure Survey analysis (1978 to 1993), Banks and Tanner (1999) conducted the first known study on charitable giving over continuous years of household-level data. They find a positive relationship between home ownership and charitable giving. Additionally, Micklewright and Schnepf (2009) find that home owners donate slightly more than the average person, and that home owners give mostly to domestic causes in comparison to overseas giving. Rooney et al. (2007: 233) explain that while 'educational attainment is a significant predictor as to who decides [to give] . . . the presence of children in the home and home ownership have a positive effect on charitable decision making'.

A different characteristic of individuals that has been found to influence their propensity to be involved in philanthropic giving is their marital status. As Bekkers and Wiepking (2007) report in their exhaustive review of the philanthropy literature, a positive relationship has generally been found to exist between marital status and engagement in philanthropic giving. Those who are married have a higher propensity to be engaged in philanthropic donations, even after controlling for other factors, such as age and income (Brooks, 2005; Feldman, 2007).

A related individual-specific characteristic that has been associated with philanthropic giving is having children. A positive relationship has been identified as existing between the number of children in a household and the propensity to be engaged in philanthropic giving (Bekkers and Wiepking, 2007). While some studies fail to find the existence of a positive relationship (Feldman, 2007), as Bekkers and Wiepking (2007) report, most studies find the existence of a strong and positive relationship.

The impact of race on philanthropic giving has been explicitly analyzed in a number of studies (Brooks, 2002; Brown and Ferris, 2007; Gruber, 2004; Steinburg and Wilhelm, 2005). The empirical evidence consistently suggests that race matters when it comes to philanthropic giving to specific types of organizations. Van Slyke and Brooks (2005) find that the propensity for Caucasians to engage in philanthropic giving exceeds that of non-Caucasians. However, this conflicts with the findings of Steinburg and Wilhelm (2005) who, along with Brown and Ferris (2007), find that black families give more to charitable organizations than families of other races, primarily due to their larger than average donation to religious institutions. Brooks (2005) finds that white families donate more to secular organizations, while Regnerus et al. (1998) find that non-whites are more likely than whites to donate to charities that help the poor and needy.

Similarly, the literature on philanthropy has found that citizens have a greater propensity to be engaged in philanthropic giving than immigrants (Osili and Du, 2005; Bekkers and Wiepking, 2007). Immigrants have consistently been found to have a lower propensity to be engaged in philanthropic giving, which, according to Osili and Du (2005), can be associated with differences in education and income levels. Mata and McRae (2000) find that mean amounts of donations increase with the number of years the immigrant has resided in the country. These findings are also consistent with Osili and Du (2005), who explain that the mean difference in donation amounts decreases as the number of years in residency increase. Schervish and Havens (2002) explain in consistency with Osili and Du (2005) that immigrants spend more on informal donations, in the form of remittances to their country of origin, than native citizens.

Lastly, for the scope of this chapter, the literature on philanthropy has considered the impact of geographic location on philanthropic donations. In particular, the size of a community has been found to be negatively related to philanthropic giving (Putnam, 2000; Bekkers and Wiepking, 2007). However, Bekkers and Wiepking (2007) point out that there are a sufficient number of contradictory findings as to warrant further research on this topic.

2.4   TWO SIDES OF THE SAME COIN?

Each of these bodies of literature has found that characteristics specific to the individual play a large role in their level of engagement in entrepreneurship and philanthropy. While this is the first commonality between philanthropy and entrepreneurship, it is only the starting point. In fact, a number of individual-specific characteristics that influence the propensity to engage in philanthropic giving also influence the propensity to become an entrepreneur.

In particular, education or human capital has a positive influence on the propensity to be engaged in philanthropy, just as it has been found to be positively related to the likelihood of being an entrepreneur. Similarly, access to financial resources has been found to be conducive to both entrepreneurship and philanthropic giving. Additionally, studies in both fields find compelling evidence that home ownership is positively related to the propensity to be engaged.

However, when comparing the findings in the two fields, certain glaring disparities emerge. The role of gender, for example, is considerably different in the entrepreneurial process than it is for philanthropy. While the literature on entrepreneurship finds a considerably greater propensity for males to engage in entrepreneurial activities than females, no such difference is discernible in the literature on philanthropy. Both males and females are likely to engage in philanthropy, although the differences in gender are correlated with giving to different types of organizations and charities.

Another disparity involves the role of age. While the literature on philanthropy generally finds that the likelihood of engaging in philanthropy tends to increase along with age, the opposite finding emerges in the literature on entrepreneurship. Age seems to be negatively related to the propensity for someone to become an entrepreneur but positively related to the likelihood of engaging in philanthropic giving. It seems natural to see more young people engage in the risky business of entrepreneurship, while older individuals, who have established and stable income, would be more likely to engage in philanthropy.

The roles of citizenship and a history of immigration are also different for individuals who engage in entrepreneurship and philanthropy. While philanthropy is clearly more associated with citizenship, this is less true for entrepreneurship. However, the role of race seems to be more similar for entrepreneurship and philanthropy. The literature shows a great diversity in the type of organizations receiving gifts and the amount of giving from specific race groups, and has fewer conclusions about which race group engages more or less than other groups.

Thus, while there are considerable similarities in the drivers of entrepreneurship and philanthropy, there are also substantial differences. Still, the similarities in individual-specific characteristics are striking, suggesting that many of the same characteristics that lead people to become entrepreneurs may also lead them to engage in philanthropy.

2.5   CONCLUSIONS

A number of the greatest philanthropists in the United States have also been among the most notable entrepreneurs. As Rockefeller (1984: 120) cajoled:

> Why not do with what you can give to others as you do with what you want to keep for yourself and your children: put it into a Trust? Let us be as careful with the money we would spend for the benefit of others as if we were laying it aside for our own family's future use . . . I beg you, attend to it *now*, don't wait.

Despite this obvious overlap between entrepreneurship and philanthropy, the phenomena of entrepreneurship and philanthropy are seemingly two distinct and unconnected activities. According to Zunz (2012: 1), 'Andrew Carnegie, who conducted large-scale philanthropy with the same obsession with which he streamlined steel operations, remembered late in his life the day when he resolved to stop accumulating and began the infinitely more serious and difficult task of what he termed wise distribution.' Certainly the scholarly literature on entrepreneurship and philanthropy are distinct and unconnected. While notable exceptions exist (Acs, 2013), few studies of entrepreneurship have considered philanthropy, just as few studies of philanthropy have considered entrepreneurship. Still, a central concern of both literatures has been what distinguishes those who engage in the activity of interest from those who do not. Thus, both literatures have generated a large body of research attempting to identify what creates differences across large samples of people who decide to engage in philanthropic and entrepreneurial activities.

This chapter has brought together the disparate scholarly literatures on entrepreneurship and philanthropy to shed light on the extent to which underlying personality and individual-specific characteristics are conducive in the same way to entrepreneurial and philanthropic impulses. This comparison between the philanthropy and entrepreneurship literatures suggests considerable, albeit not perfect, overlap. In many respects, philanthropy and entrepreneurship are, in fact, different sides of the same coin.

REFERENCES

Acs, Z. (2013), *Why Philanthropy Matters: How the Wealthy Give, and What It Means for Our Economic Well-Being*, Princeton, NJ, USA: Princeton University Press.

Ajzen, I. (1991), 'The theory of planned behavior', *Organization Behavior and Human Decision Process*, 50(2), 179–211.

Aldrich, H. (1999), *Organizations Evolving*, London: Sage.

Aldrich, H. and M. Martinez (2010), 'Entrepreneurship as social construction: a multilevel evolutionary approach', in Zoltan J. Acs and David B. Audretsch (eds), *Handbook of Entrepreneurship Research: An Interdisciplinary Survey and Introduction*, New York: Springer, pp. 387–430.

Aldridge, T. and D. Audretsch (2011), 'The Bayh–Dole Act and scientist entrepreneurship', *Research Policy*, 40(2011), 1058–1067.

Allen, I., N. Langowitz and M. Minitti (2007), *2006 Report on Women and Entrepreneurship*, Wellsley, MA: Babson College, Global Entrepreneurship Monitor.

Alvarez, S. and J. Barney (2008), 'Opportunities, organizations, and entrepreneurship', *Strategic Entrepreneurship Journal*, 2, 265–267.

Alvarez, S., J. Barney and S. Young (2010), 'Debates in entrepreneurship: opportunity formation and implications for the field of entrepreneurship', in Zoltan J. Acs and David B. Audretsch (eds), *Handbook of Entrepreneurship Research: An Interdisciplinary Survey and Introduction*, New York: Springer, pp. 23–46.

Andreoni, J. (1988), 'Privately provided public goods in a large economy: the limits of altruism', *Journal of Public Economics*, 35, 57–73.

Andreoni, J. (2001), 'The economics of philanthropy', in N.J. Smelser and P.B. Baltes (eds), *International Encyclopedia of the Social and Behavioral Science*, London: Elsevier, pp. 11369–11376.

Andreoni, J., E. Brown and I. Rischall (2003), 'Charitable giving by married couples. Who decides and why does it matter?', *Journal of Human Resources*, 38, 111–133.

Andreoni, J. and L. Vesterlund (2001), 'Which is the fair sex? Gender differences in altruism', *Quarterly Journal of Economics*, 116(1), 293–312.

Banks, J. and S. Tanner (1999), 'Patterns in household giving: evidence from UK data', *Journal of Voluntary and Nonprofit Organizations*, 10(2), 167–178.

Bates, T. (1995), 'Self-employment entry across industry groups', *Journal of Business Venturing*, 10, 143–156.

Becker, G.S. (1964), *Human Capital: A Theoretical and Empirical Analysis, with Special Reference to Education*, Chicago, IL: University of Chicago Press.

Begley, T.M. and D.P. Boyd (1987), 'Psychological characteristics associated with performance in entrepreneurial firms and smaller businesses', *Journal of Business Venturing*, 2, 79–93.

Bekkers, R. (2004), 'Giving and volunteering in the Netherlands: sociological and psychological perspectives', PhD dissertation, Department of Sociology, Utrecht University, the Netherlands.

Bekkers, R. (2006), 'Keeping the faith: origins of confidence in charitable organizations and its consequences for philanthropy', presented at the NCVO/VSSN Researching the Voluntary Sector Conference 2006, Warwick University, UK.

Bekkers, R. and T. Schuyt (2005), 'And who is your neighbor? Explaining the effect of religion on charitable giving and volunteering', Working Paper, Department of Philanthropic Studies, Vrije Universiteit, Amsterdam.

Bekkers, R. and P. Wiepking (2006), 'To give or not to give, that's the question: how methodology is destiny in Dutch data', *Non-profit and Voluntary Sector Quarterly*, 35, 533–540.

Bekkers, R. and P. Wiepking (2007), 'Generosity and philanthropy: a literature review', manuscript.

Berger, I.E. (2006), 'The influence of religion on philanthropy in Canada', *Voluntas*, 17, 115–132.

Blanchflower, D. and A. Oswald (1998), 'What makes an entrepreneur?', *Journal of Labor Economics*, 16(1), 26–60.

Bloch, Thomas M. (2011), *Many Happy Returns: The Story of Henry Bloch, America's Tax Man*, Hoboken, NJ: John Wiley & Sons.

Bobbitt-Zeher, D. (2007), 'The gender income gap and the role of education', *Sociology of Education*, 80(1), 1–22.

Brandstetter, H. (1997), 'Becoming an entrepreneur – a question of personality structure', *Journal of Economic Psychology*, 18, 157–177.

Brooks, A. (2002), 'Welfare receipt and private charity', *Public Budgeting and Finance*, 22, 101–114.

Brooks, A. (2004), 'What do "don't know" responses really mean in giving surveys?', *Nonprofit and Voluntary Sector Quarterly*, 33, 324–434.

Brooks, A. (2005), 'Does social capital make you generous?', *Social Science Quarterly*, 86, 1–15.

Brown, E. (2005), 'Married couples' charitable giving: who and why?', *New Directions for Philanthropic Fundraising*, 50, 69–80.

Brown, E. and J. Ferris (2007), 'Social capital and philanthropy: an analysis of the impact of social capital on individual giving and volunteering', *Nonprofit and Voluntary Sector Quarterly*, 36(1), 85–99.

Caliendo, M., F. Fossen and A. Kritikos (2009), 'Risk attitudes of nascent entrepreneurs – new evidence from an experimentally validated survey', *Small Business Economics: An Entrepreneurship Journal*, 32(2), 153–167.

Chaves, M. (2002), 'Financing American religion', *Directions for Philanthropic Fundraising*, 35, 41–54.

Coleman, J. (1988), 'Social capital in the creation of human capital', *American Journal of Sociology Supplement*, 94, 95–120.

Cox, J. and C. Deck (2006), 'When are women more generous than men?', *Economic Inquiry*, 44(4), 587–598.

Davidsson, P. and B. Honig (2003), 'The role of social and human capital among nascent entrepreneurs', *Journal of Business Venturing*, 18(3), 301–331.

Evans, D. and L. Leighton (1989), 'Some empirical aspects of entrepreneurship', *American Economic Review*, 79, 519–535.

Feldman, N.E. (2007), 'Time is money: choosing between charitable activities', Working Paper, Ben–Gurion University, Israel.

Frese, M. (2009), 'Towards a psychology of entrepreneurship – an action theory perspective', *Foundations and Trends in Entrepreneurship*, 5(6), 485–494.

Frese, M., M. van Gelderen and M. Ombach (2000), 'How to plan as a small scale business owner: psychological process characteristics of action strategies and success', *Journal of Small Business Management*, 38(2), –18.

Gaglio, C.M. and J.A. Katz (2001), 'The psychological basis of opportunity identification: entrepreneurial alertness', *Small Business Economics*, 16(2), 95–111.

Gartner, W. (1990), 'What are we talking about when we talk about entrepreneurship', *Journal of Business Venturing*, 5(1), 15–28.

Gaudiani, C. (2003), *The Greater Good: How Philanthropy Drives the American Economy and Can Save Capitalism*, New York: Henry Holt & Co.

Gifford, S. (2010), 'Risk and uncertainty', in Zoltan J. Acs and David B. Audretsch (eds), *Handbook of Entrepreneurship Research: An Interdisciplinary Survey and Introduction*, New York: Springer, pp. 303–320.

Gimeno, J., T. Folta, A. Cooper and C. Woo (1997), 'Survival of the fittest? Entrepreneurial human capital and the persistence of underperforming firms', *Administrative Science Quarterly*, 42(4), 750–783.

Gimpel, J., F. Lee and J. Kaminski (2006), 'The political geography of campaign contributions in American politics', *Journal of Politics*, 68(3), 626–639.

Gruber, J. (2004), 'Pay or pray? The impact of charitable subsidies on religious attendance', *Journal of Public Economics*, 88, 2635–2655.

Henrekson, M. and M. Stenkula (2010), 'Entrepreneurship and public policy', in Zoltan Acs and David Audretsch (eds), *Handbook of Entrepreneurship Research*, New York: Springer, pp. 183–216.

Hoge, D. and F. Yang (1994), 'Determinants of religious giving in American denominations: data from two nationwide surveys', *Review of Religious Research*, 36(2), 123–148.

Karlsson, C. and M. Karlsson, (2002), 'Economic policy, institutions and entrepreneurship', *Small Business Economics*, 19(2), 163–171.

Knoke, D. (1990), *Organizing for Collective Action: The Political Economies of Associations*, New York: Walter de Gruyter.

Krueger, N. and M. Day (2010), 'Looking forward, looking backward: from entrepreneurial cognition to neuroentrepreneurship', in Zoltan J. Acs and David B. Audretsch (eds), *Handbook of Entrepreneurship Research: An Interdisciplinary Survey and Introduction*, New York: Springer, pp. 321–358.

Levin, S. and P. Stephan (1991), 'Research productivity over the life cycle: evidence for academic scientists', *American Economic Review*, 81(1), 114–132.

Link, A. (1995), *A Generosity of Spirit: The Early History of the Research Triangle Park*, Durham, NC: Research Triangle Park Foundation of North Carolina.

Link, A. (2002), *From Seed to Harvest: The Growth of the Research Triangle Park*, Durham, NC: Research Triangle Park Foundation of North Carolina.

Link, A. and J. Scott (2009), 'Private investor participation and commercialization rates for government-sponsored research and development: would a prediction market improve the performance of the SBIR programme?', *Economica*, 76(302), 264–281.

List, J. (2004), 'Young, selfish and male: field evidence of social preferences', *Economic Journal*, 114(492), 121–149.

Lockett, A., S. Donald, M. Wright and M. Ensley (2005), 'The creation of spin-off firms at public research institutions: managerial and policy implications', *Research Policy*, 34(7), 981–993.

Lockett, A., M. Wright and S. Franklin (2003), 'Technology transfer and universities' spin-out strategies', *Small Business Economics*, 20(2), 185–201.

Lucas, R. (1988), 'On the mechanics of economic development', *Journal of Monetary Economics*, 22(1), 3–42.

Lunn, J., R. Klay and A. Douglass (2001), 'Relationships among giving, church attendance, and religious beliefs: the case of the Presbyterian Church (USA)', *Journal for the Scientific Study of Religion*, 40(4), 765–775.

Markman, G., P. Phan, D. Balkin and P. Gianiodis (2005), 'Entrepreneurship and university-based technology transfer', *Journal of Business Venturing*, 20(2), 241–263.

Marr, K., C. Mullin and J. Siegfried (2005), 'Undergraduate financial aid and subsequent alumni giving behavior', *Quarterly Review of Economics and Finance*, 45(1), 123–143.

Mata, F. and D. McRae (2000), 'Charitable giving among the foreign-born in Canada', *Journal of International Migration and Integration/Revue de l'integration et de la migration internationale*, 1(2), 205–232.

McClelland, D. (1961), *The Achieving Society*, Princeton, NJ: Van Nostrand Company.

Mesch, D.J. (2009), 'Women and philanthropy: a literature review', Working Paper: 4/09, Indianapolis, IN: IUPUI, http://www.philanthropy.iupui.edu/womensphilan thropyinstitute/Research/LiteratureReview.

Mesch, D., P. Rooney, K. Steinberg and B. Denton (2006), 'The effects of race, gender, and marital status on giving and volunteering in Indiana', *Nonprofit and Voluntary Sector Quarterly*, 35(4), 365–587.

Micklewright, J. and S. Schnepf (2009), 'Who gives charitable donations for overseas development', *Journal of Social Policy*, 38(2), 317–341.

Midlarsky, E. and M. Hannah (1989), 'The generous elderly: naturalistic studies of donations across the life span', *Psychology and Aging*, 4(3), 346–351.

Minniti, M. and C. Nardone (2007), 'Being in someone else's shoes: the role of gender in nascent entrepreneurship', *Small Business Economics*, 28(2–3), 223–238.

Morgan, Anne (1995), *Prescription for Success: The Life and Values of Ewing Marion Kauffman*, Kansas City, MO: Andrews McMeel Publishing.

Mosey, S. and M. Wright (2007), 'From human capital to social capital: a longitudinal study of technology based academic entrepreneurs', *Entrepreneurship Theory and Practice*, 31(6), 909–935.

Osili, U. and D. Du (2005), 'Immigrant assimilation and charitable giving', *New Directions for Philanthropic Fundraising*, 48, 89–104.

Parker, S.C. (2009), *The Economics of Entrepreneurship*, Oxford: Oxford University Press.

Parker, S.C. (2010), 'Contracting out, public policy and entrepreneurship', *Scottish Journal of Political Economy*, 57(2), 119–144.

Phelps, Edmund S. (ed.) (1975), *Altruism, Morality, and Economic Theory*, New York: Russell Sage Foundation.

Piliavin, J.A. and H.-W. Charng (1990), 'Altruism: a review of recent theory and research', *Annual Review of Sociology*, 16, 27–65.

Putnam, Robert (1993), *Making Democracy Work: Civic Traditions in Modern Italy*, Princeton, NJ: Princeton University Press.

Putnam, Robert (2000), *The Collapse and Revival of American Community*, New York: Simon & Schuster.

Rauch, A. and M. Frese (2007), 'Let's put the person back into entrepreneurship research: a meta-analysis on the relationship between business owners' personality traits, business creation, and success', *European Journal of Work and Organizational Psychology*, 16(4), 353–385.

Reed, P. and K. Selbee (2000), 'Distinguishing characteristics of active volunteers in Canada', *Nonprofit and Voluntary Sector Quarterly*, 29(4), 571–592.

Regnerus, M., C. Smith and D. Sikkink (1998), 'Who gives to the poor? The influence of religious tradition and political location on the personal generosity of Americans toward the poor', *Journal for the Scientific Study of Religion*, 37(3), 481–493.

Reynolds, P., N. Carter, W. Gartner and P. Greene (2004), 'The prevalence of nascent entrepreneurs in the United States: evidence from the Panel Study of Entrepreneurial Dynamics', *Small Business Economics*, 23(4), 263–284.

Roberts, E. (1991), *Entrepreneurs in High-Technology: Lessons from MIT and Beyond*, Oxford: Oxford University Press.

Rockefeller, John D. (1984), *Random Reminiscences of Men and Events*, New York: Sleepy Hollow Press.

Romer, P. (1986), 'Increasing returns and long-run growth', *Journal of Political Economy*, 94(5), 1002–1037.

Rooney, P., E. Brown and D. Mesch (2007), 'Who decides in giving to education? A study of charitable giving by married couples', *International Journal of Educational Advancement*, 7(3), 229–242.

Saxenian, Annalee (1994), *Regional Advantage: Culture and Competition in Silicon Valley and Route 128*, Cambridge, MA: Harvard University Press.

Schervish, Paul G. and J. Havens (2002), 'The Boston area diary study and the moral citizenship of care', *Voluntas: International Journal of Voluntary and Nonprofit Organization*, 13(1), 47–71.

Shane, S. and T. Stuart (2002), 'Organizational endowments and the performance of university start-ups', *Management Science*, 48(1), 154–170.

Shapero, A. and L. Sokol (1982), 'The social dimensions of entrepreneurship', in C. Kent, D.L. Sexton and K.H. Vesper (eds), *Encyclopedia of Entrepreneurship*, Englewood Cliffs, NJ: Prentice-Hall, pp. 72–88.

Shaver, K. (2010), 'The social psychology of entrepreneurial behavior', in Z. Acs and
    D. Audretsch (eds), *The Handbook of Entrepreneurship Research: An Interdisciplinary
    Survey and Introduction*, Dordrecht: Springer, pp. 359–386.
Shepherd, D. (2013), *Journal of Business Venturing*, available at http://www.journals.elsevier.
    com/journal-of-business-venturing (accessed August 6, 2013).
Siegel, D., M. Wright and A. Lockett (2007), 'The rise of entrepreneurial activity in univer-
    sities: organizational and societal implications', *Industrial and Corporate Change*, 16(4),
    489–504.
Solow, R. (1956), 'A contribution to the theory of economic growth', *Quarterly Journal of
    Economics*, 70(1), 65–94.
Steinburg, R. and M. Wilhelm (2005), 'Religious and secular giving, by race and ethnicity',
    New Directions for Philanthropic Fundraising, 48, 57–66.
Stephan, P. and S. Levin (1992), *Striking the Mother Lode in Science: The Importance of Age,
    Place, and Time*, New York: Oxford University Press.
Ucbasaran, D., P. Westhead and M. Wright (2006), *Habitual Entrepreneurs*, Cheltenham,
    UK and Northampton, MA, USA: Edward Elgar Publishing.
Van Slyke, D.M. and A.C. Brooks (2005), 'Why do people give? New evidence and strategies
    for nonprofit managers', *American Review of Public Administration*, 35(3), 199–222.
Wunnava, P. and M. Lauze (2001), 'Alumni giving at a small liberal arts college: evidence
    from consistent and occasional donors', *Economics of Education Review*, 20(6), 533–543.
Yen, S.T. (2002), 'An econometric analysis of household donations in the USA', *Applied
    Economics Letters*, 9(13), 837–841.
Zhao, H. and S. Seibert (2006), 'The big five personality dimensions and entrepreneurial
    status: a meta-analytical review', *Journal of Applied Psychology*, 91(2), 259–271.
Zunz, Oliver (2012), *Philanthropy in America: A History*, Princeton, NJ: Princeton University
    Press.

3. Local champions: entrepreneurs' transition to philanthropy and the vibrancy of place*
Maryann P. Feldman and
Alexandra Graddy-Reed

3.1 INTRODUCTION

Often the story of successful places is predicated on the story of an individual who was instrumental in creating institutions and making connections that were transformative for a local economy. Certainly this is the case for Silicon Valley in California and Fred Terman, the Dean of Engineering at Stanford University, USA, who offered his garage to his students, Hewlett and Packard, and encouraged other start-ups. Or George Kozmetsky, the founder of Teledyne, who created the Institute for Innovation, Creativity and Capital (IC2) and mentored over 260 local computer companies in Austin, Texas. Any reading of the lives of these individuals highlights their connection to community and motivations beyond making profits. These individuals are 'regional champions' (Feldman and Zoller, 2012) – highly connected individuals who live and work in a region and take responsibility for the stewardship of the place. This defines a class of individuals who have attachment to a community and who, through their actions, make a difference in the economic vibrancy and prosperity of a place. Driven by an attachment to a place, facilitated by a developed ability to perceive opportunity, and aided by a longer-term perspective, entrepreneurs are ideal agents for engaging the vibrancy of place. It also makes good business sense for regional champions as they expand their firms. Rather than unique individual stories, these actions appear to be fairly regular events, consistently making a difference in local economies.

Many places attempt to create vibrant economies by following the rather simple recipe that involves a heavy dose of venture capital funding, research universities as a driving force, concentrations of skilled talent and an open culture – the factors associated with the current functioning of Silicon Valley. In this chapter we explore an alternative recipe: the role of entrepreneurs who have made a difference in their local communities through business practices, complementary investments in the region and ultimately through philanthropy. According to the US Treasury Department (1965), American philanthropic foundations are 'uniquely qualified to initiate thought and action, experiment with new and untried ventures, dissent from prevailing attitudes, and act quickly and flexibly' (Treasury Department, 1965). This definition captures the essence of entrepreneurs as agents of change. We propose that through philanthropy entrepreneurs are able to influence the economy of a community. In this chapter we explore entrepreneurial ventures and philanthropy that exemplify an attachment to community that may appear to defy rational profit-maximizing behavior and speak more to an altruistic and longer-term set of objectives. A typology is developed that discusses the relative impact of entrepreneurs' decisions on the larger vibrancy of communities. The typology considers business operations, such as the provision of profit sharing and education benefits; local related and diversifying investment, such as stadiums, sports teams and real estate; and the establishment of philanthropic foundations with a local mission and community orientation.

Ewing Marion Kauffman serves as an example of a local champion who exemplifies the pattern we examine. He was born and raised in Missouri and lived in Kansas City. After what the literature defines as a strategic disagreement while working as a salesman for a pharmaceutical company, Kauffman started his own pharmaceutical company. Rather than locate in the Philadelphia–New Jersey corridor, where the industry was concentrated, Kauffman decided to stay in Kansas City, a rather unlikely place in the 1950s. He named his company Marion Laboratories, Inc., using his middle name rather than his last name to add legitimacy (Morgan, 1995). When he sold his company to Merrell Dow in 1989, the company had grown to become a global diversified healthcare giant with $1 billion in sales and employment of over 3400. Marion Laboratories was a generous employer and is noted to have provided educational and training benefits, profit-sharing plans and employee stock options before these were the norm in start-up companies. By 1968, 20 of Marion's employees had become millionaires, including a widow in the accounting department. After the merger with Merrell Dow in 1989, hundreds more employees had become millionaires (Morgan, 1995).

The impact on the local economy was significant. Kauffman was a leading benefactor of Kansas City. Although he was not interested in baseball, he purchased the Royals in 1968 to bring major league baseball to the city with the belief that a team was required in order for Kansas City to be considered a major city. The Kauffman Foundation, while well known for developing entrepreneurship as a topic of academic study, has a strong local profile contributing to education, the arts and social programs.

This path from successful entrepreneur with an attachment to a region to investments in complementary business and philanthropy to develop community capacity is the focus of this chapter. Once entrepreneurs, defined here as the founders of new companies, become successful in their fields of business, they have created a substantial amount of power and financial capital. When this success is coupled with an attachment to place, entrepreneurs may become local champions who use their standing and social capital to improve their community. This is accomplished through a series of strategic actions at their organizations, as individual community members and ultimately as philanthropists.

3.2   ENTREPRENEURS' TRANSITION TO LOCAL PHILANTHROPY

Entrepreneurs recognize opportunity and organize resources to start new organizations, develop technologies and enable change. Schumpeter (1947) views the entrepreneur as a reformer who exploits existing technology – an innovator as opposed to an inventor. North (1990), on the other hand, describes entrepreneurs as the agents driving institutional change (North, 1990; Schumpeter, 1947). Entrepreneurs actively engage with their local environment to build relationships and advocate for resources that assist their growing businesses (Feldman, 1999). Recognizing the importance of the local ecosystem, entrepreneurs develop a geographic community of common interest around their technology – building a cluster while building a firm.

Entrepreneurs use their local networks to shift norms that lead to institutional change when they transition to policy entrepreneurs – advocates who invest resources to bring about policy change (Mintrom and Norman, 2009; North, 1990). Institutions, defined as rules, norms and culture (North, 1990; Ostrom, 2009) are endogenous and subject to change. Focused on a specific objective, policy entrepreneurs are known for their political connections, persistence and push beyond the status quo to take risks. Policy entrepreneurs frame and define a mission and then use their political and institutional reach to direct resources towards that mission (Kingdon, 2002). They are distinguishable by their high levels of social acuity and their ability to define problems, build teams and lead by example (Mintrom and Norman, 2009). These policy entrepreneurs are in fact entrepreneurs who have focused their energy on opportunities to bring about institutional change.

Successful entrepreneurs can also use their wealth for socially beneficial investments. Although dominant actors in their own industry, these individuals see philanthropy as a means to achieve an elite status, acquire the power to act on a larger scale, and increase multiple types of their capital – cultural, social, economic and symbolic (Harvey et al., 2011). Social capital, the connections to others and organizations, can influence changes in other types of capital and increase total capital (Emery and Flora, 2006; Zahra et al., 2009). Thus, philanthropy can yield social, cultural and symbolic returns that then lead to economic returns; entrepreneurs are drawn to philanthropy as a source of these capitals (Harvey et al., 2011). The private and public benefits to philanthropy place it in an impure altruistic model (Andreoni, 1990). This theory allows for individuals to be both rational and altruistic in their giving and explains why despite financial incentives, not all wealthy individuals engage in philanthropy (Andreoni, 1990; Harriss, 1939). These theories help explain why entrepreneurs are predisposed to give: not only will the entrepreneur benefit from the improved economic standing of her surrounding community and increased capital, but their efforts to create resources and capacity has significant effects on the economic well-being of an area – making it a tool for economic development work (Irvin, 2007).

The US structure of philanthropy allows for many types of foundations that range in mission, size and focus. Corporate foundations receive their assets from a connected for-profit business, while family foundations have been endowed by members of a family, who stay actively engaged in the decision-making of the foundation. Independent foundations are usually funded by a single source and are set up to provide grants in specific designated areas of social assistance (Grant Space, n.d.). Community foundations are usually public charities, receiving funds from multiple donors that are then managed and dispersed to charitable grants for specific communities or regions (Grant Space, n.d.). Community foundations are arguably actively engaged in place-based economic development. Local donors pool their resources and then discuss allocation – expanding the number of voices participating in the grant-making decisions, but still rarely including other stakeholders (Ostrander, 2007). Venture philanthropy is a style of giving often used by entrepreneurs across foundation types that employs a more business-like approach to giving with greater attention to the grantee and with more expectations for returns on the investment (Letts et al., 1997).

3.3   CHAMPIONS OF THEIR LOCAL COMMUNITIES: A CONTINUUM

Entrepreneurs first assist their communities by being successful – spurring the local economy through a multiplier effect associated with export

Figure 3.1   Local champions' continuum

industries. However, entrepreneurs can also improve the quality of life in a local community through supportive employment practices, such as paying what have become known as living wages, providing profit-sharing plans, investing in employees through education and training and providing health benefits. Entrepreneurs can also diversify their business investments in the community across industry. On the social end, they provide charitable giving to the community through the firm's corporate social responsibility practices and with direct personal donations through philanthropic organizations. They work as local elites to use their own social and financial capital to improve the local community. See Figure 3.1.

3.3.1   Supportive Business Practices

Providing supportive employee practices and creating a healthy business environment offers benefits to the community and employees. A 2012 report on North Carolina organizations showed the vast majority of survey respondents provided some employee benefits with 84 percent offering on-site training and 48 percent offering employee education (Graddy-Reed et al., 2013). These benefits increase the employee's skills and the quality of life in the community and are fundamentally different than wage-cutting and incentive-seeking behavior from firms. Entrepreneurs can also engage the community through positive business practices. In the North Carolina survey, 81 percent of respondents used local suppliers (Graddy-Reed et al., 2013), which is another business practice that strengthens the community's economy by keeping resources within the area.

3.3.2   Diversified Business Investments

Entrepreneurs become local champions when they invest resources to improve communities. Many entrepreneurs improve their local community by diversifying their investments while staying local; new ventures in sports teams, newspapers, real estate and entertainment bring up the community's amenities while improving the status and advancing the motives of the entrepreneur. These diversified financial investments in the community provide improved quality of life for employees and community members, which create short- and long-term benefits for the area.

3.3.3   Corporate Social Responsibility

Entrepreneurs also improve their community by engaging their company in charitable or civic-minded activity. In the above-mentioned survey, North Carolina respondents also strongly supported their community beyond business practices: 57 percent donated the use of their facilities, 51 percent supported K-12 education and 30 percent had a company service day (Graddy-Reed et al., 2013). The work of Tony Hsieh in Las Vegas and Dan Gilbert in Detroit are other examples of entrepreneurs who are using their financial success to make local investments in their cities' urban areas. These actions may be seen as an extension of what is known in the literature as corporate social responsibility (CSR) – the action by for-profit firms to give back to their community by providing time, funding, or their specialized skills and technology towards the greater good. CSR has long been practiced in the US but appears to be gaining popularity as many firms intend to keep or expand their efforts, even in poor economic conditions (Delevingne, 2009). In terms of who is engaged in CSR, research on the transition of business leaders into greater corporate citizenship found that women and young entrepreneurs and family firms are high givers (Reis and Clohesy, 2001).

Firms consider CSR to be influential for their reputation and chances of future success (Delevingne, 2009). The literature finds two main reasons firms engage in CSR: business success and customer base. The former has found mixed results of CSR affecting business success, with the most rigorous studies finding no effect of CSR on financial performance (Aupperle et al., 1985; McWilliams and Siegel, 2000). However, there is strong support for CSR in terms of customer base as CSR is strongly desired by certain segments of the population and can boost the reputation of a firm (McWilliams and Siegel, 2000).

3.3.4   Creation of Private Named Foundations

With a deepening commitment, entrepreneurs may expand their efforts to personal involvement outside of their business life. This type of investment includes personal donations to community efforts, support of local community foundations and their projects and potentially the creation of an individual and/or family foundation focused on sustaining and growing the community. Private donations and the creation of endowments allow for the entrepreneur to remain influential in the process of community development. At the turn of the last century, the creation of universities was one avenue through which philanthropists improved their communities. Often named after the philanthropist, these private universities have become anchors in the communities where they are located.

As with their business investments, entrepreneurs champion their communities through personal philanthropic investments that include short-term efforts to address immediate problems and longer-term investments to sustain improved conditions. For example, Tom Cousins, a local developer, transitioned into social entrepreneurship when he worked to revitalize the East Lake Meadows community, an impoverished neighborhood in Atlanta, Georgia. Tom Cousins moved through the continuum of investing his own capital, pulling in the resources of his extensive network, making investments through his named family foundation and creating a dedicated nonprofit community foundation (Van Slyke and Newman, 2006). Cousins was motivated by his own 'social theory of impact' which was 'predicated on a hypothesis that redevelopment could not emerge without these other [education, job training, child care] components in place, which would contribute to sustainability over the long term' (Van Slyke and Newman, 2006: 346). Because of his efforts, home values increased and more investment followed. The original lower-income residents mostly either remained in the neighborhood or moved to other neighborhoods that were better than the original East Lake Meadows (Van Slyke and Newman, 2006).

3.3.5 Engagement with Community Foundations

Community foundations are unique entities that exist to engage in place-based economic development and were created to pool charitable resources for greater impact. There are now more than 700 community foundations in the United States with $55 billion in assets (Foundation Center, 2012) and an equal number in the rest of the world. The mandate of community foundations is local. They are continuously informed by local developments and able to respond quickly to local needs and opportunities.

Entrepreneurs support the local community through their investment in and founding of community foundations. Unlike private and family foundations, community foundations are named for the area they are meant to improve and gain assets from multiple donors. They are tax-exempt charitable organizations that provide support for a particular community or region and walk the line between foundations as grant-makers and charities as they receive funds from multiple public donors (Grant Space, n.d.). They connect a network of local champions and unite the business community to address place-based problems.

The first community foundation was the Cleveland Foundation started in 1914 by Frederick Goff, a visionary banker and lawyer. While with contemporary eyes bankers are not perceived as entrepreneurs, legal changes around the establishment of the Federal Reserve allowed for opportunities of entry. Goff, who was attorney to John D. Rockefeller, created community foundations to follow the donor's intent as charitable needs changed in an area and for this to be ensured through a board of directors, chosen by public institutions (Carson, 1994). Goff is noted to have promoted the idea using his social standing and, in part due to his proselytizing, eight more community foundations were started within a year, mostly organized by bankers and trust officers (Grogan, 2013). By 1930, there were 22 community foundations, mostly in the Midwest (Carman, 2001).

Community foundations are rising in importance because as federal support of community development declines, communities need more support from foundations and businesses (Carman, 2001). While US community foundations account for almost 10 percent of all foundation giving, providing approximately $4 billion a year, they do so by giving differently: they are more likely than their private and corporate counterparts to fund arts and culture, education and religion, while they are less likely to fund international and public affairs (Foundation Center, 2012). Table 3.1 gives details of community foundations with assets over $1 billion.

3.4   CASES OF LOCAL CHAMPIONS

We develop examples of how entrepreneurial action along the continuum affects local economic development. For small towns, local entrepreneurs are key stakeholders for the prosperity of the community by using their social capital to link professional and social networks (Tolbert, 2005). Sam Walton and the growth of Walmart, and Fred Carl and the evolution of Viking Ranges, serve as examples of single champions revitalizing rural areas in the South. Two urban entrepreneurs in Seattle, Paul Allen and Jeff Bezos, are then compared to showcase different stages of the continuum. Finally, the case of the Research Triangle Park in North Carolina is discussed to provide a counterfactual: how places respond when they lack a local champion.

3.4.1   The Waltons and Walmart: Making Northwest Arkansas an International Destination

Sam Walton, the creator of Walmart, was a modest man with a dislike for publicity (Rosen, 2009; Vance and Scott, 1992). He began his empire

Table 3.1 Community foundations with assets over $1 billion

Foundation	Assets	Founded	Founders
The Cleveland Foundation	$1.8B	1914	Frederick H. Goff (banker & lawyer)
Chicago Community Trust	$1.6B	1915	Albert W. Harris (banker)
California Community Foundation (Los Angeles)	$1.2B	1915	Joe Sartori (banker)
New York Community Trust	$1.9B	1924	11 New York financiers
The Columbus Foundation	$1.1B	1943	Harrison M. Sayre (publisher & founder of *Weekly Reader*)
The San Francisco Foundation	$1.1B	1948	Daniel Koshland, member of the Levi Strauss family
Oregon Community Foundation	$1.0B	1973	William Swindells (Willamette Industries)
Greater Kansas City Foundation	$1.2B	1978	Seven local entrepreneurs from diverse industries
Marin Community Foundation	$1.2B	1986	Leonard and Beryl H. Buck (oil industry)
Tulsa Community Foundation	$4.0B	1988	George Kaiser (oil industry and banker)
Silicon Valley Community Foundation	$2.1B	2006	Merger between Peninsula Community Foundation (1964) and Community Foundation Silicon Valley (1954)

by purchasing an existing store in Newport, Arkansas in 1945 (Vance and Scott, 1992). While there he took an active role in that community, but when he could not renew his lease, Walton left Newport for Northwest Arkansas (Hagge, 2009). He then opened his own store in Bentonville, Arkansas in 1950 and the first Walmart store in 1962, which was quickly followed by many more (Nene, 2005; Vance and Scott, 1992). Walmart went public in 1970 and continued to grow rapidly, expanding to new store types like Sam's Club and Supercenters (Nene, 2005; Vance and Scott, 1992). As of 2013, Walmart is the world's largest company and employs over 1.5 million people (Hemphill, 2005). Nine out of ten households have shopped at a Walmart in the past few months and the average household spends over $2000 a year there (Hicks, 2007).

Walmart's strategy for success is built around low profit margins on high volumes of sales. Initially the stores were concentrated in rural areas and supplied neighboring towns (Nene, 2005). They cut cost by using an innovative system of delivery through distribution centers, so vendors shipped to distribution centers which then sent out products to stores (Vance and Scott, 1992). They were also quick to incorporate technology, using computer systems for payroll and inventory in the mid-1970s and creating the largest private satellite communication system in the country in 1987 to manage inventory (Nene, 2005; Vance and Scott, 1992). Their most controversial strategy for cost-cutting has been on the supply side – by leveraging their buying power to force suppliers to cut costs of production, making them much more involved in the production process (Hagge, 2009; Hemphill, 2005).

Two sides of Walmart's impact
Walmart uses the term 'associate' over 'employee' to create a sense of equality and consensus (Rosen, 2009). The company believes it pays competitive wages and offers a variety of benefits including profit sharing, retirement plans, stock matching and loan programs, paid vacation time, health insurance, disability insurance and counseling (Hemphill, 2005). Although retail wages are low, many early employees became multi-millionaires through profit sharing (Rosen, 2009). Walton facilitated employees' purchase of stock, provided stock as bonuses, and ordered stock splits to keep the share price low and affordable for employees and customers (Hagge, 2009). Walmart has been well regarded for its corporate citizenship, especially for its work within local communities, which is heavily advertised (Hemphill, 2005). It has also invested in green buildings for the corporation (Tyler, 2012). In 2012, Walmart and the Walmart Foundation donated $1 billion in the United States to hunger relief, sus-

tainability, women's empowerment and career development (Walmart, 2013).

However, Walmart is often criticized for having poor employee benefits and discriminating against women and minorities. Walton himself admitted to not always taking care of his employees when the company was growing (Rosen, 2009). Studies have shown that Walmart stores, and any big-box store, result in a net loss of jobs and lower wages and benefits for a community (Hemphill, 2005; Nene, 2005). Further, studies have found that a large number of Walmart employees and their families receive anti-poverty public assistance and Medicaid health insurance (Hicks, 2007), which are paid by taxpayers, thus providing a public subsidy to Walmart (Nene, 2005).

In spite of these issues, Northwest Arkansas grew rapidly from the 1960s and morphed from a collection of rural towns to a thriving and diverse metro area due to the success and presence of Walmart's corporate headquarters and its suppliers. Walmart's decision to keep its headquarters in the area propelled the success of the region, bringing the banking industry in the state to the area and creating the need for the development of office parks and better housing and services, which all added to the capital of the area (Hagge, 2009; Rosen, 2009).

Sam Walton's philanthropy

Through Sam Walton's innovative strategies, Walmart has become the largest private employer in the US and, as a result, made the Waltons the richest family in the US. Their wealth has prompted the Waltons to turn to philanthropy. The Walton Family Foundation, founded by Sam Walton and his wife Helen, has assets of over $1.7 billion and supports the areas of systemic reform in K-12 education, marine and freshwater conservation, Northwest Arkansas and the delta region of Arkansas and Mississippi (Foundation Center, 2013b). Along with its focused areas of giving, the Foundation employs a venture philanthropy approach, considering its grants investments toward its specific goals and thoroughly evaluating these investments with benchmarks (Walton Family Foundation, 2013a).

The Walton Family Foundation is actively involved with its home region, following the desire of Sam Walton to improve the quality of life for Northwest Arkansas (Walton Family Foundation, 2013a). In 2012, the foundation provided grants of over $30 million to the home region to improve the education and economic development of the area (Walton Family Foundation, 2013b). The foundation is also an active funder of charter schools and school vouchers in an effort to revamp the nation's education system (Hopkins, 2004). In addition to the family foundation, the Waltons engage in individual philanthropic projects. Sam's daughter Alice

Walton created the Crystal Bridges Museum of American Art, located in Northwest Arkansas (Rosen, 2009). She was the primary financier of the over $800 million cost, which also received support from the community through a sponsorship gift from Walmart to provide free admission to the public, and an education program funded by the Walker Foundation, a local philanthropy of an early Walmart employee (Tyler, 2012).

The Northwest Arkansas community
The wealth of the area continues to be reinvested in it. The Arvest Bank, the largest in the state and the bank of Walmart, sponsored a new stadium for the minor league baseball team, which it owns (Rosen, 2009). In addition to the Walton Family Foundation, other family foundations like the Pat and Willard Walker Charitable Foundation were created with money made through Walmart's success and now support the area. The Walker Foundation with assets over $20 million invests in education, community development and health care for the area (Foundation Center, 2013c). Much of this local philanthropy was encouraged and promoted by the Waltons, who lived modestly and used their wealth to reinvest in the region (Hagge, 2009).

The large wealth in the area has also led to the creation of multiple community foundations, which have pulled wealth from many individuals to help develop the area. The Endeavor Foundation was established in 1999 and has assets of over $150 million and has provided over $60 million in grants (Endeavor, 2011). There is also the Fayetteville Area Community Foundation, established in 2004 as a regional affiliate of the Arkansas Community Foundation (Foundation Center, 2013a). With the help of Sam Walton and the success of Walmart, Northwest Arkansas has transformed from a region of rural towns into a wealthy hub of multiple industries and a community driven to keep improving its quality of life.

3.4.2   Rising Waves in the Delta: Fred Carl and the Viking Range

Greenwood, Mississippi was once the prosperous capital of the cotton industry, but mechanization favored the open spaces of west Texas, and globalization favored imports. In a familiar story of economic restructuring, Greenwood fell upon hard times. Located in the Mississippi Delta, Greenwood was a small city in the poorest region of the poorest state in the United States. In such a situation, it is difficult to engineer a comeback. While federal and state government programs were available, the lack of a tax base made it difficult to restructure the economy and to recover from the loss of a once prominent industry.

Fred Carl Jr emerged as a local champion for Greenwood, inventing a new product that provided jobs for residents, revitalizing the city through diversified investments and improving the quality of life for residents by offering human capital support. Fred Carl is indicative of a class of entrepreneurs who are dedicated to conducting business differently, with an emphasis on increasing prosperity in their home communities. This exemplifies an attachment to place and community that seemingly defies rational profit-maximizing behavior and speaks more to an altruistic set of objectives (Feldman, forthcoming).

A native of Greenwood, Fred Carl was a fourth-generation building contractor. Carl set out to create a household stove of commercial quality, which was absent from the market. After designing a prototype that combined commercial power and quality with the styling and safety of a residential range, Fred Carl gathered financing from investors and incorporated Viking Range Corporation. He quickly followed the advice of his wife's cousin and ran his company as if it was publicly traded, hiring the best accountants and lawyers (Carl, 2007). He approached his business with high expectations of quality and service to create his high-end product (Carl, 2007).

Viking Range Corporation was incorporated in 1984 (Viking Range, n.d.-a). After struggling to find partners, Carl partnered with a California manufacturer and began production in 1987. But when demand grew beyond their capacity, Carl decided to move production to Greenwood in 1989 (Kornegay, 2012; Mississippi Secretary of State, n.d.). While he had originally planned to relocate to Jackson, Mississippi, a larger and more successful city in his home state, he was moved by his feelings of disloyalty and guilt to instead move back home to Greenwood (Holliday, 2004). In 1992, Stephens, Inc. invested in Viking, allowing it to expand, growing from 32 000 to 600 000 square feet of manufacturing space; it continued to grow and branch out into other appliances (Mississippi Secretary of State, n.d.). Viking quickly became the county's largest private employer and second overall to the hospital, with over 1000 jobs at its peak (Kornegay, 2012; McMillin, 2013).

But Carl and Viking did not just bring jobs to Greenwood: they brought strong employee benefits to improve the quality of life of Greenwood. Viking has 99 percent retention and attendance rates for its employees, with an average tenure of nine years. It is repeatedly named one of the best places to work in Mississippi by the *Mississippi Business Journal* (Carl, 2007; Kornegay, 2012; Viking Range, n.d.-c). It offers a competitive salary, advancement and educational opportunities, and strong employee benefits including full medical, pharmaceutical, vision and dental coverage to full-time employees. It also offers retirement savings plans with employer matching, life insurance and disability coverage (Viking Range, n.d.-c). Employees can be reimbursed for the full cost of their tuition for high school, college or graduate degrees and can receive on-site and external training to improve their skills (Carl, 2007; Viking Range, n.d.-c).

Viking's Greenwood
Fred Carl continued to revitalize Greenwood through diversified investments within Viking. Carl and Viking bought properties in downtown, started new businesses of restaurants and shops, and facilitated others to create start-ups by renting refurbished space (McMillin, 2013). Former cotton warehouses were retrofitted to serve as manufacturing sites in downtown, and Viking headquarters are a collection of historic buildings, including the 1903 opera house (Holliday, 2004). For these efforts, the Mississippi Heritage Trust and the National Trust for Preservation have recognized Viking (Viking Range, n.d.-b).

Furthering its efforts in historic preservation, and to diversify investments, Viking renovated the Hotel Irving into the Alluvian, a five-star boutique hotel and spa, in 2003. The motivation behind this investment was in part the lack of a nice hotel in Greenwood for buyers, suppliers and dealers (Holliday, 2004). The high-end hotel also features an art collection of Mississippi artists (Viking Range, n.d.-b). The hotel along with its spa and fine dining made Greenwood into a travel destination for cooking enthusiasts (Newsome, 2007). Adding to the travel package is the presence of the Viking Cooking School, of which there are multiple sites across the country (Mississippi Secretary of State, n.d.). In 2006, the Alluvian hosted 18000 guests, which is roughly the same as the number of residents in Greenwood (Newsome, 2007).

Beyond investments, Viking has also improved the quality of life for Greenwood through service work and charitable donations. Viking sponsored a Professional Golfers' Association (PGA) tour, the Viking Classic, for five years beginning in 2007, which raised money for 90 charities in Mississippi (Newsome, 2007; Viking Range, n.d.-b). Viking employees are encouraged to volunteer and have had their own fundraising events for the American Cancer Society and the local United Way, and hosted a blood drive for the Mississippi Blood Services (Viking Range, n.d.-b). Viking's efforts have also improved Greenwood by inspiring others to invest in the city. Following their efforts, new investors have opened restaurants, museums and a nightclub (Holliday, 2004). These efforts have left a significant impact on Greenwood, revitalizing it for a modern generation.

Fred Carl's philanthropy
Fred Carl also acted on his own to promote the well-being of his hometown, financing a number of developments within the city including build-

ing renovations and a bookstore (McMillin, 2013). He also served on the Governor's Commission on Recovery, Rebuilding, and Renewal after Hurricane Katrina and was then appointed Housing Chair of Gulf Coast Rebuilding (Viking Range, n.d.-a). His effort in and leadership of Viking made him Man of the Year of the Greenwood Commonwealth in 2002. He was also awarded a national American Spirit Award in 2006 for his volunteerism and donations to areas affected by hurricanes (Viking Range, n.d.-a). Carl has supported student scholarships and student recruiting efforts at his alma mater Mississippi State University and has made his largest monetary donation to its College of Architecture with a $2.5 million donation to support the Small Town Center (University Relations, 2003). Carl and his wife have a foundation in their name, the Fred and Margaret Carl Foundation, located in Greenwood, which is an independent foundation but has not yet received a large endowment (Foundation Center, n.d.), possibly signaling that Carl is preparing for a greater presence through his foundation.

Changing roles and the future of Fred Carl, Viking and Greenwood

The success of the Viking Corporation has been waning following the recession of 2008–2009. As a result, Viking had to lay off a quarter of its workforce, decreasing it to approximately 1000 employees (Schoen, 2010). Then in January of 2013, Fred Carl announced that he had sold Viking to the Middleby Corporation for $380 million. He assured employees that little would change, but as with any shift in leadership, change was inevitable, and just one month later Middleby laid off 200 employees, half of whom were in Greenwood. In addition, Carl announced his resignation (Chandler, 2013a). The new chief executive officer (CEO), Selim Bassoul, said these would be the only layoffs and that Viking would remain in Greenwood (Chandler, 2013a). The laid-off employees did receive a minimum of four months of salary and benefits, costing Middleby $2 million (Chandler, 2013b).

In spite of this downturn, Carl remains optimistic about Viking and Greenwood and continues his investments and support in the city, including plans to open two new restaurants. On the philanthropic side, Viking donated the old Elks Lodge to Carl's foundation, under which it will be renovated and used for public and private events (McMillin, 2013). Now, Greenwood begins a new period, where Viking and Fred Carl still dominate, but it is clear that new investors are needed to sustain the vitality Carl built.

3.4.3   Two Sides of Seattle: Paul Allen and Jeff Bezos

Paul Allen and Microsoft
Paul Allen, a child of educators, was born and raised in Seattle, Washington (PGA Family Foundation, 2013). While in school in the 1960s, Allen met Bill Gates and they began the first high school computer club (Keiper, 2011). After working on small jobs together, the two quit college and launched Microsoft in 1975 as a company that made software for microprocessor computers. In 1980, they received a contract from IBM (Keiper, 2011).

In 1982, Allen was diagnosed with Hodgkin's lymphoma. He left Microsoft to treat the disease in 1983 (Keiper, 2011). Although he departed from Microsoft early on, the company continued to grow and now has over 40 000 employees in Washington alone (Microsoft, 2013). The company has a large philanthropic presence in the state and works on issues around public education, transportation and the arts to improve the quality of life for both employees and other citizens (Microsoft, 2013).

Beyond Microsoft
Microsoft went public in 1986 and Allen soon became a billionaire (Keiper, 2011). Allen had beaten cancer and decided to diversify his business ventures. He turned to his enjoyment of sports and purchased the Portland Trail Blazers basketball team in 1988 and then in 1997 purchased the Seattle Seahawks football team (Keiper, 2011). He is also part owner of the Seattle Sounders soccer team (Allen Institute for Brain Science, 2013). He described the purchase of the Seahawks as a 'civic chore' since he did not actually care for football at the time but instead saw the danger of the team moving to California and the need to keep the team in Seattle for its vitality (Keiper, 2011).

He founded Vulcan Incorporated, which manages both his business and philanthropic investments (PGA Family Foundation, 2013). In the 1990s he invested in a variety of entertainment and online companies that included services and content providers, a cable company, DreamWorks and Oxygen Media (Biography Channel website, 2013). At the turn of the century, Allen expanded his interests to space, and in 2004 he funded SpaceShipOne in an effort to put people in suborbital space. The company built the first spaceship to reach space that was not built by the government (Keiper, 2011). Then in 2011 he founded Stratolaunch Systems, a company that works on a new approach to airborne launches (Allen Institute for Brain Science, 2013). Allen has also invested heavily in real estate to redevelop Seattle's South Lake Union neighborhood (Allen Institute for Brain Science, 2013).

Allen's philanthropy

Allen has been generous and aggressive with his money, taking an involved venture approach to philanthropy. So far, he has given over $1.5 billion and has pledged to donate the majority of his fortune (PGA Family Foundation, 2013). In 1988 he and his sister founded the Paul G. Allen Family Foundation, which is largely focused on investing heavily in communities of the Pacific Northwest (PGA Family Foundation, 2013). They fund a variety of projects that support entrepreneurs, writers, artists and, following their parents' interests, fund libraries in the local area (PGA Family Foundation, 2013).

Beyond the foundation, Paul Allen also gives directly. After meeting with the experts in genomics, neuroscience and psychology in 2001, he launched the Allen Institute for Brain Science in Seattle in 2003 with a $100 million endowment. In 2006, their researchers produced the Allen Brain Atlas – a mapping of the active genes in a mouse brain, and a tool now used by hundreds of researchers (Wadman, 2007). He has since committed another $400 million to the institute (Allen Institute for Brain Science, 2013). The ultimate goal of the institute is to help cure neurological disorders like Parkinson's and Alzheimer's, a disease he witnessed firsthand with his mother (Keiper, 2011).

In 2010, Allen made a gift of $26 million to Washington State University for the Paul G. Allen School of Global Animal Health (PGA Family Foundation, 2013). He has also founded three museums: one around music and science fiction, one on aircrafts from World War II and another on computer equipment, all in the Seattle area (Allen Institute for Brain Science, 2013).

Jeff Bezos and Amazon

Also located in Seattle, Jeff Bezos is one of the wealthiest people in the US, with a net worth of over $20 billion (Cook, 2011; Gunther, 2012). The founder of Amazon stays out of the press, surrounding himself in a bit of mystery. While his family has a large expensive home on Lake Washington, they are often seen driving a Honda minivan (Ross Gardner, 2013). Born in Albuquerque, New Mexico, Bezos grew up in Houston and spent his summers working on his grandfather's ranch (Academy of Achievement, 2013). He attended Princeton University, where he studied computer science and electrical engineering, before moving to Wall Street and rising in the chain of command (Academy of Achievement, 2013).

Then Bezos was inspired by the rising use of the Internet and saw the book market was lacking a mail order shop (Academy of Achievement, 2013). He and his wife set out to start Amazon. They picked Seattle to be close to a book wholesaler and computer experts (Academy of

Achievement, 2013). The other appeal of Seattle was the small population: under the Supreme Court ruling at the time, online retailers did not have to collect sales taxes in states where they were not physically located, allowing most of his customers to not pay sales tax (Martinez and Heim, 2012). Amazon launched in 1995 and within one month, with no press, Amazon had sold books in every state (Academy of Achievement, 2013). Bezos's parents invested a large portion of their life savings into Amazon, $300 000 at the time, and then quickly became billionaires (Academy of Achievement, 2013). Their strategy has been to run a tighter profit margin while maintaining a larger share of the market (Academy of Achievement, 2013; Martinez and Heim, 2012). As of 2013, Amazon is a large and successful company, second in the Northwest only to Microsoft (Martinez and Heim, 2012).

Amazon's business and community practices
Amazon's success has not led to a strong reputation for employee or social practices. While little is known about the employee benefits it does offer, Amazon came under fire in 2011 for poor working conditions in its Pennsylvania warehouse, where employees worked without air conditioning in over 90 degree temperatures (Gunther, 2012). Following a media uproar, Amazon installed air-conditioning at a cost of $52 million (Shafer, 2013). Meanwhile, its white-collar workers appear to lack typical benefits like training: a director of a civic leadership program reported that Amazon employees who take the training say they have to cover their own cost, in juxtaposition to the other major corporations in the area that cover it for their employees (Martinez and Heim, 2012). There is also little incentive to volunteer or donate for Amazon employees, and they even face a disincentive at times: employees who would like donations deducted from their paychecks are charged a 6 percent fee from the company that processes Amazon's payroll (Martinez and Heim, 2012).

Amazon is also lacking in corporate social responsibility and support from and for its local neighbors in Seattle (Holtzman, 2011). Amazon does not publish a sustainability report, which is unusual for large corporations (Gunther, 2012). According to Amazon, employees have engaged in volunteering in many states, of which its largest contribution probably comes in the form of technology use and support as it lets nonprofits use a set of tools to generate online donations (Holtzman, 2011). It also hosts online appeals to customers, which have raised over $35 million for disaster relief efforts (Holtzman, 2011). Following the increased attention towards its lack of service, Amazon has announced efforts to increase its local philanthropy. It has pledged two $1 million endowments of professorships at the University of Washington in the computer science department and has reached out to local nonprofits to offer volunteers and donations (Martinez and Heim, 2012). It has also launched AmazonSmile which provides a 0.5 percent donation to charity when customers shop through the site (Research and Insights, 2013).

Amazon's limited social engagement runs parallel to its level of community development in Seattle. Bezos and Amazon continue to keep a low presence in Seattle, even as it expands. Even though Bezos was named 'Executive of the Year' by the *Puget Sound Business Journal* in 2011, he did not appear at the luncheon honoring him (Martinez and Heim, 2012). Further, the Amazon logo is missing from all of its buildings at its new campus in the South Lake Union area (Martinez and Heim, 2012). Seattle city planning seems happy with Amazon, however. When the company decided to move and expand to South Lake Union there were no negotiations with the city for incentives, just a desire to do it (Johnson and Wingfield, 2013). Amazon is also encouraging its employees to live within walking distance, and plans to buy a new streetcar for the light rail system that will run by its campus, as well as pay for part of a dedicated bicycle lane (Johnson and Wingfield, 2013). While Amazon does appear to be dedicated to remaining in Seattle and supportive of an environmentally conscious work environment, the move to South Lake Union has left Amazon's former neighborhood to deteriorate (Ross Gardner, 2013).

Bezos beyond Amazon
While Amazon is clearly his top priority, Bezos has begun to diversify his business ventures. He recently purchased the *Washington Post* for $250 million (in cash), though his plans for the newspaper are unknown at this time (Johnson and Wingfield, 2013). In 2004, he founded an aerospace company, Blue Origin, which is aimed at developing space travel and recreation (Academy of Achievement, 2013).

In terms of philanthropy, Bezos is beginning to leave a footprint. The Bezos Family Foundation is focused on education and improving children's ability to utilize their abilities (Bezos Family Foundation, 2013), though it has also funded cancer research (Martinez and Heim, 2012). Regarding individual acts, Bezos has donated $15 million to his alma mater Princeton for neuroscience research, $10 million to immunotherapy research to fight cancer, and funded the development of a 10 000 Year Clock in Texas (Cook, 2011; Gayomali, 2011). Bezos is beginning to donate locally, with a $10 million donation to the Museum of History and Industry in Seattle (Cook, 2011). However these efforts are small in comparison to other tech giants, especially those of his neighbors, Bill Gates and Paul Allen of Microsoft. This may be due in part to his philosophy of philanthropy: Bezos has said that he feels that for-profit models are a better way to solve problems than philanthropy (Ross Gardner, 2013). Further, he sees Amazon's most important contribution to society as its success in business and the employment it provides (Martinez and Heim, 2012). However, Bezos has also said he thinks that philanthropy takes as much work as running a successful company (Academy of Achievement, 2013), so perhaps he has not yet been able to devote the time to it he feels it requires.

Contrasting Seattle's best
Although both Allen and Bezos reside in Seattle and call it home for themselves and many of their investments, the two represent two different approaches to business and philanthropy. Allen has a clear attachment to Seattle – he was raised there, began his business there and dedicates many of his resources to improving the area. Bezos, on the other hand, is a newcomer and seems less attached to Seattle as he has invested little in the community and focused his efforts where he has a greater attachment, like his alma mater. Interestingly, both Bezos and Allen have shown an interest in the brain, focusing much of their philanthropy in the area of neuroscience research and each creating their own centers, and in space travel, both funding business ventures in the area.

Though Allen is no longer a part of Microsoft, the companies do reflect different approaches to business. Microsoft is located in the suburbs of Seattle, while Amazon is in the heart of downtown. It was with Allen's help that Amazon was able to prosper in the city, since it was Allen who invested in real estate in the South Lake Union area and later leased and sold the property to Amazon (Johnson and Wingfield, 2013). But while physically detached, Microsoft is much more involved with Seattle than Amazon, through corporate and employee donations and a program of loaning executives to local charities (Holtzman, 2011). Amazon, on the other hand, still lags in terms of corporate responsibility (Gunther, 2012). However, Microsoft was also criticized in its early days for not giving enough back to the community (Martinez and Heim, 2012). So while we may be seeing two different examples – one with Allen as a champion of place and Bezos as a detached businessman – there may be another story, where Bezos is still developing his attachment to Seattle and how he wants to actualize that support.

3.4.4   The Counterfactual: Research Triangle Park and the Lack of an Entrepreneur

The lack of an entrepreneur tied to the Research Triangle Park (RTP) in North Carolina has left it without a local advocate and without strong ties to its community. What makes RTP unusual from other industry clusters is that it was a planned, public–private strategy to change the economy of the region. Its business success is attributed to a variety of factors including the timing after World War II, a concentration of research universities in the area, a critical mass of people who continue to thrive in the area and a long-term commitment by the varied interests that formed it (Weddle et al., 2006). RTP continues to develop and change.

The idea for RTP originated in the private sector in the mid-1950s. It was a grand idea to create a mecca for research and development (R&D) in a state that was at the bottom of per capita income in the US. But the idea was too grand for the private sector. Fortunately, the Governor, Luther Hodges, a former textile mill executive, believed in the idea and created a public–private partnership. Early on, the decision was made to stick to the target of attracting R&D operations even though manufacturing offered politically important employment (Feldman and Lowe, 2011). The recruitment of R&D was intensely personal, and locals advocated and lobbied large firms to locate. Through changes in governors, political administrations and political parties, a long history of adaptive and responsive public policy in the state was able to create conditions attractive to entrepreneurship. The industrial genesis is the story of the attraction of large multinational firms to locate their R&D operations in RTP and then the encouragement of start-up firms once the larger ones went through the inevitable mergers and acquisitions, lay-offs and restructurings (Lowe and Feldman, 2014).

The strategy did pay off, although it is said to be a 50-year overnight success. RTP's achievement defies the conventional wisdom that regions need to attract venture capital financing to grow an entrepreneurial economy. RTP did so by attracting proportionally more corporate venture capital. Entrepreneurial ventures in the region had good technology, which made them attractive for corporate venture capital investment (Zoller, 2010). Corporate venture capital often invests in potential acquisition targets rather than pursuing initial public offerings. Without venture capital money, companies in the region are likely to grow through mergers. Newly merged firms maintained a presence in the region because the region was attractive. But without many initial public offerings and strong locally grown companies, there are few local champions in RTP (Zoller, 2010).

New vision, new challenges
RTP's supporting foundation, the RTP Foundation, released a new vision in 2005 that set out for RTP to 'become the world's leading regional center for innovation, technology commercialization, and quality job creation'

by 2020 (Weddle et al., 2006: 10). Based on this new vision, the RTP Foundation identified the areas it needs to improve upon: personal inter-action, networks for spin-off firms and stronger entrepreneurial capac-ity (Weddle et al., 2006). Its new focus of attention on the smaller level, whether it be the individual or new firm, points to the changing makeup of RTP: the park is no longer made up of massive firms. Instead, 56 percent of its firms employ less than ten people, with only 6 percent employing over 1000 (Research Triangle Foundation, n.d.).

The Foundation is working on the personal interaction issue by pro-viding community amenities and trying to foster relationships between employees and the community through volunteering and out-of-work activities (Research Triangle Foundation, n.d.). It expanded its com-munity building efforts in 2008 with the creation of Outreach@RTP, a program which focuses on encouraging firms to expand their CSR programs (Research Triangle Foundation, n.d.). In 2007, the Triangle Community Foundation set up a website, Triangle Gives Back, to encour-age giving and match donors to nonprofits in the RTP area (Friedman, 2009). Triangle Gives Back also started the 1 percent challenge in the Fall of 2010. The challenge tries to get firms to give at least 1 percent of their profits to local nonprofits (Triangle Gives Back, 2010). In 2008, the group published a report offering an in-depth look at giving in the Triangle region. It found that corporate giving in the Triangle is smaller than in older clustered economies, along with individual giving being below similar metropolitan areas and other cities in North Carolina. Wealthier citizens gave less than lower-income residents in the region (Guillory et al., 2008).

Giving from RTP

The lower levels of giving are not due to lower levels of need. The RTP area is currently struggling with sufficient care for children and seniors, affordable housing, education and a high poverty rate of one out of nine residents (Triangle J Council of Governments, 2008). The Triangle also has a lower number of grant-making foundations, as compared to similar regions in the United States with around 470 in the Triangle, 20 of which are corporate foundations, and only ten that give a high proportion to the local area. Of the total number of grant-making organizations, 82 gave less than 25 percent of their grants to organizations in the Triangle and 93 gave less than $10000 to Triangle organizations in 2006. The top foundations, based on giving to the Triangle in the same year, were the Triangle Community Foundation, John William Pope Foundation, Progress Energy Foundation and Blue Cross Blue Shield of North Carolina Foundation (Guillory et al., 2008). This group includes a community foundation, a family foundation and two corporate foundations. The Triangle Gives Back report also conducted a survey of a small subset of Triangle firms. Larger firms tended to publish reports on their giving, have employee-matching programs and have CSR budgets outside of a corporate foundation. Smaller firms were less likely to have annual reports on giving or have employee-matching programs, and they also gave at a lower rate than larger firms (Guillory et al., 2008). Though not surprising, as they likely operate a smaller profit margin, the result is concerning since the majority of RTP firms are small.

There are multiple factors that contribute to the lower levels of CSR and community support from RTP. One reason is the scattered nature of the area: firms are primarily located in RTP while their employees live in many of the surrounding communities in the region. This causes two problems. First, employees may not feel much connection to their work community if they are commuting a long distance; and second, firms cannot easily provide support to their employees' community if that includes many different areas (Guillory et al., 2008). Also, almost half of RTP employees were not born in North Carolina, which could decrease the sense of community felt by employees and firms alike (Guillory et al., 2008). And since the area lacks locally based headquarters, the few larger RTP firms and their executives that have corporate and family foundations are not based in RTP (Guillory et al., 2008).

An alternate reason for lower giving is that firms in RTP often serve clients outside of North Carolina and even the United States, which takes away one of the major reasons for corporate giving: increased consumer support (Guillory et al., 2008). Such firms are more likely to provide CSR to the communities they serve or work with. This is seen in the self-reporting firms provided on their levels of giving overall and in the region. GlaxoSmithKline gave $558 million overall in 2006, $5.1 million of which went to the Triangle. The firm says its CSR is focused on global health, good employment practices, human rights, access to medicine and an improved environment and supply chain (GlaxoSmithKline, 2010). Although it has a strong presence in RTP, its international focus has led to most of its philanthropy going outside of the region.

IBM reported the second-highest amount donated to the Triangle, $3.2 million out of $148.5 million. The company is also focused on stakeholder engagement and as such focuses its CSR where its stakeholders are: globally. It is contributing to a high number of employee volunteer hours through its Corporate Service Corps, which sends employees to developing nations to help solve technology problems (IBM, n.d.). Progress Energy is the third-highest donor to the region as a firm, spending $3 million out of $12 million to the area. It is not surprising that this energy company would be high on both lists given that it is interested in supporting its consumers, who include residents of North Carolina (Progress Energy, 2010). Wachovia was the fifth highest donor, but only regionally focused in its CSR activities, that region also includes its home base of New Jersey, Delaware and Pennsylvania (Wachovia, 2010).

SAS provides an interesting contrast to these firms. A locally grown firm, SAS provides an annual report on its CSR and sets goals for each year. In 2009, it was focused on the environment and stewardship. It is also focused on stakeholder engagement, which it works for by providing volunteers, grants, donations and training. Its motto for giving, 'think global, act local', explains its focus on local community support. But even given these values, it does not make the list of top ten donors to the region. This may be explained by its focus on its employees as a main element of its community. Many of its efforts are based around improving the quality of life and education of its employees as opposed to the surrounding community members. However, this has led to only 2 percent turnover in 2009, as compared to the industry average of 22 percent (SAS, 2010).

Giving from RTP is lower than it should be as seen by its comparison to other areas and the remaining needs of the region. These lower levels of support are explainable. Ease of giving is low as the RTP community is spread out, with a high concentration of firms in one area but employees living in many surrounding towns. Motivation to give locally is also low since many of the consumers of RTP firms are not in North Carolina and many firms are driven to CSR in part to garner increased consumer support. Ability to give is low for the area as large firms are typically 'better' givers but they make up a small proportion of RTP. Though the smaller firms probably have a stronger attachment to the RTP community, they have not made enough profits to offer much support. While the industrial park continues to develop and contribute to the area through economic success and employment, RTP has failed to unite and thrive as a community. Its formation from a public–private partnership and lack of any major headquarters has left it without powerful local champions. There is, however, the potential for future success in this area. If any of the small start-ups succeed and remain in the area, their founders may then be able to expand their entrepreneurial efforts in the community and shape their philanthropy accordingly.

3.5   CONCLUSIONS

So much of our imagination and policy prescriptions focus on what we might call the Silicon Valley model. Many places attempt to create vibrant economies by trying to replicate the mix of venture capital funding, research universities, concentrations of skilled talent and open culture. But these factors do not exist in most places; instead, determined entrepreneurs propel many areas with a strong attachment to a community, pushing for the prosperity of their homes. These entrepreneurs are redefining their hometowns and the approach to business. While this chapter showcases positive examples of their roles in improving the prosperity of an area, there is also great risk to the town being too dependent on one major employer, as we see with the effect of the recession on Viking in Greenwood, Mississippi. Further, a single influential person or a small group may not engage the public in order to understand the needs and resources of an area (Ostrander, 2007). These local champions also may not be most efficient in their allocations for producing public goods, as they may be more motivated by increasing their own social capital (Zahra et al., 2009). Even with these limitations, however, local champions offer an alternate path to economic development for many areas, as these individuals use their own financial success to advance the quality of life in their communities.

NOTE

* This material is based upon work supported by the National Science Foundation Science of Science Policy Program under Grant Number 1158755. Any opinions, findings, and conclusions or recommendations expressed in this material are those of the authors and do not necessarily reflect the views of the National Science Foundation.

REFERENCES

Academy of Achievement (2013, September), 'Jeff Bezos biography', available at http://www.achievement.org/autodoc/page/bez0bio-1.
Allen Institute for Brain Science (2013), 'About us: Founders', available at http://www.alleninstitute.org/about_us/founders.html.
Andreoni, J. (1990), 'Impure altruism and donations to public goods: a theory of warm-glow giving', *Economic Journal*, 100(401), 464–477.
Aupperle, K.E., A.B. Carroll and J.D. Hatfield (1985), 'An empirical examination of the relationship between corporate social responsibility and profitability', *Academy of Management Journal*, 28(2), 446–463.
Bezos Family Foundation (2013), 'About us', available at http://www.bezosfamilyfoundation.org/about-us.
Biography Channel website (2013), 'Paul Allen', available at http://www.biography.com/print/profile/paul-allen-9542239.
Carl, F., Jr (2007), 'The best advice I ever got', *Harvard Business Review*, November.
Carman, J.G. (2001), 'Community foundations: A growing resource for community development', *Nonprofit Management and Leadership*, 12(1), 7–24.

Carson, E.D. (1994), 'Community foundations, racial diversity, and institutional change', *New Directions for Philanthropic Fundraising*, 5, 33–43.

Chandler, C. (2013a), 'Former CEO Fred Carl told Viking employees in emails to expect few changes', *Mississippi Business Journal*, February 8, available at http://msbusiness.com/blog/2013/02/08/in-email-former-ceo%e2%80%88fred-carl-told-viking-employees-to-expect-few-changes/.

Chandler, C. (2013b), 'Middleby CEO: Viking staying in Greenwood is "not negotiable"', *Mississippi Business Journal*, February 8, available at http://msbusiness.com/blog/2013/02/08/bassoul-viking-staying-in-greenwood-is-not-negotiable/.

Cook, J. (2011), 'Amazon founder and brainiac Jeff Bezos donates \$15 million to Princeton Neuroscience Institute', *Geek Wire*, December 13, available at http://www.geekwire.com/2011/amazon-founder-brainiac-jeff-bezos-donates-15-million-princeton-neuroscience-institute/.

Delevingne, L. (2009), 'Surprising survivors: Corporate do-gooders', *CNN Money*, January 20, available at http://money.cnn.com/2009/01/19/magazines/fortune/do_gooder.fortune/.

Emery, M. and C. Flora (2006), 'Spiraling-up: Mapping community transformation with community capitals framework', *Community Development*, 37(1), 19–35.

Endeavor (2011), 'Who we are', available at http://www.endeavorfoundation.net/who-we-are.

Feldman, M.P. (1999), 'The new economics of innovation, spillovers and agglomeration: A review of empirical studies', *Economics of Innovation and New Technology*, 8(1–2), 5–25.

Feldman, M.P. (forthcoming), 'The character of innovative places: entrepreneurial strategy, economic development and prosperity', *Small Business Economics*.

Feldman, M.P. and N.J. Lowe (2011), 'Restructuring for resilience', *Innovations*, 6(1), 129–146.

Feldman, M.P. and T.D. Zoller (2012), 'Dealmakers in place: Social capital connections in regional entrepreneurial economies', *Regional Studies*, 46(1), 23–37.

Foundation Center (2012), 'Key facts on community foundations', available at http://foundationcenter.org/gainknowledge/research/pdf/keyfacts_comm2012.pdf.

Foundation Center (2013a), 'Fayetteville Area Community Foundation', *Foundation Directory Online*, available at http://fconline.foundationcenter.org/companion/new_page.php?row1data=androw2data=Arkansas+andcounty=androw3data=andmsa=andcd=andzip=androw4data=androw7data=androw5data=andfcTOD=andfcTOG=Community+foundationandrow6data=andexan=andtotal_giving_range=andrange_field=total_givingandrange_start=andrange_end=andsortfield=title%7Candsortorder=1andnarrow_keywords=andresults_per_page=andsearch_source=Grantmakersandid=FAYE320.

Foundation Center (2013b), 'Walton Family Foundation, Inc', *Foundation Directory Online*, available at http://fdo.foundationcenter.org/grantmaker-profile?collection=grantmakersandname=walton%20andstate=andzip_code=andSubmit=Searchandsort_by=cityandsort_order=1andkey=WALT052andfrom_search=1.

Foundation Center (2013c), 'Willard and Pat Walker Charitable Foundation, Inc', *Foundation Directory Online*, available at http://fdo.foundationcenter.org/grantmaker-profile?collection=grantmakersandname=willard%20walkerandstate=andzip_code=andSubmit=Searchandkey=WALK133andfrom_search=1.

Foundation Center (n.d.), 'Fred and Margaret Carl Foundation', *Foundation Directory Online*, available at http://fdo.foundationcenter.org/grantmaker-profile?collection=grantmakersandkey=FRED360andpage=1andstate=%22Mississippi%22andfrom_search=1.

Friedman, L. (2009), 'Web site hopes to boost giving: Site to link groups with donors', *News and Observer*, February 2, available at http://www.siptrunkingreport.com/news/2009/02/02/3955475.htm.

Gayomali, C. (2011), 'Five rich tech Titans and what they've given to charity', *Time*, March 9, available at http://techland.time.com/2011/03/09/five-rich-tech-titans-and-what-theyve-given-to-charity/slide/jeff-bezos/print/.

GlaxoSmithKline (2010), *Corporate Responsibility Report 2009*, GlaxoSmithKline, available at http://www.gsk.com/content/dam/gsk/globals/documents/pdf/corporateresponsibility/CR%20report%202009.pdf.

Graddy-Reed, A., M.P. Feldman and D. Trembath (2013), *Innovation at Work for Carolina Communities*, Chapel Hill, NC: University of North Carolina at Chapel Hill.

Grant Space (n.d.), 'Glossaries', Foundation Center, available at http://grantspace.org/Tools/Knowledge-Base/Funding-Research/Definitions-and-Clarification/glossaries.

Grogan, P. (2013), *Changing the Game: Civic Leadership at The Boston Foundation, 2001–2012*, Durham, NC: Center for Strategic Philanthropy and Civil Society, Sanford School of Public Policy, Duke University.

Guillory, F., A. Holton and T. Brantley (2008), *How the Triangle Gives Back: A Report to the Region*, Durham, NC: Triangle Community Foundation.

Gunther, M. (2012), 'Amazon's a great company. But good? Nope', Sustainable Business Forum, December 21, available at http://sustainablebusinessforum.com/marcgunther/74846/amazon-s-great-company-good-nope

Hagge, P.D. (2009), 'The new Northwest: The transformation of small-town economies in Northwest Arkansas since 1960', Master's thesis, Pennsylvania State University.

Harriss, C.L. (1939), 'Philanthropy and federal tax exemption', *Journal of Political Economy*, 47(4), 526–541.

Harvey, C., M. Maclean, J. Gordon and E. Shaw (2011), 'Andrew Carnegie and the foundations of contemporary entrepreneurial philanthropy', *Business History*, 53(3), 425–450.

Hemphill, T.A. (2005), 'Rejuvenating Wal-Mart's reputation', *Business Horizons*, 48(1), 11–21.

Hicks, M.J. (2007), *The Local Economic Impact of Wal-Mart*, New York: Cambria Press.

Holliday, T. (2004), 'The stove groupies' pilgrimage', *New York Times*, November 5, available at http://www.nytimes.com/2004/11/05/travel/escapes/05COOK.html.

Holtzman, C. (2011), 'Amazon, Microsoft, Starbucks, Nordstrom and Costco give back', *Puget Sound Business Journal*, May 20, available at http://www.bizjournals.com/seattle/print-edition/2011/05/20/amazon-microsoft-starbucks.html?page=all.

Hopkins, J. (2004), 'Wal-Mart heirs pour riches into education reform', *USA Today*, March 11, available at http://usatoday30.usatoday.com/money/companies/2004-03-11-waltons_x.htm.

IBM (n.d.), *2009 Corporate Responsibility Report*, IBM, available at http://www.ibm.com/ibm/responsibility/report/2009/index.shtml.

Irvin, R.A. (2007), 'Regional wealth and philanthropic capacity mapping', *Nonprofit and Voluntary Sector Quarterly*, 36(1), 165–172.

Johnson, K. and N. Wingfield (2013), 'As Amazon stretches, Seattle's downtown is reshaped', *New York Times*, August 25, available at http://www.nytimes.com/2013/08/26/us/as-amazon-stretches-seattles-downtown-is-reshaped.html.

Keiper, A. (2011), 'Minding Paul Allen', *Philanthropy Magazine*, Fall, available at http://www.philanthropyroundtable.org/site/print/minding_paul_allen.

Kingdon, J.W. (2002), *Agendas, Alternatives, and Public Policies*, Longman Classics Edition, London: Longman Publishing Group.

Kornegay, J. (2012), 'Viking ranges made in Mississippi', *American Profile*, October 7, available at http://americanprofile.com/articles/the-history-of-viking-ranges/.

Letts, C.W., W. Ryan and A. Grossman (1997), 'Virtuous capital: What foundations can learn from venture capitalists', *Harvard Business Review*, 75, 36–50.

Lowe, N.J. and M.P. Feldman (2014), 'Catch a wave: strategies for economic development', Working Paper, Carolina Public Policy.

Martinez, A. and K. Heim (2012), 'Amazon a virtual no-show in hometown philanthropy', *Seattle Times Newspaper*, March 31, available at http://seattletimes.com/html/businesstechnology/2017883663_amazonmain25.html.

McMillin, L. (2013), 'The Carl effect', December 11, available at http://hottytoddy.com/2013/12/11/the-carl-effect/.

McWilliams, A. and D. Siegel (2000), 'Corporate social responsibility and financial performance: correlation or misspecification?', *Strategic Management Journal*, 21(5), 603–609.

Microsoft (2013), 'Serving communities: Acting locally, globally', Microsoft Corporate Citizenship, available at http://www.microsoft.com/about/corporatecitizenship/en-us/serving-communities/acting-locally-globally/.

Mintrom, M. and P. Norman (2009), 'Policy entrepreneurship and policy change', *Policy Studies Journal*, 37(4), 649–667.

Mississippi Secretary of State (n.d.), 'Spotlight on business', available at http://www.sos.ms.gov/spotlight_on_business2.aspx?business_id=21andmonth=2009–06.

Morgan, A. (1995), *Prescription for Success: The Life and Values of Ewing Marion Kauffman*, Kansas City, MO: Andrews & McMeel.

Nene, G. (2005), 'The effect of Wal-Mart on the economic growth of Nebraska counties', Master's thesis, University of Nebraska.

Newsome, M. (2007), 'Viking simmers a strategy', *Time Magazine*, August 30, available at http://thedeltadirt.blogspot.com/2007/08/time-viking-simmers-strategy.html.

North, D.C. (1990), *Institutions, Institutional Change and Economic Performance*, Cambridge, UK and New York, USA: Cambridge University Press.

Ostrander, S.A. (2007), 'The growth of donor control: Revisiting the social relations of philanthropy', *Nonprofit and Voluntary Sector Quarterly*, 36(2), 356–372.

Ostrom, E. (2009), *Understanding Institutional Diversity*, Princeton, NJ: Princeton University Press.

PGA Family Foundation (2013), 'About the PGA Foundation', *Paul G. Allen Family Foundation*, available at http://www.pgafamilyfoundation.org/About.

Progress Energy (2010), *Strong Foundation Bright Future: 2009 Corporate Responsibility Executive Summary*, Progress Energy.

Reis, T.K. and S.J. Clohesy (2001), 'Unleashing new resources and entrepreneurship for the common good: A philanthropic renaissance', *New Directions for Philanthropic Fundraising*, 32, 109–144.

Research and Insights (2013), 'Is Amazon beginning to embrace CSR?', *CONE Communications*, November 1, available at http://www.conecomm.com/amazon-csr.

Research Triangle Foundation (n.d.), *RTP at a Glance*, Research Triangle Foundation.

Rosen, M. (2009), *Boom Town: How Wal-Mart Transformed an All-American Town Into an International Community*, Chicago, IL: Chicago Review Press.

Ross Gardner, J. (2013), 'Bezos, five ways: The Jeff Bezos you don't know', *Washingtonian*, November 26, available at http://www.washingtonian.com/blogs/capitalcomment/media/bezos-five-ways-the-jeff-bezos-you-dont-know.php#.

SAS (2010), *2009 SAS Corporate Social Responsibility Report*, SAS.

Schoen, J. (2010), 'Viking battles to keep manufacturing in US', *NBC News*, May 18, available at http://www.nbcnews.com/id/37094337/#.UrSZ02RDuRY.

Schumpeter, J. (1947), 'The creative response in economic history', *Journal of Economic History*, 7, 149–159.

Shafer, J. (2013), 'Jeff Bezos has two words for you: "No comment."', Reuters, August 19, available at http://blogs.reuters.com/jackshafer/2013/08/19/jeff-bezos-has-two-words-for-you-no-comment/?print=1andr=

Tolbert, C.M. (2005), 'Minding our own business: Local retail establishments and the future of southern civic community', *Social Forces*, 83(4), 1309–1328.

Treasury Department (1965), *Report on Private Foundations: Committee on Finance of the United States Senate*, 89th Congress, 1st Session.

Triangle Gives Back (2010), *1% Giving Challenge*, Durham, NC: Triangle Community Foundation.

Triangle J Council of Governments (2008), *Measures of the Research Triangle Region*, Presented at the Deligate Orientation, January 23, available at http://conservationsuccess.wikispaces.com/file/view/tjcogmeasures.pdf.

Tyler, K.E. (2012), 'Framing cultural capitalism: William Wilson Corcoran and Alice Walton as patrons of the American Art Museum', Master's thesis, University of Nebraska-Lincoln.

University Relations (2003), 'Delta businessman supports architecture center', July 7, available at http://web.archive.org/web/20110720004335/http://lists.msstate.edu/web/media/detail.php?id=2154.

Van Slyke, D.M. and H.K. Newman (2006), 'Venture philanthropy and social entrepreneurship in community redevelopment', *Nonprofit Management and Leadership*, 16(3), 345–368.

Vance, S.S. and R.V. Scott (1992), 'Sam Walton and Wal-Mart Stores, Inc.: A study in modern southern entrepreneurship', *Journal of Southern History*, 58(2), 231–252.

Viking Range, LLC (n.d.-a), 'Fred Carl, Jr', Viking, available at https://www.vikingrange.com/consumer/category/about-viking/the-viking-story/fred-carl--jr-?.

Viking Range, LLC (n.d.-b), 'The Viking commitment to our community', Viking, available at http://www.vikingrange.com/consumer/category/about-viking/the-viking-commitment/the-viking-commitment-to-our-community;jsessionid=9bGCDg7CtfaiGHmvLxeFdQ**.node1.

Viking Range, LLC (n.d.-c), 'The Viking commitment to our employees', Viking, available at http://www.vikingrange.com/consumer/category/about-viking/the-viking-commitment/the-viking-commitment-to-our-employees.

Wachovia (2010), 'Community involvement', Corporate Social Responsibility Annual Report.

Wadman, M. (2007), 'Biomedical philanthropy: state of the donation', *Nature*, 447(7142), 248–250.

Walmart (2013), 'Walmart community giving', Walmart Foundation, available at http://foundation.walmart.com/.

Walton Family Foundation (2013a), 'About us', available at http://www.waltonfamilyfoundation.org/.

Walton Family Foundation (2013b), 'Home region', available at http://www.waltonfamilyfoundation.org/homeregion.

Weddle, R.L., E. Rooks and T. Valdecanas (2006), 'Research Triangle Park: Evolution and renaissance', presentation to the IASP World Conference.

Zahra, S.A., E. Gedajlovic, D.O. Neubaum and J.M. Shulman (2009), 'A typology of social entrepreneurs: Motives, search processes and ethical challenges', *Journal of Business Venturing*, 24(5), 519–532.

Zoller, T.D. (2010), *The Dealmaker Milieu: The Anatomy of Social Capital in Entrepreneurial Economies*, Chapel Hill, NC: University of North Carolina at Chapel Hill.

PART II

DIFFERING PERSPECTIVES – DIFFERENT EXPERIENCES?

From the broad overview provided by the authors in Part I, we move in this section to developing an understanding of the experiences of multiple segments of the entrepreneurial world and how the entrepreneurs in these segments experience and involve themselves in philanthropy. In sequence, the chapters present insights into female entrepreneurs, Black or African-American entrepreneurs, companies transitioned or transitioning from the founder, high-tech donors in the Northeast US, and the Silicon Valley entrepreneur.

The Diana Project (Chapter 4) provides insights into the experiences of female entrepreneurs and their philanthropies. This set of leading researchers, whose individual contributions to the research focus on entrepreneurs are long-standing and widely recognized, wisely provide us with both historical and cross-sectional perspectives of female entrepreneurs' involvement in philanthropy. The historical perspective provides evidence of the significant achievements effected by female philanthropists earlier in US history. These women were generally wives or daughters of wealthy individuals. The situation was a reflection of the limited roles then available to women in the work world. However, the situation has changed so that increasingly women involved in philanthropy are entrepreneurs in their own right, a phenomenon reflected in the expanding literature on female entrepreneurs.

The research on philanthropy has examined gender differences. Notably results indicate that women have differing motivations for philanthropic engagement and different strategies as they engage in philanthropy. However, research on philanthropy has only limited examination of entrepreneurs' experiences and the study of women entrepreneurs' involvement in philanthropy is, at best, sparse. Thus the observations of the Diana Project drawn from the research literatures and popular press characterizations of selected female entrepreneur philanthropists present a clarion call for systematic investigation.

Cox Edmondson and Taylor introduce us to the Black or African-American entrepreneur's experience in philanthropy in Chapter 5. Cox Edmondson and Carroll (1999) undertook the earliest systematic investigation of this issue. In this chapter Cox Edmondson with Taylor updates the earlier findings with insights drawn from the popular press as well as recent interviews with a small sample of entrepreneurs associated with Morehouse College, USA. The results from the recent investigation appear to confirm the results from the earlier study. However, the initial study did not differentiate between the entrepreneurs' involvement in the African-American and the broader community. In the current study a minority of the interviewees indicated that they focus their philanthropic efforts on the Black community. The authors note the need to compare the experiences of the African-American entrepreneurs' engagement in philanthropy with that of other ethnic groups – an area heretofore unexplored. The chapter underscores the importance of the Black entrepreneur's success as an entrepreneur as well as the involvement in philanthropy as an important role model and contribution to the African-American community.

Hoy and Rosplock (Chapter 6) draw on their significant research and practitioner backgrounds to provide intimate profiles of family businesses and their involvement with philanthropy. Their focus in this chapter is on firms that have moved from the first generation or founding entrepreneur to the second generation or to professional management. The two authors begin with an intimate portrait of Henry Bloch's evolution from entrepreneur (co-founder of H&R Block) to philanthropist. They note that as the entrepreneur's efforts move from founding and growing the firm to transitioning to the next generation and professional management, the entrepreneurial founder is able to focus on philanthropic investments and community engagement. The scholarly literature has provided significant insights into the ownership and management succession issues, but has as yet little emphasis on how the entrepreneur and associated family manage their philanthropic interests. Recent work indicates changes are occurring to more active involvement rather than reactive response to external solicitations.

These two authors draw insights through review of the available literature, the case study of Henry Bloch, and in-depth interviews with nine individuals who provided insights about other multi-generational enterprising families who demonstrated their philanthropic commitments.

From the interview transcripts they draw four themes: enduring qualities of the entrepreneur; balancing family wealth transfer and giving; building education, continuity and cohesion; and leaving a philanthropic legacy. Each of the themes is illustrated by a mini-case and data from other interviews. The chapter provides tantalizing possibilities for future research initiatives which, as the authors note, is much needed to augment the considerable practitioner literature on family firms, their philanthropies, and their foundations.

The work of Paul Schervish as Director of the Center on Wealth and Philanthropy at Boston College has provided significant insights into the motivational underpinnings of charitable giving and philanthropy. In Chapter 7 he revisits his 2001 co-authored report, 'Agent-animated wealth and philanthropy', an important and early contribution to our understanding of the high-tech entrepreneurs and the dynamics of their philanthropic activities. The 2001 report was based on interviews with nearly 30 individuals whose wealth was derived from their involvement in high-tech firms. Schervish notes that their philanthropy is different than what he and other scholars have observed in the philanthropy realm generally. Schervish describes these individuals as highly educated, less religious and generally actively involved in their philanthropic investments. These philanthropists seek to drive greater return from their investments in the philanthropic realm. In their philanthropy they remain market-conscious of the dynamics of the needs that are presented and the undersupply, focus on the need to both utilize and build human capital to meet those needs, and drive for impact through building scale. Schervish refers to the phenomenon as 'agent-animated philanthropy'. He acknowledges that the very intensity of the drive of these highly successful individuals has been viewed by the non-profits with which they work as arrogance. But he tempers this observation by sharing the experience of a particular individual case and notes his observation of a frequent sense of gratitude for unmerited advantage among the interviewees. He concludes that the current phenomenon of the entrepreneurial engagement in philanthropy may well be yielding even more abundant and adept philanthropy than we have observed in the past.

Our final chapter in Part II complements Schervish's observations in the Northeast United States with experiences from the West Coast, specifically Silicon Valley in the San Francisco area. Stilwell and Carson (Chapter 8) provide insights into their donors who are entrepreneurs, and their observations about how the entrepreneurs approach their philanthropic activities. Their long-term experiences in providing guidance to the Silicon Valley entrepreneurs provide insights strikingly parallel to those that Schervish makes from his research in the Northeast US. The clients that Stilwell and Carson work with tend to 'move quickly', take a libertarian view on non-government involvement, and drive for a return on the investments in philanthropy just as they and their funders drove for their investment in the for-profit world. Stilwell and Carson characterized these entrepreneurs engaged in philanthropy as highly optimistic and a group for whom failure is not an option. The chapter provides us with a unique opportunity to understand the Silicon Valley entrepreneurs with whom Stilwell and Carson have long been involved.

Together the five chapters in Part II provide rich insights into the dynamics of women entrepreneurs, Black or African-American entrepreneurs, family business members and high-tech entrepreneurs in the Northeast US and in the Silicon Valley. The authors challenge us to deepen and broaden our understanding of these under-researched segments of entrepreneurs engaged in the philanthropic world.

REFERENCE

Cox Edmondson, Vickie and Archie B. Carroll (1999), 'Giving back: An examination of the philanthropic motivations, orientations and activities of large Black-owned businesses', *Journal of Business Ethics*, 19(2), 171–179.

4. Women entrepreneurs and their approach to philanthropy

The Diana Project*: Candida G. Brush,
Nancy M. Carter, Elizabeth J. Gatewood,
Patricia G. Greene and Myra Hart

4.1 INTRODUCTION: PHILANTHROPY IN THE UNITED STATES

Philanthropy can be defined in a number of different ways. In general, dictionaries provide common definitions that focus on the gifting of financial resources (*Free Dictionary*, *Miriam-Webster Dictionary*, *Oxford English Dictionary*). Other more comprehensive definitions are found, such as: 'the desire to promote the welfare of others, expressed especially by the generous donation of money to good causes' (*Oxford English Dictionary*, 2013) or 'the voluntary and unconditional redistribution of wealth by the private sector' (Acs and Dana, 2001). Still other discussions combine the dedication of time and/or effort into the discussion (Coombs et al., 2008). Our approach is that each of these definitions actually includes research questions at their heart (motivation, context and other resources, respectively) and we therefore instead accept and work from the most basic starting point of the gifting of financial resources. In addition, we work from the premise that we are exploring philanthropy at the individual level, as separate from any corporate social responsibility or outreach or even social entrepreneurship.

Philanthropy is not a modern-day phenomenon as historical studies have identified philanthropic activities in ancient civilizations of Greece, Rome and the Middle East. Certainly modern-day philanthropic activities are evident elsewhere as well. For the purposes of this chapter we will, however, confine ourselves within the boundaries of the United States. According to the Council on Foundations (2002) the general philosophy of philanthropy in the United States emphasizes mutual assistance building on the democratic principles of civic participation. While philanthropy was actually evident in the United States as early as 1638 (actually predating the actual United States), Hall (2006) labeled this activity 'indigenous philanthropy' and noted that while present, until the end of the eighteenth century philanthropy was somewhat limited in the US. What is more popularly recognized as the rise of philanthropy in the US occurred post-1850 (Hall, 2006) with the advent of the wealthy and powerful nineteenth-century entrepreneurs who amassed great wealth and distributed it to meet some social good. John Jacob Astor, Andrew Carnegie, James Buchanan Duke, Marshall Field, Andrew Mellon, J.P. Morgan, John D. Rockefeller, Charles Schwab, Leland Stanford and Cornelius Vanderbilt are among those whose names are easily recognizable as much for their philanthropic efforts as for their entrepreneurial endeavors.

Over the years, the practice of philanthropy has become more prominent both on the individual level and through organized institutions, with at least some of this growth attributed to federal governmental policies that favored charitable giving and nonprofit organizations (Hall, 2006). By one measure the number of non-profits grew from approximately 13 000 in 1940 to approximately 1.5 million by the year 2000 (Hall, 2006). Around the world the US tax policy is generally seen as helping to foster a philanthropic environment that supported the giving of $316.23 billion to charity in 2012, an increase of 3.5 percent over the previous year (Giving USA Foundation, 2013).

The examples of philanthropic individuals generally presented over the past 200 years are almost always white males who started businesses that grew to a very large scale. When focusing on philanthropy as the gifting of financial assets, the business-founding dimension is not surprising as it is one of the only ways to significantly grow family wealth so as to have it available for philanthropy. The focus on male philanthropists, despite evidence of the growing importance of women entrepreneurs in the economy and their accumulation of wealth, may be attributed to a number of factors which we will discuss in this chapter, including economic, social and even psychological factors of the donors. In order to connect these multiple aspects, we will first consider the background of philanthropy of women in general and gender differences in approaches to philanthropy. We will next look at women's entrepreneurship and segue into the philanthropic approaches of entrepreneurial women. We will conclude with a discussion of what is known to date through the lens of Bourdieu's framework of capital types, and a proposal of the next round of questions needed to ground future research.

4.2   WOMEN'S PHILANTHROPY: THE BEGINNING

Women have been only a limited part of the historical view of philanthropy; when they are included, it is most often to recognize their philanthropic activities in distributing family wealth, most often acknowledged to have been accumulated by a father or husband. These included such women as the following:

- Katharine Drexel (1858–1955) and her sisters, with money inherited from their father, founded Sisters of the Blessed Sacrament for Indians and Colored People. The sisters are credited with starting over 50 missions and schools, including Xavier University in New Orleans. Although the money given to charitable causes totaled more than $12 million, she also took Holy Orders and served as a missionary for the causes she supported (Oppedisano, 2004).
- Henriette DeLille (1813–1862), with money inherited from her family, started the Order of the Sisters of the Holy Family, of which she was a member, and built the Hospice of the Holy Family, Asylum of the Children of the Holy Family, and a number of free parochial schools, nursing homes and retirement homes that are still operating in the Gulf Coast area (Oppedisano, 2000).
- Juliette Gordon Low (1860–1927), with financial support from her wealthy husband, founded the Girl Scouts of America, which was modeled after Girl Guides, a British scouting movement. In addition to financial support, she was an active participant in the organization until her death.
- Jane Addams (1860–1935) was a pioneer settlement social worker, public philosopher, sociologist, and leader in women's suffrage and world peace. She co-founded Hull House, a Chicago facility, which served impoverished immigrants. She funded all capital expenditures to bring the facility to standards required to operate, and most of its operational funds in its early inception, from money inherited from her family. She and her partner lived at Hull House, which operated a night school for adults, kindergarten classes, girls' club, bath house, music and drama programs, book bindery and library.

There are, however, a few notable exceptions of women who were earners of the money they used for their philanthropy, including Madame C.J. Walker (born Sarah Breedlove, 1867–1919) founder of a cosmetics and hair product company and recognized as the first African-American female millionaire. Madame Walker was the largest donor for preserving the Anacostia, Washington, DC house of abolitionist Frederick Douglass, and a major contributor to other causes related to African-American education and well-being (Jasper, 2005).

The context of the times must be considered when examining the role of women as philanthropists in these earlier days, for these are years in which women not only were less likely to be in the workforce but also faced legal barriers to property rights and access to capital. Indeed, it was women becoming more visible as social activists that helped to drive the increase in philanthropy in the United States. This was particularly apparent as increasingly educated women could not find opportunities in the workforce and, therefore, turned to changing society as their work, their contribution (Scott, 1991; Waugh, 1997 in Hall, 2006; Wooster, 2002 in Oppedisano, 2004). Women increasingly served in the twin roles of staff and board members, as well as donors, of the associations that grew from their activities (McCarthy, 1982, 1991 in Hall, 2006; Oppedisano, 2004).

Hall (2006) describes the perfect storm of social forces that led to the creation by Margaret Olivia Sage of the Russell Sage Foundation:

> The Russell Sage Foundation, considered one of the earliest modern foundations, was founded in 1907 on a gift of $10 million from Margaret Olivia Sage (1828–1918), the widow of financier Russell Sage, 'for the improvement of social and living conditions in the United States of America' (see Glenn et al., 1947; Hammack and Wheeler, 1994; Crocker, 2002). The foundation, she instructed, 'should preferably not undertake to do that which is now being done or is likely to be effectively done by other individuals or by other agencies. It should be its aim to take up the larger and more difficult problems, and to take them up so far as possible in such a manner as to secure co-operation and aid in their solution.' (Sage, 1907)

Sage's gift, in a very real way, brought together all the strands of American philanthropy and voluntarism as it had developed since the early nineteenth century. A product of a New England evangelical household, she had been educated at Emma Willard's Troy Female Seminary, an evangelical institution. At her graduation in 1847, she presented an oration on those 'who spend their wealth in deeds of charity' (Crocker, 2002: 202). Sage was involved in a range of post-Civil War urban reform movements. She was an active supporter of religious causes, and she served on the board of the New York Women's Hospital and the New York Gospel Mission, as well as the New York Exchange for Women's Work and the Women's Municipal League, 'a political organization that aimed to unseat Tammany and bring more women into public life' (Crocker, 2002: 201 in Hall, 2006).

4.3   MEN AND WOMEN: DIFFERENCES IN PHILANTHROPIC ACTIVITIES

Although there are some disagreements about whether women are more likely to be involved in philanthropy (Mesch et al., 2006; Reed and Selbee, 2000), or involved at the same rate as men (Andreoni et al., 2003), there seems to be some consensus that differences are found in the type of motivations (perhaps most intriguingly, the recognition or lack thereof expected) and strategies, including the form of philanthropic activities undertaken and the approach. One notable change for women in philanthropy is a movement from volunteering to financially supporting, with a robust research finding that 'women are more likely than men to both volunteer and donate to charity and while women may donate less, the percentage of income that they do donate is the same as men's' (Jasper, 2005: 56; Capek, 2001; Daniels and Brush, 2013).

While the general motivation to give often appears to be to advance the social good, there are other reasons to give besides 'giving back': for example, to build reputation, legitimacy or a power base, or to network with influencers, including politicians, celebrities, prominent people and organizations (Shaw et al., 2011). Shaw and Taylor had earlier (1995) made these differences quite explicit with the suggestion of 'six C's' of what motivates women entrepreneurs and business leaders to give: the desire to change, create, connect, commit, collaborate and celebrate. In their research on members of the Committee of 200, these researchers identified primary motivations of 'desiring to support an issue or cause about which these women were passionate' (66 percent of respondents) and 'wanting to give back to the community' (40 percent of the respondents) (Shaw and Taylor, 1995 in Oppedisano, 2004: 175). In subsequent research on this same group of business leaders, over half (53 percent) of the women reported that their business philanthropy was due to a sense of social responsibility. Only 8 percent said their philanthropy was for an economic return, something done to benefit their business.

As research on differences between women's and men's reasons for giving has developed, a multi-level perspective has evolved. Calhoun (2006) confirmed five of the six C's proposed by Shaw and Taylor and found that compassion and community were also key reasons for women's giving. Convincing evidence shows that the pattern of women's and men's giving differs, and the reasons or motivations behind their philanthropy differ too. Coombs et al. (2008) next proposed a theoretical model of philanthropic actions in which an entrepreneur's philanthropy is seen as dependent on three types of motivations: generativity (establishing and guiding the next generation), immortality striving (identifying with self-expression) and legacy creation (leaving something behind). Gender is presented as a moderator in the relationship between these antecedents and philanthropic activities, resulting in the hypothesis that women are presumed to be more motivated by generativity and legacy creation, men by immortality striving.

Gender differences in philanthropic strategies are also seen. Women spread the amounts they give across a wider variety of organizations, whereas men take a more focused approach, giving to a few causes (Andreoni et al., 2003; Brown, 2006; Piper and Schnepf, 2008). Men are also more apt to donate in return for expectations, some kind of social rewards (Kottasz, 2004), or for recognition (naming opportunities), while women are more drawn to causes where they know someone, where the charitable cause impacts them personally, or give to make a difference (Burgoyne et al., 2005; Oppedisano, 2004; Parsons, 2004; Nowell, 1996; Shaw and Taylor, 1995). And finally, women and men have been shown to differ in the types of causes they give to, with women favoring international, community, religious institutions, health care, and youth and family organizations (Women Give 2010, Part B, 2010), while men are more likely to give to the arts (Coombs et al., 2008).

4.4   WOMEN'S ENTREPRENEURSHIP

Past research on women's entrepreneurship has been guided by a number of assumptions that apply to the discussion of women entrepreneurs and philanthropy. Early research starting in 1934 on entrepreneurship was almost entirely conducted on white males. Researchers assumed that entrepreneurship was 'generic' and therefore did not recognize the possibility that men and women would approach entrepreneurship differently (de Bruin et al., 2006) or that entrepreneurship was about business and the sex of the operant made no significant difference (Achtenhagen and Welter, 2011; Bruni et al., 2004).

By the 1970s, studies began showing that there were differences not only in characteristics of men and women, but also in aspects of business management (Schwartz, 1976; DeCarlo and Lyons, 1979; Sexton and Kent, 1981; Hisrich and O'Brien, 1981). However, these early research studies assumed a 'deficit model': that is, women did not fit the theoretical model of male entrepreneurs in terms of businesses or their ventures (Ahl, 2006) and, therefore, were less successful.

Only in the last decade have entrepreneurship researchers recognized that theory is seldom gender-neutral and begun to believe that received theory did not adequately capture the motivations, behaviors or actions of women entrepreneurs (Martin, 2000). Even more recently have researchers focused on entrepreneurial behaviors of a far broader diversity of men and women, with the expectation that the general field of entrepreneurship can benefit from the body of research on women entrepreneurs. This new approach is described as a more pluralistic approach (Jennings and Brush, 2013).

Moral development theory would suggest that women are socialized differently, and therefore have different approaches to entrepreneurship (Fischer and Reuber, 2003). As a result, they are more likely to make deliberate choices in the growth of their businesses, stressing social goals over economic goals (Carter and Allen, 1997). More recent work suggests that women are more socially conscious and focus on social relationships (Harding, 2004). Not surprisingly, then, we find that women are more likely to be social entrepreneurs. Van Ryzin et al. (2009) find that entrepreneurs with economic and social goals are more likely to be female. Sharir and Lerner (2006) also find that the leaders of social ventures in Israel are more likely to be women. In a sample of women entrepreneurs in the United Kingdom, Harding (2006) also finds that women are more likely to start social ventures than traditional ventures.

4.5   MODERN WOMEN ENTREPRENEURS AND PHILANTHROPY

Women entrepreneurs and their philanthropic activities are becoming increasingly visible around the world, with many kinds of women entrepreneurs supporting many kinds of activities (see Table 4.1).

In 2000 the Center for Women's Business Research conducted a study dedicated to advancing our understanding of the philanthropic practices of women entrepreneurs. This remains the largest and most focused study of the intersection of entrepreneurship and philanthropy by women. The study included an investigation of the donation of time (volunteering) and financial capital. From the financial perspective, women business owners were seen to donate their time and money most often to community activities (65 percent), followed by education (35 percent), religious charities (28 percent), health or disease-related causes (21 percent) and the arts (19 percent). Almost a third (31 percent) of the women reported contributing more than $5000 per year, with 52 percent reporting that they were increasing the annual amount donated. Their decision criteria as to where to give included seeing the potential donee as a well-run organization, their passion for the cause, and the way in which they were asked. Recognition was also a point of note, with 55 percent of the women preferring not to be recognized. Of the 32 percent that did want, or at least accept, recognition, 10 percent preferred a letter, 9 percent preferred to be included on a list with others, and 1 percent preferred a naming opportunity. Also of note, when looking at the differences between women entrepreneurs and women executives, 28 percent of the women business owners reported identifying with the description of 'active and engaged

Table 4.1   Modern women entrepreneurs and philanthropists

Name	Company/industry	Philanthropic activities
Dorothy Stimson Bullitt	King Broadcasting	Started an environmental preserve in the US Northwest (Oppedisano, 2004)
Swanee Hunt	Hunt Alternatives	Women Waging Peace. 'To me . . . philanthropy, at its best, means bringing together many different voices and finding ways to modulate the ones that are too loud and raising the ones that can't be heard so that you get a balance' (Marchetti, 2001 in Oppedisano, 2004: 177).
Mildred Robbins Leet	Real Estate	Co-founded United Cerebral Palsy in 1948.
Anita Roddick	Body Shop	Started Body Shop Foundation in 2000 to support human and civil rights, animal and environmental protection. Launched biannual Body Shop Human Rights Award (Jasper, 2005).
Oprah Winfrey	Harpo Productions, Inc.	Families for a Better Life.
Dara Moore	Investment company	Donated $25 million to University of South Carolina which named the business school after her (Hall, 2005 in Jasper, 2005).
Patricia Miller and Barbara Bradley Baekgaard	Vera Bradley	Vera Bradley Foundation for Breast Cancer. Vera Bradley chair in Oncology and Vera Bradley Center for Breast Cancer Research at Indiana University School of Medicine. Vera Bradley Gold and Tennis Classic (Jasper, 2005).
Eileen Fisher	Women's clothing	Supports programs on women's health, well-being, independence and empowerment (Pofeldt, 2003 in Jasper, 2005).
Catherine Muther	Three Guineas Fund	Put in $2 million as 501 (c) grant making foundation – economic equality for women and girls. Supports CoAbode House Sharing, GirlSource, Lower East Side Girls Club and National Women's Law Center (Jasper, 2005).
Pleasant Rowland	American Girl (originally the Pleasant Company)	Donates merchandise to Madison Children's Museum to raise over $8 million. Also started Pleasant Company's Fund for Children – grants to enhance children's education through arts, culture, and environment. Established Aldo Leopold Nature Center. Works globally with Kids in Distress Situations (Jasper, 2005).

philanthropist', while only 16 percent of the women executives reported the same identification.

Another approach to the topic of women's entrepreneurship and philanthropy is to explore what women entrepreneurs, as well as men entrepreneurs, bring to the philanthropic table. The ready answers include wealth (economic capital), entrepreneurial know-how (cultural capital), know-who (social capital), and reputations or brand (symbolic capital), with a goal of creating 'innovative solutions to deep-seated social problems' (Shaw et al., 2011: 584).

4.6   PHILANTHROPY EVOLVING

So far we have been looking back to see what has been learned to date to inform our understanding of the philanthropic behaviors of entrepreneurial women. Before moving to our suggested framework we also think it useful to capture a few of the more recent changes in philanthropy (Table 4.2). Many patterns in philanthropy have stayed the same for the last 100 years, for example the majority of charitable dollars went to education and religious institutions, or large human service organizations, like the American Red Cross or the Salvation Army (Brill, 2011). However, some changes have been noted, especially around strategic issues such as the timing of giving, the geography of beneficiaries, expectations around the evaluation of results, and increased levels of active involvement after the gift is made (Fulton and Blau, 2005).

New models of philanthropy are emerging, some of them uniquely tied to entrepreneurship. At the organizational level, social entrepreneurship has become an entire field dedicated to the solving of social problems through business applications (Maclean et al., 2013). With the advent of social entrepreneurship, the idea of the creation and distribution of wealth as a two-step process to solve social problems has been turned on its head. Rather than assuming that one creates wealth and then solves social problems through distribution of financial resources, social entrepreneurship focuses on directly creating social value to solve social problems. (This also questions the 'transition' model of philanthropy, moving from entrepreneurship to philanthropy, from creating wealth to solving social problems, given that some companies are created with an explicit model of building philanthropy into the business model.) Social entrepreneurship and other models have identified the need for widening the models of philanthropic behaviors. This evolving, or at least expanded view includes new mechanisms of donating financial capital, such as crowdfunding, a model that allows individual donors to give together, anywhere in the world, and focus on funding solutions to societal problems.

Table 4.2　Recent evolution of philanthropy

Old patterns or habits	Seeds of change
Giving primarily late in life	Giving throughout life
Foundations as the key institutional form	Foundations as one form among many
Social benefit equals the nonprofit sector	Social benefit can come from any sector
Philanthropy corrects for the market because the market is part of the problem	Philanthropy connects to the market because the market is part of the solution
Older, white male leadership	Diversifying leadership
Donors focus on communities where they live or have a connection	Donors focus both close to home and on systemic global problems with equal ease
Donors fund great strategies brought to them by nonprofits	Donors have great strategies and fund great strategies
Donors set general goals	Donors set specific targets
Donors make gifts	Donors make investments, award contracts, and make gifts
Money is the resource, grants the tool	Influence is the resource, money is one tool
Donors keep grantees at arm's length	Donors highly engaged with partners
Donors give independently	Donors give independently and give together
Donors content to do good	Donors try to assess impact
Donors learn from their own work	Donors learn from their work and share what they learn with others

Source:　Fulton and Blau (2005).

4.7　ENTREPRENEURIAL WOMEN AND PHILANTHROPY: CAPITAL TYPES

Shaw et al.'s discussion of Bourdieu's types of capital in the context of women entrepreneurs and philanthropy provides a useful pathway to summarize what we know to date and advance our understanding of women entrepreneurs and their philanthropic practices through the proposal of the next stage of research questions.

Pierre Bourdieu (1986) proposed a series of capital types to allow for an accounting of the structure and function of the social world in a way that moves beyond the limitations of viewing everything through only a purely economic lens. Economic capital is the category for those things that

Table 4.3   *Guiding the future of research on entrepreneurial women and philanthropy*

	Background (food for thought)	Questions for further investigation
Capital		
Economic	Women and men donors in general donate similar amounts when looking at the amount as a proportion of their salary. The creation of foundations is increasingly seen as a philanthropic strategy. Women-owned businesses tend to be smaller than those owned by men when measured in terms of revenues.	1. Are women entrepreneurs more likely to establish foundations than either male entrepreneurs or other women donors? 2. Are women entrepreneurs (not those self-defining as social entrepreneurs) more likely to wait until they have reached an economic milestone before donating?
Cultural		
Embodied	Entrepreneurship theory supports that people with entrepreneurial parents are more likely to become entrepreneurs. Moral development theory suggests that women are socialized differently.	1. What is the impact of philanthropic parents on women entrepreneurs? 2. What is the relationship between parents' entrepreneurial and philanthropic behaviors and the entrepreneurial and philanthropic behavior of women entrepreneurs? 3. Do the philanthropic behaviors of entrepreneurial parents have an effect on the timing of the first philanthropic efforts of an entrepreneurial daughter?
Objectified	Women donors tend to not put their names on the things they fund. Role models are deemed an important consideration for women entrepreneurs. Donors are increasingly looking to share what they learn from others regarding their philanthropic efforts.	1. What is the impact of role models for entrepreneurial women in their philanthropic practices? 2. Are women entrepreneurs as donors more likely to place their names on funded items than women donors in general?

Table 4.3   (continued)

	Background (food for thought)	Questions for further investigation
Institution-alized	Historically women donors were well educated yet unable to apply their education in labor markets.	1. Does formal education make a difference in why and how women entrepreneurs participate in philanthropy? 2. Are women entrepreneurs with degrees from private educational institutions more philanthropically active than women entrepreneurs with degrees from public institutions?
Social	Philanthropic leadership is seen as increasingly diversified, and influence is considered an important resource. Donors are also increasingly likely to give together as well as individually. Networks are different for men and women.	1. Do women's entrepreneurial networks also inform their philanthropic behaviors? 2. Are women entrepreneurs more likely to donate separately than male entrepreneurs or other women?

Sources: Adapted from Shaw et al. (2011) and informed by Bourdieu (1986) and Brush et al. (2001).

can be immediately and directly converted into money. Culture capital is considered as embodied, objectified or institutionalized. Embodied cultural capital captures the 'long-lasting dispositions of the mind and body' (Bourdieu, 1986: 47) built on the transmission and cultivation of culture, both innate and acquired. Objectified capital includes those things in a material state which represent culture, while institutionalized cultural capital focuses on academic qualifications which allow for the assignment of value as a 'certificate of cultural competence' (Bourdieu, 1986: 50). The final capital category, social capital, is one that underlies much of resource-based and network theorizing, in that Bourdieu describes it as, 'the aggregate of the actual or potential resources which are linked to possession of a durable network of more or less institutionalized relationships' (Bourdieu, 1986: 51). These capital types have been used as a foundation for exploration into women's entrepreneurship (Brush et al., 2001) and now lend themselves well to guide our investigation into women entrepreneurs and their approach to philanthropy (see Table 4.3).

4.8 CONCLUSION

Philanthropy plays an ever-increasing role in addressing the social challenges of the world. At the same time, more and more women are starting and growing entrepreneurial ventures. The intersection of philanthropy, gender considerations and entrepreneurship raises many questions based upon what we have learned to date about philanthropy, women donors and women entrepreneurs. Given that both entrepreneurship and philanthropy strive for the creation of value, Bourdieu's capital types are a useful tool to frame the next set of questions on the philanthropic behaviors of entrepreneurial women. The questions cover the territory of motivation and strategy while also driving toward the future of philanthropy. As such, additional research in this area will prove useful not only to practitioners, but also to entrepreneurship educators as they strive to teach about the creation of multiple types of value for both the economic and the social good of the world.

NOTE

* The Diana Project is a research consortium dedicated to the investigation of issues related to women growing businesses. Consortium members in alphabetical order are: Candida Brush, Nancy Carter, Elizabeth Gatewood, Patricia Greene and Myra Hart.

REFERENCES

Achtenhagen, L. and F. Welter (2011), 'Surfing on the ironing board – the representation of women entrepreneurship in German newspapers', *Entrepreneurship and Regional Development*, 23, 763–786.

Acs, A. and L. Dana (2001), 'Contrasting two models of wealth creation', *Small Business Economics*, 16, 63–74.

Ahl, H. (2006), 'Why research on women entrepreneurs needs new directions', *Theory and Practice*, 30, 595–621.

Andreoni, J., E. Brown and I. Rischall (2003), 'Charitable giving by married couples: Who decides and why does it matter?', *Journal of Human Resources*, 38(1), 111–133.

Bourdieu, P. (1986), 'The forms of capital', in J. Richardson (ed.), *The Handbook of Theory and Research for the Sociology of Education*, New York: Greenwood Press, pp. 241–258.

Brill, B. (2011), 'The more philanthropy changes, the more it stays the same', www.forbes. com, January 27 (accessed January 24, 2014).

Brown, E. (2006), 'Married couples' charitable giving: who and why', in M.A. Taylor and S. Shaw-Hardy (eds), *The Transformative Power of Women's Philanthropy*, San Francisco, CA: Wiley Periodicals Inc, pp. 69–80.

Bruni, Al, S. Gherardi and B. Poggio (2004), *Gender and Entrepreneurship: An Ethnographic Approach*, New York: Routledge.

Brush, C.G., P.G. Greene and M.M. Hart (2001), 'From initial idea to unique advantage: the entrepreneurial challenge of constructing a resource base', *Academy of Management Executive*, 15(1), 64–78.

Burgoyne, C.B., B. Young and C.M. Walker (2005), 'Deciding to give to charity: a focus group study in the context of the household economy', *Journal of Community and Applied Social Psychology*, 15(5), 383–405.

Calhoun, D.B. (2006), 'Philanthropic motivations of female donors to Virginia's 4-H program', Dissertation, Virginia Tech, http://scholar.lib.vt.edu/theses/available/etd-12212006-110146/unrestricted/FinalETDdbc.pdf.

Capek, M.E.S. (2001), 'Women and philanthropy: old stereotypes, new challenges', Monograph Series, St Paul, MN: Global Fund for Women, Michigan Women's Foundation, Resourceful Women, Women & Philanthropy and Women's Funding Network.

Carter, N. and K. Allen (1997), 'Size determinants of women-owned businesses: choice or barriers to resources?', *Entrepreneurship and Regional Development*, 9(3), 211–220.

Center for Women's Business Research (2000), *Leaders in Business and Community: Philanthropic Contribution of Women and Men Business Owners*, Washington, DC: National Foundation for Women Business Owners.

Coombs, J.E., A.J. Shipp and L.J. Christensen (2008), 'Entrepreneur as change agent: antecedents and moderators of individual-level philanthropic behavior', *Frontiers of Entrepreneurship Research*, 28 (21), Article 1.

Council on Foundations (2002), *An Abbreviated History of the Philanthropic Tradition in the United States*, Washington, DC: Council on Foundations.

Crocker, R. (2002), 'From gift to foundation: The philanthropic lives of Mrs. Russell Sage', in Lawrence J. Friedman and Mark D. McHarvie (eds), *Charity, Philanthropy, and Civility in American History*, New York: Cambridge University Press, pp. 188–216.

Daniels, C. and C. Brush (2013), 'Babson College Career Pathways Alumni Study', Wellesley, MA: Babson College.

de Bruin, A., C. Brush and F. Welter (2006), 'Introduction to the special issue: towards building cumulative knowledge on women's entrepreneurship', *Entrepreneurship Theory and Practice*, 30, 585–593.

DeCarlo, J.F. and P.R. Lyons (1979), 'A comparison of selected personal characteristics of minority and non-minority female entrepreneurs', *Journal of Small Business Management*, 17, 22–30.

Fischer, E.M. and R. Reuber (2003), 'Support for rapid growth firms: A comparison of the views of founders, government policymakers and private sector resource providers', *Journal of Small Business Management*, 41(4), 346–365.

Fulton, K. and A. Blau (2005), 'Looking out for the future of philanthropy: An orientation for twenty-first century philanthropists', Monitor Company Group,

Giving USA Foundation (2013), *Giving USA 2013*, Chicago, IL: Indiana University Lilly Family School of Philanthropy.

Glenn, J.M., L. Brandt and F.E. Andrews (1947), *Russell Sage Foundation, 1907–1946*, Vol. 2, New York: Russell Sage Foundation.

Hall, Peter Dobkin (2006), 'A historical overview of philanthropy, voluntary associations, and nonprofit organizations in the United States, 1600–2000', in Walter Powell and Richard Steinberg (eds), *The Nonprofit Sector: A Research Handbook*, 2nd edn, Newhaven, CT: Yale University Press, pp. 32–65.

Hammack, D.C. and S. Wheeler (1994), *Social Science in the Making: Essays on the Russell Sage Foundation, 1907–1972*, New York: Russell Sage Foundation.

Harding, R. (2004), 'Social enterprise: the new economic engine', *Business Strategy Review*, Winter, 39–43.

Hisrich, R.D. and M. O'Brien (1981), 'The woman entrepreneur as a reflection of the type of business', in K.H. Vesper (ed.), *Frontiers of Entrepreneurial Research*, Boston, MA: Babson College, pp. 54–67.

Jasper, Cynthia R. (2005), 'Women executives and business owners: a new philanthropy', *New Directions for Philanthropic Fundraising*, 50(Winter), 55–68.

Jennings, J. and C.G. Brush (2013), 'Research on women entrepreneurs: challenges to (and from) the broader entrepreneurship literature?' *Academy of Management Annals*, 7(1), 661–713.

Kottasz, R. (2004), 'Differences in the donor behavior characteristics of young affluent males and females: empirical evidence from Britain', *International Journal of Voluntary and Nonprofit Organizations*, 15(2), 181–203.

Maclean, M., C. Harvey and J. Gordon (2013), 'Social innovation, social entrepreneurship and the practice of contemporary entrepreneurial philanthropy', *International Small Business Journal*, 31(7), 747–763.

Martin, J. (2000), 'Hidden gendered assumptions in mainstream organizational theory and research', *Journal of Management Inquiry*, 9(2), 207–216.

Mesch, D., P. Rooney, K. Steinberg and B. Denton (2006), 'The effects of race, gender, and marital status on giving and volunteering in Indiana', *Nonprofit and Voluntary Sector Quarterly*, 35(4), 365–587.

Nowell, I. (1996), *Women Who Give Away Millions: Portraits of Canadian Philanthropists*, Toronto, ON: Hounslow Press.

Oppedisano, J. (2000), *Historical Encyclopedia of American Women Entrepreneurs 1776 to the Present*, Westport, CT: Greenwood Press.

Oppedisano, J. (2004), 'Giving back: women's entrepreneurial philanthropy', *Women in Management Review*, 19(3), 174–177.

Oxford English Dictionary (2013), Oxford: Oxford University Press.

Parsons, P.H. (2004), 'Women's philanthropy: Motivations for giving', Unpublished doctoral dissertation, retrieved from ProQuest Doctoral Dissertations, (AAT 3155889).

Piper, G. and S.V. Schnepf (2008), 'Gender differences in charitable giving in Great Britain', *Voluntas: International Journal of Voluntary and Nonprofit Organizations*, 19(2), 103–124.

Pofeldt, E. (2003), 'The best bosses – the nurturer: Eileen Fisher', *Fortune Online*, October 1.

Reed, P. and K. Selbee (2000), 'Distinguishing characteristics of active volunteers in Canada', *Nonprofit and Voluntary Sector Quarterly*, 29(4), 571–592.

Sage, M. (1907), 'Letter to the trustees of the Russell Sage Foundation', http://www.russell-sage.org/about/history (accessed January 24, 2014).

Schwartz, E. (1976), 'Entrepreneurship: A new female frontier', *Journal of Contemporary Business*, 5, 47–76.

Scott, A.F. (1991), *Natural Allies: Women's Associations in American History*, Urbana, IL: University of Illinois Press.

Sexton, D.L. and C.A. Kent (1981), 'Female executives and entrepreneurs: A preliminary comparison', in K.H.Vesper (ed.), *Frontiers of Entrepreneurship Research*, Boston, MA: Babson College, pp.40–55.

Sharir, M. and M. Lerner (2006), 'Gauging the success of social ventures initiated by individual social entrepreneurs', *Journal of World Business*, 41(1), 6–20.

Shaw, E., J. Gordon, C. Harvey and M. Maclean (2011), 'Exploring contemporary entrepreneurial philanthropy', *International Small Business Journal*, 31(5), 580–599.

Shaw, S. and M. Taylor (1995), *Reinventing Fundraising: Realizing the Potential of Women's Philanthropy*, San Francisco, CA: Jossey-Bass Publishers.

Van Ryzin, G.G., S. Grossman, L. DiPadova-Stocks and E. Bergrud (2009), 'Portrait of the social entrepreneur: Statistical evidence from a US Panel', *Voluntas: International Journal of Voluntary and Nonprofit Organizations*, 20 =(2), 129–140.

Waugh, J. (1997), *Unsentimental Reformer: The Life of Josephine Shaw Lowell*, Cambridge, MA: Harvard University Press.

Women Give: 2010, Part 2 (2010), 'Causes women support', Women's Philanthropy Institute at the Center on Philanthropy at Indiana University, available at http://www.philanthropy.iupui.edu/files/research/women_give_2010_report.pdf (accessed 7 January 2014).

Wooster, M. (2002), 'First suppression, then gibberish: American philanthropy's enduring historical void', *Philanthropy Roundtable*, March–April, 1–3.

5. Another look at giving back: an examination of the philanthropic motivations, orientations and activities of Black American entrepreneurs
Vickie Cox Edmondson and Marilyn L. Taylor

Wealth for Life Principle No. 10: I will strengthen my community through philanthropy. Once you've built wealth, we believe that in addition to passing it on to future generations, you must use it to preserve our institutions and uplift those in need. That thrust has always been a part of our tradition – and a way that all of us can make history. (Derek T. Dingle, Editor-in-Chief, *Black Enterprise*; Dingle, 2012: 12)

5.1 INTRODUCTION

The literature on Black American-owned businesses shows that these businesses are small compared to White-owned businesses, yet media outlets have many accounts of Black American (Black) entrepreneurs giving back to their community. The evidence suggests that regardless of firm or personal resources, many Black entrepreneurs devote substantial time and money to causes deemed capable of helping their community and beyond. One recent example is the USC gift from Black American entrepreneur Andre Young ('Dr Dre', hip hop mogul) and music executive Jimmy Lovine. Young and Lovine donated $70 million to create the USC Jimmy Lovine and Andre Young Academy for Arts, Technology and the Business of Innovation at the University of Southern California. The Academy is set to open in the fall of 2014 with an initial class of 25 students (Max Nikias, 2013). In a second recent example, the University of Wisconsin–Madison made a 2012 announcement regarding the First Wave/MC Lyte Scholarship presented by Hip Hop Sisters Network. The Network presented the scholarship on behalf of its founder, MC Lyte (Lana Moorer – pioneer Black American hip hop artist and member of Sigma Gamma Rho Sorority, Inc.). Moorer said, 'For years I've dreamed of having the ability to help our community and now finally the day has arrived ... This scholarship partnership with UW–Madison is just the beginning for what HHSF has in store' (Davis, 2012).

However, systematic study of Black or African-American entrepreneurs and their philanthropic activities remains scant. The 1999 *Journal of Business Ethics* article by Cox Edmondson and Carroll remains one of the few systematic studies which provide insights from research specifically focused on Black or African-American entrepreneurs and their philanthropic activities. To begin the process of updating these earlier insights, the authors of this chapter undertook a two-phase investigation. The first phase involved an extensive search of the literature to identify what is known about US Black entrepreneurs' philanthropic activities. The second phase involved interviews with a small sample of Black entrepreneurs recommended by local sources. The questions guiding these interviews parallel much of the study reported earlier in the *Journal of Business Ethics*.

The overall purpose of the current study is to explore any changes that may be occurring among Black entrepreneurs involved in philanthropy since the Cox Edmondson and Carroll study was conducted in 1996. Specifically this chapter provides:

- an overview of the literature on Black entrepreneurs' philanthropic activities;
- discussion of the major findings from the Cox Edmondson and Carroll 1999 study;
- a summary of the findings from the small-sample interview study;
- a discussion and future research issues.

5.2 CURRENT STATE OF THE LITERATURE

Although the Cox Edmondson and Carroll study has been cited more than 50 times, recent examination of the literature indicates little additional empirical work in this area. The dominant theme in the academic journals regarding Black entrepreneurs has been on profit maximization. The issues have included management practices and the implications for business development in the Black community as a rationale for why Black-owned business should be supported by lending agencies (Nopper, 2011; Raphael et al., 2000).

Indeed, during the last two decades there have been few peer-reviewed articles that focus on entrepreneurs in general and their activities in the philanthropic arena. Shaw et al. (2013) noted the dearth of literature. She and her colleagues have made the two recent contributions to this literature. The first is the development of a model based on the example of Andrew Carnegie. The model posits that investment in philanthropic activities can contribute to economic, social, and symbolic capital which, in turn, can contribute to an increase in economic capital (Harvey et al., 2011). Harvey, Shaw and colleagues have provided additional insights into the complex dynamics between the realm of the entrepreneur's business activities on one hand and the philanthropic activities on the other (Shaw et al., 2013). A handful of researchers have provided some insights into entrepreneurs engaged in philanthropy (Acs and Phillips, 2002; Acs et al., 2008; Bishop and Green, 2008; Schervish et al., 2001). Recently Lähdesmäki and Takala (2012) provided insights into the motivations of small business owners for engaging in philanthropy. While some of the motivation may be closely related to economic goals, there is evidence of altruism and a desire to contribute to others' welfare. Lähdesmäki and Takala suggest that in small businesses there may be fewer organizational context barriers to the expression of the owner's values through philanthropy than may exist in large businesses.

A major exception in the literature since the original study is the emergence of a new area of study, namely social entrepreneurship or the process of employing market-based methods to solve social problems (Grimes et. al., 2013; Seymour, 2012). This stream of literature has been so robust that social entrepreneurship has been accepted as a mainstream form of entrepreneurship (Acs and Dana, 2001). As posited by Hemingway (2005), social entrepreneurs may be business owners, as well as decision makers within corporations. Female social entrepreneurs have been the focus of social entrepreneurship study (Oppedisano, 2004). To date Black Americans have not. We make no speculations regarding the involvement of Black community members, especially entrepreneurs and executives, in social entrepreneurship. Social entrepreneurship is not the focus of our study and thus no review of this literature is included in this chapter.

There has been systematic examination of entrepreneurs and CSR. Prior to the Cox Edmondson and Carroll study, the race of the entrepreneurs in discussions of CSR was not adequately explored in academic journals. However, subsequently more researchers have considered Black entrepreneurs within study of the CSR phenomenon and have cited the 1999 study as evidence of the importance of the philanthropic efforts of Blacks (Campbell and Slack, 2006; Dean, 2001; Pearce and Doh, 2005; Shum and Yam, 2011).

Researchers have examined the philanthropic activities of other groups and nationalities (Campbell et al., 2002; Dusuki et al., 2008; Meijer et al., 2006; Noble et al., 2008; Worthington et al., 2006). However, much of the subsequent research addresses overall philanthropy in the Black community, rather than philanthropy as undertaken by Black entrepreneurs (Conley, 2000; Donohue et al., 2002; Jackson, 2001; Shrestha et al., 2007).

Indeed we were only to identify three works that offered fruitful insights to further our study of Black entrepreneurs' philanthropic experiences. First, Shrestha et al. (2007) informed the literature in a way that the Cox Edmondson and Carroll study had not. These scholars aimed to better understand the role of marketing philanthropy in the Black community so as to more effectively achieve its social justice purposes, namely to achieve socioeconomic empowerment. These authors did not look at entrepreneurs specifically. Rather they utilized the historical evolution of philanthropy in the Black community to develop a framework based on two concepts – the causes Blacks share and identify with and the institutions Blacks trust. Shrestha et al. posited that philanthropic activities can generally be divided into three categories: donations (giving of money and other resources), volunteering (giving of time), and social justice (cause-based activism). The Cox Edmondson and Carroll study listed motivations and ways to give back. However, those identified appeared reactive with little forethought into being actively engaged in long term change other than through giving time and money. In contrast, Shrestha et al. argue that social cause-based philanthropy is invariably intent on remedying systemic and systematic injustices and these efforts often turn into a project, mobilizing sustained efforts and resources and demanding certain policy initiatives and change. This phenomenon seems to be evident regardless of race. The Shrestha et al. study does extend the Cox Edmondson and Carroll study as it identifies a model of philanthropy that includes social justice. The drawback to the Shrestha et al. study for the current work study is that these authors discuss the patterns and evolution of Black philanthropy. However the researchers did not limit the focus of the study to Black entrepreneurs.

The second study that has been conducted about philanthropy in Black-owned businesses is that of McKinley-Floyd and Shrestha (2008). These authors identified five motivations for Blacks' involvement in philanthropy: the church, kinship and community, reciprocity ('give back'), uplifting the race, and association with organizations. They noted the need for non-profits to examine segmentation strategies in order to improve their ability to mobilize the 'black gold' or financial resources that have developed in the Black community. However, the focus of this work by McKinley-Floyd and Shrestha is from the perspective of marketing to the Black community, as contrasted to the entrepreneur's perspective that was the focus of Cox Edmondson and Carroll and the current study.

The third effort focused on trust as an influence on philosophical efforts. The argument was that trust in institutions is of upmost importance in considering which entities to support. As quoted in Guiso et al. (2006), Arrow (1972) stated, 'virtually every commercial transaction has within itself an element of trust, certainly any transaction conducted over a period of time.' Guiso et al. studied economic decisions of groups by countries. However, the researchers distinguished Americans as 'Afro-Americans' and other Americans to enlighten us specifically about Black Americans. The study found that 'Afro-Americans' more than any other group preferred redistribution of wealth to ensure equality. Thus, Guiso et al. argued, trusting the government as well as the entities to which the money is given is essential to the decision to give.

However, in spite of the significant literatures in both entrepreneurship and philanthropy, these are the only three contributions that we were able to identify. Thus, we reiterate, the academic literature is largely silent on the experience of Black or African-American entrepreneurs in the realm of philanthropy. The current study then contributes to this gap by exploring changes that have occurred among entrepreneurial firms owned by Black Americans during the last nearly two decades and discusses significant changes (if any) in Black entrepreneurs' philanthropic activities. Before overviewing the 1999 study and the current research results, however, a word about the state of US-based Black entrepreneurs is in order.

5.2.1   The State of US-Based Black Entrepreneurs

The condition of Black-owned business in the US has remained largely unchanged. The number of Black-owned businesses steadily increased from 1992 to 2007. The two most recent Census Reports show that the number of Black-owned firms grew by 45.4 percent between 1997 and 2002 and increased by 60.5 percent to 1.9 million between 2002 and 2007. This rate of increase was more than triple the national rate according to US Census data released in 2011. The number of businesses across the country increased by 18 percent in the same period (2002–2007). Although the number of Black businesses is growing rapidly, the businesses remain relatively small compared to majority-owned business. Few have paid employees, and revenues are low. However, their sales and receipts improved to 7.1 percent of businesses nationwide in 2007, compared to 5.2 percent in 2002 (US Census Bureau). As a result, Black entrepreneurs may indeed have 'black gold', that is, more discretionary funds to give back to their community than in previous years.

5.3   OVERVIEW OF THE 1999 STUDY

The goals of the Cox Edmondson and Carroll study which was conducted in 1996 were to ascertain:

1. Community or philanthropic activities of the respondents, their firms, or organizations to which they belonged and in which they participated.
2. Respondents' assessment of the activities' impact on the Black community.
3. Respondents' reasons or motivations for undertaking their philanthropic and community involvement.
4. Respondents' corporate social responsibility orientations (economic, legal, ethical and philanthropic) as articulated by Carroll (1979).

The authors used a commercial mailing list from *Black Enterprise* magazine to identify the subjects. Since Earl Graves, Sr and his wife Barbara initiated the periodical in 1970, *Black Enterprise* magazine has served as an authoritative source for news relevant to and about the Black business community. Eligibility for inclusion on the list of top companies in *Black Enterprise* required that a company must have been fully operational in the previous calendar year and be at least 51 percent Black-owned.[1] The four-page questionnaire was accompanied by a cover letter stating the purpose of the survey, asking for their participation, and informing the respondents that they could receive a copy of the results. The questionnaire and cover letter was mailed to the CEOs or owners of 498 firms, and 74 useable responses were received (15.1 percent response rate). Tables providing the summary data from the 1999 study appear at the end of this chapter.

The results indicated that philanthropy and ethical justifications in the Corporate Social Responsibility (CSR) model played more important roles in firms owned by Black American entrepreneurs than found in previous studies of non-minority-owned firms. Cox Edmondson and Carroll argued that philanthropic efforts were among the first, and, perhaps most altruistic, indicators of businesses' belief that they had a responsibility to society that extended beyond producing and distributing goods and services and making a profit. They posited that CSR had a long history in the Black community and that Black business owners feel they have a special responsibility to contribute (give back) to the Black community. However, their efforts to enhance their communities and, in particular, the Black community had not been carefully studied and documented.

Cox Edmondson and Carroll pointed out that although the number of Black-owned businesses grew from 1987 to 1992, Black entrepreneurs struggled with the limitations of small size and limited revenues. They asserted that Black-Americans have a significant stake in the success of Black-owned businesses because of the impact these businesses have in the Black community. In Black-owned businesses at least four of the five stakeholder groups identified by Carroll (1995) that are affected by the philanthropic component of CSR would most likely consist of Black Americans. Those groups affected would include: (1) the Black community; (2) employees – most of whom are Blacks; (3) owners – who are Blacks; (4) consumers – who are often Blacks; and (5) other – who may or may not be Blacks.

The authors concluded that:

1. Black entrepreneurs primarily gave back to those causes that they felt would have the most impact on the community.
2. Many Black entrepreneurs teamed up with other Black entrepreneurs in order to give back to their community more generously than if they gave back individually.
3. They desired to generate good public relations value and to support particular causes embraced by directors and top managers.
4. They recognized the benefit of the appointments of more Black individuals to the boards of major corporations and nonprofit organizations, especially those that have a high number of Black employees or other stakeholders who are Black.
5. Many Black businesses were rooted in religious faith, and the authors speculated that the Black business owners had more firmly internalized ethical reasons for their actions rather than motivation rooted in legal origins.
6. Black American entrepreneurs noted the importance of philanthropy because they had more often been the recipients or benefactors of philanthropic giving and, thus, had a higher perception of its importance or worth relative to the other components.

5.4   CURRENT STUDY: INTERVIEWS WITH A SAMPLE OF LOCAL ENTREPRENEURS

We undertook an exploratory study of a small sample of Black entrepreneurs who are located in various points throughout the United States. The 1999 study focused on the large Black-owned businesses which were included on the *Black Enterprise* commercial list, an indicator of success and ability to give back. In contrast, the current study did not consider firm size. Rather, Black entrepreneurs were identified by two sources: (1) Morehouse College Entrepreneurship Center current or former clients; and (2) members of the Morehouse College business faculty. A total of 37 entrepreneurs were approached. Seven agreed to be interviewed. The questions in the interview protocol were not identical to those used in the

Cox Edmondson and Carroll study, but they did consider three of the four issues covered in the 1996 study, namely:

1. Community or philanthropic activities in which the interviewees participated.
2. Reasons or motivations for undertaking their philanthropic and community involvement.
3. Social responsibility orientations (economic, legal, ethical, and philanthropic), as articulated by Carroll (1979).

The interview protocol did not explicitly ask for the interviewees' assessment of the impact of the activities on the Black community. However, some insights did arise regarding this issue. The purpose of the current study was to identify possible changes since the mid-1990s and to explore issues that might have been missed in the earlier study. (See the Appendix for the questions that made up the interview protocol.)

The seven interviewees included four males and three females who had been in business from six to over 30 years. Four had been in business over 20 years. The overall mean was over 20 years. The number of employees ranged from two to 175 with four of the businesses having between 20–30 employees. The overall mean of current employees was 32. The business activities included: home building and improvement, distributor of logo promotional products and uniforms, fast food chain (three locations), a food service company, a medical practice, insurance sales and service, and data analytics. All of the owners indicated they were active in their companies, although one plans to retire in 2014. All, as noted earlier, had relationships with Morehouse College.

Below we summarize the insights gleaned from the interviews organized in the following categories: (1) decision-making criteria; (2) meeting and going beyond legal standards; (3) importance of ethical leadership; (4) Black owners' sense of responsibility to the Black community; (5) ways of giving back to the Black community; (6) reasons for interest in the set of activities in which involved; (7) philanthropic activities beyond the Black community; (8) reasons for the interviewees' interest in the identified set of activities; (9) changes in philanthropic activities since starting the business; and (10) relative emphases on economic, legal, ethical and philanthropic dimensions.

5.4.1   Decision-Making Criteria

All of the interviewees indicated that they relied on an economic criterion as their primary objective when making decisions about their companies.

They were concerned about current profitability as well as long-term viability. For example, they talked about goals 'to make money', 'economic strength', 'the viability of the enterprise' or 'create a multi-generational organization'. Six mentioned other criteria. Three of the six noted product quality or service to customers, while two specifically mentioned employees as a consideration. One mentioned the objective of 'giv[ing] back to the community' in addition to assuring the long-term viability of the organization.

5.4.2   Meeting and Going Beyond Legal Standards

The interviewees indicated that they were staying in step with the legal standards that impacted their businesses through multiple means, including: working with outside professionals, especially the company's lawyer (N = 3); staying current with licensure requirements or laws governing the business (2); relying on the franchisor's rules (1); and having 'every type of insurance you can imagine' (1). When asked about going beyond compliance with the law, these business leaders indicated: they focused on trying to stay within the law (N = 3), exceeding customer expectations (2), attending seminars that were not required and staying current with literature about the laws and regulations (1), and setting 'the bar high . . . if there is a gray area, do not do it' (1).

5.4.3   Importance of Ethical Leadership

All of the interviewees indicated that ethical leadership was important to them. Two specifically invoked a Christian standard ('a Christian believes in the Old Testament' and 'represent the Lord first') and another the Golden Rule ('treat people the way you want to be treated'). Two others indicated an avoidance motivation. One said: 'wanted to be able to sleep at night' while the second expressed that 'my worst fear is to be caught on the WSJ [*Wall Street Journal*] . . . [I] prefer to err on the better side'.

5.4.4   Black Owners' Sense of Responsibility to the Black Community

Five of the interviewees indicated that they felt that Black business owners did not have a greater sense of responsibility to the Black community than owners from other races have toward their ethnic communities, or heads of companies who are female have toward other current or aspiring female entrepreneurs. The interviewees said, for example, 'All should give back and have a responsibility to give back to the community that helped them get where they are'; 'they should have a responsibility to whoever they work with'; and 'I feel that responsibility . . . there [is] an obligation to help others . . . so many people helped [me] . . . not just Black entrepreneurs have this responsibility but those of all races.'

The two interviewees who felt that Blacks do have a greater sense of responsibility to their communities than other races said, 'Yes. It is the community and those who helped us get to where they are – a commitment to helping them by given back', and 'Because of the small number of black businesses, we need to support each other, even if it is just buying an ad to support their business.'

5.4.5   Ways of Giving Back to the Black Community

The entrepreneurs identified a dozen categories of ways in which they gave back to the Black community. The categories were:

- Donating in some way to education, such as scholarship funds to their alma maters, other colleges and universities, other schools such as a charter school, and support to African students to come to US HBCs (N = 4).
- Making charitable donations to organizations such as Children's Home Society or NAACP (4).
- Giving to the Church (3).
- Supporting Black fraternities that supported scholarships (1), and another that had a charity outreach (1).
- Hiring individuals viewed as difficult to hire, such as ex-cons (2).
- Speaking in the community (2).
- Giving time as a volunteer (2).
- Giving employees time off to work with a charity (1).
- Having the business match employee donations (1).
- Supporting clients' requests for help with various issues such as youth sports (1).
- Supporting or sponsoring youth activities including sponsoring a youth essay contest regarding health (1), and little league uniforms (1).
- Sitting on boards (1).
- Mentoring college students (1).

Most of the interviewees (N = 6) reported that they contributed to the community in multiple ways, with the categories of activities ranging from two to six. The one individual who focused on 'only' one category supported two levels of education, an urban prep school with campuses in urban core areas of a major Midwestern city and a Black fraternity's scholarship program.

5.4.6   Reasons for Interest in the Set of Activities in which Involved

The interviewees' responses all had a sense of giving back or strengthening the community. The two interviewees who were explicit about giving back said: 'Because someone helped me, I do the same for those who are coming so they can pay it forward', and 'Others sacrificed for me . . . I stood on the shoulders of others.' But others gave a somewhat different perspective. For example:

- Be a role model: 'to be a role model that people can see and learn from especially in places where there are not a lot of people [that is] small rural areas, as well as urban communities', and '[Be] the image of someone who has made it successful.'
- Invest in education: '[I am a] strong believer that education is way out of poverty.' (This individual supported African college students to come to the US to study.)
- Encouraging and strengthening others: 'The people we help tend to be more disadvantaged. [It's] my way of boosting them.'
- Helping those in other countries: '[I am] interested in emerging markets [particularly African].' (Note that this interviewee accepted recommendations from Church members as to where to make these contributions.)

5.4.7   Philanthropic Activities beyond the Black Community

Five of the interviewees indicated that they were involved in philanthropic activities beyond the Black community. Two specifically indicated that they were involved in the same activities within and beyond the Black community. For example, the interviewee who had a medical practice said, 'I do the same talks that I do in the AA churches in White churches. I perform the same services even if someone can't pay, regardless of race . . . [I am] not in the business of giving away free [medical] service, but when I can I give away free medicine/free testing for analysis. [In addition] I have a healthy heart essay scholarship for students of all races.'

Others mentioned specific activities including:

- Supporting the Sheppard Center program – a spinal cord injury and traumatic brain injury rehabilitation hospital in the southeast.
- Mentoring kids and students.
- Serving as a trustee for a local university.
- Volunteering in a local program.
- Participating in the university alma mater's alumni association as a life member.

- Supporting the National Black Arts Festival (which initially had an audience of primarily Blacks but has evolved to have a strongly mixed-race following).
- Participating in philanthropic activities sponsored by the chain.
- Supporting an urban school which is mixed race.

Two of the interviewees indicated they were not involved beyond the Black community. Both of these individuals were among those who mentioned multiple kinds of activities within which they were involved. One who was active only in the Black community explained his philanthropic activities with:

> [I] try to spend money with us. It's just as important as a charitable contribution . . . [i.e.,] dollars reinvested in the [Black] community. That expands the economic impact, the ecosystem within our community. When businesses are not up to par [I] educate them on where they failed. Sometimes they [the business owners] don't know what they don't know.'

And, '[I] give and support activities close to home . . . [because one can] make more impact on things you understand.'

5.4.8   Reasons for Interest in the Identified Set of Activities

Of the five interviewees who indicated they were involved in philanthropic efforts beyond the Black community, four identified reasons for participating in philanthropic activities beyond the Black community, including:

- Influenced and helped by Blacks and non-Blacks: 'I stood on the shoulders of others . . . People from all walks of life have helped me . . . you have to be [part of] the change you want to see . . . I admire Gandhi. I may influence someone else to give back.'
- Interested in a special population: a special concern for veterans because 'we [Americans] are not taking care of our veterans with devastating war injuries'. (Inasmuch as we could determine, this individual did not have a family member or close associate who was a veteran.)
- A result of previous experiences: 'Experiences in effective organization that I had relationships with and through friendships. I got traction [i.e., in the activities] and got fulfilled.' And, '[gave to major state university alma mater because] I loved the school'.

One of the individuals who focused on activities only within the Black community indicated that there was a lack of time to undertake activities beyond the Black community. That interviewee had identified the greatest number of activities in which he was involved of all of the individuals interviewed.

5.4.9   Changes in Philanthropic Activities since Starting the Business

All seven interviewees responded to this question. Three indicated that with business success growth they have been able to give more financial support. They said:

> As the business has grown, I have been able to donate more money and employ people and provide more time . . . I have more time than money in the beginning.

> The commitment was always there . . . The real change is in the amount . . . make more, give more.

> From an economic standpoint, I am more able to give back. The accumulation of wealth affords people more opportunities to do things.

Two indicated that they had changed the type of activity. One said: 'When I came to [the area] I worked hard to learn about the community . . . very active . . . serving on a lot of community boards . . . [I have] migrate[d] from Commerce to community service organizations and focus on education.'

The second was an individual who had been in the construction industry for nearly 30 years. He identified his activities as giving to his Church as well as universities and schools. In addition, he described hiring difficult-to-employ individuals and providing them with training. When asked about changes, he said, 'When I started I thought I was smarter than I was . . . [I] spent more time on causes than on [giving] help . . . it's very easy for causes to get subverted to interest group.' An earlier comment indicated that he tried to 'give and support close to home and then go out [beyond the Black community, so that I could] make more impact on things I understand'.

The other two individuals gave quite different answers. One (female in insurance sales and service for almost 30 years) indicated, '[My] effort has not changed, but the amount depends on the state of the economy.' The other indicated that the emphasis on time versus money has shifted. That interviewee said, 'I used to give a lot of my time . . . 80 percent time, 20 percent financial. As the company has grown, [I have] now flipped . . . 20 percent time and 80 percent financial.'

5.4.10 Emphasis on Economic, Legal, Ethical and Philanthropic Dimensions

This set of questions in the interview protocol was concerned with the four dimensions (economic success, legal compliance, ethical considerations and philanthropic activities) that were utilized in the 1999 study. The interviewees were asked to quantify how important these dimensions were to them, through two measures. The first approach asked the interviewee to provide an actual rank of 1 to 4 with 1 being the item of highest importance and 4 being the item of lowest importance. The second measure asked for a rating on a Likert-scale of 5 (highly important), 4 (somewhat), 3 (neutral), 2 (not very important) and 1 (not at all important). The mean ratings and mean ranks appear in Table 5.1 along with comparison to results of the 1999 study as well as two other earlier studies.

5.5 DISCUSSION AND CONCLUSIONS

In the discussion below we first consider the 1999 study and the current interview study. Second, we consider the implications of the comparisons for future research agendas. We finalize with comments for the Black entrepreneurs themselves.

5.5.1 Comparison of the 1999 Study and Interview Study of Black Entrepreneurs

Compared to the 1999 study, the current study provides the insights from the qualitative nature of the research. Overall these Black entrepreneurs in the current study responded similarly to the entrepreneurs in the previous study. However, there were notable differences. Below we discuss the activities and prioritization of the four dimensions.

The set of activities identified were similar to the list presented in the questionnaire presented to respondents in the mid-1990s. The analysis of the current study did identify several new activities that the interviewees regarded as philanthropic. The most notable in the current study was hiring individuals who were viewed as difficult to hire. Another interesting activity that the interviewees identified was having a business policy of providing opportunity for employees to be involved in philanthropic activities by giving time off to be involved in an activity or by matching donations of financial support. We note, however, that this activity was identified by only one interviewee. The interviewees differentiated between providing support (generally in the form of monetary gifts) and being

Table 5.1 Comparison of four studies regarding the relative importance of the four dimensions (numbers in parentheses indicate the order of importance)

	Aupperle (1984)v	Pinkston and Carroll (1995)	Cox Edmondson and Carroll (1999)	t-value PandC/1996 sample	Mean ratings for current interview study (2013)	Mean ranks for current interview study (2013)
Economic	3.50 (1)	3.28 (1)	3.16 (1)	0.90	4.6 (4)	2.6 (2)
Legal	2.54 (2)	3.07 (2)	2.12 (2)	10.32*	4.9 (2)	2.3 (4)
Ethical	2.22 (3)	2.45 (3)	2.19 (3)	2.54**	5.0 (1)	3.0 (1)
Philanthropic	1.30 (4)	1.15 (4)	2.04 (4)	7.22*	4.7 (3)	2.4 (3)
Residual	0.44	0.05	0.49			

Note: In all instances the higher number connotes greatest importance among the four dimensions.

personally involved (for example, giving time as a volunteer, serving as a role model, mentoring or speaking to youth in order to enlighten them about opportunities in entrepreneurship). This differentiation has been made in other studies (Wilson et al., 2004).

The mid-1990s study did not differentiate between activities within and outside the Black community. With caution we note that overall the respondents in the current study did not markedly differentiate between targeted recipients. Two of the interviewees were very explicit that race was not a factor in their giving at all. However, we note that two interviewees were very explicit that they did not involve themselves in activities outside the Black community. The backgrounds of the entrepreneurs and their types of business (a male entrepreneur with a distribution firm of more than 20 years, and a female entrepreneur with a service company of somewhat more than six years) did not appear to contribute to an explanation. The first of these was very explicit about being a role model to the Black community. The second, even though she was definitive about not being involved in philanthropy outside the Black community, also noted that she helped with start-up businesses of which two were owned by non-Black women.

With regard to prioritization of the dimensions (economic, legal, ethical or philanthropic), the results in this study were different than in the previous studies noted in the 1999 article. The interviewees in the current study identified ethical considerations as the most important consideration (first in order in the current study, as contrasted to third in previous studies). Further, the economic dimension was identified as lower in the current study (fourth in order, as contrasted to first across all of the previous studies). Similar in all the studies, however, the philanthropic dimension was higher (third in the current study, as contrasted to fourth in the previous studies).

The responses of these Black entrepreneurs to various questions strongly affirmed their commitment to giving back and there was a strong element of encouraging others to do so. For example, entrepreneurs in the current study said:

I don't see it as a color thing . . . if someone is hungry, it doesn't matter what color they are . . .

I feel that responsibility . . . much is given much is required . . . obligation to help others . . . so many people helped [me] . . . not just Black entrepreneurs have this responsibility but those of all races – not just money, intellectual capital, and other resources.

We Americans are not taking care of our veterans with devastating war injuries. People from all walks of life have helped me . . . you have to be the change that you want to see. I admire Gandhi. I may influence someone else to give back.

All should give back and have a responsibility to give back to the community that helped them get where they are . . . they should have a responsibility to whoever they work with . . .

5.5.2   Research Agendas

The current study provides preliminary updates on Black American entrepreneurs' experiences in their philanthropic activities. The results of the two most recent investigations suggest that Black entrepreneurs have retained active interest in philanthropy over an extended period of time, in this case for going on three decades. The differences between the two studies, as well as the similarities, suggest multiple issues that remain intriguing for building on these two studies.

First, the philanthropic activities of Black American entrepreneurs call for systematic study of the phenomenon to ascertain whether these preliminary results, similar in many ways to the 1999 study, hold. The current study is exploratory only. A larger sample designed to gather sufficient data to ascertain whether changes have occurred is definitely needed. A follow-up of the entrepreneurs from the previous *Black Enterprise* list would permit longitudinal observations. A survey of the companies on the current *Black Enterprise* list would provide a basis for making more definitive observations. If the sample was sufficiently large, there would be opportunity to ascertain whether there are regional differences.

Second, systematic study of the philanthropic activities of Black American entrepreneurs compared to entrepreneurs in other ethnic groupings needs to be undertaken in order to understand how these ethnic groups invest in their ethnic communities as contrasted to the broader society. Third, the Black entrepreneurs in the current study described giving of their largesse and of themselves, their time and their talents. Both charitable giving and volunteerism (direct activity with a non-profit, or the clients or beneficiaries of the non-profit's services) are clearly important in philanthropy (McKinley-Floyd and Shrestha, 2008). These sets of activities need to be explored in terms of the investment versus pay-off in terms of economic, social and symbolic capital (Harvey et al., 2011). Study at the individual as well as community system levels is warranted. Intensive case studies of how the philanthropic investments may make a difference in the targeted ethnic community as well as broader more systematic study are also needed. The case studies would complement the broader sample designs by providing insights into the dynamic evolution of the philanthropic investment process.

Table 5.2 Summary data from 1999 study: activities, means of participating and impact on the Black community

| Activity | %* | Means of participating (%) | | | Impact on the community (%) | | | |
		You	Firm	Org.	Major	Some	Minor	No.
1. Support youth activities	90.5	58.1	68.9	21.6	61.4	33.3	3.5	1.8
2. Gifts to charities supporting Black community	87.8	63.5	66.2	13.5	42.4	47.5	8.5	1.7
3. Management advice to minority-owned firms	77.0	60.8	39.2	12.2	50.0	41.1	7.1	1.8
4. Community development programs	75.7	45.9	54.1	27.0	59.3	38.9	1.9	0.0
5. Gifts to United Negro College Fund	75.7	45.9	64.9	16.2	44.6	42.9	7.1	5.4
6. Tithes and offerings to church	74.3	70.3	6.8	2.7	37.3	39.2	17.6	5.9
7. Gifts to organizations like the NAACP	71.6	44.6	58.1	16.2	30.6	57.1	6.1	6.1
8. Support art and cultural events	71.6	50.0	59.5	24.3	23.9	41.3	28.3	6.5
9. Gifts to non-minority-based charities	68.9	45.9	56.8	9.5	16.7	50.0	31.3	2.1
10. Church activities to benefit community	66.2	59.5	35.1	12.2	56.9	33.3	5.9	3.9
11. Student internships	66.2	12.2	58.1	8.1	34.8	45.7	17.4	2.2
12. Gifts directly to Black colleges	66.2	33.8	43.2	10.8	30.6	61.2	8.2	0.0

Note: *Percentage of respondents who were engaged in this activity.

109

Table 5.3   Motivations for giving back

Possible motivations for giving back	Ranked most significant (%)	Ranked in top 3 choices (%)
Protect and improve environment in which to live, work, and do business	39.2	68.9
Practice good corporate citizenship	35.1	71.62
Give back with little or no direct or indirect company self-interest	32.4	63.5
Realize good public relations value	27	59.52
Commitment of directors or senior officers to particular causes, involvement	23	50
Realize benefits for company employees (normally in areas where company operates)	18.9	47.3
Increase the pool of trained manpower or untrained manpower	18.9	43.2
Preserve a society that enables citizens to choose between government and private-sector alternatives	10.8	37.8
Pressure from business peers, customers, and/or suppliers	2.7	16.2

5.5.3   Comments for Black Entrepreneurs

Finally, the importance of Black entrepreneurs to the Black community cannot be underestimated. First, the entrepreneurs provide important role models to other members of the Black community from economic, ethical and legal, and philosophical perspectives. Second, our observations suggest that their efforts do indeed strengthen the community. The giving-back and pay-it-forward concepts are important in the Black community. Further, finding new ways to encourage and help the Black community, as well as the broader community, effectively and efficiently undertake philanthropic activities remains among our current and future challenges as a society. See Tables 5.2 and 5.3.

NOTE

1. However, in early 2000 in a controversial move the National Minority Supplier Development Council (NMSDC) voted to allow businesses to reduce their minority equity ownership to 30 percent rather than 51 percent and still qualify for minority status. The change applies only to financial equity and not to voting control. Persons of color must retain control of at least 51 percent of a company's voting stock to be considered for contracts administered by NMSDC (Quittner, 2000).

REFERENCES

Acs, Zoltan J. and Leo Paul Dana (2001), 'Contrasting two models of wealth redistribution', *Small Business Economics*, 16(2), 63–74.

Acs, Zoltan J., Sameeksha Desai and Leora Klapper (2008), 'What does "entrepreneurship" data really show?' Jena Economic Research Papers 2008–007, Friedrich-Schiller-University Jena, Max-Planck-Institute of Economics.

Acs, Zoltan, J. and Ronnie J. Phillips (2002), 'Entrepreneurship and philanthropy in American capitalism', *Small Business Economics*, 19(3), 189–209.

Arrow, K. (1972), 'Gifts and exchanges', *Philosophy and Public Affairs*, 1(4), 343–362.

Aupperle, K.E. (1984), 'An empirical measure of corporate social orientation', *Research in Corporate Social Performance and Policy*, 6: 27–54.

Bishop, Matthew and Michael Green (2008), *Philanthrocapitalism: How Giving can Save the World*, New York: Bloomsbury Press.

Campbell D., G. Moore and M. Metzger (2002), 'Corporate philanthropy in the UK 1985–2000: Some empirical findings', *Journal of Business Ethics*, 39(1–2), 29–41.

Campbell, D. and R. Slack (2006), 'Public visibility as a determinant of the rate of corporate charitable donations', *Business Ethics: A European Review*, 15(1), 19–28.

Carroll, A.B. (1979), 'A three dimensional conceptual model of corporate social performance', *Academy of Management Review*, 4, 497–505.

Conley, Dalton (2000), 'The racial wealth gap: Origins and implications for philanthropy in the African American community', *Nonprofit and Voluntary Sector Quarterly*, 29(December), 530–540.

Cox Edmondson, Vickie and Archie B. Carroll (1999), 'Giving back: An examination of the philanthropic motivations, orientations and activities of large Black-owned businesses', *Journal of Business Ethics*, 19(2), 171–179.

Davis, V. (2012), 'UW-Madison announces First Wave/MC Lyte Scholarship presented by Hip Hop Sisters Network', *University of Wisconsin Madison News*, September 6, available at http://www.news.wisc.edu/21024 (accessed August 15, 2013).

Dean, J. (2001), 'Public companies as social institutions', *Business Ethics: A European Review*, 10(4), 302–310.

Dingle, Derek (2012), 'Preserve our rich history of philanthropy', *Black Enterprise*, 42(10), 12.

Donohue, John J., James H. Heckman and Petra E. Todd (2002), 'The schooling of Southern Blacks: The roles of legal activism and private philanthropy, 1910–1960', *Quarterly Journal of Economics*, 117, 225–268.

Dusuki, Asyraf Wajdi and Tengku Farrah Maimunah Tengku Mohd Yusof (2008), 'The pyramid of corporate social responsibility model: Empirical evidence from Malaysian stakeholder perspectives', *Malaysian Accounting Review*, 7(2), 29–54.

Grimes, M.G., J.S. McMullen, T.J. Vogus and T.L. Miller (2013), 'Studying the origins of social entrepreneurship: Compassion and the role of embedded agency', *Academy of Management Review*, 38(3), 460–463.

Guiso, L., P. Sapienza and L. Zingales (2006), 'Does culture affect economic outcomes?', *Journal of Economic Perspectives*, 20(2), 1–48.

Harvey, Charles, Mairi Maclean, Jillian Gordon and Eleanor Shaw (2011), 'Andrew Carnegie and the foundations of contemporary entrepreneurial philanthropy', *Business History*, 53(3), 425.

Hemingway, C.A. (2005), 'Personal values as a catalyst for corporate social entrepreneurship', *Journal of Business Ethics*, 60(3), 233–249.

Jackson, Tysus D. (2001), 'Young African Americans: A new generation of giving behaviour', *International Journal of Nonprofit and Voluntary Sector Marketing*, 6, 243–253.

Lähdesmäki, Merja and Tuomo Takala (2012), 'Altruism in business – an empirical study of philanthropy in the small business context', *Social Responsibility Journal*, 8(3), 373–388.

Max Nikias, C.L. (2013), 'President's Page', *USC Trojan Family Magazine*, Summer, available at http://tfm.usc.edu/summer-2013/presidents-page41 (accessed August 15, 2013).

McKinley-Floyd, L. and N. Shrestha (2008), 'Segmentation strategies for non-profits: Mining the emerging market of "black gold"', *Journal of Business and Industrial Marketing*, 23(6), 416–428.

Meijer, M., F. De Bakker, J. Smit and T. Schuyt (2006), 'Corporate giving in the Netherlands 1995–2003: Exploring the amounts involved and the motivations for donating', *International Journal of Nonprofit and Voluntary Sector Marketing*, 11(1), 13–28.

Noble, G., J. Cantrell, E. Kyriazis and J. Algie (2008), 'Motivations and forms of corporate giving behaviour: Insights from Australia', *International Journal of Nonprofit and Voluntary Sector Marketing*, 13(4), 315–325.

Nopper, T.K. (2011), 'Minority, Black and non-Black people of color: "new" color-blind racism and the US Small Business Administration's approach to minority business lending in the Post-Civil Rights Era', *Critical Sociology*, 37(5), 651–671.

Oppedisano, Jeannette (2004), 'Giving back: women's entrepreneurial philanthropy', *Women in Management Review*, 19(3), 174–177.

Pearce, J.II and J. Doh (2005), 'The high impact of collaborative social initiatives', *MIT Sloan Management Review*, 46(3), 30–39.

Pinkston, T.S. and A.B. Carroll (1994), 'Corporate citizenship perspectives and foreign direct investment in the US', *Journal of Business Ethics*, 13: 157–169.

Quittner, J. (2000), 'Can a minority business be nearly all white? A new ownership definition for contract set-asides has minority small businesses in an uproar', *TRENDS* New York, available at www.businessweek.com/smallbiz/0002/tr000209.htm?scriptFramed (accessed August 13, 2013).

Raphael S., M.A. Stoll and H.J. Holzer (2000), 'Are suburban firms more likely to discriminate against African-Americans?' *Journal of Urban Economics*, 48(3), 485–508.

Seymour, Richard (ed.) (2012), *Handbook of Research Methods on Social Entrepreneurship*, Cheltenham, UK and Northampton, MA, USA: Edward Elgar.

Shaw, Eleanor, Jillian Gordon, Charles Harvey and Mairi Maclean (2013), 'Exploring contemporary entrepreneurial philanthropy', *International Small Business Journal*, 31(5), 580.

Shrestha, Nanda, Lydia McKinley-Floyd and Mark Gillespie (2007), 'Promoting philanthropy in the Black community: a macroscopic exploration', March, available at www.faculty.quinnipiac.edu/charm/ (accessed August 13, 2013).

Shum, Paul and Sharon Yam (2011), 'Ethics and law: Guiding the invisible hand to correct corporate social responsibility externalities', *Journal of Business Ethics*, 98(4), 549–571.

Wilson, Fiona, Deborah Marlino and Jill Kickul (2004), 'Our entrepreneurial future: Examining the diverse attitudes and motivations of teens across gender and ethnic identity', *Journal of Developmental Entrepreneurship*, 9(3), 177–197.

Worthington, Ian, Monder Yusof and Trevor Jones (2006), '"Giving something back": a study of corporate social responsibility in UK South Asian small enterprises', *Business Ethics: A European Review*, 15(1), 95–108.

APPENDIX

Interview questions for current study of Black entrepreneurs and their philanthropic activities:

- Please think about your various priorities when you are making decisions about your company. [Slight pause.] What would you say is your primary objective?
- What actions does your company undertake to ensure that the firm follows laws governing businesses that are within your industry?
- How does your firm go beyond compliance with the law?
- How important is ethical leadership to you as a business owner? Ethics is defined as going beyond what the law requires in the decision-making process in an attempt to be fair and do the right thing in your business endeavors.
- Do you think Black business owners have a greater sense of responsibility to the Black community than business owners from other races or women?

If individual responds affirmatively:

- – Why do you suppose that is?
- – How is that sense of responsibility manifested in their decisions and action?

If individual responds negatively:

- – Why do you suppose that is? Why not?
- What philanthropic activities are you involved in because of a sense of responsibility to the Black community?
  - – Why are you so interested in this activity (or activities or set of activities)?
- What philanthropic activities are you involved in outside of the Black community?
  - – Why are you so interested in this activity (or activities or set of activities)?
- How has your activity (have your activities) in the community changed over time since you started your company?
- How important are each of the following to you? Highly important, somewhat important, neutral, not very important, or not at all important?

- Economic success?
- Legal compliance?
- Ethical considerations?
- Philanthropic activities?

6. Issues in multi-generation family companies
Frank Hoy and Kirby Rosplock

6.1 THE STORY OF H&R BLOCK

6.1.1 The Rise of an Entrepreneur

Henry W. Bloch and his brother Richard (Dick) started the United Business Company, a fledgling bookkeeping and accounting operation, in their hometown of Kansas City, Missouri in 1947. The Bloch brothers had a novel idea to serve the bookkeeping and accounting needs of small to mid-size businesses. Yet in the early years, the business limped along as one client would sign on but another would leave. Persistent and driven, the brothers were not afraid of hard work. Henry was a decorated B-17 bomber navigator in World War II who had flown 31 combat missions over Germany. The challenges that he and his brother faced with this budding enterprise paled in comparison to the adversity that he fought through during the war.

6.1.2 Bootstrapping the Business

In order to survive the lean times, Henry and Dick took on side work doing personal income tax returns during the tax season. The Blochs charged $5 for a federal and state return. This side business grew from a handful of returns to 160 by 1954, netting them approximately $500 apiece. The brothers worked around the clock, seven days a week, for that money. In the meantime, Henry's wife Marion raised the children and managed the household. When Marion had their second child on the eve of the tax deadline, Henry transformed the hospital waiting room into a makeshift office in order to wrap up the last several tax returns.

6.1.3 Adapting and Seizing an Idea

The following year the Bloch brothers gave notice to clients that they were no longer in the tax business. Disappointment was the common response.

Clients left saying, 'Who will we turn to then to do our tax return?' One client, John White, was determined to convince Henry and Dick that the tax business was the actual business that they should be pursuing. John was a display-advertising salesman for the *Kansas City Star*. A few days later, he returned with an advertisement clipping to show the Bloch brothers. With a bit of persuasion, White was able to get the reluctant brothers to sign up for two $100 advertisements in the paper. Both brothers feared they were throwing money away. The first day after the small advertisement ran in the paper, their office was flooded with prospective clients. White turned out to be their 'white knight' as his idea to advertise the tax services launched what would become the largest tax services business in the United States.

As their business was just taking flight, the Bloch brothers received notice that another firm in Massachusetts had a similar business name, United Business Company. Fearing that their name would be confused with that of this other firm, Henry and Dick decided to change the firm's name to H&R Block. They changed the spelling of their last name to avoid pronunciation errors.

6.1.4   Franchising Concept is Born

In the Fall of 1955, the Bloch family moved to New York City, where Henry opened seven H&R Block offices. Although the new tax preparation and planning outlets were a success, the Blochs missed the familiarity and comforts of their Midwestern home. By the end of tax season, the brothers sold the New York operation for $10 000 and 2 percent of future revenues. 'It turns out that we were among the pioneers of franchising,' Henry said. 'But at that time, we had never heard the term' (Marion and Henry Bloch Family Foundation, 2013). Not only were Henry and Dick forging a tax experiment, but they were also embracing an entirely new way of building a business through the nascent concept of franchising.

In 1957, with 17 offices in three states, the Blochs proudly announced the slogan, 'Nation's Largest Income Tax Service'. Over the years, H&R Block expanded to become the largest commercial tax preparation firm in the entire world, with a system of more than 100 00 retail locations and 100 000 tax professionals. Henry retired as chief executive officer (CEO) in 1992 and his second oldest son Tom Bloch, who had followed his father into the business many years prior, assumed the mantle of CEO. Father and son continued on the business for several more years, until Tom resigned in 1995 to pursue his passion as a teacher. Henry stepped down as chairman in 2000.

6.1.5 Business Success, Founder Gratitude and the Family Foundation

As Henry approached retirement from the family business, he increasingly felt a deep connection and indebtedness to the Kansas City community who got behind the Bloch brothers' experimental idea for tax preparation all those years earlier. He read extensively about industrial giants such as Rockefeller and Carnegie and newer wealth creators such as Bill and Melinda Gates and Warren Buffett who decided to direct the majority of their fortunes to charitable and philanthropic interests as opposed to passing as much wealth as possible to their heirs. Henry established the Marion and Henry Bloch Family Foundation in 2011. Henry and his brother had been brought up in a solidly middle-class home with hard-working parents. They valued the opportunities that they were afforded. Henry's son Tom Bloch remarked that his father accomplished a lot in building the success of H&R Block, but that the true significance in his life materialized when he was able to dedicate most of his time to giving back to the community at large. The family's focus is now on a path of charitable giving and philanthropy. The Foundation exists to transform and give back to the community that Henry felt he benefited from so many years back. Beneficiaries include post-secondary business and entrepreneurship education programs; visual and performing arts; education for the poor, disadvantaged and underserved; health care; social services; Jewish community organizations; and legacy organizations.

6.1.6 Bringing the Family Together

The family foundation has another element kindred to the family enterprise – family involvement. Tom Bloch was Henry's only child from the second generation who worked in the family business. The family never set an expectation that family members had to work in the family business. They were encouraged to follow their passions. As a result, Tom's siblings Robert, Elizabeth and Mary Jo moved forward with other interests. But with the advent of the family foundation, all members of the second generation have been appointed to the foundation's board of directors. The board also includes some non-family experts and executives; however, the majority of the board is family members and is intended to remain so during Henry's lifetime. The Board oversees the hiring of staff and is integrally engaged in developing and refining the donor intention and the grant-making process. 'In a way, the family foundation has allowed us to come together and work to do well for others as a family group. We are able to do this with our father and to celebrate our parents' lives, legacy and to better the community around us,' remarked Tom Bloch, vice-chairman and director of the family foundation. Tom provided the insight that his father reflected on the past as having two primary components: success and significance. Achieving financial success was very empowering and fulfilling, yet at this stage of the journey, the joy of being able to give back in a meaningful, measurable and impactful way provides the greatest joy for the 91-year-old entrepreneur. Henry reflected, 'True success is not measured in what you get, but what you give back' (Bloch, 2011). The entrepreneur inside Henry sees the world of opportunity ahead and that there is still so much to be accomplished.

6.2   INTRODUCTION

In the first line of *Anna Karenina*, Leo Tolstoy wrote, 'Happy families are all alike; every unhappy family is unhappy in its own way.' But those of us familiar with families in business know that each is unique, both in happiness and unhappiness. Yet, despite the uniqueness, patterns emerge. One of those patterns is that families who create wealth through their enterprises often engage in charitable giving, regardless of whether outside observers would consider the families happy or unhappy.

In the Bloch case, we observe two brothers who struggled and built the largest firm in their industry. No doubt they experienced contentious events throughout their life-long relationship. For the most part, however, interactions were positive. Their ability to get along contributed to a company culture that Henry described as 'like a family' (Bloch, 2011: 82). Henry demonstrated the values of the family by serving on the boards of charitable and service organizations beginning in the early 1960s, and creating the H&R Block Foundation with Dick in 1974. According to Tom Bloch, one of Henry's principles was, 'Make giving back part of your corporate culture' (Bloch, 2011: 170).

Henry's children were not forced to join the family firm, but their parents' values appear to have influenced them. They supported the charitable commitment Marion and Henry made to the community in which H&R Block grew and prospered. This chapter reports what scholars and practitioners have learned about family business philanthropy, and examines specific cases to determine why and how this has occurred.

Examples of philanthropy by families who earned their fortunes through business ventures are easy to find. The names of many are well known: Ford, Honda, Kellogg, Rockefeller, Rothschild, Slim – family names associated with successful, multi-generational enterprises, but names of charitable foundations as well. A study conducted in the United Kingdom documented that family businesses are more philanthropic than non-family businesses (Breeze, 2009). This chapter examines why and how families that have accumulated wealth through private enterprise choose to engage in charitable giving.

It must also be recognized that not all business families practice such behaviors. Danco and Ward (1990) found numerous negative views of business owners regarding family philanthropy. These included what they labeled a psychological hurdle, that of being the lone entrepreneur, someone who is not dependent on others. They also observed that there could be a distrust of what are purported to be 'good causes'. Philanthropy is sometimes perceived by politically conservative owners as representing a liberal practice. Owners may also acknowledge themselves as being unfamiliar with philanthropic behavior or that they are intimidated by issues associated with charity. Additionally, there is evidence that wealthy business owners may be concerned about the visibility that accompanies charitable giving. On balance, however, proactive action by family firms has been viewed positively.

To discuss the actions of family firms requires understanding what one is. There is no universally accepted definition of a family business. Because we are studying families engaged in philanthropy, we operate on the assumption that there is the expectation of family financial legacy, extending across generations. We have adopted the definition offered by Chua et al. (1999): family businesses are organizational entities in which either the individuals who established or acquired the firm or their descendants significantly influence the strategic decisions and life course of the firm. In this chapter, we refer to companies that are engaged in or have completed the transition from the owner-founder (generation 1) generation to a second, and perhaps the involvement of the third generation. In most cases, the families represent philanthropic transitions as well. In studying family philanthropy in India, Chanana and Chatti (2011) found that having children step in to run the family enterprise frees the founding generation to focus on philanthropy.

We begin with a review of previous studies of philanthropic behavior by entrepreneurial families and identify factors that stimulate or inhibit such generational transfers. Much of what has been published about family businesses has been written by practitioners. These include autobiographies of successful entrepreneurs, and books and articles by consultants to families and their firms. Autobiographies give one person's perspective, while service providers to families and businesses lean toward anecdotal descriptions of their direct observations from which they derive normative recommendations for improving the functioning of both the family and the enterprise. Some consultants, however, possess legitimate academic and research credentials. Thus their conclusions rest on more credible analyses. Academic scholars have found the contributions of practitioners to be of value in providing foundational knowledge for studying family businesses and in suggesting models for explaining the behavior and improving performance of both families and firms.

Scholarly contributions to the family business literature are remarkably recent (Sharma et al., 2007). The dominant research stream by academic scholars has been ownership and management succession. Studies of charitable and philanthropic behavior are sparse. The advent of research conferences and introduction of new journals focused on family business provide more venues for sharing the results of investigations. Most published studies to date focus more on the business than on the family (Danes, 2014). Dominant issues include governance, succession, interpersonal relationships and estate planning. Despite increases in the volume of published research, little attention has been given to the practices of firms and families in charitable giving.

Following the literature reviews, we examine specific cases shared by wealth and philanthropic advisors to some of the wealthiest enterprising families, as well as a few cases from anonymous philanthropic families. We assess key themes and observations around the charitable intentions and actions of these multi-generational enterprising families and the opportunities and challenges along the journey from founder entrepreneur to philanthropic family. From these analyses we provide some initial observations and preliminary conclusions along with subjects for further research and consideration.

6.3   LITERATURE REVIEW

Reviews of the family business literature identify subject areas of dominant research activity (De Massis et al., 2012; Sharma et al., 2012; Yu et al., 2012). Sorenson et al. (2013) went so far as to devise a taxonomy of clusters of family business outcomes from prior empirical studies. They labeled the clusters governance, performance, social and economic impact, strategy, family dynamics, family business roles, and succession. For purposes of this chapter, we consider the interface of family business with entrepreneurship. Thus, we seek to examine where the domains overlap relative to philanthropy. Prominent themes in the entrepreneurship literature that could be expected to address philanthropy are the characteristics and behaviors of entrepreneurs. For the family business literature, succession has received a great deal of attention, especially regarding preparing successors to enter the firms with entrepreneurial mindsets. There are distinctions between the domains. In entrepreneurship, acquiring and applying financial resources are studied, whereas for family firms managing and disposing of wealth are major research topics. Entrepreneurship encompasses exit strategies, while family business is concerned with legacies.

In reviewing the literature, we assess scholars' investigation into these issues as they relate to philanthropy. We include in our review observations and conclusions drawn by practitioners encompassing views of business owners, consultants to family businesses, and philanthropy professionals. The review begins with entrepreneurial behavior of family business owners relating to philanthropy. Next is a section on wealth management, followed by developing successors and other family members to be charitable benefactors, and the final section concerns the legacy sought by entrepreneurial families.

6.3.1 Entrepreneurial Behavior

Much of the family business literature gives attention to problems associated with families in business and strategies for professionalizing the operations of the firms. A breakthrough study appeared in 2005 when Miller and Le Breton-Miller published *Managing for the Long Run: Lessons in Competitive Advantage from Great Family Businesses*. Although some studies had appeared in journals documenting superior performance of family-owned enterprises over matched samples of non-family corporations, the Miller and Le Breton-Miller book provided documentation of how such family firms operated. There are now streams of research regarding how family enterprises function, with more and more emphasis placed on how these enterprises can maintain entrepreneurial cultures.

Zellweger and Nason (2008) observed multiple objectives sought by families engaging in philanthropy. These included societal outcomes, tax advantages and family harmony. The last was found to build trust relationships among managers which, in turn, facilitated innovations in both products and organizational functioning. They also explained how external stakeholders may be the motivating forces for philanthropy. Stakeholders can include the local community, interest groups, political groups and governments. Their demands often focus on such issues as social or environmental initiatives, support of nonprofit organizations, and job creation or sustainment in areas with high unemployment rates (Breeze, 2009).

We think of entrepreneurs as creators of business ventures, engaging in risk to reap profits. But the process of creation can be manifested in many ways. Eichenberger and Johnsson (2013) found that family business charitable donors like to see a balance of generosity with real opportunities.

The Orton family of Vermont is an example of opportunity-seeking and philanthropic creativity. Writing for the *New York Times*, Charles Paikert (2012) profiled the Ortons, owners of the Vermont Country Store. Launched first as a catalog in 1945 and a store in 1946 by Vrest and Ellen Orton, the company is now operated by their son Lyman along with his sons, Gardner, Cabot and Eliot. The family grew the business to recent annual sales of $100 million. According to Eliot, his grandfather had a strong sense of civic duty, wanting to improve the local economy through donations of money and time. In 1995, Lyman Orton, working with a specialist in land use planning, established the Orton Family Foundation. The mission of the foundation has been to work with citizens of small cities and towns to make changes based on shared community values. The second and third generations extended the charitable giving behavior of the founders by formalizing their philanthropy and setting objectives for their donations.

Eichenberger and Johnsson (2013) explained how the philanthropic strategies of family firms have been changing in recent years, a sign of opportunity recognition by inheriting generations. They described the old model as members of the family functioning independently, responding to solicitations rather than being proactive, choosing not-for-profit entities as recipients, and giving to general causes.

They saw a new paradigm emerging in which families learn from other family foundations and consultants, involve their children at earlier stages, initiate programs and work with donors as partners, and set specific objectives to make an impact. Eddy (2008) proposed that families formalize charitable activities beginning with drafting a mission statement.

Betsy Brill, president of Strategic Philanthropy, a Chicago-based firm that advises donors and their legal and financial advisers, described family intent in wealth distribution (Paikert, 2012):

> Businesses that are owned or controlled by families are using philanthropy as part of a business strategy and aligning the family's core values with the company's. It makes sense and can also be extremely beneficial to business objectives such as attracting and retaining great employees and improving the company's reputation as a good corporate citizen with its customers, community and vendors and suppliers.

Some family business owners envision philanthropy as an approach to infusing an entrepreneurial mindset throughout the company. Paikert (2012) quoted Kelin Gersick (2006), author of *Generations of Giving: Leadership and Continuity in Family Foundations*, as advocating employee involvement in charitable giving and activities. Gersick observed stronger connections between the family ownership group and non-family managers, and went on to say, 'It also creates a connection to the company for employees, customers and the supply chain not only through what the company makes or sells, but through what it does by improving quality of life.'

Paikert (2012) found the Vermont Country Store to be an example of Gersick's observations, reporting employee involvement in its philanthropic decisions. Employees both review proposals from management and form 'community action teams', submitting their own ideas for charitable work.

It should be noted that philanthropy, like opportunity recognition, can be influenced by economic conditions. Havens and Schervish (2009) offered an historical perspective. They tracked a 40-year period, finding that charitable giving declined by 3.9 percent per year during the four longest recessions. When organizational entities such as foundations are formed to engage in philanthropic activity, it is important to recognize that they must be managed efficiently and effectively. Economic recessions impact those organizations just as they do business enterprises (Havens and Schervish, 2009). Poor fund management or failure to adjust to changing environments can lead to personnel lay-offs or worse. Additionally, declines affect the strategies for families and may reflect anxieties regarding their businesses.

The observations of practitioners indicate that philanthropic behavior by families which have generated wealth through their businesses is often initiated informally, but tends to evolve to more structured approaches. There are many reasons behind charitable giving practices, with establishing legacies and perpetuating values cited as frequent motivations. There is evidence, however, that succeeding generations may have different values and objectives regarding the use of wealth created by their families' businesses.

6.3.2 Wealth Management

Family wealth has received attention in the family business literature in the study of estate planning, ownership transfer and interpersonal conflict. Few studies have examined philanthropic activity and how philanthropy may or may not impact both family and enterprise. One significant exception was a special issue of *Family Business Review* on family foundations. But the subject matter was acknowledged by the editor as out of the mainstream for the journal in that the journal normally focused on the business, not the dispersal of assets (Gersick, 1990).

Charitable foundations began being created in the United States in the latter half of the nineteenth century. The United Kingdom and India were experiencing similar activity at that time (Chanana and Chatti, 2011). The foundations represented family control of wealth combined with socially concerned philanthropy. They frequently functioned as holding companies, enabling the avoidance of inheritance taxes. Philanthropy provided an alternative occupation for family members in many cases. Examples have been described as both altruistic and self-interested (Hall, 1988).

In 1889, Andrew Carnegie, who built Pittsburgh's Carnegie Steel Company, published in the *North American Review* an article entitled 'Wealth', which is more commonly known as 'The Gospel of Wealth'. In the article, the self-made entrepreneur discussed the responsibility of wealth creators to be engaged philanthropists. Carnegie, regarded as one of the titans of capitalism, recognized the divide between the 'haves' and the 'have-nots' as a function of the growth of civilization, democracy and capitalism; however, he believed it was incumbent on those with means to help those without. Carnegie was not a proponent of conspicuous consumption; rather he believed that with great wealth comes great responsibilities.

In an early contribution to the study of family business philanthropy, Danco and Ward (1990) highlighted the need for recognition by peers as a motivational factor in the creation of family foundations: 'Two-thirds of America's independent foundations emphasize giving within a particular geographic locale, at least partly to satisfy benefactors' need for local recognition' (p. 349). They added that other motivational factors exist: a foundation can serve as a buffer from requests for charitable donations, to minimize taxes, to avoid pitfalls associated with leaving too much wealth to the next generation, to deal with the needs of communities better than government agencies, and to foster continuity of the family legacy.

Yermack (2009) reported a study of 150 stock gifts made to family foundations between July 2003 and December 2005. The stock gifts occurred just before price drops, suggesting private information or backdating. Such gifts may have been used in order to evade taxes.

Lungeanu and Ward (2012) gathered data on 200 of the largest foundations in the United States and found over half (specifically 111) to be family controlled, with decisions often determined by family members serving on the board of directors. A key finding associated with strategic behavior was that family foundations were more focused on grant-making than on charitable giving, when contrasted with non-family foundations.

Of course, wealth management goes beyond foundations. Jaffe (2003) presented a normative listing of six wealth dimensions. He proposed these as the guiding factors for a family concerned with conveying value to future generations. He defined the societal dimension as, 'Commitment and a sense of respect, compassion and connection to the suffering and concerns of others, taking a place of service within one's community, and using the resources to support the future of the planet' (Jaffe, 2003: 81). Jaffe visualized this dimension being expressed through proactive family involvement in the community through service and philanthropy.

One example of how individuals and organizations in practice view the relationship of family businesses and philanthropy is represented by the Coutts Prize for Family Business. Coutts & Co., an international private banking and wealth management firm based in the United Kingdom, sponsors this prize which is awarded annually to enterprises from around the globe that demonstrate excellence not only in corporate governance and family governance, but also in social responsibility and philanthropy. Specific criteria for the prize include the corporate social responsibility strategy, the corporate giving strategy, family philanthropy and social impact (Evans, 2013). Social responsibility and ethical reasons were also found to be important in a survey reported by Love et al. (2009).

Susan Winer, senior vice-president at Strategic Philanthropy, recommended that families wanting to start a company philanthropic program should construct a strategy with actionable steps. She suggested forming a committee to define goals, then dedicate management and staff to support carrying out the plan and track progress. Winer's program requires limits and specification of resources to be applied (Paikert, 2012).

Love et al. (2009) found that the majority of giving by families is planned, assessed and institutionalized. Brill's (2011) advice for families that create formal charitable giving vehicles, such as foundations or trusts, consisted of setting up mini foundations or funds with small amounts of money for heirs to manage. Structured entities can serve as training grounds, helping the next generation to learn and practice the governance and grant-making skills they will need to serve as leaders in the future. There are many structures used by families and their firms for performing or supporting philanthropy. As suggested by the example of the Blochs, some families form a private family foundation from the wealth their businesses generated. These foundations may be funded by corporate profits, shares or other family capital. Consultants often recommend drafting family protocols to provide guidelines for family collective giving (Lank and Ward, 2000).

Even if a foundation is created or if family business owners make significant donations to other charitable organizations, the board of directors of the family firm should be informed if the family retains an ownership position, according to Danco and Ward (1990). They advocated openness in the process with non-family as well as family to ensure support. They further recommended using external advisors who are specialists in structures and legal requirements for charitable giving. The family needs to decide on a legal form of organization, and it may be necessary to form a board of trustees. A written mission statement should be prepared and an administrative structure agreed upon.

Le Van (2010) described how some family foundations allocate budgets that can be spent by various family members or branches. Other foundations appoint succeeding generation members to board or staff positions. The purpose is to offer them direct participation with the recipients of the charitable gifts. He also reported that it is common for family foundations to partner with other non-profits that possess related expertise and community presence. According to Le Van, family members must learn to find balance and synergy among compassion, professionalism, and accountability.

Some families choose to channel their charitable giving through family offices. This structure appears to be especially suitable when the family has grown to multiple branches and may have several philanthropic entities (Etheridge, 2012). This assumes, of course, that the staff of the family office are trained on philanthropy issues. Sara Hamilton, CEO of Family Office Exchange, is quoted by Etheridge (2012) as listing the following responsibilities of the family office staff regarding philanthropy:

- Understanding donor intent;
- Supporting the Foundation's visions;
- Mentoring Foundation board members;
- Ensuring philanthropic impact; and
- Providing time saving administrative services.

Tax policy in the United States has contributed to the creation of a tax-exempt sector that is unique in size and scope (Leibell and Daniels, 2008). While this has resulted in opportunities for charitable giving by families, it also demands attention to changes in laws and regulations. And it raises questions as to the power exercised by charitable organizations. Tax policies have been found to influence philanthropic behavior in other countries as well, for example India (Chanana and Chatti, 2011) and Israel (Schmid and Rudich, 2009).

In practice, many families find it difficult to gain consensus about doing good (Le Van, 2010; Warnick, 2008–2009). Etheridge (2012) warned that using the family office or foundation structure is not a solution for families which do not get along. In both business and philanthropic planning, processes may be expected to involve a certain degree of conflict (Brill, 2011). Additionally, conflict may be inherent between generations. According to Pervin (2013), surveys report that 42 percent of individuals under 30 believe social change is as important as profit, compared with only 26 percent of those over the age of 45. For young wealth holders, 65 percent rated charitable activities as an important part of their wealth creation plans compared to 58 percent of those over 45. Additionally, the objectives of giving can change with generational transitions. A study of family philanthropy in Asia concluded that the older generation demonstrates a responsibility to the local community, while the younger are more inclined toward national and international causes. The older generation has concentrated on education, health and poverty. For the younger generation, the emphasis has been on the arts, civil rights and the environment (Mahmood and Santos, 2011).

Zellweger and Nason (2008) concluded that family philanthropy contributes to harmony which in turn leads to reduced agency costs. An example of cost savings is the avoidance of expensive control mechanisms, translating into increased family wealth. The assumption is that harmony leads to trust, which results in fewer monitoring and reporting requirements. Harmony is not merely a cost control issue, however. A key conclusion of both scholars and practitioners is that philanthropic decisions are not restricted to the entrepreneurial founder, but that it is a family activity.

Whatever the choices made by a family, it is reasonable to expect that planning and learning from the experiences of others are likely to improve results. Observations of both practitioners and scholars suggest that philanthropic actions should occur through structures that are well governed and value-driven. Impacts of charitable gifts should be assessed, although one survey indicated that this was the biggest challenge faced by families in their charitable efforts (Love et al., 2009). And negative consequences should be anticipated. Emotion cannot be divorced from implementation (Etheridge, 2012). Nevertheless, the experience gained through wealth management and philanthropic participation have been found useful in preparing succeeding generations for taking on leadership and other responsible positions in both the business and the family.

6.3.3 Successor Development

To date, most writing on family business philanthropy is normative rather than empirical, with descriptive behaviors resulting from anecdotal observations. There are a variety of conclusions that can be drawn from these observations and recommendations. Various authors tout philanthropy as a strategy for building skills in members of the succeeding generation. The practice of these skills can result in increased confidence – self-confidence for those acquiring the skills and confidence on the part of the senior generation that younger family members will be prepared to accept responsibility (Eddy, 2008).

Charitable initiatives often result from an objective of senior family members to prepare their successors for responsible decision-making roles, infuse values and leave legacies (Breeze, 2009). In a column for the San Diego *Daily Telegraph*, Peggy Eddy (2008) contended that 'families in business use philanthropic activities to instill values and traditions, maintain family ties, deepen social consciousness and increase personal fulfillment in family members through the generations'. Eddy saw managing funds for charity as a good way to teach financial basics.

Jaffe and Grubman (2007) viewed philanthropy as a strategy for developing succeeding generations. Based on their literature review, they recommended philanthropy as a means to educate children in financial literacy, to grasp the ethical values of the family, and to provide a sense of social responsibility. They contended that children should engage in hands-on effort, not just handing out money. Jaffe and Herz Brown (2009) further argued that collaborative activities by the younger generation can be fun, fostering lifelong habits.

Brill (2011) argued for a 'deliberate approach' to involve next-generation family members. She found formalizing family participation works better to ensure the continuation of philanthropic goals. She acknowledged that there is no single approach for involving younger family members, but that values can best be transmitted from one generation to the next while senior family members are still living.

One strategy that consultants frequently propose to families is to use philanthropic activities as a venue for sharing family history (Brill, 2011). This typically starts with storytelling by the senior generation, eventually evolving into written documents and, more recently, audio and video recordings.

Eddy (2008) described how members of family businesses can strategically help the younger generation to develop leadership, teamwork, fundraising, social awareness and family building skills. To achieve such goals, formalized structures are typically designed.

Seventy percent of respondents (skewed toward the wealthiest) in a global survey of family philanthropists reported that they involve children under the age of 21 in some way (Love et al., 2009). A logical approach to preparing younger family members would include drafting succession plans consisting of criteria (for example, age, education, volunteer service, geographic proximity) for eligibility to serve as trustees. Succession plans may contain job descriptions that articulate the responsibilities of trustees (Brill, 2011).

Much of what Brill recommended can occur through family meetings or retreats. She encouraged the use of professional facilitators. The outsider provides all participants with an opportunity to contribute to formulating a shared vision for philanthropy. Family gatherings are best held on a regular basis. They thus provide a structure for conveying values by means of family tradition. By encouraging open discussion, subsequent generations can remain flexible and express their interests.

Parent–child relationships can have negative consequences as well as positive ones. When parents fail to instill values of social responsibility in their children, the result can be a sense of entitlement that ignores the needs of other individuals or the larger community (Coles, 1977). Even simple interactions around the dinner table at which a child's proposal for charitable giving is ignored or belittled may stifle an instinct toward philanthropy (Jaffe and Herz Brown, 2009). And disagreements can occur, whether between parent and child or among other relatives (Jaffe, 2003).

Eichenberger and Johnsson (2013) described philanthropy as a means to strengthen the bond between the generations by involving the next generation. They outlined the following steps for the senior generation in dealing with their heirs:

1. to accustom them to share their resources and to give them the opportunity to do so;
2. to guide them in finding their modus operandi that will help shape their personalities;
3. to enable them to learn how to defend their point of view within the family;
4. to make them understand the value of money and teach them to work together; and
5. to explain the importance of wealth management.

Following such steps enables the senior generation to instill into the succeeding generation both their legacy and an entrepreneurial mindset for seeking their own opportunities.

6.3.4   Legacies

There are many reasons why families engage in charitable practices. Some stem from decisions by senior-generation members that relate to the role of their firm in a community or industry, or to the values held by an entrepreneur or clusters of family members. Other instigations relate to establishing a legacy for future generations. And for some families, forming foundations represents a means for new leadership roles for family members who may not join the business (Hamilton, 2004).

For some families, philanthropy is an expression of personal and spiritual values. It can translate the desire to give back to the community

(Eichenberger and Johnsson, 2013). The latter was identified by Judith Rodin, president of the Rockefeller Foundation, who described the Rockefeller family as having 'strong views that people with that much money should give it back to society' (Crary, 2013). She also acknowledged that a motivating factor for creating the foundation was to improve the image of the family, an image that many saw as empire-building by John D. Rockefeller and associated with the 'robber baron' era of economic expansion in the United States (Schwass and Lief, 2008). The Rockefeller Foundation is also credited with being a pioneer in choosing to engage in ideas-based philanthropy rather than 'just' charitable financial giving. The Foundation articulates this philosophy on its website (Rockefeller Foundation, 2013):

> Throughout its history, the Foundation has been primarily proactive in its approach to the world's problems. For example, while we do not provide emergency relief for disasters, in the wake of Hurricane Katrina the Rockefeller Foundation took the long view in supporting the creation of the groundbreaking unified plan for building a more sustainable, more equitable New Orleans in the future.

Eddy (2008) quoted a Foundation Source booklet supporting next-generation involvement in philanthropy as 'giving them the desire, confidence and skills they will need to extend your family's legacy of good works and generosity into the future'. This was echoed by Brill (2011), who reported how families in business find philanthropy can be a tool for teaching financial stewardship in, as the Rockefellers did, giving back. The motivation goes beyond perceiving wealth as an identity; instead, as a means of making the world a better place. This view was captured in the words of Andrew Carnegie (1889): 'The man who dies thus rich dies disgraced.'

By the end of his life, Carnegie had donated over $350 million (a sum of approximately $4.3 billion by 2005 figures) to a multitude of causes and charitable efforts (Carnegie, 2011). Part of his legacy and philosophy was captured in the 'Andrew Carnegie Dictum' which was: 'To spend the first third of one's life getting all the education one can. To spend the next third making all the money one can. To spend the last third giving it all away for worthwhile causes' (Carnegie, 1889). Although Carnegie felt it was his moral duty to direct his wealth to those in need at the end of his life, he did not do it to achieve notoriety, fame or public praise. Yet, his legacy as an industrial leader may be overshadowed by his tremendous philanthropic actions which resulted in the public library system that we know today in the US,[1] founding and supporting higher education such as Carnegie Mellon University, and being a proponent of the arts and sciences among other causes he supported.

The Walton Family Foundation represents an example of a family using philanthropy to extend their values to future generations (Walton Family Foundation, n.d.): 'Across diverse areas of giving, Walton family members carry forward the timeless Walton value of creating opportunity so that individuals and communities can live better in today's world.'

It is also worth noting that, whatever the motivation, there can be unanticipated consequences. These can be positive. Le Van (2010) believed, for example, that the motivational factor of seeking to enhance the family's reputation had the additional benefit of creating goodwill toward the business in the community served.

In the case of the Bloch family, we find legacies in the name of the business (H&R Block Foundation) and in the name of the family (Marion and Henry Bloch Family Foundation, and the R.A. Bloch Cancer Foundation). The legacy is most visible in Kansas City, where you can find the Bloch name attached to the fountain at Union Station, the School of Management at the University of Missouri – Kansas City, and more. Through such case examples, we uncover patterns among family businesses as founders become philanthropists and convey their values to the next generation.

6.4 EXPLORING FAMILY PHILANTHROPY IN MULTI-GENERATIONAL FAMILIES: FROM ENTREPRENEUR TO PHILANTHROPIST

When an entrepreneur begins a new venture, the goal of establishing a multi-generational family business is not usually the driving motivator. Rather, the short-term goals tend to focus on establishing a solid foundation for the business that is self-sustainable and capable of growth over time (Welsch et al., 1995). Some leaders of entrepreneurial start-ups may simply desire to survive another year of business, particularly if the operation is being bootstrapped. This was certainly the case of the Bloch brothers, whose story is featured at the beginning of this chapter. The Bloch brothers believed that they had a great concept for a business, but toiled for the first several years before their business eventually blossomed. Tom Bloch acknowledged that luck and good fortune played key factors in their success. Having the courage, tenacity, drive, fearless ambition, business acumen and self-assuredness to persevere are also core components to the entrepreneurial spirit that the Bloch brothers demonstrated. In this section, the Bloch family enterprise case will be discussed in conjunction with other multi-generational enterprise stories revealed from interviews and secondary research on other prominent enterprising families.

6.4.1   Research Method

Understanding the experience of a family business founder from the beginning as an entrepreneur to the evolution and development to a philanthropist is multifaceted and complex. No two entrepreneurs' stories and experiences are exactly alike; however, there are certain elements and themes of the individual and the family business they create, and the subsequent transitions from business-owning family to a family focused on philanthropy. This section of the chapter presents preliminary findings from a series of qualitative, non-directed interviews with a cross-section of wealth advisors, philanthropic advisors, entrepreneurs, and owners past and present of family enterprises.

6.4.2   Qualitative Research Design

Procedures

An emergent design was employed to begin exploring the phenomenon of the experience of the founder and entrepreneur of a multi-generational family business to becoming philanthropic. Because the topic is a relatively new field of study within the family business and philanthropic literature, an inductive approach was taken towards the subject matter to first observe and understand the experiences and the phenomenon.

Primary data consists of nine nondirective phone interviews (Kvale, 1996) with family members, advisors and experts to philanthropically inclined family business owners and entrepreneurs to begin to assess some observable themes. The interviews were conducted by telephone and recorded digitally for review, transcription and analysis. Content and thematic analysis was applied to examine each individual interview and to compare interviews in parallel.

In addition to the interviews, an in-depth case study describing the experience of Henry Bloch, co-founder of H&R Block, further complements the themes identified in the interview. Tom Bloch, the second oldest son of Henry Bloch, was interviewed by phone. Secondary data from articles, websites, books and the family's foundation website as well as the websites from the experts and advisors interviewed also informed the research design. The combination of data provides a preliminary base of information to identify nascent themes that may be further researched in the future.

Sample criteria

The researchers narrowed the criteria for participant involvement in the study to individuals who were: (1) entrepreneur-founder of a philanthropic family business; (2) wealth advisor to multi-generational family

Table 6.1   Interview characteristics of participants

Code	Founder/ entrepreneur	Wealth advisor	Philanthropic advisor	Philanthropist	Multi-generational family business owner
Dave	X		x	x	
Aaron	X		x	x	x
Ella			x	x	x
Sara		x	x		
Kate		x	x		
Jan		x	x		
Tom				x	x
Kevin		x	x		
Jason			x		

Note: Pseudonyms were used to protect the identities of those interviewed, and identifying details of the family were also obscured in order to protect their privacy.

business owner who is philanthropic; (3) philanthropy expert or advisor to enterprising families who are philanthropic; (4) philanthropist; or (5) multi-generational family business owner who is philanthropic. In certain cases interviewees met multiple criteria. Everyone interviewed had to either be a member of a multi-generational philanthropic family or an advisor to enterprising families who were philanthropic.

Data collection
In total, 14 individuals were approached and invited to participate in phone interviews resulting in nine in-depth interviews. The interviews with family business owners, experts and wealth advisors provided insights into the experience of the entrepreneur to philanthropist from a multi-generational perspective. Some advisors had experience advising multi-generational family enterprises beyond the second generation, and a short discussion of some of those findings is also provided. In certain cases, the operating family business remains intact and the desire to become charitable and philanthropic occurs in parallel. In other cases, the family business may go through a complete or partial liquidity event, which provides excess capital to be directed towards philanthropic activities by the founder or family members through a shared vehicle such as a family foundation, charitable trust and/or a community foundation. See Table 6.1 for an understanding of participant criteria.

The emergent design provides a basis to explore and understand the

*Table 6.2   Themes from entrepreneur to philanthropist in multi-
generational family business philanthropists*

Code	Theme 1 – Enduring qualities of the entrepreneur	Theme 2 – Balancing family wealth transfer and giving aspirations	Theme 3 – Building education, continuity and cohesiveness	Theme 4 – Leaving a philanthropic legacy
Dave	x		x	x
Aaron	x			x
Ella		x	x	x
Sara	x	x	x	x
Kate	x	x	x	x
Jan	x		x	x
Tom	x	x	x	x
Kevin	x	x	x	x
Jason		x	x	x

phenomenon, experiences and themes from family business owners and entrepreneurs who transitioned into philanthropist and/or philanthropic families. Engaging wealth advisors and philanthropic advisors to large, enterprising philanthropic family enterprises allowed the researchers to gather first- and third-party perspectives from family members and experts who typically worked with a multitude of family enterprises. Gleaning the perspectives and insights from both expert advisors as well as family owner experiences presents a more expansive vantage point of the transition from entrepreneur to family business philanthropist.

Data analysis
Following the engagement and interview process, the interview recordings were transcribed and reviewed individually and then reviewed compara-tively. Key themes and mini cases were extracted from the individual inter-views and coded. To follow is a broader discussion of those preliminary themes and mini case examples evidencing themes on the family business entrepreneur to philanthropist. From the interviews, four mini case studies are shared that are examined in conjunction with supporting insights from the Bloch family case and other interviews.

Interview themes and mini case study discussion
From the interviews, four predominant themes emerged. They have been analyzed and compared across the sample of interviews. Table 6.2 provides a matrix of each interview and which themes surfaced in each interview.

The interviews and in-depth case study surfaced four initial themes related to the multi-generational family business founder to philanthropist experience and its impact on the family. From the interviews, four mini case studies were developed that highlight themes that resonate from the experience of entrepreneurs who engage in multi-generational philanthropy.

6.4.3 Enduring Qualities of the Entrepreneur: Mini Case Study 1

During the interview with Dave, he shared that his passion for philanthropy and entrepreneurship was rooted early in his formative values and experiences as a young child. Specifically, he shared his ambition and interest in his grade school and high school days to be resourceful and creative to come up with opportunities to make money. From car washes, to lemonade stands, and other mini enterprises, Dave was inspired and driven to find creative ways to make money. And when he was presented with an opportunity as a grade school child to be part of a Jerry Lewis telethon, Dave jumped at the chance. Applying his industrious passion for entrepreneurship at a formative age, Dave raised $10 000 for the charity, a significant sum for any adult fundraiser, let alone a child. He knew at that moment that he was hooked on making a difference and applying his entrepreneurial ideas and business know-how to transforming the lives of others. Dave then went on to share his enterprise story and the creation of an online philanthropic platform to help families govern, organize and implement their family foundation giving. Because he observed the need that many families have for a virtual platform to help implement their giving, Dave was one of the first to market with an online, virtual hub where families could maintain important philanthropic documentation, search a number of national charitable foundation research websites, and virtually engage to make governance decisions for their philanthropy. Today, this company is the leader in this niche market and has grown significantly from its infancy.

In addition to his own personal experience as an entrepreneur and philanthropist, during his time growing and fostering the online philanthropic platform, Dave has worked with hundreds of clients, many of whom were founders of successful family businesses like him that were into the second, and sometimes third generation or more. He observed how the passion, excitement, dedication and hard work that the founding entrepreneurs illustrated in their originating enterprises was utilized in their approach to their philanthropy. He shared that entrepreneurs do not 'check' their entrepreneurial values when they become inspired by their philanthropic objectives. Rather, these enduring entrepreneurial characteristics are a key factor and shape how they engage with their philanthropy. Dave went on to say that the meaning and passion they have for specific causes and issues make their philanthropic efforts more targeted and engaged. He notes, 'Rather than writing checks and "spraying and praying" to make a difference, these individuals tend to apply the same business rigor and acumen to their enterprise efforts to how they conduct their philanthropy.' However, Dave's story is not unique.

In the opening case on the Bloch family, Henry Bloch's entrepreneurial spirit was an important influence for their family foundation's direction of giving. In addition to giving to museums, hospitals and other local community efforts, a significant portion of the family's philanthropic mandate is directed toward entrepreneurial education and training. Tom Bloch shared his father's belief in the importance of inspiring others to be entrepreneurial. To this day, Henry Bloch continues to personally mentor and counsel a number of young, up-and-coming entrepreneurs in the local community. Tom Bloch wrote in *Many Happy Returns* regarding his father's entrepreneurial zeal towards giving:

> For Henry, giving does not mean 'blank-check' charity. He wants to be person-ally engaged and strategic in his social investments. 'I get more bang for the buck when I am personally involved,' he says . . . As David Miles says, 'Henry is very focused. He has clear objectives, he demands the best, and he rewards people for their good performance.' (Bloch, 2011: 176)

A number of the other interviews also revealed similar elements of entrepreneurial spirit of the founder as a critical characteristic of how multi-generational families approach their philanthropy. In fact, seven of nine interviews revealed the theme of the founders' entrepreneurial values as being a driver or influencer impacting how multi-generational giving occurred.

The interview with Kevin, an advisor to numerous family business founders, shared that 'these individuals are eager to experience the impact of their philanthropic efforts'. Similar to their nature to want to be at the center of the entrepreneurial ventures, they want to effect change by leading and driving the changes they desire to see. There is tremendous gratification and fulfillment to be able to apply entrepreneurial skills that can lead to growth, transformation and opportunities for others, notes Kevin. Sometimes these philanthropic efforts provide a greater sense of accomplishment than their prior successes as successful business men and women.

Finally, an interview with Aaron, a second-generation family business owner and a successful entrepreneur of a philanthropic advisement busi-ness, indicated that often founders are seeking an 'outlet for their next business venture, and their philanthropy becomes a mechanism to direct this passion and drive'. With the same savvy and strategic planning that may have gone into their business success, Aaron notes that these individuals often know no other way to pursue their giving goals. In other words, instead of following mainstream channels of giving, these individuals are not concerned to establish a new approach or conduct research to come up with creative solutions to maximize their giving.

6.4.4 Balancing Family Wealth Transfer and Giving: Mini Case Study 2

During an interview with Sara, a wealth advisor in a multi-family office who advises a number of enterprising families with multi-generational philanthropic activities, she revealed the challenges that a number of entrepreneurs she works with face: how much to leave to heirs and how much to leave to their philanthropic interests. Sara shared that the challenge is not solely 'how much' but 'how' and 'when' it is appropriate to facilitate wealth to the next generation of family members. Should it be transferred outright? Should the wealth be transferred through a trust? If so, which type of trust structure may be most appropriate? What terms or conditions may be appropriate to protect the interests of the beneficiary from creditors, divorce situations or their own devices? At what age, and is there a good time for families to share their wealth transfer intentions with beneficiaries? What happens if 'entitlelitis' – heirs' sense of entitlement to an inheritance (Rosplock, 2014) – sets in?

Sara shared the story of one of her clients who is extraordinarily entrepreneurial and started a number of specialized businesses which resulted in significant wealth. In his mid-fifties the entrepreneur had engaged one of his children, and his other children were not interested in pursuing a career in the family business. Sara revealed that the founder, whom we will call Ray, came to a point with the management of the family's liquid wealth where he feared that the wealth might actually harm the ambitions and motivations of his children. He wanted to find a way to balance his wealth transfer intentions and align them with his goals around philanthropy. He shared with Sara and his wife his concerns that too much too early might thwart his children from understanding the importance of financial independence, self-sufficiency and the pride that results from knowing that you can make it on your own. His one daughter had already displayed some less than responsible spending behavior and did not seem to grasp that there was not an infinite well of wealth that she could draw from forever. Further, Ray was passionate about directing a good portion of his liquid wealth to doing good. He had always intended to give back once he had achieved his business and financial success. Sara discussed the various calls, visits and family meetings as they devised a strategy to: (1) prioritize goals; (2) determine the lifestyles needs of Ray and his wife; (3) understand the risks and opportunities associated with wealth transfer to heirs; and (4) conduct a capital sufficiency analysis to determine the feasibility of gifting to heirs and philanthropic initiatives.

Ray and his wife determined that, with the help of their advisors, they would first educate their youngest daughter on the responsibilities that come with wealth, and provide a baseline of financial literacy for their oldest son who was more financially responsible and employed by the business. The determination of wealth transfer to heirs was then structured through a series of trusts and integrated into their overall estate plan. A family foundation was created with the anticipation that the bulk of funding would result after Ray and his wife's death. Yet, in the meantime, $5 million was transferred to the foundation to jump-start the family's philanthropic intentions. Sara shares that the process is evolving and unfolding as the family members become more comfortable and educated with the wealth transfer and giving aspirations of their parents.

Six of the nine interviews revealed the theme of how to balance the goals of leaving wealth to heirs with their philanthropic goals. 'Not all foundations are motivated by the tax man,' explained Dave, whose mini case was shared earlier. He notes that many entrepreneurs and their families are conscious of mitigating taxes with their charitable giving; however, their motivations stem from a personal and familial value set to want to give back and make a difference. The tension for many grantors is how much is appropriate to leave the next generation. Kate, another wealth advisor to many entrepreneurs and their families, shares that the simple reality is that it all depends. Kate indicated that some desire to leave relatively very little to their heirs, and echoed Warren Buffett's intent to leave his children, 'enough money so that they would feel they could do anything, but not so much that they could do nothing' (Funk, 2012).

Henry Bloch, in the opening case, had a similar experience of determining how much was enough to leave to his children, as well as to his philanthropic aspirations. Henry Bloch studied industrialists such as Carnegie and Rockefeller as well as contemporaries such as Gates and Buffett to inform his opinion and thinking on wealth transfer to heirs and philanthropy. His determination of where and how to direct his wealth was well thought out and strategic, in order to have his wealth make the most positive impact for his heirs and for his philanthropic objectives. The fear, as Ella, a second-generation family business owner, inheritor and philanthropic advisor, indicated is that with too much wealth, inheritors lose a sense of self, passion and direction. Instead of being fortified and buoyed by their financial inheritance, the family wealth results in them becoming co-dependent, unmotivated and/or entitled. The goal is to find the balance between the amount that creates a sense of normalcy and that which creates an extraordinary financial circumstance. The opportunity for giving as a family was another theme that was identified, which leads to the next theme and case study.

6.4.5 Building Education, Continuity and Cohesion: Mini Case Study 3

During an interview with Ella, a second-generation family business owner, inheritor and philanthropic advisor, Ella shared the story of a very successful Silicon Valley technology entrepreneur, Tom, who amassed significant wealth in his early forties. By 50, Tom had sold the business and 'retired' from the tech world to focus on the management of his wealth, his family and his growing interest in philanthropy. He and his wife, Eva, have a son, Andrew, who grew up in affluence and was a 'native' to growing up in affluence (Jaffe and Grubman, 2007). Andrew was groomed to have all the opportunities, education and experiences that Tom and Eva missed growing up. Tom and Eva have grown comfortable with their financial means, despite both growing up middle class. Even with the tremendous wealth amassed, their lifestyle is not excessive or unsustainable relative to their financial means, and the biggest upgrades and changes in their lifestyle come in regards to their giving. Eva and Tom are substantial benefactors to the local art museum and the children's hospital in the city, as well as to education programs for disadvantaged children. They are very passionate about making a difference locally.

Ella described the division that emerged with their son during his teenage years as he increasingly became distant and disengaged. Tom and Eva chalked his sulking behavior as a typical teenage transition, and were not concerned until sophomore year in college when Andrew dropped out. Tom and Eva were shocked and dismayed. They called to discuss, and Andrew did not return calls or messages. The communication had been strained for some time, particularly between father and son. Finally, Andrew sent word that he had decided to 'take a break' from college to surf in Costa Rica. Meanwhile, Ella was already engaged with Tom and Eva as they further refined the foundation's giving mandate when Ella learned of the personal challenges they were facing with their son.

A week later, an email arrived of Andrew with photos of him in his wet suit with his surf board, and a number of locals around him, smiling on the beach. In his email he shared that he had become engaged with a turtle rescue effort, and his short break might turn into a semester off. He finally called his parents with his excitement regarding the non-profit work and his passion to figure out a way to do more for the turtle rescue. As fate would have it, Ella was also seasoned and experienced in aligning families around giving interest, and suggested to Tom and Eva to consider broadening the foundation mandate to support Andrew's new-found passion.

Through a series of video conference calls and further education on the foundation, Andrew, who felt uninspired in school and frustrated with his parents, turned a major corner to being interested in the family's foundation and how to become more involved. Now the foundation not only brings Tom and Eva together, but also their son, as they expand the giving objectives. Further, Ella helped to craft a process for Andrew to report back on the progress of the turtle rescue and how to evaluate and understand the impact of the financial investment being made. With this new-found passion for giving, Andrew returned to finish his college education and then went on to complete a master's degree in biology. The family foundation continues to support the turtle rescue nonprofit and has expanded giving to ecological sustainability efforts in other geographies.

As Ella's mini case above illustrates, family giving, particularly through a foundation, can be an important mechanism to align family values along giving. Where the family grew apart and fractured, philanthropy became a point of focus to bring alignment and an opportunity for inclusion. The Bloch case study similarly describes how the Bloch family foundation has provided a mechanism for Tom and his siblings to all be engaged in the family's philanthropic giving. Not all family members may have the interest, ability or drive to be engaged in the family business; however, philanthropy can be unifying and an opportunity to build continuity.

Eight out of nine interviews referenced the idea that engaging multiple generations of a family in philanthropic activities can help foster continuity, cohesion and learning opportunities. Sara, a family wealth advisor to a number of affluent, enterprising families, shared that through philanthropy, a number of her families have helped to educate and teach important financial skills to their children. From the basics of managing accounts, to writing checks and conducting site visits, Sara shares that there is a sense of responsibility and accountability that often results. Jack, who works for a philanthropic membership organization, also shared the growing interest in education programs that help support families and their family members with philanthropic education around family giving. Further, Kate shared the experience of one family who also helped teach leadership skills and business acumen to heirs who aspired and were cultivated to become members of the family's foundation board. Not all entrepreneurs will have heirs active or engaged in the business, yet for those who are able to engage children in philanthropy in a meaningful and productive fashion, greater continuity of family values, cohesion of family relationships and opportunities for learning emerge.

6.4.6 Leaving a Philanthropic Legacy: Mini Case Study 4

During an interview with Jan, a wealth advisor to a number of affluent, enterprising families, she shared the story of Stanley, a retired, successful entrepreneur in his seventies. Stanley started his career as an office boy in a large transportation corporation and worked his way up to executive vice-president by the tender age of 29. His corporate position required him to travel to faraway places in South and Central America, among other foreign locations. While traveling he took an interest in local sporting competitions that were new to the US. Stanley took the bold step of leaving his corporate position and starting a league of this new special sport in a few different locations in the US. He was able to engage top executive and board members as early investors in his venture in the 1960s and 1970s. The sport was not an overnight success, but Stanley persevered and worked long hours to build the interest and marketing for this nascent sport. By the mid-70s, the sport took off and was viewed with high regard, attracting a clientele similar to those at polo matches or dressage. As the sport grew in popularity, more locations were opened and the leagues expanded. Additional enterprise opportunities also came to fruition, including gaming and slot machines. Yet, with these changes also came challenges from local Indian tribes who were not pleased with the addition of gaming to Stanley's growing enterprise. After litigation and growing frustration, Stanley decided to sell his business in the early 2000s to an interested third party. In Stanley's memoir, he quotes Seneca, 'Every new beginning comes from some other beginning's end.' This quote appears in the epilogue as he discusses the succession of leadership in his company, as well as his efforts to involve his family in his personal philanthropic legacy. Stanley could finally focus on spending more time with his wife, Janice, and family and pursue his passion for philanthropy full-time.

Stanley's son, Brett, worked with his father in the early years of the business, but decided to pursue a separate career, not wanting to follow directly in his father's footsteps. Brett went on to have a very successful business career in his own right, married and had children of his own. Yet, as Stanley began to transition from wealth creator to wealth steward, he experienced a number of interesting realizations. First, Stanley recognized that his wealth was in fact a whole new business, a family office. For Stanley, he viewed it as an opportunity to involve his son in a more meaningful and personal way in the stewardship of the wealth. Brett and his family lived on the West Coast, which meant Stanley and his wife were able to visit with their son, daughter-in-law and grandchildren a few times a year. Yet, Stanley and Janice wanted them to be physically closer in order to spend more time with them. So Stanley offered Brett the opportunity to manage and run the family office and codify his wealth transfer intentions and legacy through the start of the family office. Brett had a number of transferable business skills to apply to his new position and also enjoyed the flexibility that working with his father would provide. Brett and his family made the move to the East Coast to establish the family office and to be closer to Stanley and Janice.

Second, Stanley realized that his son's move gave him renewed vigor and inspiration for his philanthropy and charitable work. His company had always been very philanthropic and charitable, but now Stanley saw an opportunity to make his giving a family affair. He established a private, family foundation and included his wife and Brett as board members. Brett managed the investments from within the family office and helped his father and mother conduct grant research and establish the giving mandate.

Third, the family philanthropy helped to align their philanthropic values, as Stanley encouraged his son and daughter-in-law to participate and help direct the giving so as to bridge the family's philanthropic values across generations. Although Stanley felt a tremendous responsibility to give back, he also recognized his good fortune to be in a position to have his son and daughter-in-law directly involved with this important element of his legacy. In addition to giving financially, Stanley and his family were also directly engaged through volunteer work and activism. Providing leadership and influence was another important element of the family's outreach. For Stanley, his philanthropic legacy and the management of his wealth provided the gateway to build continuity and greater bonds with his son, daughter-in-law and the establishment of a legacy predicated on stewardship and giving back.

In all of the nine interviews conducted, legacy was mentioned as a goal, outcome or result of family philanthropy. Although the word 'legacy' may have a number of differing interpretations (Rosplock, 2014), a philanthropic legacy tends to reflect the values, beliefs, actions and aspirations of the founder and/or entrepreneur with regards to giving. Henry Bloch clearly demonstrates how he is creating a philanthropic legacy in Kansas City, as he and his family are devoted to a number of regionally specific philanthropic efforts to impact the community that provided Henry and his brother Richard with their fledgling business start. Other interviews also reflected the power and influence of a philanthropic legacy on future generations, as a 'tie that binds' one generation to the next, as described by Ella, and any opportunity to 'ground the family in the foundational values', as shared by Kevin.

Similarly, Sara shared the experience of working with a third-generation family business, and the opportunity to work with her clients, Jim and Mary, to establish a family foundation. After a successful family business venture, the family foundation brought together their children and grandchildren to be a part of establishing its philanthropic values and mission. As a part of this process they also incorporated values held dear by his grandfather, Bill, and father, James, who led the family business. Capturing values across a spectrum of generations of family members enriched the meaning of the philanthropic mission and grounded the family with respect and responsibilities to the heritage of the wealth creation. The ability to bridge the family business success with their philanthropic legacy helped the family to solidify the importance and impact of their giving as a driver of the family's legacy.

As was stated earlier in the literature review, Carnegie articulated in the Carnegie Dictum the importance to 'spend the first third of one's life getting all the education one can. To spend the next third making all the money one can. To spend the last third giving it all away for worthwhile causes' (Carnegie, 1889). A philanthropic legacy in a multi-generational family provides the conduit to set in motion a family's core values to impact others and their surroundings for a more prosperous reality.

6.4.7   Limitations

Due to the limited time frame to gather data, the sample was one of convenience. This presents limitations to the generalizability of the findings; however, the research design provides a starting point for researchers to build on and further understand the experiences and phenomena that motivate, drive and compel a successful entrepreneur and founder of a family business to devote and direct financial support, time, influence and/ or power toward philanthropic endeavors.

The data collection time frame, summer 2013, presented challenges for engaging family business owners identified in the study, due to seasonal travel and family engagements. As a result, more expert and advisor interviews were relied upon for gleaning a greater number of the family business examples. These stories are relevant, valid and useful; however, they are secondary perspectives on family businesses. Because client confidentiality was paramount, additional qualifying research such as biographical data, articles or documentation from family business or philanthropic experiences was not shared.

6.5   IMPLICATIONS FOR FUTURE RESEARCH

The chapters contained in this book have been compiled with the recognition that there is much to be learned about entrepreneurs and philanthropy.

Our objectives in this chapter were to examine the state of knowledge regarding family businesses and philanthropy, particularly those businesses which are in transition or have transitioned from first to second generation. There have been some empirical studies of philanthropy by families in business, but much of what is believed to be known is anecdotal, with consultants to family businesses being a major source. Consultants and practitioners may well be accurately describing behavior and prescribing courses of preparation and action. Scholarly attention to these issues is needed to confirm the advice that is being given to family business owners.

Through our literature reviews and case analyses, we have identified subjects that have received attention:

- Entrepreneurial qualities and characteristics. Should philanthropic initiatives be viewed in the same context as venture initiation? Does participation in philanthropic behavior contribute to the development of entrepreneurial mindsets in successors?
- Wealth management and transfer. Is philanthropy a business function or should it be restricted to the family? What are the strengths and weaknesses of various structures (councils, foundations, offices, and so on) for achieving philanthropic goals?
- Family continuity and developing successors. Do successors acquire skills relevant to business management from their participation in philanthropic projects? Should philanthropy be incorporated into development strategies?
- Family and business legacy. Is philanthropy a means for transferring value systems? Are legacies objectives in and of themselves, or the results of other objectives?

In pursuing further research, scholars must consider the implications of their findings for other researchers, students, family business owners and their stakeholders, professionals in philanthropic fields, and consultants to family businesses. Investigators should anticipate that their observations may identify questions associated with ethical and legal factors associated with charitable giving.

CONCLUSION

The fields of family business and entrepreneurship have emerged relatively recently in business education and scholarship, especially in comparison with disciplines such as economics, accounting, finance, marketing and management. Within family business and entrepreneurship, research streams have been developed. Although some research has been conducted on philanthropy and family firms, it would be an exaggeration to consider the subject a stream at this stage. Nevertheless, we were able to document four areas that have received attention and appear to offer promise for further research. We conclude that the subject of business-owning family philanthropy demands attention due to its volume and influence world-wide. Scholarly research has the potential to provide valuable information and guidance to those directly and indirectly involved.

NOTE

1. Some 3000 libraries were funded in 47 states and also in Canada and the part of what was the United Kingdom and is today the Republic of Ireland.

REFERENCES

Bloch, Thomas (2011), *Many Happy Returns: The Story of Henry Bloch, America's Tax Man*, Hoboken, NJ: John Wiley & Sons.

Breeze, Beth (2009), 'Natural philanthropists: findings of the family business philanthropy and social responsibility inquiry', Institute for Family Business, June.

Brill, Betsy (2011), 'How to make philanthropy a family affair', available at http://www.forbes.com/2011/04/19/family-philanthropy.html (accessed August 12, 2013).

Carnegie, Andrew (1889), 'Wealth', *North American Review*, 148(391), 653–665, June. (Later published as Part I of *The Gospel of Wealth*.)

Carnegie, Andrew (2011), *The Autobiography of Andrew Carnegie*, New York: Public Affairs.

Chanana, Dweep I. and Karim Lukas Chatti (2011), 'Insights into UHNW family philanthropy in India', UBS, available at www.ubs.com (accessed December 8, 2013).

Chua, Jess H., James J. Chrisman and Pramodita Sharma (1999), 'Defining the family business by behavior', *Entrepreneurship Theory and Practice*, 23(4), 19–39.

Coles, Robert (1977), *Privileged Ones: The Well-Off and Rich in America*, Boston, MA: Atlantic Little-Brown.

Crary, David (2013), '100 years on, Rockefeller Foundation still busy', available at http://www.businessweek.com/ap/2013–05–12/100-years-on-rockefeller-foundation-still-busy (accessed August 13, 2013).

Danco, Lèon A. and John L. Ward (1990), 'Beyond success: The continuing contribution of the family foundation', *Family Business Review*, 3(4), 347–355.

Danes, Sharon M. (2014), 'The future of family business research through the family scientist's lens', in Leif Melin, Mattias Nordqvist and Pramodita Sharma (eds), *Sage Handbook of Family Business*, London: Sage Publications, pp. 611–619.

De Massis, Alfredo, Pramodita Sharma, Jess H. Chua and James J. Chrisman (eds) (2012), *Family Business Studies: An Annotated Bibliography*, Cheltenham, UK and Northampton, MA, USA: Edward Elgar Publishing.

Eddy, Peggy (2008), 'Family businesses and the significance of philanthropy', available at http://www.sddt.com/commentary/article.cfm?Commentary_ID=85&SourceCode=20080611tbi (accessed August 11, 2013).

Eichenberger, Etienne and Jessie Johnsson (2013), 'Philanthropy – what it provides to families in business', *Tharawat Magazine*, 10, available at www.tharawat-magazine.com (accessed August 10, 2013).

Etheridge, Anne (2012), 'Working together for common purpose: The first national study of family philanthropy through the family office', National Center for Family Philanthropy, Special Report 29, Washington, DC.

Evans, Mark (2013), 'Coutts prize for family business', available at http://www.coutts.com/private-banking/coutts-institute/family-business/coutts-prize-for-family-business/ (accessed August 17, 2013).

Funk, Josh (2012), 'Warren Buffett's kids follow dad's philanthropic lead', *Huff Post Money*, available at www.huffingtonpost.com/2012/10/01/warren-buffett-kids_n_1928665.html.

Gersick, Kelin (1990), 'Editor's notes', *Family Business Review*, 3(4), 327–330.

Gersick, Kelin (2006), *Generations of Giving: Leadership and Continuity in Family Foundations*, Lanham, MD: Lexington Books.

Hall, Peter Dobkin (1988), 'Historical overview of family firms in the United States', *Family Business Review*, 1(1), 51–68.

Hamilton, Debroah Brody (2004), 'Becoming more than we are: Ten trends in family philanthropy', *Passages*, 6(3), available at www.ncfp.org (accessed December 9, 2013).

Havens, John J. and Paul G. Schervish (2009), 'Giving in today's economy', *Trusts and Estates*, January, 42–48, available at www.trustsandestates.com (accessed August 16, 2013).

Jaffe, Dennis T. (2003), 'Six dimensions of wealth: Leaving the fullest value of your wealth to your heirs', *Journal of Financial Planning*, April, 80–87.

Jaffe, Dennis T. and James A. Grubman (2007), 'Acquirers' and inheritors' dilemma: Discovering life purpose and building personal identity in the presence of wealth', *Journal of Wealth Management*, 10(2), 1–26.

Jaffe, Dennis T. and Fredda Herz Brown (2009), 'From entitlement to stewardship: How a prosperous family can prepare the next generation', *Journal of Wealth Management*, 12(1), 1–18.

Kvale, Steiner (1996), *InterViews: An Introduction to Qualitative Research Interviewing*, London: Sage Publications.

Lank, Alden G. and John L. Ward (2000), 'Governing the business owning family', *Family Business Network Newsletter*, No. 26, May.

Leibell, David T. and Daniel L. Daniels (2008), 'Giving in America', *Trusts and Estates*, May, 16–18, available at www.trustsandestates.com (accessed August 1, 2013).

Le Van, Gerald (2010), 'Global firm identifies five attributes of family businesses who survive long term', available at http://www.uww-adr.com/zgraph-content/uploads/docs/global-firmconfirmsfamilybusinessnorms12010.doc (accessed March 7, 2014).

Love, Bruce, Susan Raymond and Josh Moore (2009), 'Giving through the generations: Demanding impact, building unity, securing legacy', BNP Paribas/Campden Research, Global Philanthropy Report, London.

Lungeanu, Razvan and John L. Ward (2012), 'A governance-based typology of family foundations: The effect of generation stage and governance structure on family philanthropic activities', *Family Business Review*, 25(4), 409–424.

Mahmood, Mahboob and Filipe Santos (2011), 'UBS–INSEAD study on family philanthropy in Asia', UBS, available at www.ubs.com/philanthropy (accessed December 8, 2013).

Marion and Henry Bloch Family Foundation (2013), 'About the founders', available at www.blochfamilyfoundation.org/foundation/founders/ (accessed August 14, 2013).

Miller, Danny and Isabel Le Breton-Miller (2005), *Managing for the Long Run: Lessons in Competitive Advantage from Great Family Businesses*, Boston, MA: Harvard Business School Press.

Paikert, Charles (2012), 'Stepping up at family firms', *New York Times*, available at http://www.nytimes.com/2012/11/09/giving/more-family-firms-make-philanthropy-their-business.html?pagewanted=1&_r=2& (accessed August 8, 2013).

Pervin, Aron (2013), 'A big conversation for the new philanthropists', Familybusinesswiki.org, Family Business Wiki's Town Square, June 24.

Rockefeller Foundation (2013), 'Our history – a powerful legacy', available at www.rockefel-lerfoundation.org/about-us/our-history (accessed August 14, 2013).

Rosplock, Kirby (2014), *The Complete Family Office Handbook*, Hoboken, NJ: Wiley/ Bloomberg Press.

Schmid, Hillel and Avishag Rudich (2009), 'Elite philanthropy in Israel: Characteristics, motives and patterns of contribution', Hebrew University of Jerusalem, Article no. 7.

Schwass, Joachim and Colleen Lief (2008), 'About family, business and philanthropy', Perspectives for Managers, No. 165, November, available at http://www.imd.org/uupload/ IMD.WebSite/MicroSites/family-business/pdfs/articles/About-Family-Business-and-Phil anthropy.pdf (accessed December 6, 2013).

Sharma, Pramodita, James J. Chrisman and Kelin E. Gersick (2012), '25 years of *Family Business Review*: Reflections on the past and perspectives for the future', *Family Business Review*, 25(1), 5–15.

Sharma, Pramodita, Frank Hoy, Joseph H. Astrachan and Matti Koiranen (2007), 'The practice-driven evolution of family business education', *Journal of Business Research*, 60(10), 1012–1021.

Sorenson, Ritch L., Andy Yu, Keith H. Brigham and G.T. Lumpkin (eds) (2013), *The Landscape of Family Business*, Cheltenham, UK and Northampton, MA, USA: Edward Elgar.

Walton Family Foundation (n.d.), 'Creating opportunity so individuals and communities can live better in today's world: Our legacy', available at http://wff.cotcdn.rockfishhost-ing.com/documents/76022f5d-f9e0-44aa-929c-1c2e26f219ac.pdf (accessed March 7, 2014).

Warnick, John A. (2008–2009), 'When times are tough – a call for compassion and creative boldness', *Journal of Practical Estate Planning*, December–January, 13–15.

Welsch, Harold, Gerald Hills and Frank Hoy (1995), 'Family impacts on emerging ventures in Poland', *Family Business Review*, 8(4), 293–300.

Yermack, D. (2009), 'Deductio' *ad absurdum*: CEOs donating their own stock to their own family foundations', *Journal of Financial Economics*, 94(1), 107–123.

Yu, Andy, G.T. Lumpkin, Ritch L. Sorenson and Keith H. Brigham (2012), 'The landscape of family business outcomes: A summary and numerical taxonomy of dependent vari-ables', *Family Business Review*, 25(1), 16–32.

Zellweger, Thomas M. and Robert S. Nason (2008), 'A stakeholder perspective on family firm performance', *Family Business Review*, 21(3), 203–216.

7. High-tech donors and their impact philanthropy: the conventional, novel and strategic traits of agent-animated wealth and philanthropy
Paul G. Schervish*

7.1 INTRODUCTION

This chapter contains an original section in addition to drawing on the Boston College Center on Wealth and Philanthropy 2001 report, 'Agent-animated wealth and philanthropy' by Paul G. Schervish, Mary A. O'Herlihy and John J. Havens, conducted between January and March 2001 on behalf of the Association of Fundraising Professionals (Schervish et al., 2001), and hereafter also referred to as the High-Tech Donors Study. My goals are to depict the meaning and practice of high-tech donors as they approach the world of wealth and philanthropy; to provide nonprofit organizations, community foundations, fundraisers and today's impact-oriented philanthropists with knowledge to improve their endeavors; and to offer the general public accurate information that will counter some misunderstandings and encourage fresh thinking about the attitudes and activities of high-tech donors. The leading questions of the research revolve around discerning: (1) the relationship between how high-tech wealth holders accumulate their money in business and how they allocate it to philanthropy; (2) the range of personal, business and philanthropic issues that surround high-tech wealth and philanthropy; (3) the implications of the findings for understanding and improving the trajectory of the philanthropy carried out by high-tech donors; and (4) the application of this new information to further our understanding of the emerging problems and prospects of philanthropy in general. The research was conducted on behalf of the Association of Fundraising Professionals (formerly the National Society of Fund Raising Executives) and was initiated and funded by Dr Robert B. Pamplin, Jr, President and Chief Executive Officer (CEO) of the R.B. Pamplin Corporation in Portland, Oregon. Ultimately the research provides a case study on the meaning and dynamics of agency and hyperagency in the realm of philanthropy.

The findings of the study are based on confidential telephone interviews with 28 high-tech wealth holders involved in philanthropy, as well as two co-participating spouses, three well-informed individuals who work with and among high-tech philanthropists, and an additional interview with a high-tech executive subsequent to the report. I dedicate a section to this interview because it accurately exemplifies what I have heard over the years from many wealth holders when they recount their transition from focus on financial accumulation to philanthropic allocation. Respondents were promised complete confidentiality, and so all identifying information has been changed.

In the next section, I review the research landscape concerning the so-called venture or new philanthropy in which our study takes place, and describe the characteristics of the respondents in the sample. In the third section, I discuss what is not so new and several core aspects about what is new or has received a reinvigorated emphasis among 'new' or 'impact' philanthropists. In the fourth section I differentiate among three philanthropic strategies often lumped together under the rubric of impact or social venture philanthropy. In the fifth section, I describe, as a typical example, the process by which the additional respondent takes up his heightened nexus to philanthropy. In the sixth section, I draw out some of the ways in which high-tech donors manifest some of the basic dynamics of philanthropy of wealth holders in general. In the conclusion, I bring together my analysis by indicating a positive future for philanthropy by the respondents and other wealth holders. A more detailed review of the literature and analysis of the findings can be obtained in the complete report (Schervish et al., 2001).

7.2 THE RESEARCH LANDSCAPE

Several chapters in this book review the contemporary literature on the new philanthropic approaches variously called social venture, entrepreneurial and impact philanthropy. I call your attention to them. As the background for the historical context of our study, I mention just some of the sources we drew on as we conducted our high-tech donor study. At that time we discovered over half a dozen different formulations and descriptions of the so-called 'new philanthropy': from media (*Time Magazine*, 2000); academe (Dees, 1998; Letts et al., 1997; Borden and Koudsi, 1999; Lee et al., 2000); the nonprofit world (Carlson, 2000; Sievers, 1997; Community Foundation Silicon Valley, 1998; Morino Institute, 2001, 2000); the financial services industry (Prince and Grove, 2001; HNW Digital, 2000, 2001; Schervish and Havens, 2000; US Trust, 2000); New Economy reports (Atkinson and Court, 1998; Atkinson et al., 1999; Edwards, 1999; Florida,

2000); and our own research on philanthropy by the wealthy (Schervish and Herman, 1988; Schervish et al., 1994; Schervish and Havens, 2000; Schervish, 2000, 1990).

It became clear, as one commentator put it, that high-tech wealth holders are 'the new celebrities and rock stars' (Prince and Grove, 2001: 4) and receive the same levels of adulation and attack. We found that the 'new philanthropy' and high-tech donors were popularly viewed as being new in history; as critical and suspicious of nonprofits' effectiveness; as desiring hands-on involvement in philanthropy; as being 'cyberstingy'; as wanting to apply the lessons of business to every nonprofit, namely, strategic thinking, measurable results, scalability, accountability and sustainability; and, for all their claims of radicalism, as being fundamentally conservative in their philanthropy, focusing primarily on education and on the environment, rather than embracing more unusual approaches or causes. We concluded from our review of the research landscape that there was much room to deepen the understanding of 'venture philanthropy' and high-tech wealth holders; and that it would be fruitful to look behind the stereotypes to learn the inner workings of philanthropy as practiced by members of the high-tech community.

7.3   CHARACTERISTICS OF RESPONDENTS

I define a high-tech business as one that produces hardware or software for computers and communications, or a company which although not involved in research and development, depends completely upon the application and leveraging of software for its entrepreneurial success. In turn, I define high-tech wealth holders as persons who have made or are making the majority of their wealth from direct participation as an owner or as a top executive with equity holdings in a high-tech business. Given our small sample, it did not seem to be necessary or useful to segment our definition of 'high-tech' further, and, indeed, none of the respondents whom we asked to describe the meaning of 'high-tech' defined the term in relation to a specific product. In addition to the production or principal use of computer hardware and software, they designated a set of elements which differentiate high-tech enterprises from older business models, including:

- rapidity of change and the speed of cycles of learning;
- need for constant innovation to stay ahead of the market;
- the youth of staff in positions of responsibility;
- reliance on 'unseen [human capital] wealth' (Blair and Wallman, 2001) rather than on physical capital assets for success;

- financial reward for collaboration, teamwork and mastering intellectual challenges;
- a drive to expand the scale of their enterprise; and
- relentless innovation and global horizons governing their business strategy.

The study sample, all from the US, consists of 20 males and 10 females in 28 families, both spouses having been interviewed in two families. Of those reporting racial or ethnic affiliation, one respondent was black, one reported no racial or ethnic affiliation, one reported Jewish, and the remaining 25 were white. The respondents ranged in age from 26 to 57, with an average of 42 years. Twenty-two of the participants were married or living with a partner; four were single; and four were separated or divorced. Eighteen of the 28 families had one or more children or stepchildren. The participants were well educated with two holding PhDs, eight holding master's degrees and 11 holding bachelor's degrees, out of the 23 participants reporting their educational attainment. Most of the 28 high-tech entrepreneurs, 15 persons, were still working full-time in a high-tech business; eight participants had retired from the high-tech industry; and one was on a year-long work break (of these aforementioned nine, all were working full-time or part-time in philanthropy); and the remaining four respondents were semi-retired, still employed part-time and were either also working in philanthropy or exploring opportunities in the nonprofit world.

Table 7.1 summarizes our findings on the respondents' net worth, annual income, charitable giving and volunteering in 2000 (sampled in 2001). Family net worth of the participants at the time of the interview ranged from $1 million to $1.15 billion, with an average of $159 million and a median of $43 million for the 26 families reporting their net worth. Most of this wealth had been earned in the high-tech industry, although 19 percent, on average, was earned from subsequent investments, and approximately 2 percent, on average, was inherited or derived from other sources. The annual family income of the participants for the year 2000 ranged from a loss of $75 million to a positive income of $30.1 million, with an average of $4 million and a median of $750 000, for the 24 families reporting their family income. Since participation in philanthropy was a selection criterion for inclusion in the study, all the participants were involved in philanthropy. Their total family contributions (exclusive of political contributions) in the year 2000 amounted to $127 million in combined contributions for the 25 participants reporting contributions. These contributions ranged from $500 to $65 million per family with an average of $5.1 million and a median of $325 000. The number of gifts per family ranged from one to 200, with

*Table 7.1   Economic status and philanthropy of 2001 sample, in 2000
dollars*

	Number of respondents
Family net worth	
Under $5 million	6
$5 million to under $100 million	9
$100 million to under $500 million	8
$500 million to under $1 billion	1
$1 billion or more	2
Not reporting	2
Total	28
Range $1 million – $1.5 billion	
Mean $159 million	
Median $43 million	
Family income	
Under $100 000	4
$100 000 to under $500 000	7
$500 000 to under $1 million	3
$1 million to under $5 million	3
$5 million to under $20 million	3
$20 million or more	4
Not reporting	4
Total	28
Range $75 million – $30.1 million	
Mean $4 million	
Median $750 000	
Family contributions	
Under $50 000	10
$50 000 to under $100 000	1
$100 000 to under $500 000	2
$500 000 to under $1 million	1
$1 million to under $10 million	7
$10 million or more	4
Not reporting	3
Total	28
Range $500 – $65 million	
Mean $5.1 million	
Median $325 000	
Personal volunteer time	
10 hours or less per month	4
11 hours to 20 hours per month	6

Table 7.1   (continued)

	Number of respondents
21 hours to 40 hours per month	3
41 hours to 100 hours per month	6
101 hours to 200 hours per month	4
More than 200 hours per month	3
No. of respondents not reporting	2
Total	28
Range 0–258 hours per month	
Mean 73 hours per month	
Median 42 hours per month	

most families giving ten or more gifts in the year 2000. The average number of gifts was 44 and the median was 18 for the 22 families reporting the number of gifts they made during the year. Nearly all the high-tech wealth holders (25 of the 26 reporting) also volunteered their time to charitable causes in the year 2000. One participant of the 26 reporting had done no volunteering. The combined total number of hours per month for the 26 who reported their specific hours was 1902 hours per month. The volunteer time ranged from 0 to 258 hours per month per person, with an average of 73 and a median of 42 hours per month.

Table 7.2 updates the 2001 sample characteristics to 2013 in order to portray the financial wherewithal and level of charitable giving in today's dollars. Personal volunteer time, of course, remains the same in the two periods.

In order to obtain respondents, we used a branching technique whereby we asked various initial respondents to help us contact others in their circle for interviews. Thus the high-tech philanthropists that we interviewed are not representative of the entire population of high-tech donors. The respondents are likely to be more philanthropically active, and are not likely to be good informants about those who are not so highly involved. Still, the respondents were diverse enough and spoke consistently enough for us to identify an array of motifs which I believe are common to high-tech donors:

- As a group, high-tech donors are self-made, usually from modest means.
- They are well educated and have leveraged their education and intellect to achieve great success.
- Their wealth has come rapidly and has taken some getting used to.

Table 7.2   Economic status and philanthropy, in 2013 dollars

	Number of respondents
Family net worth	
Under $6.6 million	6
$6.6 million to under $132 million	9
$132 million to under $660 million	8
$660 million to under $1.32 billion	1
$1.32 billion or more	2
Not reporting	2
Total	28
Range $1.32 million – $2.0 billion	
Mean $210 million	
Median $55 million	
Family income	
Under $135 656	4
$135 656 to under $678 281	7
$678 281 to under $1.36 million	3
$1.36 million to under $6.78 million	3
$6.78 million to under $27.13 million	3
$27.13 million or more	4
Not reporting	4
Total	28
Range $102 million – $40.8 million	
Mean $5.4 million	
Median $1 017 422	
Family contributions	
Under $67 828	10
$67 828 to under $135 654	1
$135 654 to under $678 281	2
$678 281 to under $1.36 million	1
$1.36 million to under $13.57 million	7
$13.57 million or more	4
Not reporting	3
Total	28
Range $678 – $88.2 million	
Mean $6.9 million	
Median $440 883	

- They have an equal partnership with their spouse, working as a team in philanthropy and in rearing their children, with specific concerns about the special opportunities and pitfalls of wealth.
- Several were highly engaged with political parties and causes, but only half had donated to political causes. Most said they were generally non-political, did not believe that they could effect change through a political donation, and became involved in social and political issues only to the extent that such involvement was directly related to their specific interest in conservation, education or human rights.
- They are not much involved in religious congregations. Among the 26 high-tech respondents who completed the supplemental survey, only two reported being regular church-goers, 12 reported no religious affiliation, one was in search of a Church having been brought up with no religious affiliation, and the remainder stated they were spiritually inclined, but did not regularly go to church.
- The majority had young families – the average age of the oldest child was ten-and-a-half and the median was seven.
- For most, their frame of reference has been bounded by work, their relationship with their spouse, their education, and their upbringing; only a few have had a relatively long acquaintance with substantial philanthropic involvements.

7.4 PHILANTHROPIC STRATEGIES OF HIGH-TECH DONORS: AGENT-ANIMATED PHILANTHROPY

The focus of the research is how high-tech wealth holders carry out their philanthropy, especially how they participate in that highly engaged mode of philanthropy commonly referred to as 'new' or 'venture' philanthropy. Our findings and previous research indicate that neither term is strictly accurate. The philanthropy of high-tech wealth holders is not so much new as it is distinctive. Before turning to the new and distinctive aspects of high-tech philanthropy, I clarify what is not novel.

7.4.1 What Is Not New

There is a set of elements surrounding the philanthropy of high-tech donors that properly warrants the appellation 'distinctive'. However, these elements are not what commentators regularly mention. According to the popular view, new philanthropy entails an explicit effort by donors to apply the lessons learned in business – strategic thinking, focus on measurement, accountability, scalability, investment and return on investment – to ensure that the charities they support are effective in producing outcomes and not just outputs, in documenting those outcomes, and in becoming creative risk-takers rather than quasi-bureaucratic protectors of their organizational survival. I agree that the intercessional or impact-oriented temperament that high-tech wealth holders bring to all their philanthropic approaches is integral to what high-tech donors look for in a nonprofit or try to advance when contributing to nonprofit organizations, introducing new directions in these organization, or initiating their own philanthropic ventures. However, it is not historically novel for philanthropists to keep an eye on these objectives. In fact, throughout the twentieth century, virtually every significant philanthropist or foundation has implicitly or explicitly insisted on these characteristics, as our interviewees themselves were at pains to mention:

> You're a baby boomer like me. We have always thought we were somehow different from any generation that ever lived and we probably aren't . . . I'm not an expert on these old guys like Carnegie and Rockefeller but I know when Carnegie put a big investment in the library system, he probably was thinking it was a good investment.

Second, our interviews with 140 wealth holders from 1985 to 1987 in the Study on Wealth and Philanthropy reported in 'Empowerment and beneficence: strategies of living and giving among the wealthy' (Schervish and Herman, 1988) enabled us many years ago to discern an already well-entrenched commitment by many philanthropists to the issues of effectiveness, innovation, venture investment, managerial assistance and entrepreneurship. Furthermore, venture, managerial and engaged philanthropy are not the only strategies through which high-tech donors carry out their philanthropy: we also found ample evidence of them practicing the entire gamut of strategies we found in our previous research, from the adoption philanthropy of a software entrepreneur who had 'adopted' his nieces and nephews, paying their college costs; to the consumption philanthropy of many high-tech donors to schools and environmental issues which have benefited, now benefit, or will benefit them and their family directly; to the brokering philanthropy of high-tech donors who solicit the help of members of their business network for their favorite charity (see Schervish, forthcoming).

Third, high-tech donors seldom limit their philanthropy to causes in which they are personally involved. In fact, impact-oriented donors are perfectly happy to offer financial support to established organizations, which they believe are effective and have missions with which they identify, often without any strings attached; for example, a donation to the capital campaign of an alma mater. Indeed, high-tech donors often make some of their earliest as well as repeated gifts to the universities they or their spouse attended. Without much to-do, they will even make incidental contributions to organizations that do not meet the criteria of effectiveness and engagement:

> Now, I'm not against this organization, and I've wanted to support it anyway. Even though I see it sometimes does some bad things, at least, people got excited about doing it. And in fact, even though the model is not perfect, I think they kept doing a better and better job. I mean, they realized some of these mistakes and they kept doing a better job at it.

One participant described this mixing and matching of approaches. He combines time, money and skills to both the stage of his business and family life and to his philanthropic involvement, 'putting together the pieces perhaps in a different mix, like a recipe that is in keeping with today's values and today's individuals who are interested in doing the work'.

7.4.2   What Is Distinctive

All the respondents are involved in a variety of philanthropic approaches, many of which, as I said, are quite familiar and conventional. Their motivations vary as much as any set of donors; and they admit that their 'venture philanthropy' approach is not new in history. Still, there is something that is distinctive about high-tech philanthropy, perhaps even new, although I do not insist on the latter adjective. This distinctiveness does not reside merely in the fact that high-tech donors participate in venture philanthropy or in other forms of activist approaches, for example, managerial and entrepreneurial philanthropy. However, there is a combination of skills and approaches specific to the high-tech industry, which I see our high-tech donors bringing to philanthropy:

- An insistence on research and 'due diligence' for the start of any new venture.
- A strategic-thinking approach that combines both a global view and a broad-systems approach.
- A strong belief in the centrality to success of teamwork, partnering and collaboration rather than competition.
- An idealistic and optimistic belief in the capacity of the individual to make a difference, especially on an intellectual level, which comes from seeing the revolutionary effect that their problem-solving approach has had in business.

- A fundamental belief in the development and application of human capital as the basis for solving society's problems.
- A conviction that innovation, constant change and a reassessment of circumstances are crucial to progress.

The foregoing descriptive characteristics manifest the underlying motifs of agent-animated philanthropy. In this practice donors transfer the dispositions and practices surrounding the accumulation of financial capital to their allocation of philanthropic capital. I will focus on three particular aspects which characterize both high-tech business and philanthropy, namely: a strong market consciousness; an unwavering belief in the transformative power of intellectual and human capital; and constant attention to innovation and expansion of business horizons. But the most fundamental aspect of agent-animated philanthropy is, as I will describe, the fact that the donor is engaged in philanthropy, as in commerce, in such a way as to directly affect the rate of return of the investment.

7.4.3   Market-Consciousness

The initial ingredient of a successful business is to identify some need for which the current or anticipated future demand outstrips the supply, and for which people are willing to pay. This, of course, is common knowledge in the business world. But our high-tech respondents emphasized how crucial it is for them to be especially precocious in discerning market demand. One software entrepreneur described the need he discerned in the high-tech arena, and which he expects his company to fill:

> Everybody is familiar with walking into a retail establishment in any country of the world. There's a well-understood ritual that takes place between you and the merchant that does not exist in the electronic world. Our goal is to put in place that standardized methodology for what I believe is going to be a revolution in how people consume information, and entertainment and education content electronically.

There are at least two reasons why this attention to market demand is crucial. First, high-tech producers are vigilant about discovering the need not so much for a discrete product as for a multiplex process. In other words, consumers are looking not for a furniture catalog, but for a way to browse catalogs. Internet retail companies are in need not of a cash register, but of an electronic system of processing orders and payments. High-tech creates reusable, multifunctional tools that are designed to meet a rationally logical or emotionally appealing chain of needs. For high-tech entrepreneurs to be effectively attentive to the market means being especially attentive to sequences or interconnected arrays of needs. The second reason why high-tech entrepreneurs turn out to be particularly sensitive to their market is that they pay heed not just to emerging needs. They also focus on how creative technology can meet a backlog of needs that were previously impossible to meet. By researching, inventing, developing and producing new technologies, the high-tech industry is able to create a stream of new products to meet qualitative, and not just quantitative, pent-up demands. Taken together these two market conditions teach high-tech donors the necessity and reward for honoring consumer sovereignty.

High-tech donors are as market-conscious in philanthropy as they are in business. They are alert to the needs of nonprofit organizations, but even more so to the needs of the ultimate beneficiaries being served by nonprofits. Because their development of high-tech products and services necessarily takes place within a broad-systems context, they tend to bring that comprehensive vision to their mission of philanthropy. They regard the role of philanthropy as to meet the needs of beneficiaries, but believe that it does not always do a good job of doing that. It is not poor intentions or a lack of dedication that evoke their concern. Rather, it is that current practices of philanthropy too often fail to perform well in discerning the needs of recipients, and allow modest successes to become an obstacle to greater accomplishments. High-tech donors, educated in the school of high-tech business, believe that existing charitable organizations must become more perceptive about the needs of the people they serve. Such needs are for a sequence of processional outcomes within the context of a complex social system rather than for any discrete product. Thus, inner-city school children are in need not just of a better education: they also need a series of socially interconnected intercessions that will produce a course of change in their lives. In order to succeed financially and meet the need for rural hospitals and clinics to quickly fix their sophisticated machinery and monitors, workers in Kenya need more than the requisite technical skills and certification. They need a new network of hospitals and clinics that trust their credentials and call upon them repeatedly for repairs.

Not only do high-tech donors have an eye for viewing beneficiaries' needs as causally linked; they also have a particular fix on the interconnected needs of existing charities. In the view of many high-tech donors, established charities and foundations have become stuck in old perceptions of the requirements of their clients or have subtly allowed pressing organizational demands to hamper their work on behalf of their target population. This critique, while never presented with severity, was universal among respondents. When high-tech donors believe there is potential to improve the market consciousness and the responsiveness of the charities they care about, they offer their time and money to actualize that vision. When they believe there is a need to start afresh, given the resources of time and money, they will start new philanthropic ventures. In all cases, they are vigilant about the threat of goal displacement. They fear the substitution of both organizational survival for organizational growth and bureaucratic imperatives for market imperatives. For this reason high-tech donors, either alone or through the many venture partner associations which have sprung up across the US, work to provide the managerial expertise and multi-year financial support to unfetter nonprofit organizations from the constraints that threaten what would otherwise be market-conscious and market-responsive enterprises. Only when beneficiaries' needs for a series of outcomes rather than outputs are on the radar screen will charities garner their impact.

7.4.4   Intellectual and Human Capital

The second characteristic, which brings a distinctive edge to high-tech entrepreneurship in business and philanthropy, is the belief that knowledge is the primary force of production. The most consistent finding of the 2001 High-Tech Donors Study is the esteem in which high-tech donors hold the strength of ideas and the importance of gathering a team of workers with exceptional intellectual capacity. For one of our respondents, the high-tech world is simply this: '[the application of] intellectual capital – which is just smart people and methodologies – to create efficiencies for businesses, for people'. In all eras, ideas are an important factor of production, but only in recent decades, and especially for the high-tech industry, have ideas been elevated to the primary factor of production, surpassing plunder, natural resources, physical labor and physical capital as the dominant source of added value. Knowledge is the wealth of nations and ideas are the coin of the realm.

High-tech donors believe that human capital is the key to human development. To the familiar question about whether money or ideas are more important for improving the human lot, high-tech donors answer that it is ideas. Money is important; but even without large sums of money, good ideas are the principal factor of production. Money spent without the intelligence to make it effective is not just squandered wealth; it is squandered efficacy. High-tech donors, rightly or wrongly, believe that philanthropy is in many ways as young as their industry. The best ideas are yet to come and any attention devoted to uncovering and applying new thinking is a worthy effort. Creativity and intellectual thirst are in shorter supply than money and, besides, the application of good ideas with a small amount of money will become a magnet for attracting added dollars.

For high-tech donors, it is not just that philanthropists need to become more endowed with insight, but that the very goal of human development is essentially an undertaking that fosters human capital. Not only is human capital seen as the principal tool of philanthropy, it is also its principal output. Thus, it is not startling that knowledge-industry philanthropists focus on education, research, the arts, early childhood development, teacher-training and for-profit ventures which foster new businesses. The debate over which should have the higher priority – the development of capacity or the advancement of economic distribution – is superseded by the focus on the distribution of human capital as the foundation for the distribution of wealth. What matters is neither the production of wealth nor its distribution, but the dispersion of the productive capacity of wealth. For high-tech donors this is not just supposition, it is their personal experience. One respondent describes how he had leveraged his connections in the venture capital world to convene a meeting between international entrepreneurs and US venture capitalists. He strives to build the confidence of young high-tech workers by giving them the opportunity to have their skills recognized and rewarded, he gives them not a handout, 'but a leg up, so that they are capable of doing all these things . . . and eventually they don't need you anymore'.

Despite this dedication to the power of ideas and human capital development, there remains a potential obstacle. As successful entrepreneurs, high-tech donors are children of the Enlightenment. They believe that people and organizations are corrigible and that both can be directed to generate greater well-being. In the nonprofit world, where the object of production is often to bring about change in the way human beings think and act, knowledge is not the only determinant. Custom, habit, emotion, self-interest, lack of capacity and simple resistance come into play as well. The human beings whom nonprofits hope to benefit are themselves agents who will not be changed by ideas alone. The same is true for the human beings who work in nonprofits. Much of the misunderstanding between agent-animated donors who are trying to engender philanthropic outcomes, on the one hand, and nonprofit professionals, on the other, can be traced to an overappreciation of the compelling authority of knowledge by the former and an underappreciation by the latter.

7.4.5 Impact: Outcomes versus Outputs, Innovation and Growth

The third characteristic of high-tech engagement in business and philanthropy is its unabashed and sometimes unforgiving drive for impact. But before impact comes the need to read the innovative content and velocity of change in markets, to anticipate and create the near-term and long-term evolution of those markets, and to constantly innovate. All industries face changing markets. However, high-tech entrepreneurs encounter and foster an increase in the velocity of change and a corresponding growth in efforts to monitor and respond to the dictates of that change. In this dynamic environment, locating what people need now and what they will need in the near future, rather than imposing what they do not need, is the surest path to success. It is the difference, said several respondents, between marketing and selling, or between good selling and bad selling, as another respondent insisted. Selling is getting people to buy what you need them to buy; marketing, as the respondent uses the term, is providing what people need. As such, high-tech business owners and equity investors need to anticipate and meet the needs of consumers for goods and services, rather than push consumers to meet the needs of a business for revenue. One respondent described how well he meets the needs of customers as 'disruptive' in the sense that he exceeds expectations in quality, quantity and price: 'We introduce the technology with almost all the functionality that people expect, and at ten or five percent of the price.' High-tech business owners not only introduce the world to change; they are introduced to change by the world. Their prosperity depends on how readily and astutely they recreate themselves and their enterprises.

As with their businesses, high-tech donors consider that growth in the scale of a philanthropic enterprise is a necessary indicator of success. Respondents repeatedly stated that most established charities are too often growth-oriented only in revenue and personnel, not in widening their impact. Too many nonprofit professionals believe they will never have large enough or consistent enough financial support and so too readily seek to maintain the scale they have already or, at best, to increase their scale only marginally. This dynamic of maintenance rather than 'scaling' jumps out at high-tech entrepreneurs as an oddity of time and place, rather as if they had been transported to a strange land with strange customs and unfamiliar norms. If what a nonprofit is doing is so important, why then, ask high-tech donors, should it not strive to expand its impact and become a model for others to emulate? Breaking the nonprofit's self-reinforcing cycle of scarcity thinking and subdued aspirations becomes the natural insertion point for high-tech donors into philanthropy. They are inclined to see their unique ability as philanthropists to be, first, their managerial expertise and creative intelligence; and second, their financial wherewithal. As to conventional charities, high-donors view them, sometimes wrongly of course, as too interested in financial wherewithal and not enough in reconstituting their purposes and organizational management for impact.

For high-tech donors a more successful production of philanthropic effect requires a measured attention to outcomes or impact, and not just of outputs. This will attract the convergence of two enhancements. It will spur more organizational flexibility, analytical suppleness and entrepreneurial instinct. It will also stimulate the infusion of enough financial capital to allow nonprofits to develop their organizational capacity and expand their accomplishments. High-tech donors view themselves as able to coach the former and tender the latter.

7.4.6 Agent-Animated Philanthropy

The way in which high-tech donors strive to be productive of outcomes in philanthropy is the same way they have been, or continue to be, formative of outcomes in their business ventures in the knowledge economy. I call this 'agent-animated philanthropy'. Just as a high-tech business must be both market-conscious and knowledge-based to succeed, so too must philanthropy. Agent-animated philanthropy is market-conscious, because as in business, high-tech wealth holders recognize the absolute necessity of accurately comprehending the needs presented to them. It is knowledge-based, because in both spheres they recognize the unqualified importance of applying their and others' intellectual capital to meet those needs.

As mentioned previously, not all high-tech philanthropy is agent-animated in the sense of bringing to bear new knowledge, new methods and new organizational operations. However our respondents tell us that the most consequential contributions they and their peers make or plan to make are agent-animated. They create new directions within existing organizations, inaugurate venues to tackle needs in a fresh way, and in general apply the principles they have adhered to in business. Utilizing their state-of-the-art commercial is the way they can effectively contribute to well-being.

Despite the criticisms I heard from nonprofits about the arrogance of high-tech donors in thinking they have the solution to every social problem, our respondents often told us that they believe in sticking to what they know. And yet they do recognize that they must get to know how the nonprofit world works. As one respondent put it, negotiating the landscape of philanthropy as a novice is both 'intimidating' and frustrating: 'I had given lots of dollars on an *ad hoc* basis to every fireman's spaghetti feed, or national lung campaign, you know, you name it. It didn't feel very structured; it didn't feel like I was maximizing leverage.'

To learn how to conduct philanthropy in a way congruent with his high-tech experience, he gravitated quickly to Social Venture Partners (SVP). In this forum he became educated by SVP members about how to employ 'capital and hands-on intelligent skills . . . to whatever the particular target opportunity was'.

While recognizing these distinctive characteristics, we must be careful not to erect an insurmountable wall around high-tech philanthropy. Many donors who are not involved in the high-tech industry approach their businesses and philanthropy in relatively the same way as do high-tech donors. And, conversely, there are high-tech donors here and there who do not undertake an explicit or full-blown agent-animated philanthropy. Still, the dominant theme that surfaces from the accounts of every person with whom we spoke is the effort to shape philanthropy in the way they have learned to shape their high-tech businesses. They will mold the present and future of philanthropy because they embrace the insight that, in an ever-changing world, insight is the lever for extended significance, service and effectiveness.

Just as the exponential growth in technology and knowledge means that we are only at the beginning of new business horizons, high-tech philanthropy is still in its nascent phase. Just as we do not know all the future formations of business, we do not yet know the transfigurations in store for today's agent-animated philanthropy. In both business and philanthropy, entrepreneurs harbor a strong sense of experimentation. As I write, new forms of commercial and philanthropic enterprises are daily in the news. What is happening now may well be supplanted by a sequence of innovations in business, philanthropy, and the combination of the two.

7.4.7   Varieties of Agent-Animated Philanthropic Strategies

Strictly speaking, 'venture capital', the term that spawned the analogous 'venture philanthropy', denotes the more or less active dedication of an investor's money and expertise to propel an entrepreneurial activity initiated by someone else. It is marked by the following characteristics:

- Successful philanthropy requires the rational calculation of an expected rate of return in the form of specific outcomes.
- Investment philanthropy fosters a partnership relationship between donor and recipient. The donor underwrites the recipient to pursue a set of goals and the recipient recognizes the donor as an active stakeholder whose interests merit attention.
- Investment philanthropists tend to subordinate financial to intellectual capital. While appreciating the genuine instrumentality of money, they view the success of a nonprofit as primarily a function of the ideas behind the venture.

In recent times, we have come to use the term 'venture philanthropy' to encompass all versions of agent-animated philanthropy. In common parlance the term refers to a range of approaches that are in fact more widespread and multifaceted than the strict parallel to venture capital business investment. I find that much of what is regularly included within the category of venture philanthropy is more accurately called 'managerial philanthropy' or 'entrepreneurial philanthropy'. Managerial philanthropy is the contribution of organizational expertise without the contribution of financial resources to elevate the effectiveness of a charitable organization. Its chief characteristics are:

- An attempt to recapitulate, in the realm of philanthropy, various business standards that are used in running an efficient commercial enterprise.
- An overriding concern with the production and measurement of philanthropic outcomes as the primary mechanism for achieving efficiency and cultivating business discipline.
- The contribution of time and effort mainly in the form of holding a formal or informal leadership position in the nonprofit organization.

Entrepreneurial philanthropy is the joint contribution of both human and financial capital of a wealth holder to inaugurate either a new charitable enterprise or a new component within an existing charity. The distinctive elements of entrepreneurial philanthropy, like those of venture philanthropy, parallel the elements that surround efforts in the for-profit sector:

- Direct engagement by the wealthy philanthropist in founding, rather than simply contributing to or advising, a philanthropic organization.
- Achieving social and moral change by the application of innovative ideas.
- The aspiration to generate a sizable impact by leveraging the influence of an embryonic initiative.

In my view, venture philanthropy is that 'middle' form that infuses managerial advice and financial resources into a philanthropic effort, but does not interject the hands-on daily direction that is the hallmark of an entrepreneur.

Our respondents provided numerous examples of the three intercessional forms of philanthropy. An example of each form should help to properly distinguish among managerial, venture and entrepreneurial philanthropy. One respondent, whose wealth is tied up in a Silicon Valley Internet start-up, contributes some money but much managerial expertise to her alma mater to help with fundraising and to develop better fundraising methods. A Boston software entrepreneur, who has started his own family foundation, is nonetheless also contributing both venture capital and skills to help others get their charity off the ground, assisting them with goal definition, planning and advice about how to leverage funding. Finally, one Austin high-tech founder expends the majority of his philanthropic dollars and time overseeing his entrepreneurial start-up of a charity dedicated to overcoming the digital divide among urban youth.

The myriad engagements by our respondents in these three philanthropic strategies suggest that carrying out one or more of these intercessional philanthropic strategies is a leading characteristic of high-tech donors. In order to understand more accurately what high-tech donors are actually doing, and in order to better alert them to the variety of intercessional strategies they may wish to pursue, it is necessary to recognize the differences among managerial, venture and entrepreneurial philanthropy. Indeed, the future of so-called venture philanthropy or, better, of venture philanthropists engaged in various venture partner organizations, is more likely to revolve around entrepreneurial philanthropy to the extent that these high-tech donors solidify their wealth, garner more time to pursue their philanthropic purposes, and discover the causes and people on behalf of which they desire to exert their hyperagency. I propose that considerations about the connection between enterprise and philanthropy need to be expanded beyond the term 'strategic philanthropy' to the specific types of strategic philanthropy (see Schervish, forthcoming/2014 for a review of 13 strategies) pursued by donors. More directly relevant for our concerns in this book, we need to stop using the generic term 'venture philanthropy' when in fact the strategy may instead be managerial or entrepreneurial. The three approaches are similar in that each entails a practice of organizational leadership and a disposition focused on improving effectiveness; but they are radically different in the personal mode of engagement carried out by donors.

7.4.8   Dilemmas of Care and Control

In the three foregoing strategies, wealth holders in general, and high-tech donors in particular, are institutional architects. As such, they are endowed with the expectation, confidence and capacity to be world-builders. The caliber of the philanthropic worlds they beget depends upon the caliber of their intercessions. Without abundantly more information and wisdom it is at best presumptuous, and at worst ethically indefensible, for us to declare that any agent-animated donor is clearly more a servant of care or dominion in how they intercede with their time and money. And so I refrain from doing so.

Still it is necessary and possible to retain a critical eye because high-tech donors possess such overwhelming capacity to generate much care and much control. Being thoroughly aware of the Janus-faced prospects is crucial because the characteristic that makes high-tech donors constructive is simply the obverse of what makes them destructive: the resolute determination and financial wherewithal to carry out their will. We see high-tech donors benefiting a cause by spurring creative directions; helping an organization to distinguish between and measure outputs and outcomes; knowing when to step aside and turn a venture over to others; and developing relationships of mutual respect. On the other hand, there are temptations, such as for activist philanthropists to insist on implementing their views despite countervailing opinions by front-line professionals or community activists; to push a pet project that a community may neither need nor want; to sidetrack a worthwhile project; to insist on an accounting scheme too narrow for effectiveness; or, finally, to pressure a charity to shift from its existing undertakings in order to scale up, thereby disrupting how it currently serves its beneficiaries.

7.5   FROM HERE TO THERE: SHIFT IN EMPHASIS FROM BUSINESS TO PHILANTHROPY

7.5.1   Turning to Philanthropy: The Transitional Secret of Focus from Accumulation to Allocation

More important here for our argument is how, in the light of meeting their goals for financial independence, high-tech entrepreneurs turn to philanthropy as the realm in which they will begin to focus their intellectual, emotional, and financial capital. I call this the 'transitional secret of focus from accumulation to allocation'. It is transitional because it leads to a shift in orientation. It is a secret because it is rarely articulated by wealthy entrepreneurs or by researchers and yet in practice it can be discovered and implemented. To say there is a transition in focus from accumulation in business to allocation in philanthropy does not mean there was no previous, even substantial attention to philanthropy. Nor does it mean that intensifying philanthropic involvement ends all attention to business endeavors. It does mean that there is more intellectual, emotional and behavioral attentiveness to charitable giving either during business involvements, during a period when business activity has terminated, or before new business activities commence. There is no model that all donors follow. They each choose over time the sequencing or combination of business and philanthropy. But an increased focus of their capacities on philanthropy takes place in a constellation of considerations that we can see in David Hendricks's (pseudonym) evolution. He is a typical example of how wealth holders reallocate their attention from financial accumulation to charitable allocation. He is emblematic in that he evinces the general pattern of the transition in focus from business to philanthropy. Considering him an ideal type means that not everyone who makes this shift will follow his exact pattern, and not everyone will shift as fully or completely from business when philanthropy takes on a higher priority.

David Hendricks is a 45-year-old, now cashed-out equity partner of a high-tech venture capital firm, who graciously granted an interview over two sessions of more than four hours. His shift from finances to philanthropy finds him calculating his financial security, undergoing a positive reversal in his previously cynical view about the value of philanthropy, and narrating the familiar experiences that mobilize his giving to benefit the education of disadvantaged students. Among several such experiences, he identifies personally with the fate of students in need of education and responds to his gratitude for the gift of his own education.

7.5.2   Financial Security

Our findings from two surveys of wealth holders (Schervish and Havens, 2000, 2011) and Independent Sector studies (e.g., Hodgkinson and Weitzman, 1996) based on household income up to what would be today around $200 000 in annual income, point to the importance of trust in future financial well-being for higher levels of charitable giving. The higher-wealth individuals rate themselves on financial security and middle-income people rate themselves on confidence in their family's financial future, the more they give to philanthropy than their economic peers who rate themselves lower. Personal interviews (e.g. Schervish and Herman, 1988) also reveal that economic events such as cashing in stock options, sale of a company or engaging in a public offering often, but not invariably, lead wealth holders to turn to philanthropy as their primary vocation. Those who have solved the economic problem for themselves and their heirs indefinitely into the future face a new and fuller range of choices – one of which is continued business activity, and the second of which is to focus more on using their wealth, their time and their skills for philanthropy.

For David Hendricks his shift to a greater focus on philanthropy begins his emblematic path to philanthropy with his recognition of financial security, which he defines as:

> basically having a very, very low chance that you will go broke even if you don't have a job, given an acceptable lifestyle. I have a computer model that I built that reaches out to when we're [he and his wife] ninety years old that factors in infla-

tion and that plays out all this growth stuff and what the random fluctuations of the stock market could possibly be. And it lays out a thousand versions of the way the world might play out and in only one time out of a thousand will we go broke given the lifestyle that we've chosen. And that's financial independence.

He goes on to explain that as a mathematician and computer programmer, and as one who is exceptionally risk-averse when it comes to long-term financial independence, he was able to construct a simulation model that:

randomly simulates the way the stock market will play out over the years, using history as a guide for what numbers you should put in there. And the question for me was, do you have enough squirreled away so that basically we can maintain the lifestyle that we've chosen through our old age and have a very low probability of having either inflation or a lack of appreciation in the stock market make us go broke?

For Hendricks, the amount designed for financial security is a present value resource stream in 2002 of $6 million in present value ($8 million in 2013 dollars), net of prospective taxes, net of inflation and net of potential negative shocks to the stock market.

What Hendricks explains next is crucial to the transition in focus to philanthropy for all who make this shift. What he enunciates is often obscured from perception – both for those who go through this transition, as well for us researchers who seek to excavate that distinctive inner dynamic that leads to a greater focus on philanthropy rather than continued business enterprise or extended leisure. Why, after all, turn to philanthropy, since doing so is not inevitable? What is it about philanthropy that inclines individuals to dedicate devotion to it? What is that usually un-annunciated and unstudied experience that leads to philanthropy instead of alternative directions?

Hendricks makes it clear that any serious pursuit of philanthropy would only be a 'romantic' rather than a 'pragmatic' pursuit had he not first achieved financial independence. But note: although Hendricks explains the role of financial capacity in making philanthropy possible, this still does not explain why he turns his attention to philanthropy:

You need wealth to actually act on that ideal because, I'm sorry, I enjoy so much the lifestyle you can achieve with wealth. The pragmatist in me, like the squirrel, says, 'save your chestnuts and the sooner you get that done, the sooner you can rise up a Maslovian level and do the other things'. And beware trying to rise up the Maslovian level before you are ready to do it. Be very, very sure that you are ready to do it because it is tough to turn back.

Prior to affirming his material and psychological financial security, Hendricks was already a small contributor to charities. But why does he plan to cut back on his business activity and cash out his equity share in his venture capital firm? It need not be to take up philanthropy; many other options present themselves to someone like Hendricks, as I said, from increased leisure to new business enterprises. He chooses philanthropy because he learns the transitional secret: the happiness of caring directly for people in need. He is attracted to pursue what he calls the 'ideal' of doing something 'unambiguously socially positive'. It is now time, he recounts, for him to pursue more wholeheartedly something in the realm of philanthropy. He commences in earnest to investigate ways to dedicate his money, skills and time to philanthropy in a qualitatively effective and quantitatively ample manner. As he puts it:

> I've always kind of rolled my eyes a little bit when I hear about do-gooders because I have this image in my mind – not grounded at all on any experience – they will be lightweight type of stuff, full of petty politics. So I've always steered away from the world of philanthropy or nonprofit and pooh-poohed it somewhat. But there is a side of me that says that maybe I can tune in a little bit more and do something that is unambiguously socially positive and see how that feels. I would like to see how that feels and if I find myself getting up in the morning very excited about how I am spending my time if indeed, I do find something that is unambiguously socially positive. This is something that struck me really very profoundly: those simple pleasures of being a contributor and being able to map how those contributions fit into the larger scheme of things. A kind of social welfare, if you will.

Hendricks's previous statement is replete with expressions of feeling, highlighting his anticipation of the 'simple pleasures of being a contributor'. What Hendricks feels is a chance to enter more fully into what Aristotle considers the greatest virtue and most inviting engagement: *philia*. This root of the word 'philanthropy' is not primarily a definition, but a relationship and an experience. Philanthropy is more profound than the conventional etymology *philia+anthropos* or love of human beings. Philanthropy is best understood as the experience and practice of friendship love for human beings that brings mutual nourishment. 'A friend is another myself,' says Aristotle, with such friendship nourishing both parties. Friendship love is the principal virtue leading to happiness. So what leads Hendricks to philanthropy? He attains an attraction to replicate and extend his sense and sensibility of *philia* into the public and organized world of philanthropy, as a path to self-fulfillment and fulfillment of others. Not everyone replicates Hendricks's learning of the transitional secret. But many do answer positively the question raised by financial security: how to convert a vast quantity of choice into a deeper quality of choice. Like Hendricks, they link through philanthropy their own and others' growth in effectiveness, meaning and compassion. He deems that he and others would flourish more by caring for others directly. That is, just because they are in need, not because they can express their need through dollars as in a commercial relationship. Aristotle says the attractive potency of *philia* as friendship love arises from the joy and happiness of the parent–child relationship and then develops throughout life into the fulfillment of close personal acquaintances, workmates, and even those in fair contractual associations. Hendricks, we hear, begins to understand the mutuality of philanthropy and that something positive is in store for his own fulfillment as he cares for others.

7.5.3 Identification

Hendricks's sense of fulfillment comes from an array of ultimately inseparable experiences that lead him to the dispositions, decisions and deeds of the transitional secret of philanthropy. The first is identification. I have already discussed identification as well as other mobilizing experience at some length in other writings (Schervish, 1997, 2007). But its ability to animate the philanthropy of a wealth holder can be appraised by a brief look at how Hendricks connects what he considers to have been the comparative advantage of being well educated with the plight of those whose lack of quality education excludes them from the knowledge economy. Hendricks recounts that both he and his wife, Meagan, have gotten ahead in life due to the intellectual capital they garnered from their extensive top-tier university studies and, besides, 'between Meagan and me we've got so many educators everywhere' in the family, that a concern for education has been 'imprinted in us'.

Hendricks considers the poor who are 'education have-nots' as like him, his wife, and his children – but in reverse. And he aspires to make a subvention for this group commensurate to the privileges he and his family enjoyed. 'I'm very concerned about a bifurcation of the educated and the educated-nots in our society,' explains Hendricks, 'because I see increasingly that our economy is driven by knowledge-worker types, problem-solvers. So I have real concerns about how to democratize education.' Especially for the poor, 'education is very important 'cause what we're talking about is people who would otherwise be burger-flippers'. As was true for him, 'the comparative advantage to them [poor children] is an affordable education, which in turn allows them to get jobs in the knowledge economy'.

7.5.4 Gratitude

The experience of identification is complemented by a particularly strong sense of gratitude for unmerited advantages or, as some say, 'blessings' in reaching financial success. In our 2001 High-Tech Donors Study we found that most participants do not credit their wealth solely to their own efforts and skills. They understand that at various points in their careers there was always risk of failure. Thus, they credit their wealth at least in part to luck, breaks and good fortune, and for those who are religiously inclined, to God's grace or blessing. Such experience of blessing and gratitude further animates them to seek ways to help individuals and causes with which they identify.

The dynamics of gift and gratitude leading to care for others is precisely what Hendricks describes as generating his concern for the vocation of education as a 'noble thing'. 'The other piece of it,' he continues, moving from identification to gratitude:

> is I personally got so much out of my education. It has enriched me beyond measure. Not only the practical aspects of it, for instance in my career, [but also] to have a sense of irony, and to build an intellectual richness in life that for me has just meant so much as a gift . . .
> The gift of knowledge you might say – the gift of how to think, how to write, how to communicate, how to analyze as well as the gift of all the touchstones that an education gives you – the building of commonality in a community. You know, if everybody has read Shakespeare, there's a commonality that comes out of that which makes for better life. I do believe in having touchstones – that communities have points of reference that are rich and deep which can be commonly held and therefore allow people to not feel alone and to have confidence in the like-mindedness of their fellows.

7.5.5   Hyperagency

In addition to identification and gratitude, another mobilizing experience derives from the particularly active way wealth holders have made their money. Like Hendricks, they desire to be as entrepreneurially productive in the realm of philanthropy as they are in the realm of commerce. An analysis of several years of the Federal Reserve Survey of Consumer Finances indicates that the majority (approximately 93 percent) of wealth holders acquired most of their wealth through their own skills and efforts (including investments) rather than through inheritance (7 percent). Their major road to wealth has been business in the sense that they have owned and operated their own enterprises, most often as entrepreneurs. And those who are not directly involved in running a business are active investors. Our research findings continually confirm that the fundamental common trait of wealth holders is what we call hyperagency (Schervish and Herman, 1988). Hyperagency is the ability to be a producer and a creator of the organizational life of a society rather than simply a supporter and participant. As institution-builders in commerce, politics and philanthropy, hyperagents do not simply seek to find the best environment within which to work, live or give. Rather, in all three realms, hyperagents are able to do alone or with a few other individuals what would take a substantial social, political or 'mass philanthropy' (Zunz, 2012) movement to achieve. When they choose to do so, hyperagents on their own can start new ventures, apply new ideas and methods, and set new institutional directions for existing organizations. Also, as we have often seen in recent years, they create new products and methods to solve global problems, spur giving pledges among billionaires, and jump into electoral politics, leapfrogging established candidates. The wealthy thus bring to their philanthropy not just an overarching expectation and confidence about being effective, but also a wide range of skills revolving around 'questions of how to manage change', as Hendricks puts it. Such skills include an understanding of finance, management, investment leverage, personal connections, leadership talent, and a can-do attitude bred by success. In particular, wealth holders, the longer they are members of a community, often have assembled such an array of informal and formal associations within their communities and through board memberships and other leadership positions that they become, as a matter of daily schedule, intimately knowledgeable about, interested in and responsible for philanthropic initiatives and nonprofit management and innovation. When coupled to the fact of earlier financial security and longer life expectancy, many wealth holders have both the time and energy to devote deeper thinking and vigor to the people and causes about which they care.

In philanthropy, as in commerce, politics and civic life in general, the desire to be productive hyperagents is an active motivation that is part of the general inclination of wealth holders to be as publicly purposeful in allocating their wealth as they were privately purposeful in accumulating it. Hendricks demonstrates this third motivation in addition to those of identification and gratitude. His disposition to be involved in philanthropy requires working through a 'high performance culture':

> I want strong intellectual problem-solvers who are also interested in really getting a lot done. It's not just getting a lot done, but I am just a more cerebrally oriented person, I think, and will find it difficult being effective and happy in a more politically oriented culture or in a more ideologically oriented culture than maybe other people will be.

His objective to make a far-reaching impact leads Hendricks to look first at local education but, speaking as a hyperagent, he says, 'at the end of the day I have an ambition to be able to look at the magnitude, how far reaching the things are that I do. I'd like to see if I could affect thousands of people positively and meaningfully.' He seeks to apply the 'Jesuit premise' of leveraging and measuring change so as to solve the 'bottleneck' in inner-city education due to 'the expense of real estate and the scarcity of good teachers, who can be effective'. In his view, the use of technology is one tool to 'change the student-to-teacher ratio' and to create better education 'which is one-hundredth as expensive on a per-student basis'. But his goal is not to simply affect this or that school, but to produce new and measurable advances for the educational enterprise in general. Hendricks does not insist that his approach will be the answer but he does look to produce a widespread approach to an old problem: 'Will you be able to attract leadership and build an institution that allows for the continuous improvement' of education for the poor, he asks, so that once started the innovations in such education can keep up with the next waves of development in business and technology? Put simply, he says, 'there's an institutionalization aspect to this' and it is a clear example of 'an unambiguously positive type of thing that could have far-reaching impact'. This hyperagency, it should be added, infuses all the philanthropic endeavors of high-tech donors, but it shows up in particular in the agent-animated philanthropy that I highlight in this chapter. Whether through a charitable vehicle or personally, at a distance or close to home, it is the possibility and practice of 'making a difference' that undergirds the determination and dominion of high-tech philanthropists.

7.6   HIGH-TECH DONORS AND ENDURING THEMES OF PHILANTHROPY

Hendricks is not alone in experiencing the mobilizing experiences that unveiled the transitional secret for him. His experiences generate charitable giving in virtually all those we have interviewed in our 30 years of research on wealth and philanthropy, including high-tech donors. Among other factors, such as the gratitude that Hendricks experiences, high-tech donors are similar to all the wealth holders we have interviewed who devote their wealth and abilities on behalf of the commonwealth. They take up their philanthropy as a result of their experience of identification with others in need; the networks of association which bring them into contact with others and expand their circle of care; the desire to make an uncommonly large difference in well-being; and learning the spiritual vocation of wealth.

7.6.1   Identification as the Foundation of Care

A principal finding about philanthropic engagement that we discovered in all our previous research and again in the 2001 High-Tech Donors Study is that the school of care is identification, and the school of identification is association. The key determinant for improving the probability that high-tech wealth holders will answer in a positive way the call to care is the extent to which they experience the fate of others as linked to their own. It is for this reason that several high-tech donors are accordingly proud givers to their parents, kin, in-laws, and nieces and nephews, for they understand care as a single fabric that extends outwards from the self and immediate family.

Furthermore, throughout the interviews we found that the causes high-tech donors tend to support are those that recapture the concerns they, their families and those with whom they have been associated have experienced. A beneficial elementary school or college education breeds a concern in later life with early childhood education or research at a university. A life-long participation in hiking and mountain climbing generates a special care for preserving the environment. The death of a loved one from cancer leads to establishing an oncology center at a hospital. Being a musician leads to contributions to the arts. Explicitly, or just beneath the surface of their narratives, we hear accounts of how the most familiar – both in the sense of already in their purview and in the sense of being familial – experiences of empathetic connection to what high-tech donors most care about determine their philanthropy.

7.6.2   Association: The School of Identification

The disposition of identification does not grow in isolation. The school of identification is the constellation of communities, organizations and media reports from which donors learn about the needs of those people with whom they come to identify. Over the years, we have discovered that the propensity to give time and assets across the economic spectrum is due to more than differences in income, wealth, religion, gender and race. What matters most is not one's morals or finances, but one's abundance of 'associational capital' in the form of social networks of invitation and identification (Schervish and Havens, 1997).

High-tech donors by age, origins, religious disposition and business industry comprise a group with a comparatively low level of associational capital. They are relatively young and so have not accumulated the network of involvements that often come from living and conducting business affairs in a community. In addition, they are either unmarried, recently married, or have young children. As such, many are not yet incorporated into their community life in the manner that any parent comes to understand as children enter school and participate in music and sports programs. Also, high-tech donors more often than not end up conducting their business operations in a locale in which they did not grow up. Another factor that we have found is that the respondents, with only a few exceptions, were neither religiously involved in a Church nor politically involved. They tend to be rather non-ideological, with neither the religious nor political passions that their parents felt. Finally, their businesses tend not to produce the kinds of retail goods and services that would enmesh them in their communities: given available talent, most could run their businesses anywhere. The major associations of high-tech entrepreneurs are with their own employees, other people and firms in the high-tech arena, and their own families and friends. These associations foster an appreciation of knowledge-based needs in education, research, the arts, early child development, teacher training and parent support. In order to expand their appreciation of the multiplicity of needs in their communities, given their rather 'loose connections' to these communities (Wuthnow, 1998), our high-tech entrepreneurs needed to be brought into contact with the needs of others locally and elsewhere in order to kindle their feelings of identification and provide an outlet for their feelings of gratitude. For this reason, many respondents emphasized the importance of their and others' venture-partner activities, giving circles, and even socializing with other donors. A co-founder of one SVP summarized this advantage of the organization:

> The strategy for Social Venture Partners is not as a generator of funds to distribute, although it does in fact do some of that. The main thing that it does is, because you get some of these people involved in even giving the amount of money that they do, it allows them to make a connection with organizations that need the money. And I don't think that they would be able to cross that gap without it.

High-tech donors readily understand how their philanthropy is teaching them about the needs of others and about themselves. Philanthropy is, organically and welcomingly, pulling them out of themselves, their encompassing business obligations and their firms, and into care. The fruit of such associational capital is being harvested today as high-tech donors increasingly involve themselves in philanthropy not as a second stage of life but from the outset of their success. More and more are replicating Hendricks's march to philanthropy, except they are learning the transitional secret to philanthropy earlier from their counterparts, making community involvement a regular matter of their financial attainment.

7.6.3   The Spiritual Vocation of Wealth

Like the wealth holders we have interviewed in all our previous studies, reaching a level of financial security that allows them to provide for self, spouse and family for the future leads high-tech donors to confront the spiritual vocation of wealth and to discover the empowerment of their hyperagency, as well as its attendant dilemmas of care and control.

The spiritual vocation of money is how I describe in more general terms the transition to philanthropy that Hendricks undergoes. The spiritual vocation of wealth is the experience by which wealth holders plumb the depths of the blessings that made them prosperous, the lack of blessing that makes others not prosperous, and the implications for the prosperous to provide the needed breaks, assistance and blessings others require to improve their well-being. The spiritual vocation of wealth is the softened heart that realizes that all people's lives result from effort and blessing, and so those in need are just like us except for the blessings that we can offer. The experience of fortune as partially undeserved or as resulting in large measure from luck and breaks, as noted previously, creates for many wealth holders a sensitivity that others live equally under the influence of the hand of fate. It is the impetus of increased financial security that leads wealth holders, and financial confidence for those lower on the economic continuum, to shift their attention from the quantity of their interests, to the quality of their needs and happiness – and the needs and happiness of others. Here I paraphrase what John Maynard Keynes says (Keynes, 1963). When individuals cease to be economically purposive for themselves, they remain economically purposive for their neighbor. One respondent describes his experience of wealth through the analogy of being lost in the desert and discovering an inexhaustible cache of food and water: 'you [have] achieved financial freedom [and] you can turn your attention to other things. It might be working on your golf game; it might be giving back to the community.'

A major component of this shift to a deeper horizon of care is the realization by wealth holders that their wealth is not completely due to their own actions. If advantage is not experienced simply as the result of merit, then disadvantage cannot by corollary simply derive from the lack of merit. Throughout the course of the study we repeatedly hear respondents testify that their vast amount of wealth, the speed with which it was amassed, their stumbling upon a successful product, and the assistance they received from others to succeed, represent the grace of fortune, not just their own merit. They are conscious that they have been dealt a valuable hand through parental upbringing, education, assistance from spouses, financial breaks and the availability of the expertise of others. At the same time, they have no false humility: it has been up to them to exert the proper strength of character and hard work to play that hand successfully. Opportunity is granted, but virtue takes advantage of opportunity. Hence, we find that all high-tech wealth holders are an enigmatic mixture of both humility and gratitude on the one hand, and self-assurance and pride on the other. Some tend more toward the former, others toward the latter, but all harbor a mixture in their hearts. It is this experience of blessing or luck that first causes wealth holders to think about expressing their gratitude through allocating their wealth for the good of others.

7.7   CONCLUSION: THE EMERGING VOCATION OF PHILANTHROPY FOR HIGH-TECH DONORS

The snapshot of high-tech donors presented in the foregoing sections is not a static picture. There is evidence that much of what we found by way of dedication to philanthropy is in fact just an indication of an emerging fuller commitment with new modes and forms of social innovation (see Martin, 2013). Those who do so can be said to have or to be formulating a philanthropic identity, the development of a self-conception and a way of life that focuses on allocating wealth for the care of others instead of mainly on the accumulation of wealth. Still, some wealth holders who are young in chronological age or in business tend currently to be more infused with a business than a philanthropic world-view. But this, as I said, is changing. Today, however, it is becoming more the norm that both business and philanthropy develop together, even when the major focus remains on business evolution. Older high-tech donors who have been active in business and philanthropy for years are already substantially engaged in well-conceived and well-executed philanthropic projects to which they have contributed large sums of their wealth, and have brought their philanthropic activity to the forefront of their self-conception or have made it equal to their business role. For those not substantially yet involved in philanthropy, however, there is still an explicit anticipation of an even greater contribution of time and money in the future, when current limitations such as achieving more wealth, liquidity and business success have been accomplished. These respondents state that they are still learning about the world of philanthropy and about their place in it, seeking answers to questions about what their priorities might be, about what others are currently doing and how well, and how much money and time they will devote now and in the future. Philanthropy is a calling they already feel; it is a vocation they desire to follow now and more vibrantly as time goes by.

Whenever the freedom of choice and personal capacity that wealth holders currently enjoy is refined in the furnace of personal discernment and reflection, wealth holders are more likely to develop a caring philanthropic identity, to make wise decisions about allocating their wealth, and to experience the reinforcing satisfactions that accompany generous charitable giving and volunteering. With such forces in play, high-tech donors will become even more inclined, rather than simply pushed or coaxed toward increasing the quantity and quality of their philanthropy. We have written elsewhere that:

> [a supply-side approach to charitable giving] drawing on the inclinations of donors to care about the issues and people with whom they identify and to desire to effect change in the world around them . . . [by approaching] donors as knowledgeable decision makers who are to be tutored through a process of personal discernment rather than instructed how much to give and to whom [is the most effective way to evoke charitable behavior]. (Schervish and Havens, 2002)

Our interviews with high-tech philanthropists and other recent research (Schervish and Havens, 2011) have reinforced our belief that donors are more inclined to donate their time and money when they reach that phase in their business life when the urgency of causes with which they identify joins, or even surpasses, their sense of urgency about accumulation. This differs from the scolding or cajoling model. This approach tries to elicit giving by 'twisting my arm', as one donor put it, tries to force expanded philanthropic involvement by invoking the overly prevalent rebuke that 'you are not giving enough, to the right causes, at the right time, in the right ways!' The supply-side approach does not ignore the demand of needs or focus solely on the donor; rather, it tries to bring both together in a relationship that works inductively with the dynamics of liberty and inspiration, rather than deductively with the dynamics of compulsion and imposed duty. In contrast to the scolding model, the inclination model asks, 'What would you like to do with your wealth? That meets the needs of others? That you can do better than commerce or government? And that expresses your gratitude and identification with others in their need?' In fact, it asks the very same questions that our interviewees have told us they pose and grapple with on a daily basis.

High-tech philanthropy is a fast-moving, expanding and changing landscape. Many of our interviewees are at the very beginning of their family lives and their careers, and their philanthropic identity is newborn. The balance they are trying to achieve between family, business and philanthropy will certainly change over the next 40 to 50 years as circumstances change and their experience of philanthropy, both positive and negative, grows. For now, most of those with whom we spoke are not even certain how their fortunes will fare in the years to come. Later in their lives, they will think more about their wealth in the light of death and the desire to leave a legacy – topics about which at least half of the respondents have so far thought little.

Wealth and hyperagency are not new in history, nor is agent-animated philanthropy. But what is new is that from the beginning of accumulation, wealth holders are thinking about how to be wise and generous about the allocation of their wealth. It is not just so much a question of what is new about high-tech philanthropy, as it is a question about its future. High-tech philanthropists pick up themes from the past. They combine them with what is distinctively contemporary about their businesses and themselves. They seek opportunities to advance as students of care. They work to create new nonprofit organizations or monitor existing charities' organizational workings and measurable impact. And they are poised to be among the next generation of teachers about how to advance the well-being of people across the globe.

NOTE

*   I am grateful to the Association of Fundraising Professionals for giving us the opportunity to conduct this research and, in particular, to Michael Nilsen, for assisting us in seeking out and contacting respondents. I am also grateful to the sponsor of the study, Dr Robert B. Pamplin, Jr, President and Chief Executive Officer (CEO) of the R.B. Pamplin Corporation in Portland, Oregon for generously supporting our research and graciously providing this intellectual opportunity. Thanks are also due to all those who assisted us in making contacts with potential respondents: Paul Shoemaker of SVP Seattle; J. Donald Monan, S.J. of Boston College; Jan Kreamer of the Greater Kansas City Community Foundation; Dalene Bradford of Community Foundations of America; Andrea Kaminski of the Women's Philanthropy Institute; the Forum for Women Entrepreneurs; Women in Technology International; and those respondents who connected us to other respondents, but whose direct acknowledgement would compromise their anonymity. I am indebted to our interviewees and our anonymous informants for being so forthcoming with their time and thoughts. I also would like to thank Maria Aiello, Kelly Fargo, Mark McGregor, Meghan McGuinness, Caroline Noonan, Shelley-Ann Quilty, Jill Weidner, Daniele Wilson and, especially, my two co-authors of our original report – Mary A. O'Herlihy and John J. Havens – without whose competent and dedicated research assistance and research colleagueship the project could not have succeeded. I am grateful also to the editors of this volume for inviting my contribution and for their leadership in our field. Finally, I wish to thank the Ewing Marion Kauffman Foundation of Kansas City, Missouri, and the Wieler Family Foundation of Baltimore for supporting the writing of this chapter.

REFERENCES

Atkinson, R.D. and R.H. Court (1998), 'The new economy index: Understanding America's economic transformation', Progressive Policy Institute Technology, Innovation and New Economy Project.

Atkinson, R.D., R.H. Court and J.M. Ward (1999), 'The state new economy index: Benchmarking economic transformation in the States', Progressive Policy Institute Technology and New Economy Project.

Blair, M.M. and S.H. Wallman (2001), *Unseen Wealth: Report of the Brookings Institution Task Force on Intangibles*, Washington, DC: Brookings Institution Press.

Borden, M. and S. Koudsi (1999), 'America's forty richest under forty: They're young, smart, and on the Net', *Fortune Magazine*, September 27, available at http://money.cnn.com/magazines/fortune/fortune_archive/1999/09/27/266173/ (accessed October 10, 2012).

Carlson, N. (2000), 'Enlightened investment or excessive intrusion', *Grantsmanship Center Magazine*, Fall, Los Angeles, CA.

Community Foundation Silicon Valley (1998), 'Giving back, the Silicon Valley way: The Culture of Giving and Volunteerism in Silicon Valley Report'.

Dees, J.G. (1998), 'The meaning of social entrepreneurship', Stanford, CA: Kauffman Center for Entrepreneurial Leadership.

Edwards, C. (1999), 'Entrepreneurial dynamism and the success of US high-tech', United States Joint Economic Committee, Report to Chairman. Growth and Prosperity Series, Vol. III.

Florida, R. (2000), 'Competing in the age of talent: quality of place and the new economy', report prepared for the R.K. Mellon foundation, Heinz Endowments, and Sustainable Pittsburgh.

HNW Digital, Inc. (2000), *Survey of Wealth and Values*, New York: HNW Digital.

HNW Digital, Inc. (2001), *Survey of Wealth and Giving*, New York: HNW Digital.

Hodgkinson, V.A. and M.S. Weitzman (1996), *Giving and Volunteering in the United States: Findings from a National Survey*, Washington, DC: Independent Sector.

Keynes, John Maynard (1963), *Essays in Persuasion*, New York: W.W.Norton & Co.

Lee, C.M., W.F. Miller, M.G. Hancock and H.S. Rowen (eds) (2000), *The Silicon Valley Edge: A Habitat for Innovation and Entrepreneurship*, Stanford, CA: Stanford University Press.

Letts, C.W., W. Ryan and A. Grossman (1997), 'Virtuous capital: What foundations can learn from venture capitalists', *Harvard Business Review*, March–April, 2–7.

Martin, M. (2013), 'Making impact investible', Impact Economy Working Papers, Vol. 4, available at http://www.impacteconomy.com/papers/IE_WP4_EN.pdf (accessed January 23, 2014).

Morino Institute and Venture Philanthropy Partners (2001), 'Venture philanthropy: the changing landscape report', prepared by Community Wealth Ventures, Inc.

Morino Institute Youth Social Ventures (2000), 'Venture philanthropy: landscape and expectations', prepared by Community Wealth Ventures, Inc.

Prince, R.A. and H.S. Grove (2001), 'eWealth: Understanding the Internet millionaire', online paper from *Institutional Investment* newsletters, available at http://www.iihighnetworth.com.

Schervish, P.G. (1990), 'Wealth and the spiritual secret of money', in R. Wuthnow and V.A. Hodgkinson (eds), *Faith and Philanthropy in America: Exploring the Role of Religion in America's Voluntary Sector*, San Francisco, CA: Jossey-Bass, pp.63–92.

Schervish, P.G. (1997), 'Major donors, major motives: The people and purposes behind major gifts', *New Directions for Philanthropic Fundraising: Developing Major Gifts*, 16, 85–112.

Schervish, P.G. (2000), 'The modern Medici: Patterns, motivations and giving strategies of the wealthy', paper presented on the panel, The New Philanthropists, at the inaugural forum, What is 'New' About New Philanthropy, of the University of Southern California Nonprofit Studies Center, Los Angeles, CA.

Schervish, P.G. (2007), 'Why the wealthy give: Factors which mobilize philanthropy among high net-worth individuals', in A. Sargeant and W. Wymer (eds), *The Routledge Companion to Nonprofit Marketing*, Abingdon: Routledge, pp.165–181.

Schervish, P.G. (forthcoming), 'Beyond altruism: philanthropy as moral biography and moral citizenship of care', in Vincent Jeffries (ed.), *Altruism, Morality, and Social Solidarity: Establishing a Field of Study*.

Schervish, P.G., P.E. Coutsoukis and E. Lewis (1994), *Gospels of Wealth: How the Rich Portray Their Lives*, Westport, CT: Praeger.

Schervish, P.G. and J.J. Havens (1997), 'Social participation and charitable giving: A multivariate analysis', *Voluntas: International Journal of Voluntary and Nonprofit Organizations*, 8(3), 235–260.

Schervish, P.G. and J.J. Havens (2000), 'Wealth with responsibility study', Social Welfare Research Institute, University of Massachusetts Survey Research Center, Bankers Trust Private Banking, New York: Deutsche Bank.

Schervish, P.G. and J.J. Havens (2002), 'The new physics of philanthropy: The supply-side vectors of charitable giving, part 2: the spiritual side of the supply side', *CASE International Journal of Higher Education Advancement* 2 (3): 221–241.

Schervish, P.G. and J.J. Havens (2011), 'High net worth households that make very high charitable gifts: Finding on four under-studied concepts', report presented to the John Templeton Foundation and the Bill and Melinda Gates Foundation, Center on Wealth and Philanthropy, Boston College, Chestnut Hill, MA.

Schervish, P.G. and A. Herman (1988), 'Empowerment and beneficence: Strategies of living and giving among the wealthy', final report from the Study on Wealth and Philanthropy, Chestnut Hill, MA: Boston College Social Welfare Research Institute.

Schervish, P.G., M.A. O'Herlihy and J.J. Havens (2001), 'Agent-animated wealth and philanthropy: the dynamics of accumulation and allocation among high-tech donors', Center on Wealth and Philanthropy, Boston College, Chestnut Hill, MA, USA, http://www.bc.edu/content/dam/files/research_sites/cwp/pdf/hightech1.pdf.

Sievers, B. (1997), 'If pigs had wings: it's sexy to compare grantmaking to venture capitalism. It's also dead wrong', *Foundation News and Commentary*, November and December.

Time Magazine (2000), 'The new philanthropy', *Time*, 156(4).

US Trust (2000), 'US Trust survey of affluent Americans', prepared by Financial Market Research, Inc., XVIII: Professionals in the technology sector.

Wuthnow, Robert (1998), *Loose Connections: Joining Together in America's Fragmented Communities*, Cambridge, MA: Harvard University Press.

Zunz, Oliver (2012), *Philanthropy in America: A History*, Princeton, NJ: Princeton University Press.

8.   Facilitating entrepreneurs' transitions to philanthropy: the case of the Silicon Valley Community Foundation
Emmett D. Carson and Leigh Stilwell

8.1   INTRODUCTION

Many entrepreneurs look to community foundations[1] for guidance and support as they seek to find their place in philanthropy. Silicon Valley Community Foundation (SVCF) is the largest US community foundation working with entrepreneurs who seek to become engaged in philanthropy. Headquartered in Northern California, SVCF works with more than 2600 individual and family donors, a significant share of them entrepreneurs who become involved in philanthropy with its assistance. Many of these entrepreneurs helped create and shape Silicon Valley's innovative culture, politics and interconnectedness in the global economy, and this history informs their perspective on philanthropy and how they wish to engage in it. This chapter describes the Foundation's experience working with entrepreneurs across the age continuum to support them as they define, pursue and evaluate the impact of their goals for giving. It draws on the authors' combined 40-plus years of experience working with entrepreneur donors and partnering with them to achieve their philanthropic goals. The hope is that these insights offer a useful basis for comparison with the experience of others and will inform more in-depth research.

SVCF is today the largest community foundation in the United States, with more than 2600 individual and family donors and $4.7 billion in assets. The Foundation was created in 2007 through the merger of parent organizations that together had nine decades of history working closely with those who helped create and shape Silicon Valley's innovative culture, politics and interconnectedness in a global economy, and it credits this history with fundamentally shaping its approach to working with today's entrepreneurs as they find their place in philanthropy. In the years since the merger, SVCF has experienced extraordinary growth, celebrating its fifth anniversary as it passed the $1 billion mark in grant-making. In 2013, from its base in Mountain View, California, SVCF received contributions of $1.4 billion and made 10,300 grants worth $367 million. The Foundation is the fifteenth-largest international grantmaker based in the

US. In 2013, grants were made to 37 countries. SVCF donors are individuals, families and corporate partners in the San Francisco Bay Area and throughout the world.

This chapter consists of five further sections. We begin by describing how and why donors decide to partner with SVCF. We then discuss how a libertarian ideology helps shape the world-view of some entrepreneurial donors and describe their values and problem-solving characteristics. The next section provides more detail about the unique 'DNA' of the entrepreneurial donor and its influence on how they approach their philanthropy, and we conclude with observations about how the philanthropy of these entrepreneurial donors can achieve significant change in the world.

8.2   DEFINING THE PATH FOR GIVING

The typical entrepreneur who works with SVCF initiated that relationship at the recommendation of their tax, investment or legal advisor, although personal referrals from other entrepreneurs also are common. Under these conditions, the foundation's development team (which has considerable expertise in tax planning and charitable-giving vehicles) consults with the referring professional advisor and their client to understand the prospective donor's needs and goals. The selection of the appropriate vehicle or mix of vehicles by which to support the donor's philanthropy is guided by several factors. These include, among others, the level of control the donor wishes to maintain, the time horizon for their giving, the level of involvement they intend to have, their preferred investment strategy and the tax deduction they wish to realize. Depending upon the entrepreneur's interests and needs, the options they most commonly consider are the creation of a donor-advised fund, the creation of a supporting organization or the creation of a private foundation. Each, of course, has its own unique benefits and costs. We find that entrepreneurs with considerable wealth often have complex goals, and these donors are likely to select a combination of charitable vehicles to meet their goals.

Our foundation has specialized divisions to support donors based on the vehicles they ultimately choose. In addition to strategic advisory services focused on grant-making, we offer a comprehensive suite of services that offer a donor the opportunity to hire and maintain a dedicated staff, build a brand for their giving, engage with the public, work with prospective grantees, leverage public policy as a tool in their giving, or some mix of the aforementioned. In all cases, the Foundation works with the entrepreneur to ensure that they comply with all governmental requirements of the US and the State of California. It is also the Foundation's role to work with entrepreneurs to ensure they do not engage in any activities that are prohibited by the US Internal Revenue Service or could otherwise create legal or reputational risks for the donor. It is our experience that entrepreneurs appreciate knowing of all relevant legal parameters and, where explicit legal regulations do not exist, they are interested in what we consider 'best practices' to inform their philanthropy.

It is our experience that entrepreneurs typically want to move quickly, and we must be ready to act promptly and responsively to their ideas and interests in order to retain their interest and help them move to active philanthropy. Often, these entrepreneurs have been successful because they envisioned opportunities for which society had not considered or established norms, values or laws, and they acted quickly to exploit them. Further, many have been successful because they are comfortable working at the edge of what the law allows. Their engagement in philanthropy is no different. It is our experience that while entrepreneurs will follow the letter and the spirit of the law, they will also, as is their nature, explore the boundaries of what is allowed.

8.3 THE VALUES OF SILICON VALLEY ENTREPRENEURSHIP AND THEIR IMPLICATIONS FOR PHILANTHROPY

To understand the values that drive many Silicon Valley entrepreneurial donors, it is important to understand the overall culture within Silicon Valley that helps shape their thinking. Specifically, it is our experience that many Silicon Valley entrepreneurs exhibit the cultural mindset of libertarianism. In other words, they tend to subscribe to a relatively liberal social agenda coupled with the view that government is more likely a hindrance than a help. Libertarians take the view that if the action doesn't hurt someone else, it should probably be allowed. It would be a mistake, however, to assume that people with this ideology are liberals. While liberals often believe in a larger role for government, libertarians (like conservatives) tend to be more likely to view government as ineffective and best limited in scope. We do not find it surprising that successful entrepreneurs at the edge of innovation find nineteenth- and twentieth-century laws constraining when developing new products for the twenty-first century and beyond. Many of these innovators find that the markets for new tools and approaches often are constrained by and mired in laws and regulations that were created by individuals who never contemplated the implications of their inventions. If one drives wearing Google Glass, should it be illegal? Should Amazon be allowed to deliver packages to customers using drone technology? Should there be limitations on what can be made using 3-D printers and, if so, who decides? If a passenger is reclining in a driverless Google car and there is an accident, who is liable? The list of complications goes on and on. From a societal perspective, these questions are necessary to ask, but in Silicon Valley, they become the bane of entrepreneurs' existence when they are working to bring great ideas to market. And it is these libertarian values and orientation that many entrepreneurial donors bring with them as they begin to define their philanthropic values and work.

8.4   FUNDAMENTAL QUESTIONS: VALUES, PROBLEM-SOLVING AND ROI

Many of our entrepreneur donors come to the Foundation with a preliminary sense of a problem they want to solve, though they may not be aware of why the issue compels them. We have learned that it is very important to understand the 'why' of this interest because it is fundamental as a starting point for the journey ahead. It connects the entrepreneur donor's past with their future in giving and provides a ballast for the inevitable challenges that will arise in any long-term pursuit, regardless of whether the entrepreneur donor is becoming a full-time philanthropist or remains primarily focused on their business enterprise.

We focus our earliest conversations, framed as a series of questions, with the donors and others whom they may choose to involve in their giving (for example, a partner, spouse, children), on mapping values. The results of these conversations often provide the entrepreneur donor with a profound moment of discovery, or rediscovery, of who they are and what they stand for. When prospective and current entrepreneur donors come to us with a defined problem that they wish to address through their giving, we challenge them to draw the connection between the values they have identified and the issue or issues they wish to invest in. If, after some reflection, they are unable to do this, we encourage them to consider how they came to identify the issue area as important and whether the issue will sustain their interest over time.

We have found, when this conversation involves others in the entrepreneur donor's life, that it creates a significant opportunity for them to identify those values that are distinct and those that are shared among all involved. This often sparks yet another important moment to explore how these distinctions will manifest in the couple's or family's giving; will the entrepreneur donor's values drive all giving or will each individual's unique perspective or framework inform decisions for how the wealth is reinvested in the world? It is not unusual that the entrepreneurs and their partner or other family member will decide to have the partner lead the couple's giving, so that the entrepreneur can continue to operate their business. However, when this is the case, it is important to assess how these choices will impact the partner's satisfaction with their philanthropy. Further, when those other than the entrepreneur are going to manage the couple's or family's philanthropic activity, it becomes essential to determine how they will allocate resources among their shared interests, if they exist, and how to address those that are unique to one or the other.

Building on these fundamental decisions, it then becomes important to engage the entrepreneur donor in discussions that will enable us to understand the entrepreneur donor's expectations and preferences for both their philanthropy's problem-solving approach and their return on investment. To do so, we engage the entrepreneur donor in an interactive exercise that challenges them to identify the lens or lenses they tend to bring to solving a problem; this becomes a proxy for their preferred approach to philanthropy. We find that entrepreneur donors will tend to exhibit a preference toward one or two of four general lenses as they consider their philanthropy. These lenses are:

- A crisis lens – the donor views their philanthropy as an opportunity to invest at critical moments in the life of an individual, an institution or a community.
- A community lens – the donor views their philanthropy as an opportunity to invest to improve the well-being of a group of individuals and institutions.
- An upstream lens – the donor views their philanthropy as an opportunity to invest in tackling the root causes of significant problems to alter a trajectory or otherwise impact future results.
- A systems lens – the donor views their philanthropy as an opportunity to invest to create a ripple effect or large-scale change.

It has been our experience that our entrepreneur donors tend to employ both upstream and systems lenses. For example, one entrepreneur shared at an initial meeting that he wanted to provide scholarships for promising students otherwise unable to afford college. Like many successful leaders in Silicon Valley, he'd been a student in need 30 years earlier and knew that his achievements had been made possible by the generosity of a stranger. During subsequent conversations about both problem-solving and literacy (it is not uncommon to conduct parallel conversations with these curious men and women), he identified himself as an upstream problem-solver. When informed of research that indicated that a child's likelihood to attend college is largely determined by their ability to read at grade level by third grade, he changed course. He decided he would focus his philanthropy not on college scholarships but on early childhood education.

Donors who identify as systems-thinkers, and many entrepreneurs do, tend to focus on large-scale issues – education reform, immigration reform, stem cell research, as examples – and quickly come to appreciate the role of public policy. They are learners and so are typically motivated and persuaded by data.

We have found that it is important to understand a donor's expectations for return on investment (ROI) because, for these entrepreneur donors, ROI can be a significant driver for their long-term engagement in philanthropy. Given the entrepreneur donor's strong focus on ROI in their professional life, these conversations are among the most interesting we have. These conversations are guided by a set of questions that help to ascertain the levels of connection and risk and the process with which the donor is comfortable:

- Does the donor wish to engage directly with the leadership of the organizations they support, or maintain a more distant relationship, including remaining anonymous?
- Do they need to be able to personally see and experience the results of their giving, or is it enough to be informed of progress against goals?
- What level of risk tolerance exists with regard to grantee organizational leadership, organizational strength and the complexity of the grantee's business model?
- Does the entrepreneur donor have a need to see immediate and quantified results or do they have the willingness and patience needed to wait for results over the long term?

The results of this analysis not only inform the recommendations for philanthropic giving options that we will offer the entrepreneur donor, but will also inform the way we will plan to work with the donor over time.

It is our experience that, as we support the work of these entrepreneur donors across decades, we are likely to see changes in what they value most about their giving. Three particular types of change that we have observed in these entrepreneur donors' long-term interests are:

- a sharper focus on the legacy they wish to leave;
- a greater desire to see the results of their giving in their lifetime; or
- an increase in anonymous giving as a strategy to invest in what

matters to them without fanfare or further solicitation from the recipient nonprofit organization or other nonprofit organizations.

8.5 THE UNIQUE DNA OF THE ENTREPRENEUR DONOR

We have come to believe that each donor brings a unique frame or orientation to their giving. Each donor's experience, even when employing very similar grant-making strategies and portfolios, will be different. Among the factors we find are likely to manifest themselves in the entrepreneur donor's decisions about and experience with their philanthropy are age, family history and family experience with philanthropy and giving practices, their homeland or place of origin, the nature and level of their education, their political orientation, and the industry in which they developed their business (for example, high-tech versus finance). As a foundation, one of our most important roles is to help the donor become more aware of these influences, and we are most successful in our work with these entrepreneur donors when we help the donor understand the relevance of these influences to their options for philanthropy.

Reflecting on our work with this fascinating group of donors and what it takes to achieve a positive and successful impact for the experience of the donor as well as for the organizations that ultimately are the beneficiaries of their philanthropy, we have identified the following.

First, these donors are curious. They have a gift for inquisitiveness that expresses itself through boundless questions and new ideas. Successful nonprofit leaders working with these donors will recognize this as one of the qualities that makes possible the donor's philanthropy and they will embrace the opportunity it brings to their organization.

Second, these donors invest in learning about how and why things work the way they do which allows them to make astute observations about behavior that, ultimately, will inform their grant-making decisions. They are skeptical of those who do not share their appreciation for failure as part of the learning process, and suspicious of those who claim perfect track records. Because they believe strongly in testing to create an ever-improving product or service, they tend to be attracted to those organizations that are committed to the same desire for continuous improvement through experimentation in pursuit of their missions. In some quarters, there has been harsh criticism of entrepreneur donors, particularly high-tech donors, who focus relentlessly on innovation. However, it is our experience that what these individuals seek from a nonprofit organization is a world-view that includes the process of ongoing improvement to achieve their mission. Contrary to some of the public narrative about entrepreneur donors, it is our experience that they are willing to make investments in small, 'traditional' nonprofits that are led by forward-thinking executive directors.

Third, entrepreneur donors have the capacity to make connections among seemingly unrelated areas. For example, many years ago one of our entrepreneur donors, an engineer, was in Central America with our staff visiting a project focused on tracking biodiversity. When he saw that scientists were physically tracking animals and insects and manually recording their observations, he suggested they explore a more efficient process: attaching transistors to the fauna being tracked and erecting radio-telemetry towers to assign computers the work of tracking. This was a revolutionary idea to those at the institute, though an obvious conclusion for the donor. After Foundation staff completed their due diligence, this donor helped fund a new project to develop and implement this idea, and this method of tracking biodiversity is today considered a best practice by premier institutions in the world that do this work.

Finally, we find that entrepreneur donors are uniquely optimistic. They come to philanthropy with a strong belief that complex problems can be solved with the right resources, correctly applied. This perspective often expresses itself in a 'bet on multiple horses' approach that involves investing in multiple organizations working on the same issue. These donors encourage organizations to track and share information on their progress so that the mistakes of one can be avoided by others and their successes can be shared. We also find that this can lead the donor to employ philanthropic tools beyond grant-making, such as program-related investments, charitable investments in for-profit enterprises, and support for competitions that result in prizes. Their enthusiasm also carries with it the power to bring other like-minded donors along. One of our greatest responsibilities as a foundation is to help our entrepreneur donors by unlocking networks and linking sectors to multiply the power of their efforts.

8.6   ENGAGEMENT FOR THE LONG TERM

The results of the philanthropy of the entrepreneur donors described in this chapter is felt throughout the world in large and small ways every day. These results range from the creation of a new institute to advance stem cell research, to the renovation of a rural high-school football field that gives thousands of families a stronger experience of community and promising student athletes a chance to learn the value of competition.

Beyond the billions of dollars these entrepreneur donors invest through their giving, they are also reshaping the way younger generations view and will approach philanthropy for decades to come. They are not waiting until their later years to bring their time, talent and treasure to bear in making the world a better place. We believe they are making giving more accessible and more interesting through their enthusiasm and curiosity.

NOTE

1. In the US, community foundations are a unique form of foundation that is very different from a private foundation. Three basic characteristics distinguish community foundations from private foundations (Hoyt, 1996). First, whereas private foundations are created from the wealth of a single donor, family, corporation or other private source, the assets and endowments of community foundations are derived from the gifts, grants and donations of many donors and no single one or two donors have primary control over their assets and grant-making. Second, community foundations usually exist to serve specific geographic communities, localities or constituencies. Their grant-making may or may not be limited to the geographic community, but the people they serve (donors and other stakeholders) usually reside or work in the relevant geographic location. Third, community foundations are public charities and, as public charities, they must meet the US Internal Revenue Service's 'public support test'. The public support test requires that the charity (that is, community foundation) must demonstrate that it receives ongoing financial support from many donors and that its funds are not primarily from only a few sources.

    Community foundation grant-making occurs in three general ways. Some grants distribute the earnings from the community foundation's own general fund endowment. These funds are the most flexible, with the community foundation deciding how they should be used. Special interest or 'field-of-interest' funds are funds whose grants are earmarked for a specific interest area such as the arts, the environment, and so on. Designated funds are funds that are earmarked to benefit a specific nonprofit organization. Donor-advised funds are discrete funds comprised of the donations of individual donors for which those donors retain the right to advise or make recommendations for the grants derived from 'their' fund. In addition, some community foundations such as the Silicon Valley Community Foundation (SVCF) will work with donors to create separate foundations that are legally distinct yet affiliated with (and sometimes staffed by) the host community foundation. All of these options are of potential interest to entrepreneurs as they design their approach to their philanthropy.

REFERENCE

Hoyt, Christopher (1996), *Legal Compendium for Community Foundations*, Washington, DC: Council on Foundations.

PART III

PERSPECTIVES ACROSS THE GLOBE

The chapters of Part III bring an explicitly multinational and intercontinental perspective on the phenomenon of entrepreneurs' engagement in philanthropy and the various ways that we might begin to understand its similarities and differences. Through the eyes of these authors, we are able to gain a greater appreciation for and initial understanding of the perspectives and practices of entrepreneurs in these different parts of the world. These chapters are not structured as a set to enable direct comparison across nations and continents. Instead, they offer foundational insights into the practices and extent to which entrepreneurs engage in philanthropic behaviors and help inform our understanding of the implications of these varying contexts for these entrepreneurs' engagement in philanthropy.

In Chapter 9, Roza and colleagues offer very useful historic as well as contemporary insight into the evolving practice of philanthropy in Europe. They describe four relatively distinct models of European philanthropic tradition and discuss the implications of each for the philanthropic roles and activities of the modern-day European philanthrepreneurs. These models, which range from Anglo-Saxon to Rhine to Mediterranean to Scandinavian, derive from particular geographic and cultural regions and the unique religious and civil-societal traditions and values of those regions. The authors offer an intriguing explanation of each model, discuss how they contribute to and shape contemporary philanthropy, and illustrate philanthropy within the context of each through the use of four exemplary case studies. Each case offers a rich and nuanced source of information and perspective on the nature and form of philanthropic engagement of a specific European philanthrepreneur and how their journey in philanthropy has evolved with experience over time.

Zhao and colleagues take us to a dramatically different part of the world in Chapter 10 with their illuminating chapter on the philanthropic behaviors and the evolving practices of Chinese entrepreneurs. Contemporary research on philanthropy in China is in a formative and fast-developing state, and this chapter offers fundamental insights that contribute to our understanding of the evolving legal, cultural and socio-political contexts for both entrepreneurship and philanthropy. Philanthropic behavior has deep roots in Chinese culture and history, yet its practice has been very limited in recent decades and it has only recently gained broader interest and support within the comparatively small but growing population of the entrepreneurial and corporate elite. The opportunity to practice entrepreneurship on a scale comparable to that of many other nations is also a very recent phenomenon. This chapter shares insights into a very dynamic context in which entrepreneurs may engage in philanthropy, and offers an extensive assessment of the challenges and opportunities that lie ahead for these entrepreneurs. Zhao and colleagues help us begin to understand how modern-day entrepreneurs in China are beginning to embrace a new era of opportunities for both corporate and personal philanthropy, and also how potential changes in China's laws and policies might enhance (or diminish) the extent to which China's new generation of entrepreneurs chooses to and is allowed to become more actively engaged in philanthropy. This substantive information and interpretation of the fast-changing environment of China offers welcome insights for those of us who are not in a position to directly observe these changes.

In Chapter 11, Anyansi-Archibong and Anyansi offer an extensive and thought-provoking set of case-based insights into the philanthropic traditions of African nations and how they are being practiced today by some of Africa's leading philanthropic entrepreneurs. The chapter begins with a general synopsis of the modern literature on the philanthropy of entrepreneurs and discussion of its relevance to the African context, including the significance of historic and cultural traditions of philanthropy. This sets the stage for the authors' report on their recent research to examine the philanthropic practices of ten very wealthy African entrepreneurs. This research project involved a set of case studies of the philanthropy of ten of the wealthiest of African entrepreneurs (subjects drawn from the Forbes 2013 list of the top 40 African millionaires and billionaires), sorted to create a cross-national sample of those who are philanthropically active. The chapter offers a profile of each philanthropist, and these profiles serve as the foundation for this qualitative exploratory study of the philanthropy of these entrepreneurs and the characteristics, motives, challenges and impacts of their philanthropy. The results of this study offer important insights that will serve as an important foundation for the next generation of studies of African entrepreneurs' engagement in philanthropy.

In the final chapter of this part of the *Handbook*, Tyler (Chapter 12) offers unique and instructive insights into the relationships among entrepreneurial behavior, philanthropy and the seminal principles of freedom embodied in two documents that are central to the founding of the United States of America: the Declaration of Independence and the Constitution of the United States of America. Tyler helps us to understand how the philosophical and policy foundations of the US, as codified in these documents, inform and shape options for modern policy and practice for entrepreneurs, philanthropists and, especially, for entrepreneurs who choose to become increasingly actively engaged in philanthropy. As Tyler emphasizes, the basic freedoms that are granted to Americans to engage in entrepreneurship and philanthropy are more than provisions of law – they are central to freedoms the nation's founders sought to ensure for all citizens. This chapter is especially interesting to consider in parallel with the chapters that address the historical, cultural and policy environments (or ecosystems) within which European and Chinese philanthropy and entrepreneurship have emerged and continue to develop.

The chapters of Part III of this *Handbook* offer unique yet complementary insights that help us better understand how and why entrepreneurs' options for and engagement in philanthropy differ across the globe, even as we see an extensive array of commonalities and similarities. The variations described in this part of the *Handbook* remind us that it is important to avoid overgeneralization from the similarities and misinterpret them as standards or universal characteristics. The historical, cultural, social, political and legal foundations and climates within which both entrepreneurship and philanthropy function are of consequence, and they function and intersect in different ways in different parts of the world. Further, it is through improved understanding of the similarities and differences across the globe that we have the potential to gain important insights and perspectives that make it possible for entrepreneurs and their communities to achieve the outcomes they seek as they engage in their own preferred forms of philanthropy.

9. Contemporary European E2P: towards an understanding of European philanthrepreneurs

Lonneke Roza, Marjelle Vermeulen,
Kellie Liket and Lucas Meijs

9.1 INTRODUCTION*

Philanthropy by the established rich has existed since the Greek times in Europe. In the eras of antiquity, 'doing good' was common practice for those who had family fortunes. The succession of self-made European entrepreneurs who started to get involved in the redistribution of their wealth can be traced back to the early modern era. For example, in 1521 the Fuggerei, a social housing complex for the needy, was founded by the banker and businessman Jakob Fugger (Häberlein, 2012). From that period onwards, an increasing number of entrepreneurs became involved with charitable giving. However, most of these entrepreneurs became philanthropists just before they passed away, redistributing their wealth to the public good through the endowments they created.

It was not until the late nineteenth century, with the industrial revolution, that a class of entrepreneurs arose who actively engaged in philanthropy during their lifetimes. This development had another boost around 1980, facilitated by neo-liberalist ideologies that have dominated the European socio-economic landscape since that time. Neo-liberalism has led to the rise of a large group of extremely wealthy individuals who earned their fortunes within their lifetimes. At the same time, this rise of neo-liberalism has created a growing gap between the wealthiest and the poorest people all over the globe (Krugman, 2009). This inequality has also become increasingly visible, motivating a growing number of successful entrepreneurs to engage in philanthropy.

The main research questions that guide this chapter concern the identity of the European philanthrepreneur, for which we adopt the definition of Harvey et al. (2011): entrepreneurs engaged in 'the pursuit ... on a not-for-profit basis of big social objectives through active investment of their economic, cultural, social and symbolic resources' (p. 428). Next, we turn to the motivation of this entrepreneur to engage in philanthropy, the process of transition to this different sector, and the focus and influence of the entrepreneur in the decision-making process.

Our analysis starts with a historical contextualization of philanthropy in Europe. Derived from this historical context we conclude by proposing four different civil society models in contemporary Europe which will form the context of our cases. From there we move on to analyze the phenomenon of contemporary philanthrepreneurs in the UK, which are mostly in line with philanthrepreneurs in the US. Next, we present three continental European case studies that are selected through a purposeful sampling strategy, based upon different civil society models, to provide valuable insights into the motivations and practices of contemporary European philanthrepreneurs. After analyzing the three cases and comparing them with each other and the literature, we conclude that there might be a universal type of philanthrepreneur in Europe, at least in regard to their motives, their focus and their governance.

9.2   HISTORICAL CONTEXT OF EUROPEAN PHILANTHREPRENEURS

The contemporary philanthropic sector in Europe has been shaped by religious, social and political developments throughout Europe's history. A study of the development of European philanthropy in the early modern regimes, the modern era and the postmodern era indicates that as nation-states developed in Europe, the role of the philanthropist changed from 'traditional, religion based charity to pluralist provider of quasi-public goods' (Anheier, 2001: 14). However, European philanthropic history is highly complex, as Europe has a rich history of different types of regimes and nation-states. There is no universal development in Europe leading to different civil society models in which the role of philanthropy differs. Below we explain how these contemporary civil society models are shaped throughout history and the context for the philanthrepreneurs in different parts of Europe. This contextualization will frame our subsequent exploration of contemporary philanthrepreneurs in Europe, highlighting the influence of different civil society models on philanthrepreneurship.

9.2.1   Early Modern Regimes

The basis for self-made entrepreneurs turning to philanthropy is clearly affected by developments in the overall European philanthropic tradition. Some researchers have argued that the Christian tradition inspired current philanthropic behavior (Defouny and Nyssens, 2010). At least in the early modern regimes, Christian charitable associations attached great importance to battling poverty, supporting hospitals and giving alms. This Christian or Catholic way of philanthropic behavior was mainly motivated by fear of going to hell for living a sinful life. Philanthropists hoped that those they helped would pray for their souls.

In contrast to the Catholics, Protestants did not believe that a charitable organization could save your soul. According to Calvinism, rich men had a direct responsibility to follow the will of Christ (Harvey et al., 2011), which implied that donating to (Catholic) charities in order to save the soul was not sufficient (Heerma Van Voss and Van Leeuwen, 2012). They were expected to engage in philanthropic behavior themselves. The change from giving inspired predominantly by fear to more humanistic and intrinsic motivations has influenced modern motivations, resulting in a broader basis for giving. Purely religious-based motivations for giving have evolved to individual and non-religious motivations to give back to the community. This results in a broader base of giving in general and also for entrepreneurs turning to philanthropy. Still, religion remains an important indicator of giving behavior in our contemporary society.

Due to the Reformation in the sixteenth century, declining feudalism, positive economic developments and, consequently, strong urbanization, the traditional Catholic rhetoric lost popularity. Consequently, the doctrine of duties, donations and charities was under debate. Catholic charities became victims of the secularization in reformed countries, where Protestants used media techniques such as the art of printing (Robbins, 2006) to spread the belief that taking care of the poor was the responsibility of local governments. As a consequence, in reformed nations such as the Netherlands, many Catholic charitable organizations were destroyed with the help of the state (Robbins, 2006). At the end of the sixteenth century, only 7 percent of all charities in England (still) had a religious character (Jordan, 1961; Acs, 2003). In reformed countries, the role of the local authorities increased, both in poverty relief and in organizing the philanthropic sector. In addition, the poor and needy became perceived as an unreliable and corrupt part of the population (Robbins, 2006). This shift affected the way in which philanthropic donations were made, inspiring a change from giving directly to beggars to giving to centralized and secular institutions that focused on the rehabilitation of the poor.

Consequently, as Robbins explained, 'philanthropists increasingly preferred to patronize disciplinary institutions. Officers and instructors could promise more economical and effective acquisition of orderly public welfare through social reform' (Robbins, 2006: 25). Moreover, it is due to the Reformation that a more broadly based philanthropic sector has arisen; a sector that is able to operate beyond religious institutions.

Philanthropists increasingly donated their capital voluntarily through private non-religious charitable institutions (Safely, 1997; Anheier, 2001; Robbins, 2006; for an example see Box 9.1). The philanthropic sector further developed after the 1700s, with an increasing number of philanthropic foundations that functioned as private tools to further public needs (Anheier, 2001). In the eighteenth century, mercantile wealth increased, eliminating the traditional 'high social prestige and governing power' in European societies (Anheier, 2001: 25; Safely, 1997). Consequently, a mixed system of welfare arose, where philanthropic institutions were increasingly positioned outside the original structures of local governments and the Church (Heerma van Voss and Van Leeuwen, 2012). This development of a mixed welfare system created a philanthropic sector that was accessible for those who historically lacked the required status. A conscious middle class arose in which entrepreneurs played an important role, becoming more visible and respected (Teeuwen, 2012; Landes et al., 2010). As a result, the traditional conception of philanthropists as men with social prestige and governing power changed (Safely, 1997; Anheier, 2001). These events in history are still noticeable in the context of the current philanthropic sector in which philanthrepreneurs operate.

9.2.2   Modern Era

As a consequence of industrialization, which led to extensive economic growth in Western Europe, the wealth of the middle class improved immensely and in turn they gained growing power and influence in society. The combination of the new opportunity to act on philanthropic intentions with the rise of philanthropic foundations in the early modern regime, and the increased welfare of entrepreneurs during the industrialization, led to increased involvement of entrepreneurs in philanthropy in the modern era (Anheier, 2001). As such, the middle class and the sub-elite and subsequently the entrepreneurs became major forces in establishing private philanthropic foundations (Anheier, 2001; Teeuwen, 2012).

The types of different European nation-states in this era influence the role of the philanthropic sector (Anheier, 2001) significantly. In nineteenth-century France the state had a strong position as it managed a hegemonic, anti-liberal regime. The state established itself as a representative of the public needs. As a result, the development of the philanthropic sector stagnated (see Anheier, 2001). At the same time in Spain and Italy, traditional Catholic philanthropic foundations retained their influence. In Switzerland, new reformed and secularized philanthropic foundations arose. The Netherlands and Sweden followed a different path with the establishment of many public–private partnerships. In contrast, in Britain new philanthropic

BOX 9.1   EARLY MODERN PHILANTHROPIC INSTITUTION: COMPAGNIA

Even in the early modern regime, cases can be found of entrepreneurial individuals who established innovative mechanisms to facilitate their philanthropic deeds. On 25 January 1563, seven notable citizens of Turin (France), including two lawyers, a priest, a notary, a soldier, a merchant, and an artisan, founded Compagnia. 'Piety and power' are mentioned as possible motivations for its establishment (Cantaluppi and Watkiss, 2008: 56). In the early modern era, Compagnia established various philanthropic foundations. While the focus in the sixteenth century was on helping the poor and needy in order to regain Church members, this focus shifted during the seventeenth and eighteenth centuries. In the seventeenth century, Compagnia contributed to the funding of a hospital, where it also intervened with the financial structure of the hospital and provided management assistance (Cantaluppi and Watkiss, 2008). In the same period, Compagnia had a good reputation with a significant number of important members, many of them who had roles at court or in the government. The role of the traditional Catholic charity disappeared; in the seventeenth century Compagnia was no longer only focused on helping the poor, but focused on financial activities as well. Compagnia started to invest in real estate, and its influence was expanded to the state and city government. Compagnia slowly became a political instrument, which was used during the absolute monarchy in early modern France (Ancien Régime) to maintain a state-controlled bureaucracy.

Compagnia's development during the early modern era illustrates how the relationship between the nation-state and the Christian doctrine can influence philanthropic institutions. In the sixteenth century, Compagnia was only focused on poor relief according to the traditional Catholic form of charity. However, in reformed nations like France, Protestants assigned a role for the government. Consequently, the religious character of Compagnia decreased. This decreasing religious character is noticeable in the changing types of activities carried out by the institution. Following this development, in the seventeenth century Compagnia attracted members with roles in local authorities. At the end of early modern France, Compagnia was used and deployed as a political instrument to acquire and maintain power.

foundations were formed without any interference from the state. Here, welfare services and subsidies for the arts were completely executed by British industrialists and philanthropists (Anheier, 2001). Following the effects of different developments on philanthropy, it is likely that these regimes influenced the development of philanthrepreneurs in all kinds of ways. Indeed, in the beginning of the twentieth century many examples of British philanthrepreneurs establishing foundations are known, such as Rowntree (1904), Lord Nuffield (1943) and Leverhulme (1925). At the same time, in anti-liberal regimes like France, there were few opportunities for philanthrepreneurs, and to date, philanthropy is still quite a sensitive topic. However, in Catholic countries such as Italy, the influence of philanthrepreneurs is limited as well, because traditional (mostly religious-based) philanthropic foundations retained their strong position in society. In contrast, in those countries where secularized philanthropic foundations arose such as the United Kingdom, there were more opportunities for wealthy individuals, including entrepreneurs, to establish philanthropic institutions.

In the first half of the twenty-first century, the development of the philanthropic sector was stunted by World War I, the economic crisis of 1929, and World War II (including the Holocaust). For example, the Nazis destroyed numerous philanthropic organizations and increased the public control of these organizations (Anheier, 2001). This resulted in a major setback in the development of the philanthropic sector in Europe.

In most European countries, after the 1950s the relationship between the nation-state and the philanthropic sector changed, especially in (Northern) welfare states. For charities, and consequently for philanthrepreneurs specifically, this meant a different role in society, but also a different scope and size. The political and economic conditions were more stable and prosperous than in the first half of the century, which led to an increase in emerging foundations. Nonetheless, their size and scope were constrained by relatively high levels of personal taxation in most European countries (OECD, 2003). At the same time, the development of foundations was restrained by cultural factors. European welfare state taxes support a comprehensive social safety net, and as a result many citizens feel that welfare should be provided by the state, rather than through private means (OECD, 2003). This results, in some countries, in a culture in which philanthropy is not common, well respected or accepted. It was not until the late 1980s that the philanthropic sector underwent a new renaissance, similar to that during the Middle Ages and industrialization (Anheier, 2001; Rey and Puig, 2010).

In a climate where the philanthropic sector is important, there are more opportunities for private money, since governments in this type of political climate have a less important role in civil society. As a philanthrepreneur, it is easier to execute complementary philanthropic activities

---

BOX 9.2   MODERN ERA PHILANTHREPRENEUR:
ROBERT BOSCH (GERMANY)

Robert Bosch was born in Albeck (Germany) in 1861, and has become one of the most famous entrepreneurs and philanthropists in Germany. In his early career, he successfully worked for a diversity of companies, but made his mark as an entrepreneur and philanthropist early in the twentieth century. His philantrepreneurial career started off with a donation of DM1 million to the technical university in Stuttgart in 1910, and he subsequently set up several foundations, including a homeopathic hospital in 1916. Next, he made several large donations to a variety of causes. For example, in 1920, he donated in total DM20 million for charitable purposes.

Heuss et al. (1994) wrote a biography and explained that Robert Bosch became a philanthrepreneur mainly because of his background. He came from a rural middle-class family and his good nature and benevolence naturally led him to care for others, especially the poor. As a result, he aimed both in his entrepreneurial as well as in his philanthropic career to improve the conditions of life for those in need by emancipating them. Robert Bosch died in 1942 and even after his death the Bosch family remains engaged in philanthropy through the Bosch Stiftung, which was set up in 1968, and other means.

---

successfully when the government has little philanthropic activity on the political agenda. Moreover, the attitude of the government towards philanthropic institutions is also of interest. In the Rhine countries, such as the Netherlands and Germany (for a German example see Box 9.2), the government partners with philanthropic organizations, working cooperatively. It becomes different when the state takes up complete responsibility for welfare in a country. For example, in Scandinavian countries, the link between the state and welfare remains strong in the post-war period, limiting opportunities for private philanthropy and consequently for philanthrepreneurs (Anheier, 2001).

9.2.3   Postmodern Era

In the 1970s and 1980s most European countries saw relatively high levels of unemployment (Defourny and Nyssens, 2010). Economic growth in

European countries stagnated or went into reverse. The state retrenched and interfered less with the well-being of the people. The caring role that the government rejected in that period was taken over by the philanthropic sector in Europe. As a consequence of a withdrawing state, wealthy individuals, including philanthrepreneurs, were needed again to address the prevailing poverty, diseases and other global challenges (Maclean et al., 2013; Harvey et al., 2011). Consequently, private money was needed to step into the gap that was left by the government. The period after the 1980s is often referred to as the philanthropic renaissance (Anheier, 2001).

We assume that philanthrepreneurs can more easily execute complementary philanthropic activities when the government is less active, as less interference from the government leads to a higher involvement of private initiatives. In addition, at the end of the twentieth century many entrepreneurs established philanthropic organizations as a vehicle to safeguard the wealth they had created throughout their lives. Anheier (2001: 18) noted that establishing philanthropic foundations is a way for middle-class entrepreneurs 'to solve the succession problem for owner-managers of medium-scale enterprises, and to help provide stability in terms of ownership and control'.

In addition to the institutional developments in this era, the growing consciousness of global issues inspired the development of philanthrepreneurs (for an example, see Box 9.3). During the past 30 years, people have been more able than before to travel around the globe, experiencing different cultures, traditions and also (local) issues. Moreover, information from all over the world is increasingly available and easy to access. This accessibility led people from Western developed countries to see that developing countries are in need of substantial support. Indeed, many contemporary European philanthrepreneurs are involved in international aid (Shaw et al., 2010).

9.3   CONTEMPORARY PHILANTHREPRENEURSHIP: DIFFERENT COUNTRIES, DIFFERENT MODELS

Due to the major differences between philanthropic traditions in Europe, the potential role of philanthrepreneurs in the various countries may vary greatly. The history of the different countries has led to four models of civil society: the Anglo-Saxon model, the Rhine model, the Latin or Mediterranean model and the Scandinavian model (MacDonalds and Tayart de Borms, 2008; Hartnell, 2008). These various models also shape the climate in which philanthrepreneurs develop and flourish today.

BOX 9.3   POSTMODERN PHILANTHREPRENEUR:
LILIANE BETTENCOURT (FRANCE)

Liliane Bettencourt was born in 1922 in Paris. At the age of 15, she
joined her father's company (L'Oreal), and through her entrepreneurial qualifications she took the company public in 1963. With
this move, she became the wealthiest woman in the world with an
estimated net worth of US$30 billion. In addition to her reputation
as an entrepreneur and businesswoman, she was also known for
her philanthropic activities. In 1987 she founded the Bettencourt
Schueller Foundation (la Fondation Bettencourt Schueller) to
support and develop medical, cultural and humanitarian projects.
The foundation has an endowment of €150 million, and its annual
budget is approximately €15 million. After setting up her own foundation, she continued to donate substantial amounts of money to
other charitable causes. For example, in 2012 she donated £60
million to the Swiss Save our Seas Foundation with the money she
earned from selling her private island.

9.3.1   The Anglo-Saxon Model

In this model, the philanthropic sector functions as a counterweight to the
state. The United Kingdom is the only example of a country in Europe
that has a civil society that can be described according to this model, and
is very similar to the context in the United States. It is characterized by a
strong philanthropic tradition. In the Anglo-Saxon model, donations and
gifts are stimulated by fiscal regulations, and there is a strong culture of
volunteerism. Moreover, the public trust of private philanthropic foundations is relatively high in comparison to the trust in government, and the
public trusts those who spend their private money to contribute to public
needs, with significant trust in individual wealthy people. These conditions
create a philanthrepreneur-friendly environment.

9.3.2   The Rhine Model

The countries with a Rhine model in Europe are the Netherlands, Germany
and Belgium. They are characterized by societal corporatism, where state
and the philanthropic sector cooperate. Even though the civil society is
independent from the government, its funding partly depends on the state.
Donations and gifts are not, for the most part, stimulated by means of

fiscal regulations. As a philanthrepreneur, there are increasing possibilities to contribute to the philanthropic sector, though a co-production kind of relationship with the state is likely. Due to the cooperative relationship between the state and the civil society, both the philanthrepreneurs and the government can execute complementary public and private activities for the public good.

9.3.3　The Latin or Mediterranean Model

In countries with this civil society model, such as Italy, Spain, Greece and Portugal, the relationship between the state and the (Catholic) Church is still relatively strong. The Church is dominant in the philanthropic sector. Therefore, it is difficult for individual and autonomous actors to operate in the civil society or to engage in private philanthropy. Consequently, it will be difficult for philanthrepreneurs to play a part successfully, unless they successfully integrate religious and state interests.

9.3.4　The Scandinavian Model

Scandinavian countries have historically had strong welfare states, where the civil society and philanthropy are less important for responding to public needs. Traditionally, the citizens trust in the government, expect the government to take care of the citizens, and are willing to pay high taxes. This tradition of high involvement from the state leads to a less friendly environment for philanthrepreneurs as they have little to no legitimacy to get engaged in welfare issues. However, there are opportunities in other philanthropic areas, such as environmental issues, the arts or international aid.

Table 9.1 summarizes the context based on the findings from the literature.

9.4　PHILANTHREPRENEURSHIP IN AN ANGLO-SAXON CIVIL SOCIETY MODEL: FINDINGS FROM LITERATURE

The academic knowledge of entrepreneurs' transition to philanthropy is, at least in our understanding, limited to the context of the Anglo Saxon civil society model. In this section, we will systematically assess the European academic knowledge of philanthrepreneurs from this Anglo-Saxon perspective, which we can compare with the three case studies later in this chapter.

Table 9.1 Overview of the context in the four different civil society models in Europe

Anglo-Saxon civil society model	Rhine civil society model	Scandinavian civil society model	Mediterranean civil society model
Small government	Dominant government	Dominant government	Dominant government
High public trust of private philanthropy, low public trust in government	High to moderate public trust in civil society, high trust in government	Low acceptance of private philanthropy in social welfare; high public trust in society in general and thus in government and civil society	Low public trust of private philanthropy, low trust in civil society and government
High fiscal regulation stimulation	Moderate fiscal regulation stimulation	Low fiscal regulation stimulation	Low fiscal regulation stimulation
Strong philanthropic tradition	Moderate philanthropic tradition	Moderate philanthropic tradition	Religion-based philanthropic tradition
Low government intervention in civil society	High to moderate government intervention in civil society (civil society funding partly dependent on state, societal corporatism)	High government involvement mostly in social services, civil society works alongside government (strong welfare system, high taxes)	High government involvement in civil society
High philanthrepreneur-friendly environment	Moderate philanthrepreneur-friendly environment	Low philanthrepreneur-friendly environment	Low philanthrepreneur-friendly environment

Numerous differences exist between philanthrepreneurship and other contemporary approaches to philanthropy, such as venture philanthropy and traditional forms of charitable giving. Often philanthrepreneurs are more heavily oriented towards seeking solutions that address the root causes of social problems, rather than trying to fight the symptoms (Bishop and Green, 2008; Shaw et al., 2010). It has been argued that this is caused by their experience as business entrepreneurs, which also involved the identification of creative, innovative and sustainable solutions (Shaw et al., 2013). UK-based research suggests that philanthrepreneurs have a wider variety of philanthropic interests than traditional philanthropists (Shaw et al., 2010). Philanthrepreneurs are active in one area of interest, but this area of interest varies and may include youth development, international aid, environmental sustainability, science, health, social welfare, culture, sports and religion (Shaw et al., 2010). This phenomenon seems to reflect a general difference between philanthrepreneurs and traditional European philanthropists, as the former are found to focus more heavily on global problems such as international aid or poverty reduction (Gordon, 2011). At the same time, there are also differences between the operating models of traditional philanthropists and the entrepreneurs that go beyond their areas of interest. For philanthrepreneurs, philanthropy is often yet another way to express their innovative and creative capacity as entrepreneurs. Philanthrepreneurship enables entrepreneurs to involve their innovative thinking, which can affect the established norms in the entire philanthropic sector (Steyaert and Katz, 2004).

Previous research has applied capital theory to analyze and explain the characteristics of philanthrepreneurs and their motivations for engaging in philanthropic activities, as well as the added value for recipient organizations (Bourdieu, 1986). This theory suggests that there are different forms of capital that can be used for the benefit of individuals, groups, organizations, institutions or society. Some have argued that European philanthrepreneurs possess four types of capital that, taken together, distinguish them from traditional philanthropists. Please note that in the European context (given the differences in philanthropic history, traditions and policies), the value placed on the different capitals may vary, as agency and power are found to be context-specific (Shaw et al., 2013). First, as with all philanthropists, philanthrepreneurs have a certain amount of financial capital (for example, money and assets). Additionally, philanthrepreneurs might have cultural capital as they tend to be highly educated and have certain qualifications and a certain amount of business experience (Shaw et al., 2013). Moreover, they often also have strong reputations, which can be favorable for their pursuits in philanthropy (symbolic capital). For example, their reputations can ensure that others trust their operations and decisions. Finally, philanthrepreneurs might have a relatively large network that they can use in practicing their philanthropy (social capital). Therefore, philanthrepreneurs are often able to influence societal decision-making processes, resource flows, institutional changes and public opinion, which facilitates the realization of their philanthropic goals (see, e.g., Burt, 2000).

In addition to motivating entrepreneurs to become philanthropists, these forms of capital can also be seen as the benefits that European entrepreneurs reap from becoming philanthropists. As these entrepreneurs all have a certain amount of financial resources at their disposal, the benefits they may seek by becoming philanthropists could include strengthening these and other types of capital (Harvey et al., 2011). For example, they might aim to improve their reputations, their legitimacy, or their network of influential and prominent individuals. Research has suggested that legitimization matters especially to philantrepereneurs, as they are self-conscious about their images as individuals who redistribute their wealth, as opposed to entrepreneurs who focus only on their business interests to become even wealthier (Shaw et al., 2013). Moreover, some philanthrepreneurs may desire to be recognized as part of an elite group (Harvey and Maclean, 2008; Harvey et al., 2011; Maclean et al., 2006, 2010; Ostrower, 1995).

From the perspective of organizations receiving these entrepreneurs' philanthropic support, the types of capital that the entrepreneurs possess can be of substantial value to the organizations. Philanthrepreneurs can add to their network (social capital), can train their employees, and can transfer their knowledge (cultural capital) (see also Gordon, 2011). The organization can also benefit from being affiliated with the philanthrepreneur's reputation. The philanthrepreneurs' awareness of their potential added value for recipient organizations may often be part of why they choose to engage in philanthropy. For example, contemporary Anglo-Saxon philanthrepreneurs tend to favor a partnership approach with recipient organizations. Their approaches are characterized by active investments of their resources, such as their skills, knowledge, networks and reputations. Moreover, they tend to be more selective, choosing organizations that have a higher potential for positive social returns (Harvey et al., 2011). The involvement of philanthrepreneurs with their recipient organizations can be described as an intensely iterative, interactive and engaged process (Gordon, 2011).

These characteristics of the relationship between the philanthrepreneurs and the recipient organizations also influence the strategic decision-making within the relationship. Gordon (2011) explains that, in contrast to many traditional forms of philanthropy, the decision-making processes between these parties are often based on intensive cooperation. This process starts with the joint identification of opportunities for the philanthrepreneur to develop projects that will address the root cause of a social problem with a solution that has the potential for sustainable impact, preferably one that will be fairly easy to scale. Together with the recipient organization, they will develop a proposal, which may need the approval of a foundation's board (Gordon, 2011).

This historical background and contemporary view of the tradition of European philanthropy and philanthrepreneurs indicates that institutional and contextual factors influence the possibilities for entrepreneurs to become engaged in philanthropy. Moreover, we identified four motivations based on capital theory that explain the inspiration for this transition. There is, however, limited evidence of the influence of personal experiences on the motivations of entrepreneurs to engage in philanthropy (for example, the influence of important life events). As Shaw et al. (2013) have suggested, primary inductive qualitative research is needed 'to shed further light on the complex and multiple reasons why wealthy entrepreneurs engage in philanthropy' (p. 17). Moreover, there is little in the literature about the way in which the entrepreneur organizes their philanthropic behavior, and whether this organization differs from that of other types of philanthropists. Third, we identify a gap in the literature regarding the influence of the entrepreneurs in the way in which they run their philanthropic organizations. Finally, we determine that the contemporary knowledge of philanthrepreneurs is based solely on evidence from the Anglo-Saxon perspective. Therefore, in order to further develop our understanding of contemporary European philanthrepreneurs, we develop three contemporary case studies representing the three other civil society model perspectives: from the Rhine model, the Scandinavian model and the Latin or Mediterranean model.

9.5   METHODOLOGY

9.5.1   Case Selection

We selected a purposeful sample (Easterby-Smith et al., 2002) because we wanted to include information-rich cases for our analysis. Three criteria were used to select our cases. First, the cases should focus on successful entrepreneurs who have become philanthropists during their lifetimes with the resources they have accumulated through their enterprises. Second, the philanthropic donations of these entrepreneurs must be a considerable amount on an annual basis. Third, as this chapter is fully devoted to the European perspective, we only included cases that are present in Europe.

We did not include any hybrid cases such as European philanthrepreneurs who are living in and conducting philanthropic activities in the United States or on any other continent; all cases are European-based.

9.5.2   Research Strategy and Method

As knowledge of contemporary European philanthropists is rather limited, we follow an inductive research approach. For this purpose, we follow a research strategy based on primary and secondary data. The primary data is from semi-structured interviews with three philanthrepreneurs. We conducted 35–120-minute interviews with the philanthrepreneurs, focusing on their motives to become philanthropists, the processes their foundations underwent, the focus of their endeavors and their involvement in the decision-making process. In two of the three cases, part of the interview was devoted to the philanthrepreneurs' life history, allowing the researchers to capture more complex social data and creating a holistic view with regard to the subjects of our analysis (Denzin, 2009). In the Mediterranean case, we also talked to the director of the foundation. Next, to obtain secondary data, we analyzed the foundation website and publicly available information on the entrepreneur.

9.5.3   Results

The following three cases of European philanthrepreneurs represent examples of such behavior and activity in the three models of civil society for which there is no other research: the Rhine model, the Latin or Mediterranean model, and the Scandinavian model. As such, they collectively constitute initial insights into a non-Anglo-Saxon perspective on philanthrepreneurship. Three themes are explored in each case: philanthropic motivation, which comprises the entrepreneur's inclination towards philanthropy; philanthropic focus, which comprises the intention or purpose of the entrepreneur's philanthropic efforts; and philanthropic governance, which comprises the entrepreneur's influence on the governance structures of philanthropic entities. These themes are delineated within four chronological phases of the entrepreneurs' philanthropic behavior: birth, characterized by the early philanthropic endeavors of the entrepreneur before institutionalization; growth, characterized by the amelioration of the entrepreneur's philanthropic efforts; consolidation, characterized by the stabilization and fortification of the entrepreneur's philanthropic entities; and succession, characterized by the entrepreneur's efforts to ensure philanthropic sustainability, and the entrepreneur's subsequent withdrawal.

9.5.4   Case 1: Petter Stordalen

The Norwegian entrepreneur Petter A. Stordalen started his career selling strawberries. Today he is one of the world's most prominent hotel owners and a major property developer. Through his company, Nordic Choice Hotels, Mr Stordalen owns over 170 hotels and employs roughly 12 000 people. He is a staunch environmentalist, following a triple-bottom-line philosophy in all his entrepreneurial endeavors. He pursues his philanthropic objectives together with his wife, Gunhild A. Stordalen, a medical doctor holding a PhD in orthopedic surgery.

Phase 1: birth (2011–2012)
Ever since Mr Stordalen's businesses became profitable, he has made donations to multiple initiatives as a means of sharing his good fortune. For much of that time, his donations were made in an unorganized manner and without any overarching strategy. In 2010, he married Gunhild, a long-term environmentalist with a strong belief in strategic philanthropy who wants to ensure that their philanthropic ideas and efforts are sustained indefinitely. The couple decided to combine their strengths and interest in utilizing private money as a catalyst for change. In 2011 they set up the Stordalen Foundation. Their motivation to achieve measurable outcomes through grant-giving was initiated early on when GreeNudge was established, an independent foundation that started as a core project under the Stordalen Foundation. Its objectives are to initiate and fund research measures to create behavioral change in a sustainable direction. Norway does not have a strong tradition of philanthropy and establishing private foundations, and it is not usual for philanthropists to communicate with the government upon formation. Moreover, many large-scale philanthropists remain quiet about their efforts, as large-scale philanthropy is not a topic people tend to discuss. However, Mr and Mrs Stordalen feel that they have a theme that needs some attention, and feel they have received a surprisingly positive public response.

The initial scope of the Stordalen Foundation is relatively wide but emphasizes a core focus on linking environmental issues and health issues, a marriage between the interests of both founders. The couple aim to focus on supporting projects that emphasize the co-benefits of connecting climate change with health issues in areas of human behavior such as transportation, eating habits, habitation, and so on.

Mr Stordalen played an important role in the establishment of the foundation, providing valuable input on organization structures and processes. However, he immediately transferred control of the foundation to Mrs Stordalen, who became the working chair. This reflects his entrepreneurial philosophy of trusting others with their expertise and responsibilities. He maintains a board position and has significant influence on foundation strategy, grant-giving, and supporting and structuring new foundation initiatives in their initial phases. As the chair of the Stordalen Foundation and chief executive officer (CEO) of GreeNudge, Mrs Stordalen is therefore entrusted with fulfilling both founders' philanthropic needs. Through extensive travel and board experience, the couple learn from other efforts internationally and go about supporting and initiating projects under the Stordalen Foundation flagship. At the same time, Mr and Mrs Stordalen are active in improving the sustainability of Mr Stordalen's business interests, such as Nordic Choice Hotels.

Phase 2: growth (2013–)
Mr and Mrs Stordalen's initial strong motivation to utilize their private capital as a catalyst for change is further emphasized and supported in the next phase of their philanthropic efforts. Through their experiences thus far they have developed a greater awareness of the need for a mixture of philanthropy and sustainable business, as well as a closer dialogue between public, private and nonprofit sectors in Norway.

The Stordalen Foundation's broader range of activities have been gradually streamlined to align with the core objectives of environmental issues and health issues. This strategic policy initiative was championed by Mrs Stordalen after taking the helm of the organization. In addition, the couple's entrepreneurial inclinations further focus the activities of the foundation towards private sector engagement, where sustainable business models are recognized as a necessary tool for lasting change. As such, philanthropic grants are accorded more often to sustainable business projects aimed at social innovations within the foundation objectives.

Mr Stordalen maintains his influence on the foundation through his board position, as well as through entrepreneurial advice, particularly regarding the organization's activities with private sector engagement. The couple's awareness of the potentially strategic role of philanthropy in Norway further prompts the Stordalen Foundation to collaborate more closely with public institutions such as the Department of Environment, and to initiate substantial media coverage as a means of influencing local perceptions. By becoming more open and transparent and by expanding their network and influence by taking up board positions in both nonprofit organizations (NPOs) and businesses, the couple magnifies the impact of their efforts.

Phase 3: consolidation
As the Stordalen Foundation is only a few years old, it has not yet entered a consolidation phase.

Phase 4: succession

The Stordalen Foundation will continue to focus on the intersection between environmental issues and health issues, and in its efforts demonstrate that collaboration between parties from all sectors is the proper means to the desired end. Mr and Mrs Stordalen thus envision the foundation stimulating and developing a cluster of organizations that work together to address such issues and to help build and scale sustainable business practices. They therefore believe that strategic philanthropy has a significant role in catalyzing everyone to do something.

The couple are also hopeful that the next generation of Stordalens will share their philanthropic motivations and join the board of the Stordalen Foundation, becoming increasingly involved with the operations, strategy and influence of the organization in Norwegian society. Personally, they maintain the philosophy that it is time to step down or move on once an appropriate candidate is found for their roles. Mrs Stordalen has already appointed her successor in GreeNudge, and she is hopeful that the same thing will happen when she has reached the same point in her next appointment, as it increases the sustainability of the organization and allows it to grow effectively. In any case, the couple are convinced that they will always have strong relationships with the foundation. Maintaining an entrepreneurial spirit is also important to the founders; they see a need to continuously evaluate current processes, seek new solutions and build supportive networks to allow the foundation to truly live up to its potential.

Figure 9.1 illustrates the development process of the Stordalen Foundation.

9.5.5   Case 2: Guido Giubergia

The Italian entrepreneur Guido Giubergia was always destined to follow in the footsteps of his entrepreneurial forefathers, who founded the Ersel Group in 1936 as Studio Giubergia. In 1983 it became the first mutual fund management company in Italy, and in 2000 it again led the industry in the hedge fund sector. As the CEO, Mr Giubergia is part of the third generation of family members running the company today, whose core business is asset management and highly specialized private banking services.

Phase 1: birth (1993–1998)

In 1993, Mr Giubergia arrived at a point in his life where he felt settled and wanted to give back to those who are less fortunate. His father and grandfather were always very engaged in the community and donated parts of their wealth to the local community when they encountered

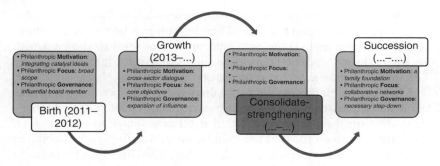

Figure 9.1   Development process, Stordalen Foundation

projects of interest. Motivated by their legacy, Mr Giubergia decided to engage in large-scale philanthropy, as he wanted to contribute something substantial. He therefore decided to organize his philanthropic endeavors formally into a foundation: the Giubergia Foundation.

In this birth phase, Mr Giubergia developed an interest in disadvantaged children and wanted to provide a future for those who are less fortunate. He argues that children are the future and wants to help them build one.

He installed a director of the foundation early on and took a seat in the board. In this way, he ensured that a qualified professional was running the foundation, but he still had some influence in the decision-making processes. The director underwent additional training, completed large-scale market research, and talked to foundations all over the world about how they run their organizations. In this phase, the foundation solely provided financial resources to the projects it supported, and operations were minimal, reflecting the difficulty that the foundation faced in grasping the complex issue it had chosen as a focus. At the same time, interaction with the state was negligible, as there was a social distrust of both state and philanthropic-based welfare interventions. In fact, it was only after five years of existence, in 1998, that the organization was officially recognized by the state as an official charitable organization that provides social value to the community.

Phase 2: growth (1998–2002)
The foundation underwent a name change from the Giubergia Foundation to the Paideia Foundation. *Paideia* refers to an ancient Greek child rearing and education system based on intellectual, moral and physical refinement, thus emphasizing an ideal member of society, and thereby developing the socialization of children within society. As such, the name fit with the mission of the organization. The name was changed for two reasons:

(1) Mr Giubergia strongly believed that the foundation should not remain just a family foundation but should develop towards becoming a community foundation; and (2) the entrepreneur did not want to show off with his philanthropic endeavors, as he was not doing it for fame but because he wanted to make a difference in society.

Based on the market research and discussions with practitioners in the child welfare sector, Mr Giubergia realized that children are extremely dependent on their families and that it takes a village to raise a child. Therefore, the main focus of the foundation shifted from merely children as the beneficiaries to also including families. The Giubergia Foundation subsequently developed and became more engaged in the community surrounding Turin. In addition, the foundation shifted from solely providing financial support to projects aligned with its objectives, to also developing programs and projects itself.

At this point in the philanthropic journey, both Mr Giubergia and the director of the foundation agreed that the Paideia Foundation should be managed as a company, striving for professionalism, efficiency and effectiveness. As such, it was influenced by Mr Giubergia's entrepreneurial background and structured along corporate lines, maintaining many typical business components such as organizational departments.

Phase 3: consolidation (2002–2013)

Mr Giubergia stressed the importance of delivering high-quality services to the community and argued that he wants the foundation to become a well-known and established foundation within its sector. It seems that he is motivated not only to do good, but also to set an excellent example in the field.

Consolidation is reflected in the acceptance of the Paideia Foundation by Italian society and other key stakeholders, a process that took 10 to 15 years to accomplish. The foundation has subsequently developed into a well-known and well-respected co-creator in the sector, particularly admired for its focus on child welfare. It has had to continuously prove itself as an important player in the sector through both its financial support as well as internal development of successful innovative projects in child welfare. Nevertheless, it is becoming clear that the organization has a reputation within the sector as a foundation that holistically addresses relevant issues through innovative, cross-discipline and cross-sector initiatives. While the focus of the organization therefore remains the same, the Paideia Foundation nevertheless experiments with increasingly collaborative and innovative efforts.

Due to the success of certain residential projects in the surrounding areas of Turin, the director and Mr Giubergia realized that they could replicate their projects in other areas in Italy. In this phase, therefore, they are not only consolidating what they have built, but also starting to expand geographically to other areas of Italy. Moreover, they recognize the importance of impact measurement, and are taking steps towards identifying the strengths and weaknesses of the organization through the development and implementation of such measurement tools. This refocuses the governance efforts towards ensuring the strategic relevance of the Paideia Foundation.

Phase 4: succession (2013–)
Mr Giubergia has invested significantly in his foundation, which represents his beliefs and ideals. As such, he expects the future leaders of the foundation to share these sentiments. This means that such leaders would share his dreams as a means of ensuring the continuity of the foundation's vision. The best way forward is therefore to inspire as many individuals and organizations as possible to commit to the foundation's cause and collaborate towards its objectives.

To this end, the foundation increasingly focuses on collaborative efforts, where multiple external parties and stakeholders are approached as a means of instilling collective ownership of child welfare. The focus therefore moves from an entrepreneurial-pioneer approach to a more social-inclusion approach of addressing the foundation's objectives.

While Mr Giubergia is still active in Ersel as the CEO, he plans to retreat and allow his daughter and son-in-law to take over. He currently spends 20 percent of his time supporting the foundation and 80 percent of his time running Ersel. In time, he hopes to reverse these commitments. This is not only because he enjoys knowing that he has helped people, but also because the director has asked him countless times to commit his social capital, cultural capital and symbolic capital to the Paideia Foundation as a means of opening as yet closed doors. His status, reputation and entrepreneurial instincts are seen as useful boosts to the organization, particularly when applied to the increasingly collaborative objectives of the organization.

In the long run, however, Mr Giubergia is convinced that the foundation should not become a family foundation. Rather, his aim is to develop the Paideia Foundation in such a way that it becomes a community foundation. This means that the Giubergia family and the Ersel company will not be the primary funders of the organization in the long run. Instead, other organizations and individuals from the community are expected to take over these functions as a means to entrench a communal disposition for child welfare. This does not mean that he is no longer interested in investing in the foundation, but rather that he would like to see the aims

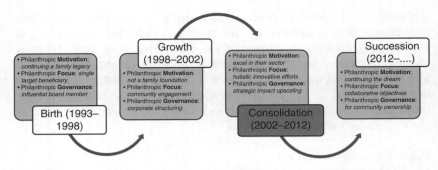

Figure 9.2   Development process, Paideia Foundation

of the Paideia Foundation become widely accepted and supported by the broader community.

9.5.6 Case 3: Paul Baan

The Dutch entrepreneur Paul Baan founded a software company, Baan Corporation, in 1987 with his brother. It made software for running corporations' internal operations and was to become one of the great success stories of the 1990s, having a highly successful initial public offering (IPO) in 1995 and competing strongly with industry powerhouses such as SAP. After Mr Baan exited the business at its peak in 2000, he applied himself full-time as the director of the Noaber Foundation.

Phase 1: birth (1994–2000)
Mr Baan believes that giving back to society is part of life, a perception that is linked to his personal norms, values and religious upbringing under the Dutch Reformed Church. However, considering his significant business obligations at this time, Mr Baan's attempt at institutionalizing his philanthropic efforts by establishing a foundation at the peak of his company's success resulted in the ad hoc funding of numerous solicitations from organizations that he felt were in need of support.

Starting with his own core competencies developed in the market, Mr Baan slowly introduced a focus on issues that can be solved through information and communication technology (ICT) to his as yet low-key and undeveloped foundation. This philanthropic focus evolved in this phase, where Mr Baan's belief that ICT can play an important role in the philanthropic sector extended towards a dedication to translating abstract ideas into workable practical solutions. His participation in a health ethics course at the Free University further directed his focus towards social issues in the fields of welfare and health care. He introduced the name 'Noaber' to the foundation, meaning 'neighborliness', thereby combining his vision on technology, ethics and collaboration.

Although Mr Baan introduced an ICT focus to Noaber Foundation projects, his time commitment to the foundation was nevertheless limited considering his overwhelming business obligations. In this phase the foundation was not yet very active and the board made most of the decisions on an ad hoc basis during their annual meetings. With the limited time he could spend on the organization, Mr Baan was able to exercise little entrepreneurial influence.

Phase 2: growth (2000–2004)
It was only when Mr Baan quit his business and committed to the foundation in 2000 that he recognized a peculiarity in the dominant logic of large-scale philanthropy: namely, the tendency of wealthy philanthropists to work really hard to earn their fortune, and then equally hard to spend it on philanthropic opportunities. Challenging this logic, he advocated for balance between philanthropy and entrepreneurship through an integrative approach which, coupled with his strong religious norms and values, propelled him towards influencing his foundation's ambitions as well as those of his children.

In line with the integrative approach of Mr Baan, the Noaber Foundation set an ambitious vision for the development of the health care sector as a whole, as well as a clear perspective of the position and role of the foundation in society and how it will be effective. Specifically, the foundation experimented with projects that were structured as investments and demanded intense involvement: venture philanthropy. This approach was adopted to advance Mr Baan's ambitions to include entrepreneurial models in philanthropy practices and as a means to tackle entrenched silo thinking in the health care sector. In addition, realizing that legitimacy was necessary to command a license to operate, Mr Baan entered into an intensive dialogue with the Dutch government on philanthropic foundation legislation, arguing for venture philanthropy adjustments that would allow foundations to make investments aligned with their mission where returns are reinvested into social initiatives.

In this phase, Mr Baan dedicated himself fully to actively running the Noaber Foundation, taking control of all aspects of its operations. He started with a grand research expedition in Europe and the United States, visiting large foundations and assessing their philanthropic models. Shocked by the extent to which entrepreneurial thinking is lacking in the sector, Mr Baan recognized that his entrepreneurial competencies were vital to effectively address the complexity of social issues. He set about applying his entrepreneurial inclinations within the foundation, looking for opportunities to integrate his expertise with his philanthropic ambitions as a means to deliver real change in society.

Phase 3: consolidation (2004–2013)

Every decision Mr Baan makes is now motivated by a more strategic approach after learning about venture philanthropy from US counterparts. Health care and aging in particular have become more central in his life, gaining urgency from personal experiences with the health care system. In addition, Mr Baan has turned back to entrepreneurship through his philanthropic convictions and established numerous parallel yet affiliated initiatives aimed at relieving stress in the Dutch health care system.

Due to these developments in Mr Baan's personal life, the focus of the Noaber Foundation has further converged towards health and aging. The foundation is particularly active in facilitating the transition from a 'treatment system' to a 'prevention system' that will alleviate current system stress resulting from a demand surplus, as well as counter national welfare support withdrawal trends. Institutional changes regarding the boundaries of the philanthropic sector are required to fully realize the foundation's potential, and the low-key Noaber Foundation therefore continues its dialogue with the Dutch government. In this phase, it is campaigning for legislation that will allow philanthropic organizations to facilitate the aforementioned shift and address emerging social issues. These efforts ensure that social impact is becoming the leading objective of the Noaber Foundation.

Multiple structural changes occurred to accommodate both the principal social impact objective as well as Mr Baan's personal circumstances. In 2004, he relegated active leadership of the Noaber Foundation but stayed involved on the board, moving into a bigger-picture role and triggering a process of management professionalization. Moreover, the foundation restructured into two divisions: Philanthropy, which donates funds to 'impact-only' nonprofit initiatives; and Ventures, which invests funds in 'impact-first' nonprofit or for-profit initiatives that are likely to deliver a return.

Phase 4: succession (2013–)

The question of succession is becoming increasingly important to Mr Baan, who is mindful of his aging capabilities. He deeply values and enjoys the involvement of his children in his philanthropic endeavors and therefore wants them to become more active in the Noaber Foundation as well as his other affiliated organizations, but without neglecting his own areas of interest. He is therefore mapping their interests and ideas to balance

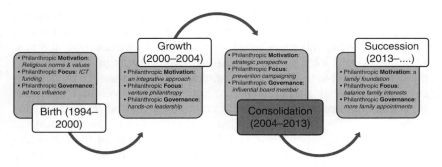

Growth
(2000–2004)

• Philanthropic **Motivation**:
  Religious norms & values
• Philanthropic **Focus**: *ICT
  funding*
• Philanthropic **Governance**:
  ad hoc influence

• Philanthropic **Motivation**:
  an integrative approach
• Philanthropic **Focus**:
  venture philanthropy
• Philanthropic **Governance**:
  hands-on leadership

Birth (1994–
2000)

• Philanthropic **Motivation**:
  strategic perspective
• Philanthropic **Focus**:
  prevention campaigning
• Philanthropic **Governance**:
  influential board member

Succession
(2013–....)

• Philanthropic **Motivation**: *a
  family foundation*
• Philanthropic **Focus**:
  balance family interests
• Philanthropic **Governance**:
  more family appointments

Consolidation
(2004–2013)

Figure 9.3   Development process, Noaber Foundation

them with his own and thus ensure a smooth transition of leadership and ownership.

Although the Noaber Foundation has deeply embedded its objective of generating social impact through venture philanthropy, facilitating the potential succession of Mr Baan by his children requires more focus area flexibility to accommodate their varied philanthropic interests. While the current focus remains the health care sector, therefore, the foundation must start to balance family members' interests in new sectors in order to expedite their involvement.

Making the foundation sustainable for multiple family generations is Mr Baan's aspiration. Indeed, in all phases of his philanthropic endeavors he has included his family by constructing governance and advisory positions within either the Noaber Foundation or its affiliate organizations that allow them to use their talents optimally and fulfill their philanthropic ambitions. Mr Baan has a large family of 11 children and 18 grandchildren of whom many, including his wife, eldest son and two daughters, are already incorporated into the foundation. The sustainability of the foundation is further assured with the professionalization of senior management through new incoming leadership that directly follows Mr Baan's transfer to a more supervisory position on the board.

9.6   ANALYSIS AND DISCUSSION

Before discussing the main themes, the cases show interesting additional information which we did not anticipate. We were able to create figures that show a clear process towards philanthrepreneurship occurring for each entrepreneur entering the philanthropic sector. This process has been categorized into the four chronological phases of entrepreneurs' philanthropic behavior: birth, growth, consolidation and succession. This is used as a means of delineating the progression of philanthropic motivation, focus and governance over time. This demarcation was possible through the identification of distinct habits occurring in each phase, mainly attributable to the developing motivations of the entrepreneurs as represented by their philanthropic time commitments. As such, the entrepreneurs would more or less form a preliminary interest in philanthropy in the birth phase, commit themselves to their philanthropic ambitions in the growth phase, secure their philanthropic endeavors in the consolidation phase, and ensure the continuity of their philanthropic interests in the succession phase. Importantly, however, not all interviewed entrepreneurs had progressed through all of the phases, as can be seen in Figures 9.1, 9.2 and 9.3 where their current phases are marked in dark gray. This further emphasizes the fact that an entrepreneur's engagement with philanthropy is very much a process. Moreover, besides cumulatively forming an entrepreneur's philanthropic life-cycle, these chronological habits also influence clear philanthropic motivation, focus and governance patterns within these phases; the descriptions in the accompanying case figures refer to progressions in these philanthropic themes. These patterns are further alluded to in the following section where the continental European cases above are compared to the current Anglo-Saxon literature understanding of philanthrepreneurs. Below we constitute the philanthropic motivation, philanthropic focus and philanthropic governance for each case and turn to an analysis and discussion of the similarities and differences across these cases as well as with the literature case, the Anglo-Saxon philanthrepreneur. Table 9.2 provides an overview of the main findings per category. Our objective here is to determine the extent to which European philanthrepreneurs are distinguishable, as a means to ascertaining an accurate profile of such individuals in Europe.

9.6.1 Motivation

We found that all the entrepreneurs from the three cases were motivated to engage with philanthropy more or less at the time that they felt secure in their respective business endeavors. This seemingly universal attribute might also explain their inclination towards utilizing philanthropy as a means to create lasting change. That is, the philanthrepreneurs seemed to envision themselves as strong change agents, being very much aware of the utility of their cultural, financial, social and symbolic capital. Mr Baan and his Noaber Foundation, for example, have dedicated much of their time and energy to lobbying the Dutch government for regulation changes in the nonprofit sector. Similarly, Mr Stordalen and Mr Giubergia are

Table 9.2 *Similarities and differences between European philanthrepreneurs*

	Philanthrepreneur in Anglo-Saxon model	Philanthrepreneur in Rhine model	Philanthrepreneur in Scandinavian model	Philanthrepreneur in Mediterranean model
Motivation	Strong drive for lasting change No information on influence of personal experiences or interests	Strong drive for lasting change Personal experiences determine beneficiary	Strong drive for lasting change Personal experiences determine beneficiary	Strong drive for lasting change Personal interests determine beneficiary
	Link between philanthropic interest and business interest	Link between philanthropic interest and business interest	Link between philanthropic interest and business interest	Link between philanthropic interest and business interest
Focus	Address root causes of social problems Focus on global problems	Address root causes of social problems Focus on local problems	Address root causes of social problems Focus on global and local problems	Address root causes of social problems Focus on local problems

Table 9.2 (continued)

	Philanthrepreneur in Anglo-Saxon model	Philanthrepreneur in Rhine model	Philanthrepreneur in Scandinavian model	Philanthrepreneur in Mediterranean model
Governance	Little knowledge of involvement of philantrepreneur in organization	Intensive involvement of philanthrepreneur in organization	Low involvement of philanthrepreneurs in organization	Moderate involvement of philanthrepreneur in organization
	High value of philanthrepreneur's alternative capital: cultural, symbolic, social	High value of philanthrepreneur's alternative capital: cultural, social	High value of philanthrepreneur's alternative capital: cultural, symbolic, social	High value of philanthrepreneur's alternative capital: symbolic, social
	No information on organizational structure	Holding organization, Corporate-divisional structure	Holding organization, Corporate-horizontal structure	Single organization, Corporate-functional structure
Contextual influence	Philanthropic sector counterweight to the state	Philanthropic sector cooperates with the state	Philanthropic sector supplements the state	Philanthropic sector competes with the state
	High independence from government	High independence from government	Low or high independence from government, depending on social issue	Low independence from government

both emphatic supporters of their respective foundations' objectives, often trying to influence public policy and social change in their countries. This implies, therefore, that having reached their entrepreneurial or personal goals, such philanthrepreneurs subsequently seek to tackle new issues in a new sector by applying their entrepreneurial spirit and vigor.

However, the shift is not entirely intrinsic, nor is it immediate. Indeed, extrinsic stimuli such as (early) life circumstances influence the entrepreneur to progressively engage with philanthropy. While this is a gap in the literature on Anglo-Saxon philanthrepreneurs, our exploratory research indicates that personal circumstances can be a vital driver of philanthropic behavior amongst entrepreneurs. This is reflected in all case studies where religious norms and values (Mr Baan), personal convictions (Mr Stordalen) or parental influence (Mr Giubergia) caused the entrepreneurs to initiate their philanthropic behavior. Later, actual life experiences motivated their choice of beneficiaries, particularly around the time that they decide to institutionalize their philanthropic efforts through the formation of foundations. For Mr Baan, for example, the impetus to focus on health care came from his personal experience with providers as well as an educational program that he enrolled in. For Mr Stordalen, it was his marriage to Mrs Stordalen that prompted a focus on environmental issues, a cause that he was not altogether unfamiliar with. Only Mr Giubergia's desire to aid disadvantaged children was not explained through personal experience. Rather, it is a personal interest. Nevertheless, it supports the implication that life events, circumstances and personal experience or interests are significant underlying forces that propel the entrepreneur towards the philanthropic sector and influence the motivation for particular beneficiaries.

Finally, as shown in Table 9.2, there also seems to be a link between the philanthropic interest of each entrepreneur and their respective business interests. Mr Stordalen, for example, introduced environmental sustainability practices in his hotel chains and other businesses which mutually enforces his philanthropic objectives. Mr Baan, on the other hand, initially wanted to pursue ICT-related philanthropy as it related to his business competencies. For Mr Giubergia, however, no link was found. Nevertheless, these findings imply that entrepreneurs make calculated risks even in philanthropy once they have institutionalized their efforts, starting first in topic areas that they are familiar with from business experiences, or by applying competencies that they have forged from business experiences.

9.6.2 Focus

When looking at the philanthropic focus of the entrepreneurs, Table 9.2 shows that in all of the cases the philanthrepreneurs chose to address the root causes of the social problems their respective foundations tackled, rather than simply alleviating the symptoms. Such a strategic approach to philanthropy probably stems from their business experiences and is in line with findings from Anglo-Saxon philanthrepreneurs.

When looking at the philanthropic interests of each individual entrepreneur, however, we see the first divergence from the current literature's understanding of philanthrepreneurs: namely, the entrepreneurs' concentration on local problems. Literature shows that philanthrepreneurs tend to focus on global problems (see Gordon, 2011) rather than local ones. Yet our cases clearly indicate that continental European philanthrepreneurs confront issues locally. This is true for all three entrepreneurs, although the Stordalen Foundation also incorporates global efforts into its objectives. This is an interesting point of divergence within continental European philanthrepreneurs, as the Stordalen Foundation is the youngest of the three foundations studied. This means that Mr Baan and Mr Guibergia have chosen to retain the national objectives of their respective foundations through all successive stages of their philanthropic endeavors. While this may be generational – Mr Stordalen is also the youngest entrepreneur – it is more likely to be influenced by personal preferences and the development of the foundation. As mentioned in the literature on the Scandinavian civil society model (see MacDonalds and Tayart de Borms, 2008; Hartnell, 2008), the high involvement of the state often forces philanthrepreneurs to focus on non-welfare issues such as environmental issues or international aid. There is therefore a clear separation from the Anglo-Saxon philanthrepreneur, but also a potential division between continental European philanthrepreneurs due to the context (for example, the civil society model) in which they operate. Moreover, it seems that the phase of the philanthropy life-cycle also influences the entrepreneur's scope of interest. For example, both Mr Baan and Mr Giubergia also experimented in their birth phase with global issues, wanting to address problems on a large scale. After increasing their involvement in their respective foundations, however, they recognized that local manifestations of such issues were equally complex, and narrowed their scope to a local or national level. It could be, then, that Mr Stordalen will also move towards a more national scope as he and his foundation progress through the philanthropy life-cycle phases.

9.6.3   Governance

The degree of intensity of involvement of the philanthrepreneur among our cases varied depending on the phase of the philanthropy life-cycle each entrepreneur was in, as well as their level of business involvement. In the first birth phase, for example, all of the cases showed minimal interaction with their foundations, each choosing instead to focus on their business interests. However, once business interests faded and the entrepreneurs dedicated more time to their foundations, the level of cooperation magnified. Mr Baan, for example, who is in the succession phase, has committed 100 percent of his time to the Noaber Foundation, but is now tapering down his involvement to allow his family members to become more engaged. This may indicate that for family-oriented philanthrepreneurs the intensity of cooperation builds under the growth and consolidation phases, but then lessens during the succession phase. On the other hand, Mr Giubergia, who is in the consolidation phase and whose foundation is not family-oriented, currently commits 80 percent of his time to the Paideia Foundation and 20 percent to his business; a commitment which is expected to increase over time as his children take on more responsibilities in his business. Only Mr Stordalen currently maintains a lower degree of involvement with his foundation. He does so for two reasons: (1) he is still very much involved with his business interests; and (2) he has delegated responsibility of his philanthropic ambitions to his wife, who runs the Stordalen Foundation on a day-to-day basis. Nevertheless, Mr Stordalen is still actively involved through the board, as explained in the case. Overall, therefore, we observe that both the stage of the philanthropic life-cycle of the philanthrepreneur as well as the degree of business involvement are important in determining the degree of involvement of philanthrepreneurs in the philanthropic entity. In any case, all three philanthrepreneurs exercise significant influence on the governance and decision-making of their respective foundations, whether on a day-to-day basis as a director or through a position on the board.

Regardless of the level of intensity of involvement, however, it is clear from the findings that the foundations highly value their benefactors' alternative capital, as shown in Table 9.2. This is a unanimous sentiment across all cases. Mr Giubergia, for example, has been asked countless times by the director of the Paideia Foundation to commit his social, cultural and symbolic capital as a means of opening as yet closed doors. For this reason alone it is in the interest of each foundation to be able to utilize their benefactors' alternative capital. However, it depends on whether such capital is provided to the foundation, which in turn depends on how much or how valued such alternative capital is of the entrepreneur in question and how comfortable they are in exploiting such capital for philanthropy. Multiple factors influence the strength of alternative capital, including, amongst others: life experience, business experience and context. For Mr Baan, for example, the Noaber Foundation capitalizes on his social and cultural capital but less so on his symbolic capital, which may be due to the fact that it is not commonly accepted to 'stand out' in Dutch society. The same is true for the Paideia Foundation's use of Mr Giubergia's alternative capital, which is a conscientious choice of the founder to restrict personal reputational benefits, but may also be due to the fact that most Italians are skeptical of private philanthropist motivations. The Stordalen Foundation, on the other hand, fully capitalizes on all aspects of Mr Stordalen's alternative capital as he has worked hard to draw attention to all three through media exposure concerning his business and personal experiences. Interestingly, Mr Stordalen may be doing so as a means of overcoming or compensating for the lack of a philanthropic tradition in Norway, thereby pioneering a positive public image of private philanthropy. In all cases, therefore, it seems that cultural and social capital is always bestowed on philanthropic endeavors. Entrepreneurs are more cautious with their symbolic capital, however, when related to their philanthropic efforts. Although the added value for foundations of alternative capital is therefore highly dependent on a number of factors, continental European philanthrepreneurs often choose to actively invest their resources, such as skills, knowledge, network and reputation, for the benefit of their respective foundations, which is in line with the Anglo-Saxon philanthrepreneur (see e.g. Shaw et al., 2013).

Unfortunately, the gap in current literature on the organizational structures of philanthrepreneurs makes it impossible to distinguish European philanthrepreneurs as different from the current Anglo-Saxon literature understanding. However, the structures of Mr Baan's foundation and Mr Stordalen's foundation are very similar to each other, and collectively different from that of Mr Giubergia's foundation. The former two use a holding-company structure where their foundations have ownership of affiliate organizations, whether nonprofit or for-profit, while Mr Giubergia's foundation is a single organization without affiliates or subsidiaries. This implies that organizational structures of non-Anglo-Saxon philanthrepreneurs have at least some level of divergence, yet how akin they are to Anglo-Saxon philanthrepreneurs is still indeterminable. The reasons behind this variation in structure are difficult to pinpoint but can generally be attributed to each philanthrepreneur's personal philosophy on management as developed from their entrepreneurial experiences. Mr Baan, for example, mentioned the creation of two divisions within the Noaber Foundation as a means to capitalize effectively on his two approaches to philanthropy: 'impact-only' (grant-making) and 'impact-first' (venture philanthropy). Similarly, Mr Giubergia stated that it was clear early on that he wanted to structure his foundation like his business: along departmental lines, where each department could concentrate on effectively executing a particular function. Mrs Stordalen also commented on Mr Stordalen's structural philosophy, indicating that he preferred flatter organizations where the work environment is based on trust and responsibility.

9.6.4 Context

According to the literature review, in Europe there should be a difference in the way philanthropy in general is executed due to the different civil society models. For example, we concluded that the Anglo-Saxon model is a highly philanthrepreneur-friendly environment due to the role of philanthropy in society and the small government and high fiscal regulation stimulation, among other factors. Next, the Rhine model is a moderately philanthrepreneur-friendly environment, because of the high involvement of the state in social issues. At the same time, philanthropy is widely recognized within society as an important institution that works collaboratively with government. Lastly, we concluded that both the Scandinavian model as well as the Mediterranean civil society model are less philanthrepreneur-friendly environments. This is mainly due to different circumstances in each country, but in both countries the state is very dominant.

Interestingly, we see little influence of the context of the civil society models on the way the philanthrepreneurs execute their philanthropy in our cases. Nonetheless, we do see a different relationship to the state. In the Anglo-Saxon-based literature we see that philanthropy and philanthrepreneurs are acting as a counterweight to the state. In the cases, however, we see differences in the three different examples in the models. First, in the Dutch case, the state is an important stakeholder to take into account, and the philanthrepreneur is trying to collaborate with both private and public organizations. In the Norwegian case, we clearly see that the philanthrepreneur is active alongside what the government is providing. The government is mainly active in social services, while the philanthrepreneur is active in environmental issues. Where this bridges into the theme of health, there is a dialogue with the government and public to influence their behavior. They are not excluding them, rather they acknowledge them as an important stakeholder. Lastly, we argue that in the Italian case the philanthrepreneur is active in the same sector and similar social issues as the government. As such, the philanthrepreneur is convinced that service provision can and should be more effective and efficient. Nonetheless, because of the dominance of the government in that civil society model, the philanthrepreneur is bound to collaborate to a certain extent with public agencies. Nevertheless, we argue that in that civil society model, the philanthrepreneur is competing with the state. This may be explained in part by the philanthrepreneur's significant independence from the government. In fact, due to the strong capitals they all possess (cultural, social, symbolic and financial) they can operate very independently from any other actor in society. In other words, because of their fortunes, the foundations are not dependent on any other source of capital. The philanthrepreneurs' reputation, network, business experience and financial capacity allow them to have much freedom in how they run the organization within the given legislation in their country. Besides legislation and the relationship with the government, we find little contextual influences in any of these cases. We do see them on a detailed level, but not on a generalizable level – not to the extent that we can say that continental European philanthrepreneurs are different than Anglo-Saxon philanthrepreneurs. Similar to the context, on the level of motivation, focus and governance, we also see small differences between the philanthrepreneurs on a detailed level, but again it seems that there are no significantly distinguishable attributes between the cases that would warrant a designation of different types of European philanthrepreneurs outside the current Anglo-Saxon literature understanding.

Stemming from the above outlined analysis and discussion, it seems that philanthrepreneurs are a distinct flavor among philanthropists. It seems that they are potentially a subgroup within philanthropists. It is seen that they are keen on having a business-like approach within their foundations, and are highly cooperative with market and even public organizations in most cases. Moreover, they all strive to be innovative and creative social agents, using their capital to catalyze their goals. These similarities in approach potentially can be explained by what is called 'isomorphism' (DiMaggio and Powell, 1983): the tendency of organizations to become more similar as a result of resembling organizations under similar constraints. We distinguish two types of isomorphism which seem to occur particularly in the (sub)group of philanthrepreneurs.

First, mimetic isomorphism, in which an organization imitates the structure of other established organizations because the organization thinks that the organization will be beneficial. All the philanthrepreneurs talked to (successful) other philanthrepreneurial foundations, which inspired them to govern their organization accordingly. Second, normative isomorphism, or professionalization, in which the tendency of organizations is to hire people from within the same industry, from a narrow range of training institutions, through common promotion practices, and from skill-level requirements for particular jobs (DiMaggio and Powell, 1983: 152). Typical for philanthrepreneurs is that all foundations combine employees from the business and the nonprofit sector, each hired to excel in their field and bring unique insights to the foundation. For example, in the case of the Noaber Foundation, Mr Baan included venture investments specialists along with people who are known within the health care sector. Both the Italian and the Dutch cases also indicate that the foundations are run by directors who have experience in the field, which complements the expertise of the entrepreneur.

9.7 CONCLUSION AND SUGGESTIONS FOR FUTURE RESEARCH

This chapter has described philanthrepreneurs' motivation, focus and governance in different European civil society models. We argue that philanthrepreneurs are a distinct flavor in contemporary philanthropy as they have an unique way of approaching philanthropy. The main finding of this chapter is that there are many similarities between the philanthrepreneurs. In conclusion, all philanthrepreneurs have a strong drive for lasting change and are guided towards philanthropic areas of interest through personal experiences. In addition, most philanthropic efforts of philanthrepreneurs are, at least initially, linked in some way to their business interests. In addition, they share the communality of addressing the root cause of social issues rather than their symptoms, a seemingly universal attribute of philanthrepreneurs' work. However, continental European philanthrepreneurs tend to concentrate on local rather than global issues, as opposed to their Anglo-Saxon counterparts, even though they address both global and local issues in the initial phase. Moreover, it seems that European philanthrepreneurs exercise a strong influence on the governance of the organization by investing their alternative capital. However, we do see a slight divergence in organizational structures despite the common corporate structure approach. This is postulated to be caused by the personal philosophy of each philanthrepreneur as influenced by their business experiences or philanthropic sector research, rather than by context, and is therefore also likely to differ on a case-by-case basis. We speculate that a larger sample of philanthrepreneurs would have resulted in an equally diverse range of organizational structures, regardless of context. Moreover, due to the increase in the transparency and accessibility of information around the globe, the way entrepreneurs pursue their philanthropic activities has become more similar, potentially leading to isomorphism. As such, this potentially might lead to a universal European philanthrepreneur. Interestingly, we have also concluded that although the different society models do influence philanthropy in general within the different models (as discussed in the literature review), we have little indication that it influences philanthrepreneurs and their activities, besides their relationships with the state.

We acknowledge that this chapter should be seen as explorative research in a phenomenon which is highly under-researched by academics. We are well aware that our research is based on mainly secondary data and complemented with three primary data sources. We have many suggestions for future research; one of the main suggestions is to look into the process in more depth. In this chapter, we briefly presented a process of development for the motivation, focus and governance throughout the development of the foundations. It would be interesting to set up a more longitudinal research study on the long-term development process of the philanthropic activities, as we were only able to look in retrospect at this process. Also, it would be interesting to look into examples of countries in which philanthropy does not have a strong tradition, such as countries in Eastern Europe. Until the mid-twentieth century, communist regimes were prevalent in these countries. These regimes did not allow any philanthropic activity, as the state was the only actor of importance. It was even forbidden under the communist regime to pursue any philanthropic activity. In the last few decades, these countries have been rapidly building their civil society and therefore it would be of interest to look into those countries and how that develops. Even more interesting in light of this book is the role of entrepreneurs in building civil society and, consequently, a philanthropic tradition.

NOTE

*   We would like to thank Sander Fleuren for his support and helpful insights to develop this chapter. Furthermore, we would like to thank Gian Paolo Barbetta for his support in selecting the Mediterranean case.

REFERENCES

Acs, Z.J. (2003), 'Entrepreneurial capitalism: If America leads will Europe follow?', *Journal of Small Business and Enterprise Development*, 10(1), 113–117.

Anheier, Helmut K. (ed.) (2001), 'Foundations in Europe: A comparative perspective', Centre for Civil Society, London School of Economics and Political Science.

Bishop, Matthew and Michael Green (2008), *Philanthrocapitalism: How Giving Can Save the World*, London: A. & C. Black.

Bourdieu, Pierre (1986), 'The forms of capital', in John G. Richardson (ed.), *Handbook of Theory and Research for the Sociology of Education*, New York: Greenwood, pp. 241–258.

Burt, R.S. (2000), 'The network structure of social capital', *Research in Organizational Behavior*, 22, 345–423.

Cantaluppi, Anna and David Watkiss (2008), 'Compagnia di San Paolo', in Norine MacDonald and Luc Tayart de Borms (eds), *Philanthropy in Europe. A Rich Past, a Promising Future*, London: Alliance Publishing Trust, pp. 53–68.

Defourny, J. and M. Nyssens (2010), 'Conceptions of social enterprise and social entrepreneurship in Europe and the United States: Convergences and divergences', *Journal of Social Entrepreneurship*, 1(1), 32–53.

Denzin, Norman K. (ed.) (2009), *The Research Act: A Theoretical Introduction to Sociological Methods*, Piscataway, NJ: Transaction Publishers.

DiMaggio, P.J. and W.W. Powell (1983), 'The iron cage revisited institutional isomorphism and collective rationality in organizational fields', *Advances in Strategic Management*, 17, 143–166.

Easterby-Smith, Mark, Richard Thorpe and Andy Low (2002), *Management Research: An Introduction*, London: Sage Publications.

Gordon, Jillian C. (2011), 'Power, wealth and entrepreneurial philanthropy in the new global economy', Doctoral dissertation, University of Strathclyde.

Häberlein, Mark (2012), *The Fuggers of Augsburg: Pursuing Wealth and Honor in Renaissance Germany*, Charlottesville, VA: University of Virginia Press.

Hartnell, C. (2008), 'European foundations' support for civil society: A means to an end or an end in itself?' in Nurine MacDonald and Luc Tayart de Borms (eds), *Philanthropy in Europe. A Rich Past, a Promising Future*, London: Alliance Publishing Trust, pp. 245–258.

Harvey, C. and K. Maclean (2008), 'Capital theory and the dynamics of elite business networks in Britain and France', *Sociological Review*, 56(1), 103–120.

Harvey, C., M. Maclean, J. Gordon and E. Shaw (2011), 'Andrew Carnegie and the foundations of contemporary entrepreneurial philanthropy', *Business History*, 53(3), 425–450.

Heerma van Voss, L. and M.H. Van Leeuwen (2012), 'Charity in the Dutch Republic: An introduction', *Continuity and Change*, 27(2), 175–197.

Heuss, Theodor, Susan Gillespie and Jennifer Kapczinsky (1994), *Robert Bosch: His Life and Achievements*, New York: Henry Holt & Co.

Jordan, W.K. (1961), 'The English background of modern philanthropy', *American Historical Review*, 66(2), 401–408.

Krugman, Paul R. (2009), *The Conscience of a Liberal: Reclaiming America from the Right*, London: Penguin.

Landes, David S., Joel Mokyr and William J. Baumol (eds) (2012), *The Invention of Enterprise: Entrepreneurship from Ancient Mesopotamia to Modern Times*, Princeton, NJ: Princeton University Press.

MacDonalds, Norine and Luc Tayart de Borms (2008), *Philanthropy in Europe. A Rich Past, a Promising Future*, London: Alliance Publishing Trust.

Maclean, M., C. Harvey and R. Chia (2010), 'Dominant corporate agents and the power elite in France and Britain', *Organization Studies*, 31(3), 327–348.

Maclean, M., C. Harvey and J. Gordon (2013), 'Social innovation, social entrepreneurship and the practice of contemporary entrepreneurial philanthropy', *International Small Business Journal*, 31(7), 747–763.

Maclean, Mairi, Charles Harvey and John Press (2006), *Business Elites and Corporate Governance in France and the UK*, London: Palgrave Macmillan.

OECD (2003), 'Philanthropic foundations and development co-operation', Off-print of the DAC Journal, 4(3), 1–80.

Ostrower, Francie (1995), *Why the Wealthy Give: The Culture of Elite Philanthropy*, Princeton, NJ: Princeton University Press.

Rey, M. and N. Puig (2010), 'Understanding the organized philanthropic activity of entrepreneurial families', *Business and Economic History*, 8, 1–30.

Robbins, Kevin C. (2006), 'The nonprofit sector in historical perspective: Traditions of philanthropy in the West', in Walter W. Powell and Richard Steinberg (eds), *The Nonprofit Sector: A Research Handbook*, New Haven, CT: Yale University Press, pp. 13–31.

Safely, Thomas M. (1997), *Charity and Economy in the Orphanages of Early Modern Ausburg*, Boston, MA: Humanities Press International.

Shaw, E., J. Gordon, C. Harvey and K. Henderson (2010), 'Entrepreneurial philanthropy: Theoretical antecedents and empirical analysis of economic, social, cultural and symbolic capital', *Frontiers of Entrepreneurship Research*, 30(7), 6.

Shaw, E., J. Gordon, C. Harvey and M. Maclean (2013), 'Exploring contemporary entrepreneurial philanthropy', *International Small Business Journal*, 31(5), 580–599.

Steyaert, C. and J. Katz (2004), 'Reclaiming the space of entrepreneurship on society: Geographical, discursive and social dimensions', *Entrepreneurship and Regional Development*, 16(3), 179–196.

Teeuwen, D. (2012), 'Collections for the poor: Monetary charitable donations in Dutch towns, c. 1600–1800', *Continuity and Change*, 27(2), 271–299.

10. A study of Chinese entrepreneurs and philanthropic behavior*

Shuming Zhao, Xiaoming Bai and Yixuan Zhao

10.1 INTRODUCTION

With the rapid growth of the Chinese economy over the last three decades, the Chinese people are beginning to become more involved in philanthropic activities and other public services, especially entrepreneurs. Entrepreneurs have a great deal of wealth and other resources and are, therefore, better equipped to take on social responsibility and promote its development in Chinese society as a whole. For example, many entrepreneurs[1] have begun paying attention especially to the needs of their hometowns or regions of birth, educational development in rural areas, religious and cultural development, as well as development of public utilities and infrastructure in those areas. Entrepreneurs have invested and have played a very important role in the rescue process after natural disasters, including earthquakes, hurricanes and tsunamis. Philanthropy is considered an important part of the redistribution of resources, transferring wealth from the rich to the poor, and promoting the development of the society toward being more harmonious and balanced (Yan and Zhu, 2008).

10.2 THE TRADITIONAL CHINESE CULTURE OF 'KINDNESS'

The concept of 'kindness' is deeply rooted in Chinese traditional culture (Zhou, 2013a). This societal value is so deeply embedded in Chinese culture that people are said to be 'born' to devote human and financial resources to philanthropic activities. Entrepreneurs have contributed significantly to the overall development of Chinese society, contributed to educational support, and provided assistance for the Qinghai Province and the Wenchuan[2] earthquakes in Sichuan Province, China. In these and other ways, entrepreneurs demonstrate the tendency to be 'kind' with their philanthropic actions.

Traditional Chinese culture originated with a combination of Confucianism, Taoism and Buddhism. Teachings from these three philosophies have had great influence on the thought and behavior of Chinese people. All three philosophies encourage people to do good deeds. The motivation behind individuals' gestures of kindness may be a desire to help others. Their motivation for kindness may also be for their own benefit. Or instincts for kindness may stem from both motivations (Wang, 2011).

In traditional Chinese culture, the concept of 'being kind to others' includes the ideas of seeking harmony between man and nature, as well as trying to help the poor. There is a deep traditional virtue and a humanitarian spirit in the connections among these three aspects of the culture. In China's modern commercial civilization, China's merchants in the Fujian and Shanxi regions played an important role when faced with natural disasters by providing people with a great deal of help and support, actions which reflect the traditional Chinese pursuit of 'kindness' (Zhao, 2007).

10.2.1 Benefiting Other People

Being charitable to others is part of traditional Chinese culture. There is a Chinese saying that people should 'perform a good deed every day to accumulate kindness and virtue'. The broader understanding of the 'kindness' concept contributes to the Chinese people's sense of responsibility and mission. Entrepreneurs stepping up to assume the mantle of social responsibility to some extent is driven by the concept of 'justice and benefit' in Confucian culture. Indeed, the 'justice and benefit relationship' derives from the core of Confucian culture (Liu, 2010). A similar saying, 'Just do good deeds, do not ask for the future', appears in the book, *The Wisdom of Ancient Aphorisms* (Che Wanyu, Qing Dynasty period). The proverb refers to doing good deeds in the moment and not considering the impact of doing the good deed on oneself.

A saying from *The Works of Mencius: Gong Sun Chou* says that everyone has sympathy. Sympathy means that if one sees a child about to fall into a well, even if one is not the child's parent, one should try to save the child. In this effort, the individual should eschew personal motivations such as using the opportunity to make friends with the child's parents, attempting to enhance one's reputation among their friends, or helping the child because they dislike hearing the child's cry. An individual who does not act to save the child lacks a heart of mercy and, therefore, is not 'human'. Mencius thinks that whether a person has 'sympathy' is an important standard in distinguishing between human and inhuman. This idea deeply influences individuals' outlooks in China. Therefore, in traditional Chinese culture, people cannot bear to see others suffer. There is a deep-seated belief that individuals need to give help and support when they see the needs of those poorer than them.

In China, there is a Confucian ideology about 'cultivating oneself, bringing order to the family, governing the country, and bringing peace to all'. Philanthropic actions can greatly contribute to the cultivation of one's moral values, improve one's personal character, and contribute to the purpose of 'cultivating oneself'. At the same time, philanthropic actions help others gain the 'basic necessities of life' and live in peace. Philanthropic actions achieve the personal goal of 'bringing peace to all'. Under the influence of traditional ideological 'kindness', donors often want to help the most people who need help, rather than just benefit only a few people. This ideology also includes the concept of 'benevolence and the world in great harmony', which greatly influenced the development of Chinese philanthropic ethics (Zhou and Zeng, 2007a; Zhou, 2011).

10.2.2   Benefiting Oneself

The concept of 'kindness' in the traditional Chinese culture does not preclude the objective of benefiting oneself (Huang et al., 2011). In Buddhism, there is the concept of 'karma'. Karma refers to one's personal experiences, the situation that one faces, and what one faces as the result of everything one has done. This concept of karma has influenced Chinese society and traditional culture enormously (Gong, 1999; Chen, 2004). Retribution refers to the good and bad things one has done in life, and the corresponding reward or punishment that one will receive. This concept, as noted, has great influence on Chinese society and may provide a good interpretation of retribution. For example, the saying, 'Virtuous deeds will receive rewards, evil deeds will be given evils', is similar to the American and Canadian phrases, 'What goes around comes around', meaning that anything one does will have consequences. This reflects the concept of 'kindness' in regards to benefiting oneself. 'Virtuous deeds' means that one has to conduct good deeds in order to accumulate merits; this not only brings good luck to oneself, it also can bring blessings to one's family (Yang and Zhang, 2008). The concept of karma is mentioned in Taoism (Zhou and Zeng, 2007b); in *The Book of Changes* there is a saying that, 'Families that do good deeds will have a good reward later, and a family that does not do good deeds will be given evils later.' If a person does many bad things, it will bring disaster to their family.

In *The Analects of Confucius*, Confucius wrote: 'Now the benevolent man, wishing himself to be established, makes others established first, and wishing himself to be successful, sees that others are successful first.' To feel and care for others, it can be said, is the best way to implement the benevolence. Therefore, benevolence as advocated by Confucian culture promotes a mutually beneficial win–win situation. If a person hopes to be successful, they must help others be successful as well, because by assisting others one helps oneself (Zhang, 2013).

The social system and mainstream values have a great influence on people's thinking and behavior (Wu, 2008). Chinese entrepreneurs are significantly influenced by traditional Chinese culture; therefore, entrepreneurs engaging in 'philanthropy' inevitably have grounding in traditional Chinese culture (Wu, 2010). The traditional Chinese culture can strengthen entrepreneurship, promote the entrepreneur's engagement in philanthropy (Wang, 1999) and pursue better social identity. The traditional culture improves and perfects one's personality under the influence of altruistic motives (Hu, 2010). And in this way, entrepreneurs will conduct more charitable donations actively; entrepreneurs believe that it is their responsibility to help others. Philanthropic donations can improve corporate reputations and the entrepreneurs' individual reputations. Enhanced social reputations can potentially satisfy entrepreneurs seeking attention and recognition, and let them have 'face'. Having 'face' is an important influence on corporate philanthropy and the corporation (Wang and Shi, 2008). Social reputation at the same time increases the opportunities for political participation (Liang et al., 2010), as the social relationship asset of a corporation (Wang et al., 2010), indirectly meets the endogenous demand of the corporation (Li and Wei, 2012). It can also improve the social influence of the enterprise, as well as enhance the company's brand value (Fang, 2011; Zhang and Zheng, 2013). Through charitable donations, entrepreneurs can effectively improve the social atmosphere and promote entrepreneurs' moral and social recognition (Zhou, 2013b). Corporations obtain income through the exchange of goods, and through entrepreneurial philanthropy, this special 'commodity' exchange, there is access to social recognition and the implicit contract between the corporation and the society (Huang et al., 2008) to obtain a higher customer loyalty. Through charitable donations, entrepreneurs also meet employees' needs for charity, and enhance the cohesion of the internal staff (Xu, 2007), as well as ultimately promote the development of the corporation. Whether in compassion for others, or in their own self-interest, entrepreneurs are eager to participate in charitable donations and fulfill their social responsibility (Wang, 2011).

10.3   THE DEVELOPMENT OF CHINESE ENTREPRENEURS' PHILANTHROPY

10.3.1   History

The establishment of the China Charity Federation[3] in 1994 is considered the starting point of the modern and contemporary Chinese philanthropy revival (Zhou and Zeng, 2007c; Zhou, 2013a). The China Charity Federation has now become one of China's largest, most influential charities. China's political and economic environment has greatly improved as a result of the continuous effort to 'bring order out of chaos' from the Cultural Revolution (1966–1976), as well as the economic reform and opening-up policy that has been ongoing since 1978. Accordingly, Chinese thinking has been further liberated (Zhou and Zeng, 2007c). In the former political environment the government did not allow private participation in social affairs, and large charitable efforts were operated by the government. However, under the new political conditions, private participation is allowed, even encouraged, in social affairs. In essence, 'kindness' had been released, and many people have begun to engage in charitable donations. At the same time, since the economic environment changed from a highly centralized planned economy to a socialist market economy (Yan and Zhu, 2008), people have been encouraged to build wealth first. The first people who achieved success under the reforms not only provided basic necessities for their families, but also built a surplus of funds. Such individuals used the surplus funds to make investments in more enterprises and also to affect a transfer of wealth through their charitable donations. As the gap between rich and poor grew, the opportunity for private participation in charitable donations also rose. After the 1980s and the problem of insufficient funding, China's state welfare agencies began to seek reform initiatives. Meanwhile, awareness of social responsibility in China began to develop rapidly (Yu et al., 2011). With the optimization of the social environment, philanthropy has made substantial development, as the government also began to support social organizations (Chen, 2008; Wang and Jia, 2002). The first social enterprises emerged (Zhao, 2012), along with a commercial business model, leading to the goal of establishing a non-profit organization (NPO). This development shows that more enterprises and entrepreneurs have demonstrated a better understanding of how to assume their social responsibilities.

A current research project, chaired by Shuming Zhao and supported by the National Natural Science Foundation of China (Project No. 71172063), calls for 'A study of occurrence mechanism and countermeasures of labor conflicts in Chinese enterprises under the transitional economy.'[4] For this study, questionnaire surveys were distributed to more than 500 companies nationwide. Each company received one questionnaire (addressed to the deputy general manager),[5] and a total of 311 questionnaires were collected as of January 2013. The questionnaire return rate reached 62.2 percent and includes 116 companies in Jiangsu, 71 companies in Shandong, 54 companies in Guangdong, 37 companies in Fujian, 18 companies in Tianjin and 15 companies in Jiangxi. The companies surveyed were determined by the geographical region of the companies as well as the anticipated questionnaire return rate. Since some of the questionnaires were not returned on time, a total of 278 questionnaires from four provinces were used; these provinces were Jiangsu, Shandong, Guangdong and Fujian.

In order for all levels of the corporation to better understand the operational situation, including the human resources (HR) policies, each questionnaire was completed by a deputy general manager, a human resources manager and eight other employees from each company. The deputy general manager's questionnaire focused on aspects of the company culture. We used the following four categories (Tsui et al., 2006) to measure the attitude toward a company's social responsibilities: (1) the importance of social responsibility; (2) the company's mission to serve society; (3) emphasis on both economic and social benefits; and (4) the importance of the company's long-term development to society.

In an analysis of 278 questionnaires from companies' deputy general managers, we find that 82.4 percent of the senior managers believe that the company's mission is to serve society, 89.2 percent think that their companies attach great importance to social responsibility, 85.2 percent think that the company culture encourages both economic and social benefits, and 84.9 percent consider the company's long-term development to be of great importance to society. Therefore, the vast majority of Chinese business managers appear to be fully aware of the importance of social responsibility and the promotion of the development of society.

The Hurun Philanthropy List has maintained data on the history, process, and structure (see Table 10.1), as well as the 50th Donation Amount, and the 100th Donation Amount from individuals. The Chinese donations listed have an increasing trend, from about US$3.33 million on average that entrepreneurs contributed through donations in 2004, to US$16.32 million in 2012, with an increase of 391 percent and an annual growth rate of 22 percent. Even with fluctuations during this period, these data reveal a substantial upward trend overall. The Hurun Philanthropy List is based on total personal donations. Based on the statistics of the National Bureau of Chinese Industrial Statistics Division (2012), as of December 2011, China has 325 629 industrial enterprises above the designated size, in which small and medium-sized and micro enterprises

Table 10.1 The Hurun Philanthropy List by year

Year	No. of People	Average amount of donations (million USD)	The 50th donation amount (million USD)	The 100th donation amount (million USD)	No. 1 donor	No. 1 donation amount (hundred million USD)	Average age
2012	100	16.32	6.45	2.71	The Cao Dewang Family	5.87	51
2011	100	19.53	4.84	2.18	The Cao Dewang Family	7.28	52
2010	50	26.48	1.73		Yu Pengnian	5.16	53
2009	50	12.55	2.34		Huang Rulun	1.37	52
2008*	100	20.71	7.13	4.27	Yu Pengnian	4.84	52
2007*	100	15.27	4.84	2.42	Yu Pengnian	3.23	51
2006*	100	9.18	2.44	0.97	Yu Pengnian	3.23	48
2005*	50	3.52	0.85		Huang Rulun	0.47	48
2004	50	3.32	0.48		Huang Rulun	0.34	48

Notes:
The Hurun Philanthropy List was originated in 2004 by the Hurun Research Institute. The slogan of the Hurun Philanthropy List is 'In Search of China's Carnegie'. It released the 100th (or 50th in 2004, 2005, 2009 and 2010) donation amount of each year (from April 1 to March 31 of next year). If the entrepreneur holds more than 50 percent of the company, the donation of the company will be added to the individual's donations.
* Accumulated donation amount by year. Before 2009, the Hurun Philanthropy List shows the individual philanthropist's previous donation (since 2004); starting in 2009, it began listing the individual philanthropist's current donation amount.

Sources: Based on the 2006–2012 Hurun Philanthropy List and the China Enterprise Philanthropist List of 2004–2005.

accounted for 97.2 percent. For the small and medium-sized enterprises, the main business income reached 57.33 percent above all other industrial enterprises, and profits 56.96 percent above all industrial enterprises. As with other countries (Ardic et al., 2011), small and medium-sized enterprise is an important part of the national economy. The majority of entrepreneurs with small-scale enterprises have less personal wealth, and their donation amounts will be less and, therefore, not listed. However, the Hurun Philanthropy List shows the direction of future Chinese personal charity, as it reflects actual donations in China.

10.3.2 The Distribution Structure of Chinese Entrepreneurs' Philanthropy

The Hurun Philanthropy List presents information for the top 100 entrepreneurs according to donations including donation category, birthday, birth place, industries, companies, and company locations. The donation category includes information such as education, religion, health and construction in the hometown. This information is released by the Hurun Philanthropy Report. Distribution analyses can be conducted based on the birth place, company headquarters location, industry, and entrepreneur donation category.

Geographic distribution

As shown in Table 10.2, Fujian merchants by birthplace accounted for 40 percent of the top 10 philanthropists on the 2012 Hurun Philanthropy List, and Guangdong merchants accounted for 20 percent.

As shown in Table 10.3, 25 of the 100 entrepreneurs shown on the Hurun Philanthropy List were born in Guangdong, 15 were born in Fujian, accounting for 25 percent and 15 percent, respectively. Entrepreneurs who set up their company headquarters in Guangdong and Fujian represent 28 percent and 13 percent respectively. As Table 10.3 demonstrates, the profile of regions in which the entrepreneurs were born is similar to the distribution among the regions in which they set up their company headquarters, with the exceptions of Beijing and Shanghai. These exceptions are likely because Beijing is the political and cultural center of China while Shanghai is the business center of China. Although only 5 percent of the entrepreneurs were born in Beijing, and only 1 percent of entrepreneurs were born in Shanghai, Beijing still attracts about 12 percent of the entrepreneurs and Shanghai attracts about 5 percent. At the same time, there were more entrepreneurs with company headquarters in the Guangdong, Fujian, Zhejiang and Jiangsu regions, as well as entrepreneurs who were born in these regions. Therefore, entrepreneurs' charitable donations are probably geographically distributed. Overall, the entrepreneurs in the

Table 10.2   Top ten entrepreneurs on the Hurun Philanthropy List

Ranking	Name	Donation amount (million USD)	Donation category	Birthplace	Industry
1	The Cao Dewang Family	587.10	Social welfare, education, aiding the poor, environmental protection, culture	Fujian	Manufacturing
2	Xu Jiayin	120.97	Social welfare, aiding the poor, education	Henan	Real estate
3	Wang Jianlin	45.16	Culture, social welfare, education, environmental protection	Sichuan	Real estate
4	Huang Rulun	40.32	Social welfare, education, aiding the poor, culture	Fujian	Real estate
5	Huang Wenzai	38.71	Aiding the poor, social welfare, education	Guangdong	Real estate
6	Lin Xiuchen and Lin Zhiqiang	35.48	Aiding the poor, education, social welfare	Fujian	Steel
7	Xu Zengping	32.26	Education	Shandong	Real estate
8	Hou Changcai	30.65	Social welfare, education	Fujian	Real estate
9	The Zhu Mengyi Family	27.42	Education, aiding the poor, social welfare	Guangdong	Real estate
10	Sun Menghuan	22.58	Social welfare, education, environmental protection	Liaoning	Real estate

Source: The 2012 Hurun Philanthropy List.

Table 10.3 *Regional distribution of entrepreneurs on the Hurun Philanthropy List*

Rank	Region	Birthplace	Company headquarters
1	Guangdong	25	28
2	Fujian	15	13
3	Zhejiang	8	3
4	Beijing	5	12
5	Henan	5	4
6	Hunan	5	3
7	Jiangsu	4	6
8	Shandong	3	3
9	Hubei	3	4
10	Liaoning	2	5
11	Sichuan	2	1
12	Shanxi	1	3
13	Hebei	1	3
14	Shanxi	1	1
15	Jiangxi	1	1
16	Shanghai	1	5
17	Chongqing	1	2
18	Ningxia	1	1
19	Yunnan	1	1
20	Hong Kong	0	2
21	Guizhou	0	1
22	Guangxi	0	1
23	Hebei	0	1
24	Inner Mongolia	0	1

Source: 2012 Hurun Philanthropy List.

south donate more than entrepreneurs in the north, as southern entrepreneurs account for about two-thirds of the total number of entrepreneurs on the list.

Comparing Table 10.3 and Table 10.4, we find that many of the entrepreneurs on the Hurun Philanthropy List were born in Zhejiang Province, with 22 percent of the total, and 14 entrepreneurs located their company headquarters in Zhejiang Province, second only to Guangdong. Among the 100 individual philanthropists from the 2012 Hurun Philanthropy List, 57 of them also donated in 2011 and were listed in the 2011 Hurun Philanthropy List. Although entrepreneurs on the Hurun Peregrine Standings and the Hurun Philanthropy List do not correspond (for example, Fujian entrepreneurs rank number 4 on the Peregrine standings,

Table 10.4   *Regional distribution of entrepreneurs on the Hurun Peregrine Standings*

No.	Region	Birthplace	Company headquarters
1	Zhejiang	22	14
2	Guangdong	16	22
3	Jiangsu	10	7
4	Fujian	8	5
5	Sichuan	8	4
6	Shandong	7	5
7	Hebei	6	4
8	Beijing	3	7
9	Liaoning	3	2
10	Shanghai	3	12
11	Gansu	2	0
12	Anhui	2	0
13	Xinjiang	1	1
14	Jiangxi	1	1
15	Jilin	1	1
16	Hubei	1	1
17	Henan	1	0
18	Chongqing	1	0
19	Shanxi	1	0

Notes: Hurun Peregrine Standings was originated in 1999 by the Hurun Research Institute. 'Hurun Peregrine Standings' reveals the nature of China's economic and social transformation. It released the 1000th donation amount for each year (from August 16 to August 15 of the following year), and it released the 50th donation amount before 2000, and the 100th donation amount between 2001 and 2007.

Source: The 2012 Hurun Peregrine Standings.

but are number 2 on the Hurun Philanthropy List), the percentage of Fujian and Guangdong entrepreneurs who participate in charitable donations on the Hurun Philanthropy List is much higher than the number of entrepreneurs from this region on the Hurun Peregrine Standings. To a certain extent, this comparison indicates that entrepreneurial wealth and entrepreneurs' charitable donations are not the same. However, in both Tables 10.3 and 10.4, the provinces listed at the top are more developed provinces and with higher regional economic levels. Corporations, therefore, are more likely to start businesses in those provinces. Entrepreneurs' philanthropic acts, then, have a certain relationship with the region's economic development level (Zhao and Wan, 2012).

*Table 10.5   Industry distribution of entrepreneurs on the Hurun Peregrine
Standings*

Industry	Real estate	Manu-facturing	Building construction	Finance and investment	Energy	Others
Number of people	43	17	9	9	9	13

Source: The 2012 Hurun Philanthropy List.

Industry distribution

As shown in Table 10.2, among the top ten philanthropists on the Hurun
list, eight are real estate developers. Table 10.5 indicates that on the Hurun
Philanthropy List, 43 entrepreneurs are in real estate, 17 are in manufacturing, and 9 are in architecture, finance and investment, and energy.
Real estate entrepreneurs account for a significant number of those on
the Hurun list. Among the top ten Hurun Peregrine Standings, five are
real estate developers; and among the 1000 entrepreneurs on the Hurun
Peregrine Standings, the industries that account for the largest number are
manufacturing, real estate, finance and investment, and energy, which is
consistent with the results of the Hurun Philanthropy List. As a 'systems
integrator' (Song, 2009), real estate has become a pillar industry of the
national economy (Ge and Jia, 2011). The real estate industry has a long
industrial chain and has played an important role in the development of
other industries. Real estate and citizens' basic living rights are closely
related (Sha, 2012), so the real estate entrepreneurs are more willing to
participate in the charitable giving of the community. Also, overall real
estate prices are high in China, and there is an ongoing need for housing.
In this situation, the reputations and social images of real estate companies and real estate entrepreneurs are challenged by the citizens. Therefore,
based on the above reasons, the behavior of real estate enterprises and
real estate entrepreneurs will get more attention from society. Real estate
entrepreneurs must participate in social welfare, whether in order to help
others in need, to enhance their own social images, or to obtain greater
wealth through a more respected social identity. This can satisfy the public's perception of the entrepreneur's behavior, as well as establish a good
social reputation. If the real estate entrepreneurs cannot actively participate in social donations, society's questioning and possible resistance will
ultimately affect the development of the corporation.

China is currently in a period of economic transition. A large part
of Chinese economic growth is still dependent on extensive resource

Table 10.6   Primary fund donations by category

Category	2012 (%)	2011 (%)	2010 (%)	2009 (%)	2004 (%)
Education	36	24	26	18	39
Social welfare	32	29	20	15	7
Aiding the poor	20	9	10	10	15
Disaster relief	3	26	28	43	27

Sources: Based on the 2006–2012 Hurun Philanthropy List and the China Enterprise Philanthropist List of 2004–2005.

dependency, and the dense population. According to the sixth population census in 2010, 8.93 percent of people per 100 000 in China have a junior college degree or higher education. The traditional manufacturing industry and the construction industry, then, still absorb a large proportion of labor in China. At the same time, the real estate and construction industries have the characteristics of a long industrial chain (Kuang, 2010).

With 30 years of reform and opening up, China's financial industry has made tremendous progress (Wang, 2010), and the economy has become more financially oriented (Yang, 2009). It should focus on cultivating strategic emerging industries. The Twelfth Five Year Plan, written under the government's guidance, indicates that the new energy industry will be further developed and become the national economy's pillar industry. These reasons have caused entrepreneurs' philanthropic behavior to differ among the different industries.

Fund donation category distribution
Table 10.6 shows the percentage of philanthropic giving that went into four categories of activities for the years 2004–2013. Donations to educational activities are consistently the largest amounts. Entrepreneurs tend to donate large amounts of money to build schools and establish scholarships. They especially devote efforts to further developing and building their alma mater schools. One such example occurred with Nanjing University's Du Xia Library. Du Xia graduated from the master's program at the School of Business at Nanjing University in 1982 and became a successful businessman. In 2007, he donated RMB 30 million yuan (about US$4.84 million) to Nanjing University to build the Du Xia Library on Nanjing University's Xianlin campus. The library was completed in 2012. There also tend to be more charitable donations in years when there are large, visible natural disasters. For example, between 2009 and 2011, more donations were made to disaster relief, due to the 2008 Wenchuan earthquake, the southern snow disaster, and the 2010 Yushu earthquake, as well as other natural disasters.

An entrepreneur's social responsibility and participation in charitable donations is related not only to the region and industry, but also to whether the company is listed and the type of ownership. For instance, entrepreneurs from listed and state-owned enterprises are more likely to engage in philanthropy (Ge and Wang, 2010). The entrepreneurs' willingness to fully participate in social responsibility is influenced by many factors, and the situation leads to the current issues that Chinese entrepreneurs face in the process of engaging in philanthropy. Only by understanding these issues can we better anticipate entrepreneurial philanthropy in the future.

10.3.3 Factors that Affect the Development of the Chinese Entrepreneur's Philanthropic Activities

For many motivations (Zhou, 2013b) and reasons, more entrepreneurs participate in charitable donations and promote the development of philanthropy and the welfare of the society.

Entrepreneurs' transition to taking on social responsibility
Entrepreneurs realize that a good social environment is a necessary condition for the development of the corporation as well as the entrepreneurs themselves. A relatively stable social environment is necessary for the corporation's positive development. Entrepreneurs must recognize the interdependence between a company and society (Porter and Kramer, 2006). Modern management guru Peter Drucker (2006) explains in his book *Management Practices* that the purpose of the enterprise must be in the enterprise itself, because the enterprise is an organ of society. As the 'citizens' of the society, corporations are developing but at the same time must fulfill their social responsibilities (Zhang et al., 2010; Wang, 2013). Only through the promotion of a healthy and orderly society can companies have good business and a healthy business environment in which to operate. With the continued improvement of the philanthropic environment, entrepreneurs have more channels to obtain charity information. In this case, the entrepreneur's moral motivations (Liu, 2011) are constantly stimulated.

As a representative for the corporation (Guo, 2012), the entrepreneur's wealth base is closely linked with the enterprise's financial performance. Therefore, entrepreneurs must recognize the necessity for social transformation. This involves a transformation from the managers' and owners' perspective to involvement in undertaking social responsibility and actively fulfilling social responsibilities, in order to improve the reputation of the company. At the same time, participation in social charity can optimize the relationship between the government and the corporation, thereby creating a more suitable environment for company development and growth. Werhahn (2011) suggests that entrepreneurs are actually public servants. Since they hold the resources that ordinary people do not have, they must assume relevant social responsibilities (Tian, 2010, 2012) in order to make a valuable contribution (Reinhard, 2005).

Company interests and social cognition

As more entrepreneurs in China make charitable donations, their participation will pressure other corporations and entrepreneurs (Liu, 2011) and lead to more entrepreneurs participating in philanthropy. After the 2008 Wenchuan earthquake, for example, many companies provided aid to the earthquake-stricken areas and donated money to support post-disaster reconstruction. Mengniu[6] took the initiative to donate, and the donation from Wong Lo Kat was RMB100 million yuan (about US$16.13 million). Such charitable donations enhance the image of a company, its social identity (Zhao, 2007; Liu and Wang, 2012), and the value and market competitiveness of its brand (Qiu, 2002; Bi, 2007). Corporations' and entrepreneurs' charitable donations can help attract customers and maintain higher customer loyalty (Tian and Fan, 2010); at the same time, social identity helps entrepreneurs gain positive social reputations (Tang, 2013).

The reason that entrepreneurs participate in charitable donations appears to be largely because they recognize that entrepreneurs themselves and their companies are affected by the effects of the activities that charitable donations support. Especially important are the external and internal social effects. Internally, charitable action can produce strong appeal and cohesion in the company and further promote the development of the company. Externally, charitable donations can reduce the competition pressure of corporations when they are fulfilling their social responsibilities as well as participating in charitable donations (Sun, 2010; Liu, 2011). This can also help corporations develop good community relations and political relations, create a good environment for the company's further development, and create favorable conditions for the entrepreneurs' personal development (Zheng et al., 2012). Therefore, through product differentiation strategies (Gao et al., 2012), such a strategy can further influence the social reputation and brand value of the company (Qiu, 2002).

Religion and traditional culture

As previously mentioned, traditional Chinese culture has a foundation of 'kindness'. Therefore, with the innate sense of mission that is rooted in Chinese cultural values, Chinese entrepreneurs with higher moral standards would have the drive to involve themselves in social welfare consciously. At the same time, entrepreneurs from different regions in China exhibit different characteristics. As noted earlier, in the Hurun Philanthropy List, many of the entrepreneurs come from Guangdong, Fujian and Zhejiang. This disproportionate representation was significantly higher than it was in the Hurun's Peregrine Standings. That is to say, a greater portion of entrepreneurs from these three regions actively participate in charitable donations than those from other places. The development of traditional religious culture is one of the most important reasons (Weller, 2006, 2009; Gan, 2011). Fujian Province, for example, has retained precious scenic spots and cultural relics that constitute symbols of traditional religion and cultural values. Those native to Fujian Province may actively participate in social welfare and make charitable donations as a result of the influence of traditional religious values.

10.3.4 Method and Types of Chinese Entrepreneur Philanthropy

Direct donation
Direct donation is the easiest way for an entrepreneur to participate in charity. Those entrepreneurs who make direct donations reduce the transfer of funds and materials and reduce the information loss during the donation process. They have a more direct and comprehensive understanding of the needs of the donation recipient, and they avoid rent-seeking behavior in the donation process. They are better able to meet the practical needs of donation recipients on a timely basis. At the same time, direct donation can establish channels for the entrepreneurs to become involved in social welfare, which broadens the ways in which entrepreneurs can fulfill their social responsibilities. Through the establishment of a more open private charity channel, entrepreneurs are better able to oversee and guide the flow of donation funds.

Direct donation is an important way for Chinese entrepreneurs to participate in charity. One such direct donation program, Project Hope,[7] has achieved positive results. Some entrepreneurs will donate money to schools in rural areas directly, or donate to Project Hope. Other entrepreneurs donate money to universities where buildings are named for them, such as the Yifu Building at many universities. In recent years, direct donations have slowly replaced 'government donations' and are becoming one of the two most important channels for Chinese entrepreneurs' charitable donations. There is evidence that participation in these organizations benefits the donors and their companies. For example, Chen Guangbiao is an active donor and publicizes his company during these charitable events. His message is that the company values 'benefiting others and oneself' as well as 'win–win' results.

Influencing others to participate in charity

Through direct donation channels, entrepreneurs can establish good communication with donation recipients. However, individual entrepreneurs often do not have enough time to develop this level of communication with recipients. The individual entrepreneur's personal capability may be limited and, in addition, an individual entrepreneur often cannot provide sufficient funds to achieve adequate scale in the charitable activities to make a significant difference. An alternate strategy is for an entrepreneur to leverage their reputation and visibility to encourage others to make charitable donations to specific social welfare projects. The aggregate efforts of multiple donors can result in significant effects. The scale of charitable donations can increase the scale of operations and thus benefit more people who have social needs. The strategy of influencing others can generate positive benefits for the companies and the entrepreneurs. For example, the strategy can increase their social capital, build their social networks, provide for a better environment for themselves and their employees, and promote the positive effects of philanthropic activities with resulting ripple effects through the geographical region or the industry.

Using the company itself (or its funds) to participate in charity

In China, entrepreneurs and businesses are closely linked. Entrepreneurs tend to see the business or family as their private property. That is to say, entrepreneurs and corporations are symbionts (Chen, 2007). Therefore, it is not clear if the source of the donor funds is the entrepreneur or the corporate donor. In other words, it is difficult to distinguish the money donated by the entrepreneurs from the money donated by the enterprises. Many of the entrepreneurs' companies can participate in charitable activities through a combination of the previous two methods. Some entrepreneurs do not contribute personal charitable donations, but they may direct the company to contribute to a specific fund or into the company's public accounts, and thereby make the donation by the company (or its funds) collectively.

Certainly entrepreneurs can make charitable donations through their own companies, but the company's participation is simultaneously an important part of an entrepreneur's philanthropy. However, there is a difference between these two kinds of charity. Since making charitable donations through a company involves a large number of people and large amounts of money, there is a degree of risk. If the charitable donation fund or organization is not well organized, the results could have a negative impact. In addition, Chinese law is still developing. Depending on the directions that policies and regulations take, the autonomy of a charitable organization could be eroded. It is possible that a charitable foundation will face problems during its operation.

10.4 PROBLEMS IN CHINESE ENTREPRENEURS' PHILANTHROPY

More entrepreneurs and their companies are embracing social responsibility (Lin and Wu, 2012). However, philanthropy in China still faces many challenges. These challenges persist because Chinese entrepreneurs' philanthropy is in the growth phase. These challenges must be faced, and in order to do so, it is very important to have a deeper understanding of these issues in order to solve the problems and promote the further development of Chinese entrepreneurs' philanthropy. Below we address some of the most prevalent problems.

10.4.1 Problems and Shortcomings in the Development of Entrepreneurial Philanthropy

The non-systematic characteristic of entrepreneurs' philanthropy

Volunteering is quite common in China (Kong and Deng, 2013); however the scale of formal charity in China is still small (Liu et al., 2006), and the social value as interpreted within the society is still immature. There is a lack of the 'corporate citizen' concept (Zhou and Lin, 2004; Chi and Wang, 2010), and there is no long-term strategic plan. Chinese entrepreneurs' philanthropy has not yet evolved into a system that is broadly understood (Zhao, 2007). Indeed, philanthropy within China is often initiated only by accident and often involves only isolated passive participation (Ge and Cai, 2009). Often there has been no deliberate initiative or clearly defined purpose. Therefore, this cannot serve as an effective driver or guide for corporations and society. Companies often participate in a particular charity because of the interests of the entrepreneurs and managers who themselves value charitable behavior (Zhou et al., 2011). Due to the lack of social entrepreneurs to participate in charitable organizations, managers of these charities can utilize only limited resources (Wang and Jia, 2002), and charitable organizations lack adequate management consciousness (Chen, 2008).

The non-autonomous characteristic of entrepreneur philanthropy

China lacks a large body of entrepreneurs who pursue philanthropy (Zhao, 2008). The concept of philanthropy is not yet well developed. Although Chinese entrepreneurs presumably have personally absorbed the concept of 'kindness' from traditional culture, such 'kindness' is often based on the premise of benefiting oneself. At the same time, because of the influence of the Cultural Revolution, some social values were weakened (Chen, 2007; Wang, 2007b). In fact, Wu (2000) argues that Chinese entrepreneurs tend to lack consciousness of a moral sense and humanistic caring. Only during major natural disasters do some entrepreneurs respond (Pang and Yan, 2008), albeit passively, to the needs of society; and when they do, they donate to the hardest-hit areas due to social pressure (Bi, 2009). At the same time, Chinese entrepreneurs' philanthropic behavior is considered as 'utilization' in that some entrepreneurs may hide internal labor relation-related issues that are of concern to society through charitable donations (Gao et al., 2012). Therefore, to a certain extent, entrepreneurs' philanthropy is considered to be a kind of 'face' and 'image project' (Hu, 2010). Porter and Kramer (2002) suggests that the desire to improve one's reputation by itself would not be a sufficient motive for entrepreneurs to participate in charity. Fang (2009) argues that a timely response to a need for donations may lead to a negative effect. There is a serious gap between the rich and the poor in China, and there exists a widespread misunderstanding that 'the rich are cruel'. At the same time, China's 30 years of reform is a process of continuous improvement of the Chinese business environment. Some entrepreneurs will use the imperfection of the system to promote the development of their corporations, and therefore some people will think that entrepreneurs are the original sin (Zhao, 2009b; Wu, 2009). Therefore, the Chinese society has an obvious 'revenge on the rich' phenomenon. Based on Fang's explanation, entrepreneurs are not willing to donate because they would reveal themselves as being rich, and that could have negative consequences for themselves and their companies (Zhao, 2007). It may also lead to 'hidden charity'[8] behavior (Yu, 2010). 'Hidden charity' to some extent reflects the entrepreneurial moral of 'helping', but it loses the purpose of charity in general, and it cannot help the community to actively respond to active charity.

If companies in China want to achieve strong development, they must establish a good relationship with the government; otherwise, the companies will face many obstacles in their course of development. The Chinese government hopes that entrepreneurs can become more involved in charitable donations (Jing and Gong, 2012). However, in this case, entrepreneurs are not willing to participate in charitable donations, because they are under 'standardized' pressure to maintain the 'legitimacy' of the 'compulsory' behavior (Ge and Wang, 2010). If there is not charitable donation behavior, some entrepreneurs will be considered as not complying with group norms; or the government will forcefully push for charitable donations (Huang et al., 2008; Niu and Zhu, 2012). If the entrepreneur does not donate, it might be hard for corporations to conduct normal business operations. A good relationship between government and business is the basis for the existence and development of companies. 'Moral coercion' (Zhang, 2010) may also occur, as no charitable donations may be considered socially irresponsible and as evidence of no moral standards, which may have a serious impact on the corporations' social and brand images. Entrepreneurs may not want to donate money under government pressure, but the government will force entrepreneurs to do so. However, some corporations when facing public discussion and social moral pressure, as well as government pressure, may donate in the name of having good moral standards.

The single form of entrepreneurs' philanthropy
Entrepreneurs currently participate in a very simple form of charity (Zhao, 2007). Indeed, many people think of philanthropy as simply donating money (Liu, 2012). But in fact, charity can also provide opportunities for the poor and people in disaster areas, especially in the form of education, job creation and improvements in public infrastructure. Such benefits can certainly improve individuals' living environment. While philanthropy is often monetary donations, it also can focus on the physiological needs of the recipients. In fact, people in the poor or disaster-stricken area, or who were affected by the difficult environment, would often be in a negative mental state. And this negative psychological mood cannot always be eased and changed. So the entrepreneurs should pay more attention to the spirit and social needs of the recipients. And now more and more entrepreneurs have started to pay closer attention to this situation. Many entrepreneurs have begun donating time, especially in becoming volunteers (Yu and Wang, 2011), to better participate in charity. Time is the most valuable resource; entrepreneurs have adopted this form of 'time donation' to enhance the effect of charity demonstration, and to meet the social needs of the recipients.

The non-equilibrium of entrepreneurs' philanthropy
According to Table 10.3 and Table 10.4, the philanthropic Chinese entrepreneurs are mainly concentrated in the areas where the economy is relatively well developed. An economically underdeveloped region is limited by the lack of philanthropy and its development (Wang, 2007a). Entrepreneurs' philanthropy is mainly concentrated in the areas that are relatively rich. Therefore, the geographic distribution is extremely uneven. Chinese entrepreneurs donate funds mainly for poverty alleviation, education and disaster relief (Liao, 2004), and the scope of activities is limited (Wang and Jia, 2002). This is closely linked to the imbalance of the Chinese economic situation.

10.4.2 Causes for Existing Problems

There are several possible reasons for problems regarding entrepreneurs' philanthropy in China, including personal, company, societal and legal explanations.

Personal reasons

Each person has different personal, moral and cultural values. Some may not recognize the necessity of making charitable donations, or lack recognition of corporate social responsibility (Chen and Yu, 2007), and are, therefore, not willing to help others who have difficulties. This leads to a non-systematic characteristic and single form of Chinese entrepreneurs' charitable behavior. If a company's managers are ineffective, it may limit the entrepreneur's participation in social welfare activities. Since the entrepreneurs do not treat the charitable donations as an important strategic business development, they do not have good plans for charitable giving. Moreover, entrepreneurs are not professionals engaged in philanthropy, and they cannot successfully manage and control the flow of their donations, which leads to the non-systematic character of Chinese entrepreneurs' philanthropy. Entrepreneurs do not distribute equally in China, and they have different personal backgrounds and preferences, so they will donate money to different categories. This leads to a lack of equilibrium in entrepreneurial philanthropy.

Company reasons

According to the Chinese Entrepreneurs Survey System (2007)[9] studies, the main reason that entrepreneurs participate in charitable giving is for the purpose of enhancing the organization's image. That is, entrepreneurs provide charitable donations for the purpose of promoting the company's brand. If the enthusiasm of Chinese entrepreneurs to participate in social welfare diminishes, the company's strategies for social welfare will be negatively affected. If the company does not maintain cash flow and does not have sufficient funds, then it may not be possible for the company to allocate resources to charitable actions. When a company enters the mature stage and has the resources to do so, the company should demonstrate social responsibility (Chinese Entrepreneurs Survey System, 2007; Sha, 2010; Liu, 2012). Companies should take measures according to the resources available at the stage in the organizational life-cycle. Corporate philanthropy must match the characteristics and current operating conditions of the company (Yi and Han, 2012). Company charitable culture and the applicable social mechanisms are currently imperfect; therefore, corporate philanthropy cannot bring forth corresponding strategic benefits to companies (Wang, 2009).

Social reasons

Entrepreneurs may be reluctant to participate in social welfare activities because of the imperfections in the current state of China's philanthropy laws. For example, before December 2010, The One Foundation was a part of the China Red Cross,[10] but had no legal status to engage in independent public fund raising. At the same time, the lack of social creditability for organizations such as The One Foundation is one reason that companies are not willing to engage in charitable donations. If relevant social management organizations or offices cannot adequately fulfill their responsibilities, and charitable organizations have a strong administrative background (Pang and Yan, 2008), companies will abandon intentions to make charitable donations (Liu, 2012).

Many entrepreneurs who participate in charity are influenced by the dual pressures of public opinion and the government (Li, 2012). On one hand, concern regarding public opinion inspires most entrepreneurs to think that donations are the social responsibility of companies. These attitudes negatively affect the development of individual entrepreneurial philanthropy (Gan, 2011). The situation is such that continuation of the Chinese traditional culture of 'kindness' will be increasingly difficult. At the same time Western business ethics systems will not operate well in China (He and Wang, 2011). Thus, a means to develop the set of cultural values and practices that will encourage Chinese philanthropy, and especially philanthropy among Chinese entrepreneurs, is an important challenge ahead for the country. One of the important reasons is that philanthropy is not often publicized, which leads to a lack of understanding (Zhu and Chen, 2011).

Legal factors

China's legal system lacks laws that are focused on charitable donations, and the money from charitable donations are often not managed well. Currently China lacks a complete and timely disclosure system (Pang and Yan, 2008). As a result, it is difficult to ensure effective constraint and guarantee the reasonable, legal use of donated funds. Some charities lack the reassurances of improving operational efficiency (Guo, 2009), resulting in a lack of donor confidence in charities and a lack of ability to promote social donations (He, 2011). The participation of corporations and entrepreneurs in charitable activities is affected. For corporate and entrepreneurs' philanthropy, the government lacks tax policies that encourage and guide donations (Pang and Yan, 2008), including a lack of gift taxes (Zhu and Chen, 2011), and the deduction proportion is low in donation taxes (Kong and Deng, 2013). Therefore, legal factors potentially hinder the ability of entrepreneurs to engage in philanthropy.

10.5   PROSPECTS AND POLICY SUGGESTIONS FOR THE DEVELOPMENT OF ENTREPRENEURS' PHILANTHROPY

Entrepreneurs in China play a significant and meaningful role in Chinese philanthropy. However, the current development of Chinese entrepreneurs' philanthropy is restricted by many factors. In order to promote the development of entrepreneurs' charitable donations and, through the exemplary contributions of entrepreneurs, to lead the development and growth of social welfare, we must solve some crucial problems. Below are several policy suggestions and recommendations.

10.5.1   Policy Suggestions

Establishing business ethics that coincide with market ethics
Business ethics arise from entrepreneurs' ethical standards. Entrepreneurs' individual value judgments will affect whether their companies will take on social responsibilities, which is in line with market logic. Society should promote the Chinese traditional culture of 'kindness' and promote that 'kindness' in Chinese entrepreneurs. Entrepreneurship activities, namely innovating and addressing technical and market uncertainty, are important assets in a company. Companies realize their values through exchange behavior (Xia, 2011). China needs to retain its distinct Chinese culture and, at the same time, widely absorb market ideas and practices from Western countries. Integrating Chinese traditional philanthropic values with Western market competition concepts is a necessary step and a significant challenge for the country as it moves on into the twenty-first century. Encouraging corporations to engage in philanthropy to enhance their competitiveness, and giving awards like honorary titles to corporations and entrepreneurs who actively participate in social welfare, may help the country meet this challenge (Liu et al., 2006; Wu, 2009).

Implementation of strategic corporate social responsibility
Entrepreneurs must have foresight and come to a consensus with regards to what constitutes modern strategic corporate social responsibility. They must do so in order to effectively integrate company development into social development, as well as to actively pursue the benefits of both companies and society (Zhao, 2009a). An enterprise must not forget an enterprise's social responsibilities and should seek to become a conscientious enterprise even while it drives for economic benefits. Philanthropic actions and charitable giving, both at the individual and the company levels, are integral aspects of individual and corporate social responsibility. In order

to maximize the social and economic value of its philanthropic investments, a company should establish a vision for its philanthropic activities that can improve employee morale, and execute a strategy of investing in charitable activities that can enhance the enterprise's long-term competitiveness. By focusing on the market environment, a company can create enormous value that meets the expectations of its investors. By carefully planning and executing strategic corporate social responsibility which includes their philanthropic activities and charitable giving, companies can improve their strategic value when making charitable donations. As others argue, companies can change the environment within which they operate in such a way so as to enhance their further development (Porter and Kramer, 2002; Larson, 2002).

Changing the leading role of government
Since entrepreneurs have higher social status as well as wealth, they naturally become the target of organizations seeking charitable donations. Entrepreneurs play an important role in the country's overall philanthropy. It is necessary, therefore, to change the traditional way of having the government dominate such philanthropic activities (Pang and Yan, 2008), and give more freedom to companies to participate in the social welfare process. This must be done because entrepreneurs have objectives that affect their interest in and level of willingness to participate in philanthropy. If companies and entrepreneurs are free of political pressures when they make decisions about their charitable donations, they can invest their money in charities that can help promote the development of the company. At the same time, the government should vigorously promote and support (Zhao, 2010) the development of non-governmental organizations (NGOs) and professional organizations which specialize in the management of social affairs (Wang and Jia, 2002), or let charity progress back to society (Guo, 2009), and form a better interaction between the government, corporations, individuals and charity organizations.

For companies to participate in social welfare activities, the government should provide policy support. The *Guidelines of China Philanthropy Development (2011–2015)*, issued by the Ministry of Civil Affairs of the People's Republic of China (2011), clearly indicates that China needs to strengthen talent in the area of philanthropy. The country must build volunteer teams, expand charitable resources, improve the philanthropic supervision system, and expand the culture of philanthropy throughout the society.

Improve the legal system
To improve the legal system, especially to develop charity law as soon as possible, the legal system should regulate the operation of charitable

organizations, individuals and organizations as well as charitable donation behavior. It must also strengthen social supervision and correct charitable organizations' unreasonable behavior. At the same time, it is recommended that there be improvement in the personal income tax law, by raising the inheritance tax and enhancing the motivations for entrepreneurs to participate in charitable donations (Zhu and Chen, 2011; Chen et al., 2013). By standardizing the personal income tax law, the government can severely crack down on tax evasion behavior and increase the tax amount raised. Donations in person can improve the direct deduction of the amount of taxable income ratio, thereby reducing the cost of individual donation (Gong, 2009). The legal system should guide corporations and entrepreneurs in terms of philanthropy and tax-related issues. The corporate donation expenditure is positively related to the corporate income tax (Zhu, 2010).

Social environment
Public appreciation for philanthropy may be cultivated through education (Wang, 2007), lectures, performances and other efforts to 'broaden the love' and create a better social atmosphere for encouraging philanthropy (Lou, 2009). Only when people hold a positive view of wealth and its contributions to society will they conduct better service to the community, as well as contribute to society. To better promote the development of philanthropy, it is necessary to attract more entrepreneurs. Only when income levels improve (Deng, 2013) can people be more involved in charitable activities. At the same time, increasing the income of residents can reduce the public's 'revenge on the wealthy' psychology (Wu, 2009). When trying to establish a better supervision system, it is necessary to introduce supervision and an accountability system at the same time, to ensure the rational use of charitable funds, and strengthen the trust in charity, so as to form a cycle of charity.

10.5.2   Factors Affecting the Development of Public Welfare

Improving individual awareness
With the development of society, people are more deeply aware of the relationship between social welfare and their own interests. The more aware they are of the relationship, the more their willingness to participate in charitable donations is reinforced. People are more willing to promote the development of society through their individual efforts. Entrepreneurs will consciously increase the use of their own influence, and call on other people to participate in social welfare activities, thus expanding the scale of social welfare, so that more people benefit from charitable donations and

philanthropic activities. People's individual consciousness will improve, and they will be more willing to supervise (Deng, 2010) charity commitment from charity donations and public figures (Deng, 2010). At the same time, the entrepreneur should strengthen communication with the donation recipients; only in this way can they better understand the urgent needs of the use of funds and the recipients, in order to better conduct charity donations. This kind of giving and receiving between charity parties requires communication between the two parties, and there also needs to be a strengthening of appreciation education among recipients of donations (Deng, 2013; Zhu and Ge, 2013), so the donated funds can be put to better use, and also to increase the will for the donors to donate.

Improving social awareness

As more people participate in social welfare activities, more people are able to better understand the benefits of and the cultural meaning underlying charitable donations. With the continuous improvement of the social system, corporations and entrepreneurs obtain wealth by providing products and services. The recognition of legitimate income has broken the existing 'questioning of sin' (Liu et al., 2006; Wu, 2009). Therefore, for those who actively participate in social welfare activities, society should give more recognition. Doing so will further improve the image of philanthropists. The interaction between entrepreneur, company and society can become beneficial for all.

Improving social welfare

With people developing a higher consciousness and improved social awareness, the corporation's philanthropic actions are increasingly recognized by society and are not merely considered a show. The social welfare environment can be further improved. In such an environment, entrepreneurs can better fulfill their social responsibilities, and not because of government pressure or public opinion. After improving the public environment, entrepreneurs who want to participate in social welfare activities will not be subject to policy restrictions, and they will have more enthusiasm to perform public duties themselves.

10.6   CONCLUSION

The transition from entrepreneur to 'philanthropy entrepreneur' is an inevitable phenomenon in the process of social development. With the ongoing development of society, the relationship between companies and society is increasingly close, and the interests of the community and its role are becoming increasingly obvious. In this process, entrepreneurs should conform to the trends in society, actively participate in social welfare activities, consciously help to solve some of society's existing problems, promote social progress and development, and create a more favorable environment for company survival and development.

Entrepreneurs are influenced by many factors when participating in charity, but overall, entrepreneurs' charity contributes to a positive reputation, a good brand image, and influences business performance. Entrepreneurs should not be passive or negative when responding to societal demands, but instead entrepreneurs need to consider how to participate in charity and social welfare activities with strategic thinking. Through strategic social responsibility and charity, companies can more effectively respond to the increasingly powerful influences of globalization, increasing demands of customers, and volatile market changes. Being strategic in their responses in the social environment will better enable companies to be able to strengthen their own core competitiveness.

For entrepreneurs to grow into becoming 'philanthropy entrepreneurs', they cannot just rely on their own efforts and personal transformation. Government and society should provide entrepreneurs as well as companies with responsible policies. Only through various efforts can Chinese corporate philanthropy become more standardized, Chinese entrepreneurs participate more – and more enthusiastically – in philanthropy, and Chinese companies, as well as the Chinese society, become better developed.

NOTES

*   This chapter is based on research which is supported by the Ewing Marion Kauffman Foundation in Kansas City, MO and the National Science Foundation of China (Project No.: 71172063).
1.   In this chapter, entrepreneurs are defined as founders and chairpersons of firms.
2.   The 2008 Wenchuan earthquake struck on May 12, 2008. It originated in Wenchuan, Sichuan, China. A total of 69 227 people were killed, 17 824 were missing and 374 643 were injured. The direct damage of the Wenchuan earthquake amounts to RMB 84.51 trillion. According to the China Audit announcement, before September 30, 2009, donations of 79.7037 billion yuan were made for the Wenchuan earthquake recovery (including the special party dues, there are 68.79 billion yuan of funds, goods converted into money 10.913 billion yuan), of which domestic donors were responsible for 72.305 billion yuan; Hong Kong, Macao and Taiwan donated 3.35 billion yuan, and international organizations and overseas Chinese and other foreign countries donated 4.048 billion yuan. Eight entrepreneurs in the top ten on the richest list donated 160 million yuan, 45 entrepreneurs in the top 100 on the richest list donated 637 million yuan and 112 entrepreneurs donated 874 million yuan; http://en.wikipedia.org/wiki/2008_Sichuan_earthquake,http://www.audit.gov.cn/n1992130/n1992150/n1992 500/2302218. html, accessed September 20, 2013.

3. China Charity Federation (CCF) is a nationwide non-governmental charity organization. It was established in 1994, with approval from the Chinese government, and was legally registered as an independent entity. Its members, all of whom work on a voluntary basis, include private citizens, businesses, and social institutions interested in charitable causes. There are over 260 affiliates of CCF throughout China; http://cszh.mca.gov.cn/article/english/aboutus/, accessed September 20, 2013.
4. Harmonious labor relations is an important part of entrepreneurs' social responsibility. A regulatory role in the conflict management strategies may present a coupling effect between the occurrence and labor environment labor conflicts. From the perspective of conflict management, this study looks for solutions to the 'black box' of labor conflicts and provides a solution for new human resource management practices to resolve these conflicts, as well as theoretical support and a practical basis for the creation of harmonious labor relations.
5. Our questionnaires included three parts: one questionnaire for the deputy general manager, one for the HR manager and eight for employees. We measured 'social responsibility' only in the questionnaire for deputy general managers; thus, we received 278 questionnaires from the deputy general manager at 278 companies.
6. Mengniu Group is a leading dairy product manufacturer in China. Mengniu Group was founded in 1999 and in 2012 had $5.88 billion in revenues with $1.48 billion in profits. The firm is headed by its founder Ms Yiping Sun, who is considered a leading woman entrepreneur in China.
7. Project Hope is a Chinese public service project established by the China Youth Development Foundation (CYDF) and the Communist Youth League (CYL) Central Committee on 30 October 1989. It aims to help children in the poverty-stricken rural areas of China to attend schools and complete elementary school education; http://www.cydf.org.cn/sub.asp, accessed 20 September 2013.
8. According to Yu Zhiqiu's (2010) definition, hidden charity refers to corporations or individuals who are unable to donate directly or cannot be included in the related charitable donation statistics for other objective reasons.
9. Chinese Entrepreneurs Survey System (CESS) is an investigative institute approved by China's State Council Development Research Center in 1993. Its purpose is to understand the current state and the law of the growth and development of Chinese entrepreneurs accurately. CESS provides scientific evidence for government decisions, empirical data for theoretical study, and guidance for the development of entrepreneurs. Since its founding in 1993, CESS has conducted a nationwide large-scale survey every year. It has investigated 50000 companies, with more than 800 million relevant data points, and has completed more than 20 surveys; http://cn.chinagate.cn/enterprises/2007–04/28/content_2374466.htm, accessed September 20, 2013.
10. Under the current legal framework in China, non-profit organization cannot fundraise from the public. One Foundation did not own a separate account and official seal. It could only use the account and seal of the Chinese Red Cross. One Foundation registered as a 'private foundation' in December 2010. Therefore, it has a separate legal identity and was allowed public fundraising; http://www.onefoundation.cn/html/43/n-643.html, accessed September 20, 2013.

REFERENCES

Ardic, P.O., N. Mylenko and V. Saltane (2011), 'Small and medium enterprises: A cross-country analysis with a new data set', World Bank Policy research working papers, available at http://elibrary.worldbank.org/doi/pdf/10.1596/1813–9450–5538 (accessed November 11, 2013).
Bi, S.H. (2007), 'Study on the charity behavior of contemporary Chinese entrepreneurs', master's thesis, Suzhou: Suzhou University.

Bi, S.H. (2009), 'Righteousness, benefit and love: The ethics of entrepreneurs charitable actions', *Nanjing Social Science*, 10, 35–39.

Chen, C.W., J.P. Chen and F. Xiao (2013), 'On the personal income tax reform and development charity', *Journal of Shanghai University of Finance and Economics*, 15(1), 11–18.

Chen, J. (2008), 'A preliminary study on the social entrepreneur Chinese', masters thesis, Nanjing: Nanjing University of Science and Technology.

Chen, J.B. (2007), 'Study on the donation of private entrepreneurs China', masters thesis, Xiamen: Xiamen University.

Chen, X.D. and X.D. Yu (2007), 'Current status and evaluation of the private enterprise society responsibility consciousness', *Journal of Zhejiang University (Humanities and Social Sciences Edition)*, 37(2), 69–78.

Chen, X.F. (2004), 'The source of Chinese traditional retribution: Views of the spring and autumn period ideas on karma', *Seeker Magazine*, 4, 170–171.

Chi, A.M. and Q. Wang (2010), 'The theory of social responsibility of enterprises and charitable donation concept', *Journal of Shandong Normal University (Humanities and Social Sciences Edition)*, 55(4), 146–150.

Chinese Entrepreneurs Survey System (2007), 'The entrepreneur's awareness and evaluation of corporate social responsibility – 2007 investigation report for growth and development of Chinese enterprises', *Management World*, 6, 75–86.

Chinese Ministry of Civil Affairs (2011), *Guidelines of China Philanthropy Development (2011–2015)*, July 15, available at http://www.mca.gov.cn/article/zwgk/mzyw/201107/20110700167556.shtml (accessed July 31, 2013).

Deng, G.S. (2010), 'The role and responsibility of government in charity development', *Journal of National School of Administration*, 5, 27–30.

Deng, W. (2013), 'City residents' charitable consciousness influence factor analysis and mobilization strategy', *Journal of Chongqing University (Social Science Edition)*, 19(3), 143–150.

Drucker, P. (2006), *The Practice of Management*, transl. R.L. Qi, Beijing: Mechanical Industry Press.

Fang, J.X. (2009), 'Donation, winning market applause?', *Economic Management Journal*, 31(7), 172–175.

Fang, J.X. (2011), 'Corporate donations and economic rationality – a reexamination of donations from Chinese listed companies after the Wenchuan earthquake', *Journal of Shanghai Lixin Accounting College*, 1, 17–26.

Gan, M.T. (2011), 'Traditional religious culture and Chinese entrepreneur charity – research on Fujian entrepreneur groups listed on the Hurun Philanthropy List', *World Religious Culture*, 2, 1–6.

Gao, Y.Q., Y.J. Chen and Y.J. Zhang (2012), '"Red scarf" or "green scarf": A study of private corporate philanthropy motivation', *Management World*, 8, 106–115.

Ge, J.H. and L.P. Wang (2010), 'Wealth, power and prestige: Institutional analysis and empirical study on private entrepreneurs' actions', *Economic Theory and Research*, 10, 74–80.

Ge, X.C. and N. Cai (2009), 'Comparative study of strategic corporate philanthropy', *Chongqing University Journal (Social Science Version)*, 15(1), 30–34.

Ge, Y. and C.M. Jia (2011), 'Analysis on the development path China real estate', *Economic Review*, 10, 35–38.

Gong, M.C. (2009), 'Model and system analysis of individual donations', *Social Scientists*, 2, 110–113.

Gong, S.P. (1999), 'The ethical significance of Samsara thought', *Voice of Dharma*, 12, 3–6.

Guo, L. (2009), 'The path of obstacles and countermeasures of social aid recovery reconstruction after the Wenchuan earthquake', *Reform of the Economic System*, 5, 58–61.

Guo, S.H. (2012), 'Analysis of the entrepreneur acts of charity on the economy', *Social Welfare (Theory Edition)*, 10, 25–29.

He, L.P. (2011), 'Development of the charity brand building and charity', *Journal of Henan Normal University (Philosophy and Social Sciences Edition)*, 38(3), 135–138.

He, W.Q. and J. Wang (2011), 'Research on the operation mechanisms of company social responsibility during a period of social transformation', Guangzhou: Guangdong People's Press.

Hu, J.X. (2010), 'Adaptive variation in the cultural inheritance and national social psychological deviation', *Jianghan Forum*, 10, 135–139.

Hu, R. (2013) 'China Philanthropy List', April 10, available at http://www.hurun.net/usen/HRCpl.aspx (accessed May 10, 2013).

Huang, J., X.G. Wang and Z.L. Tong (2011), 'The entrepreneur's social responsibility view of moral development: The interpretation based on local culture', *Statistics and Decision*, 21, 184–186.

Huang, M.X., X.L. Li and H.W. Zhu (2008), 'The enterprise "forced donation" phenomenon: The mass "irrational" or enterprise "unscrupulous"? ', *Management World*, 10, 115–126.

Jing, Y.J. and T. Gong (2012), 'Managed social innovation: The case of government-sponsored venture philanthropy in Shanghai', *Australian Journal of Public Administration*, 71(2), 233–245.

Kong, X.L. and G.S. Deng (2013), 'The charity organizations and poverty alleviation: Institutional dilemma and development suggestion – an empirical study based on Guangdong Province', *New Horizon*, 1, 72–76.

Kuang, W.D. (2010), 'The real estate related industries and China economic growth', *Dynamic Economics*, 2, 69–73.

Larson, B. (2002), 'The new entrepreneurs: new philanthropy or not?', *New Directions for Philanthropic Fundraising*, 37, 79–86.

Li, F. and X. Wei (2012), 'A study of corporate donations and the types of social capital', *Seeker Magazine*, 10, 32–34.

Li, S.H. (2012), 'Managerial background characteristics and corporate donation behavior', *Economic Management*, 34(1), 138–152.

Liang, J., S.Y. Chen and Q.E. Gai (2010), 'Private enterprises' political participation, their governance structure and philanthropies', *Management World*, 7, 109–118.

Liao, L.M. (2004), 'A discussion of the philanthropy of the modern Chinese social philanthropist group', *Seeker Magazine*, 12, 251–253.

Lin, K. and H. Wu (2012), 'Government charity and folk charity: Key questions in China's philanthropy development', *Zhejiang University Journal (Social Sciences)*, 42(4), 132–142.

Liu, C., Z.W. Liu and B. Ye (2006), 'Improving institutional arrangement of charity donation in China', *International Economic Review*, 3, 41–44.

Liu, G. (2010), *Traditional Chinese Culture and Organizational Management – Based on the Perspective of Stakeholder Theory*, Beijing: China Renmin University Press.

Liu, J.H. and J.Q. Wang (2012), 'Corporate social responsibility and capital restraint – evidence from Chinese listed corporations', *Management Review*, 24(11), 151–157.

Liu, M. (2011), 'A study of the motivation of the charitable donations of Chinese private enterprises', master's thesis, Kunming: Yunnan University of Finance and Economics.

Liu, X. (2012), 'Research on motives of private entrepreneur charity – analysis of 5 private entrepreneurs based on interviews', Master's degree thesis, Beijing: Political Science of China Youth University.

Lou, H.X. (2009), 'On the function of the charities in the national income redistribution', *Studies in Ethics*, 4, 40–45.

Niu, H.P. and S. Zhu (2012), 'Corporate donation, market cognition and informativeness of accounting earnings', *Economic Theory and Business Management*, 4, 84–94.

Pang, F.X. and H.G. Yan (2008), 'Discussion on the system of encouragement and protection of social donation – thoughts from the 5·12 Wenchuan earthquake donations', *Modern Finance and Economics*, 28(9), 14–19.

Porter, M. and M.R. Kramer (2002), 'The competitive advantage of corporate philanthropy', *Harvard Business Review*, December, 5–16.

Porter, M. and M.R. Kramer (2006), 'Strategy and society: the link between competitive advantage and corporate social responsibility', *Harvard Business Review*, December, 1–13.

Qiu, Y.L. (2002), 'Integration of entrepreneur life values and management values', *Fujian Forum (Humanities and Social Sciences)*, 5, 22–24.

Reinhard, M. (2005), *Entrepreneur Social Responsibility*, transl. X.L. Shen, Beijing: Citic Press.

Sha, Y.F. (2010), 'Social responsibility of entrepreneurs and entrepreneurship', *Commercial Economic Review*, 11, 36–37.

Sha, Y. (2012), 'Research on competitiveness of commercial real estate enterprises under the social enterprise perspective', *Social Sciences in Nanjing*, 8, 41–48.

Song, Z.Y. (2009), 'A study of the corporate social responsibility and the competitive advantage of the real estate: Evidence from the strategy perspective', *Corporate Economics*, 3, 132–135.

Sun, W.X. (2010), 'A study of the motivation and mechanism of corporate donation', *Special Zone Economy*, 3, 294–296.

Tang, W.X. (2013), 'Investigation and analysis on the charity donation and subjective well-being of the SME private entrepreneurs in Wenzhou', *Zhejiang Social Sciences*, 8, 151–155.

Tian, X.Y. (2010), 'Influence of philanthropy donation on competitive advantage: From the perspective of corporate social capital', *Journal of Convergence Information Technology*, 5(8), 233–241.

Tian, X.Y. (2012), 'Empirical research on organization performance and the influential factors of corporate philanthropy', *International Journal of Digital Content Technology and its Applications*, 6(13), 520–432.

Tian, Z.L. and S. Fan (2010), 'A study of competitive interaction of corporate market and nonmarket behaviors in China's real estate industry', *Management Review*, 22(2), 86–96.

Tsui, S.A., H. Wang and R.K. Xin (2006), 'Organizational culture in China: An analysis of culture dimensions and culture types', *Management and Organization Review*, 2(3), 345–376.

Wang, C.R. (1999), 'Entrepreneurship and Confucian ethics', *Beijing Social Science*, 3, 33–39.

Wang, H. (2007a), 'Charity and business: on the rise of charity organizations in modern Shanghai', *Journal of Social Sciences*, (10):154–161.

Wang, H. (2011), 'Seeing charitable donations from an economic person perspective', *Contemporary Economic Research*, 11, 48–52.

Wang, L.F. (2007b), 'Research of charity culture reconstruction in China', master's thesis, Xiamen: Xiamen University.

Wang, L.P., W. Gao and X.Y. Zhang (2010), 'Political connection of private enterprises: a multi-perspective analysis', *Journal of Business Economics*, 12, 18–23.

Wang, L.Z. (2009), 'China's corporate philanthropy from Webb's theory of social action perspective – thoughts from the Wenchuan earthquake', *Theory Observe*, 2, 94–96.

Wang, M. and X.J. Jia (2002), 'An analysis of China's NGOs', *Management World*, 8, 30–45.

Wang, S.B. and Y. Shi (2008), 'The dimensions, characteristics and effects of Chinese culture', *Theory Monthly*, 5, 165–169.

Wang, Y. (2010), 'The summary of the 21st century China forum on sustainable development of financial industry', *Economic Research Journal*, 11, 156–159.

Wang, Y.T. (2013), 'On the relationship between corporate citizen behavior and inclusive growth based on the perspective of ethical boundary extension', *Modern Finance and Economics – Journal of Tianjin University of Finance and Economics*, 2, 94–103.

Weller, P.R. (2006), 'Religions and philanthropies in Chinese societies', *Society*, 44(1), 42–49.

Weller, P.R. (2009), 'Religion and public interest of Chinese society', *Journal of Peking University (Philosophy and Social Sciences)*, 46(4), 82–88.

Werhahn, H.P. (2011), *The Entrepreneur's Economic Effects and Social Responsibility*, transl., L.B. Lei, Shanghai: East China Normal University Press.

Wu, J.Q. (2009), 'The original sin of private enterprise and the policies of government', *Social Science Front*, 3, 217–223.

Wu, K. (2008), 'Deconstruction and reconstruction on the "Mianzi"', *Jiangsu Social Science*, 1, 152–158.

Wu, X.B. (2000), *Big Fiascos of Chinese Enterprises*, Hangzhou: Zhejiang People's Publishing House.

Wu, Y. (2010), 'Confucious and Mencius concepts of justice and benefit: Culture basis for Chinese entrepreneur social responsibility', *Nanjing Social Sciences*, 10, 144–170.

Xia, M. (2011), 'Benefiting oneself or benefiting others? Perspective of enterprise ethics under market ethics', *Fujian Forum (Humanities and Social Sciences)*, 9, 146–151.

Xu, X.S. (2007), 'Study on corporate philanthropy', master's thesis, Shanghai: Tongji University.

Yan, K. and J.L. Zhu (2008), 'Economic thoughts on philanthropy based on the strength of donations during the Wenchuan earthquake', *Accounting Research*, 20, 63–70.

Yang, R.W. and B. Zhang (2008), 'From "merits" to "enantiosemy"', *Language Planning*, 89(4), 59–63.

Yang, X.L. (2009), 'Research on financial development, employment effect and adjustment of industrial structure in China', *Journal of Guangdong University of Finance*, 24(4), 5–12.

Yi, B.N. and Q.L. Han (2012), 'Empirical studies on the relevance of China's private enterprises charitable donations and corporate value', *Seeker Magazine*, 9, 30–32.

Yu, X.M., Q. Zhang and Z.F. Lai (2011), 'Chinese social enterprise from the international comparative perspective', *Comparative Economic and Social Systems*, 1, 157–165.

Yu, Y.F. and J.H. Wang (2011), 'Entrepreneurs' charitable behaviors: review and theoretical perspectives', *Journal of East China Jiaotong University*, 28(1), 117–124.

Yu, Z.Q. (2010), 'A study of invisible charitable benefactions of non-state-owned enterprises – case of the non-state-owned corporate donations in Ruian', master's thesis, Beijing: Chinese Academy of Social Sciences.

Zhang, B.P. (2010), 'The dilemma and the outlet: the reflections over the phenomenon of "moral menace" in philanthropical donation', *Journal of Southwest University (Social Sciences Edition)*, 36(6), 71–76.

Zhang, L. and L. Zheng (2013), 'Public welfare marketing and corporate profitability – a strategic philanthropy perspective', *Economic Survey*, 2, 89–94.

Zhang, W.Y. (2013), *The Game Theory and Society*, Beijing: Beijing University Press.

Zhang, Y., Q. Xiao and X.Q. Wang (2010), 'Management culture premise and commercial interests of corporate citizenship', *Statistics and Decision*, 22, 176–178.

Zhao, B.A. (2010), 'The "soft" international strategy of multinational private enterprises – evidence from the charity perspective', *Academic Forum*, 4, 138–142.

Zhao, H.L. (2008), 'Entrepreneur and philanthropy – discussion on China's social responsibility', *Society Observation*, 1: 9–11.

Zhao, M. (2012), 'The social enterprise emerges in China', *Stanford Social Innovation Review*, Spring, 30–36.

Zhao, S.M. (2007), 'A study of corporate philanthropy in building a harmonious society', *Jianghai Academic Journal*, 1, 100–105.

Zhao, S.M. (2009a), 'A review of current research on corporate responsibility elements, factors and strategy', *Foreign Economics and Management*, 31(1), 2–9.

Zhao, W. (2009b), 'The main problems of the Chinese private entrepreneurs wealth ethics in the transformation of China', *Macroeconomics*, 11, 69–75.

Zhao, X.Q. and D.F. Wan (2012), 'Exploring the feature of province in corporate philanthropic disaster response: an empirical study of "5·12" Wenchuan earthquake', *Management Review*, 24(2), 171–176.

Zheng, Z.G., D.X. Li, R. Xu, R.T. Lin and X.J. Li (2012), 'A longitudinal study on the influencing mechanism of customer's sexual harassment on front-line employees' service performance: the moderating roles of the employee's traditionalism and the team's emotional climate', *Management World*, 10, 146–157.

Zhou, Q.G. and G.L. Zeng (2007a), 'The thought origin of Chinese charity', *Journal of Social Science of Hunan Normal University*, 3, 135–139.

Zhou, Q.G. and G.L. Zeng (2007b), 'Analysis of the content and features of modern Chinese philanthropy', *Journal of Social Science of Hunan Normal University*, 6, 121–127.

Zhou, Q.G. and G.L. Zeng (2007c), 'Contemporary China philanthropy development review and prospect', *Cultural Studies*, 5, 14–22.

Zhou, Q.G. (2013a), 'Research on "Chinese contemporary history of philanthropy and charity development"', *Journal of Historical Science*, 3: 5–9.

Zhou, Y., X.M. Feng and H.S. Zhang (2011), 'Strategic donation – a path of China's long-term development on corporate charity', *China Market*, 22, 144–145.

Zhou, Y. and L. Lin (2004), 'The social responsibility of the Chinese private corporate under the new situation', *Finance and Economics*, 5, 15–19.

Zhou, Z.Z. (2011), 'Charity ethics between ideal and reality in contemporary China', *Journal of Hebei University (Philosophy and Social Science)*, 36(3), 192–198.

Zhou, Z.Z. (2013b), 'Moral evaluation of philanthropy behavior of entrepreneurs', *Journal of Shanghai University of Finance and Economics*, 15(2), 3–9.

Zhu, L. and L. Ge (2013), 'The inspiration of virtuous cycle for the construction of China's philanthropy cause', *Social Sciences in Nanjing*, 3, 54–61.

Zhu, Y.C. (2010), 'The incentive effects of tax policy on China's corporate charitable donations: an empirical study based on China's corporate data in 2007', *Contemporary Finance and Economics*, 1, 36–42.

Zhu, Z.G. and X. Chen (2011), 'A study of the tax policy to support the development of philanthropy', *Finance and Accounting Monthly*, 36, 49–51.

11. African entrepreneurs and their philanthropies: motivations, challenges and impact
Chi Anyansi-Archibong and
Peter M. Anyansi

> If you keep something for yourself, it decays. If you give it away, it blossoms (Ugandan proverb)

> Africans give anonymously for personal and spiritual reasons (Aliko Dangote)

11.1 INTRODUCTION

In the past decade the media has reported increasing entrepreneurial activities in Africa (for example, *Ventures Africa, This Day Live Africa, Forbes* and *CNN Africa*).The increase in the number of private enterprises in the continent is very visible, although specific contributions to the economies are yet to be determined. Many of these successful entrepreneurs are also becoming philanthropists, as also reported by the media (for example see Oladoye, 2012). Their motives are not always clear, but speculation includes the influences of culture, especially religion or belief, as well as social consciousness.

The Ugandan proverb above captures the type of culture of caring expectations prevalent in many African countries. The culture of the extended or large family system demands that the rich or wealthy members of the family bear the responsibility for the well-being of the less fortunate. This culture may be tied to the popular saying, especially in West Africa, 'The shame of poverty and homelessness is not on the victim but on the wealthy members of the family'.

Religiously, the Muslim or Islamic society demands that the Imams and wealthy take the responsibility of feeding the poor who gather in their homes every evening, especially on Fridays. Islamic or Muslim philanthropy indicates that 'giving' is integrated into Islamic culture and law. Specifically, one of the five pillars of Islam – the essential practices to which the majority of Muslims submit in obedience to Allah – is 'almsgiving'. Also, most Muslims give at least 10 percent of their income to religious or secular charities. The cultural reasons for this Muslim giving are yet to be explored.

This near-common African culture of giving is further expressed in the statements by Alhaji Aliko Dangote, a Nigerian entrepreneur and philanthropist, when he donated $2 million to the United Nations World Food Programme (UNWFP) as part of the efforts to help the Pakistani nationals affected by the 2010 flood. In making this donation, Alhaji Dangote said:

> The hearts of all Africans go out to the people of Pakistan as they go through this ordeal. Africa is not only a recipient of humanitarian aids, but is also able to help her brothers and sisters in Pakistan and elsewhere where there is suffering. Helping our family, in this case our global family, is part of Africa's traditional values. (http://Dangote.com/newsandevents/pressrelease)

Nfonobong Nsehe, a *Forbes* writer, stated that, 'While Africans in general are extremely charitable lot, only a small fraction of its 40 richest people are noteworthy givers' (Nsehe, 2011). In response Alhaji Dangote defended African wealthy entrepreneurs during his 2012 interview with Luisa Kroll of *Forbes*. Kroll reported that Alhaji Dangote 'hinted that there are a considerable number of unknown African philanthropists who prefer to shun conspicuous philanthropy, opting instead to give anonymously – possibly for spiritual and personal reasons' (Nsehe, 2013). This statement may provide some support for the limited number of identified African philanthropists.

In spite of the reported growth in African entrepreneurs and their philanthropy, limited academic and management research has examined the experiences, motives, challenges and logic behind their behavior. This chapter explores the characteristics of the African entrepreneurs, their philanthropies and philanthropic motivations. We also consider how culture may influence Africans' philanthropy, address whether philanthropy is culturally or genetically based, and discuss the potential socio-economic impact of this philanthropy on the continent.

Given the limited research on this topic, this study employed a qualitative case study for purposes of capturing the process of transition or evolution of the entrepreneurs and their philanthropic ventures. This chapter discusses African philanthropists in general and compares the concept of philanthropy in light of the above-noted African cultures. It explores the traditional need for the rich to care for the poor and compares it to the Western concepts of philanthropy. The concept of entrepreneurship in the African context is equally explored. In his books about African entrepreneurs and their stories, David Fick (2013, 2002), defined African entrepreneurs as 'the engines that get the economic trains moving. Entrepreneurs organize and direct business undertakings. They assume the risk for the sake of the profit. An entrepreneur has exceptional vision, creativity, and determination, and frequently creates entirely new industries'. It is difficult to agree on one definition of 'entrepreneur' (Howorth et al., 2005). However, other researchers and authors echo dimensions of Fick's definition (see, e.g., Schumpeter, 2012; Olakitan, 2012). Others in Olakitan's (1982) 'Conceptions of entrepreneurs' explain that the entrepreneur characteristics include the capabilities for innovation, introducing new technologies and generating new products. Various authors credit entrepreneurs as the force that builds the economy or a 'catalyst for economic change' (Dilts, 2000). Successful entrepreneurs are defined as business leaders and innovators of new ideas and business processes. They have management skills and strong team-building abilities. Some psychologically driven studies show that entrepreneurial behavior is dependent on social and economic factors. The authors of these studies conclude that countries with healthy and diversified labor markets tend to favor 'opportunity-driven' rather than 'necessity-driven' entrepreneurs. Shane and Venkataraman (2000) argue that the entrepreneur is solely concerned with opportunity recognition and exploitation, while Ucbasaran et al. (2001) argue that there are many different types of entrepreneurs, contingent upon environmental and personal circumstances.

Specifically, this study explores the various types of entrepreneurship and philanthropic concepts with the objective of classifying the African entrepreneurs. Profiles of the entrepreneurs, their businesses, their philanthropic activities, as well as potential motives, challenges and impact are explored and presented.

11.2 METHODOLOGY

This study employs a case study approach, a qualitative research methodology most appropriate for an exploratory study. A case study, when well planned and executed, often effectively produces a sequence of transitions among the group of subjects studied. This approach includes collection of data through both primary and secondary sources, including interviews, published articles and reports in business journals, company documents and Internet sites. It involves the documentation of the phenomenon, exploration of the boundaries of the phenomenon and integration of information from the various sources above (Glaser and Strauss, 1967; Eisenhardt, 1989; Taylor and Søndergaard, 2014/forthcoming; Yin, 1994). This approach also includes the sifting of information collected, and making connections from the information in the context of the situation. This is the first step in theory building (Glaser and Strauss, 1967).

The potential production of a sequence of steps in the transition to philanthropy allows authors to identify and define potential motives, challenges and the impact made by the subjects' activities. Furthermore, because of the scarcity of materials on African entrepreneurs and their philanthropic activities, theories selected or formulated prior to the field study may be inappropriate. The best fit, therefore, for this study is the exploratory, qualitative (case study) evaluation rather than a reductionist approach.

11.2.1   Scope and Sample Selection

The study scope is limited to a select number of noted African entrepreneurs engaged in some form of established philanthropy. These individuals have business operations in Africa and are of African origin. The list of wealthy African entrepreneurs has been growing (Dolan and de Morias, 2013). This pilot study is based on a limited sample of such individuals.

The *Forbes* list of top 40 African millionaires serves as the population for selecting the sample (Dolan, 2012). However, some of the millionaires listed do not have any identifiable philanthropic activity, thus the authors selected entrepreneurs associated with some evidence of philanthropic activities. Entrepreneurs selected have registered foundations for philanthropy. Ten business entrepreneurs were identified and profiled, but only the ones with adequate published data were used for analysis of motivations, challenges and impact on the society. In selecting the entrepreneurs with philanthropic activities, the authors were careful to identify individuals or families from the diverse geographic areas of Africa including those from countries located in the north, south, east and west areas of the continent. Table 11.1 presents the profile of the top ten entrepreneur philanthropists in Africa (Oladoye, 2012). The authors also diversified by including female entrepreneurs who were cited for engaging in philanthropy. Resources constraint prohibited interviewing the entrepreneurs. Thus the data was limited to examination and analysis of published documents, organization records, the press and the Internet.

11.3   LITERATURE REVIEW

This section reviews the literature on the entrepreneurship and philanthropy with a particular focus on applications in the African setting. There is an extensive literature on entrepreneurs, with major studies on classical entrepreneurs and their contributions to the economy (Yu and Ogawa, 2012). There is also an extensive literature on philanthropy (Bekkers and Wiepking, 2011). However, there is only a limited set of studies on entrepreneurs' transition to philanthropy even in industrialized society. These include Harvey's work based on historical analysis of the case of Andrew Carnegie (Harvey et al., 2011), subsequent conceptual development by Harvey and his colleagues (Shaw et al., 2013), altruism as a context and motivation for understanding philanthropy among small entrepreneurs (Lähdesmäki and Takala, 2012), a report on high-tech executives who were founders or early associates in high-tech firms (Schervish et al., 2001), and the work of Acs and colleagues which looked at the interface between capitalism and philanthropy (Acs and Phillips, 2002; Acs, 2013).

The press highlights the philanthropic activities of the successful entrepreneurs, including awards made to such noted success stories as Warren Buffet and Bill Gates, and publicity through the list of the Billionaires' Club events. The Billionaires' Club is a group initiated by Warren Buffet and Bill Gates requiring members to sign the 'giving pledge'. Pledgees commit to give away 50 percent of their wealth for 'good causes' (Clark, 2010). Some successful entrepreneur philanthropists have elected to share their experiences in starting and managing their philanthropies.

In a keynote speech to the 2007 National (US) Philanthropic Trust Forum, successful entrepreneur Mario Morino (2007) focused on what entrepreneurs bring to philanthropy and the challenges they face. The forum described philanthropic organizations as those comprised of foundations for providing grants and jobs, with philanthropists interested in social change. Katherine Fulton, President of the Monitor Institute and a partner of the Monitor Group, has suggested that the trend among modern philanthropists is to give while living rather than leave their wealth base to heirs (Fiduciary Trust of Canada, 2008). Many of the modern philanthropists embody the well-known entrepreneurial traits (resourcefulness, ability to see problems and opportunities, aptitudes for new ways of solving problems, impatience with the status quo and traditional thinking, perseverance, focus on results, and so on) in establishing their philanthropic activity or organizations. Entrepreneurs who transition to philanthropy have the need or want to make a big impact. As such as they bring money to the philanthropy, but they also want to be part of the solution. They find ways to leverage the money and efforts; they believe in their talents. Their involvement in their philanthropic activities is an attempt to protect their investment. They believe that if it works in business, it ought to be part of managing philanthropy. Morino (2007) termed this orientation as being in 'the entrepreneurs' DNA'. He also indicated that philanthropy is broadening and increasingly going global. Further, philanthropists are not afraid to partner with others to achieve greater impact.

One question that arises is whether the entrepreneurial traits and strategies for business transfer effectively into philanthropic organization. It should be noted that entrepreneurs often work concurrently in

Table 11.1   Profiles of African top entrepreneurs

Name of entrepreneur/ business owner	Net worth	Citizenship	Rank in Forbes 40	Education	Religious/ ethnic affiliation	Self-made/ inherited
Aliko Dangote*	$16 billion	Nigerian	1	University	Islam	Self
Anthony Elumelu	$3 billion	Nigerian	NR	University	Christian	Self
Folorunsho Alakija	NK	Nigerian	24	University	Muslim	Self
Francois van Niekerk*	NK	South African	NR	NK	NK	Self
Allen Gray*	NK	South African	NR	University	NK	Self
James Mwangi	NK	Kenyan	NR	University	NK	Corp
Mo Ibrahim	$1.1 billion	Sudanese	NR	University	Arab/ Nubian	Self
Ashish J. Thakkar	$100 million	Ugandan	NR	High school	Muslim	Self
Mark Shuttleworth	NK	South African	NR	University	NK	Self
Throphilus Y. Danjuma	$600 million	Nigerian	24	Military Academy	Muslim	Government/self

their for-profit business or businesses as well as in their philanthropic activities. Thus, philanthropy is not always an exit from entrepreneurial activities. Some major challenges noted in Morino's (2007) speech include the importance of remembering that the social sector is different from the private; the focus should be on relationship as opposed to process; the context is more important than the content in philanthropy; and social complexity in the social sector comes with diverse nuances. The challenges may include identification of the needy, potential abuse of funds, and other environmental factors including government regulations.

Lessons for the entrepreneur planning to transition to philanthropy, according to Morino (2007), include the need to understand that checks and balances present in for-profits are non-existent in philanthropy; that some market forces do not carry over; and that the entrepreneur must learn to be patient in the philanthropic realm, understand the importance of empathy and respect, note that there is a different set of stakeholders, and navigate formal and informal systems. Morino summarized his suggestions to entrepreneurs aiming to transition to philanthropy as follows:

Type of industry/ year established	Years in business	Multi-national operations?	Legal form	Type of entrepreneur	Honors/ awards
Multiple, 1977	35+	Yes	Conglomerate	Classic	Multiple
Multiple, 2010	3+	Yes	Conglomerate	Classic	Multiple
Multiple/Fashion and oil	33	Yes	Corporation	Classic	Multiple
Multiple	NK	NK	NK	Classic/serial	National
Financial	35	Yes	NK	Classic	NK
Corp/Bank micro finance	21	Yes	Corp.	Intrap/social	Multiple
Tele-Communications	24	Yes	Corp.	Serial	Global
Telecomm/MNC	17	Yes	Conglomerate	Classic	Global
Telecomm	NK	Yes	NK	Serial	NK
Oil/Gas	12	Yes	Corp.	Lifsyle/ Social	NK

Be meaningful, be willing to learn, be transparent, invite scrutiny, be collaborative with purpose, be yourself, and have a positive attitude for meaningful
impact. The goal is to ensure that the impact is positive and sustainable. This
is possible if the entrepreneur steps back, learns, and adapts to the ways of the
world beyond the private sector. (Morino, 2007)

The achievement of the above goals is feasible depending on the type
of philanthropic agenda proposed by the entrepreneur. Just as there are
various types of entrepreneur (for example, classic, lifestyle, intrapreneur,
serial and social entrepreneurs), there are also differences in philanthropic endeavors including corporate, traditional and entrepreneurial
philanthropy.

Corporate philanthropy is regarded as the most common approach to
fulfilling corporate social responsibility (CSR). This type of philanthropy
includes monetary donations and aid given to local and non-local nonprofit
organizations, and communities. Donations in areas such as arts education,
education, housing, health, social welfare and environmental causes are
included, but political contributions and commercial sponsorship of events
are excluded (Tilcsik and Marquis, 2013). This type of philanthropy-based

approach to CSR has been criticized for not helping the corporation to build on the skills of local populations. Many favor community-based development in which foundations fund specific projects, arguing that these activities generally lead to more sustainable change.

Philanthropy has been described as 'a form of humanitarianism, not a technique of international development – much less a driver of economic growth' (De Lorenzo and Shah, 2007). De Lorenzo and Shah (2007) differentiate between traditional and private (entrepreneurial) philanthropy. The traditional philanthropists, according to these two authors, 'look for babies to feed, children to educate, and wounds to heal'. Their investments are not for profit. Furthermore, the authors state that, 'the farther philanthropic endeavor is from the "grubby" details of wealth creation, the closer it hews to the canonical image of the selfless helper'. They thus argue, 'Philanthropists and the establishment foundations have historically eschewed nurturing local for-profit companies and improving the investment climate in developing countries'. This effort could be likened to the saying that 'Give a man a fish and you feed him for a day. Teach him to fish and you feed him for a lifetime.'

De Lorenzo and Shah's (2007) views on traditional philanthropy seem to align with the Tilcsik and Marquis (2013) view on corporate philanthropy. The arguments from both sets of authors partially support Morino's views on the challenges of transferring business development approaches to philanthropic activities. Emphasis should be on the motivation, the goals, and the purpose of the entrepreneur and their philanthropy. The trend is toward the identification of a new breed of philanthropists – the entrepreneurial philanthropists. In contrast to traditional and corporate philanthropy, entrepreneurial philanthropy is on the cutting edge of both social and economic development. Entrepreneurial philanthropists defy the notion that philanthropy does not support economic development and growth. The focus, it appears, is to 'teach a man how to fish and not to feed him'. The new breed of philanthropists provide credit and business education to small businesses and support potential entrepreneurs. They are entrepreneurial because they believe that profitability and accountability are the best ways to reach sustainable development. Their actions are designated philanthropic because they do not seek to make personal money from their efforts.

Other studies present various views of entrepreneurs and entrepreneurial philanthropists. These include Acs (2006), who examined entrepreneurship in the context of its contributions to economic development; and Harvey et al. (2011), who defined entrepreneurial philanthropy as 'the pursuit of big social objectives through active investment of ... economic, social, cultural, and symbolic resources'. For other researchers, 'Entrepreneurial philanthropists are dominant economic actors who operate within the field of power' (Maclean et al., 2010). The above perspectives are contrary to the views held by Mario Morino. This set of authors seems to be saying that there is a need to transfer business skills to achieve philanthropic gains.

One may rightfully ask how the entrepreneurial philanthropist differs from the social entrepreneurs. Given the above characteristics of the entrepreneurial philanthropist, is it appropriate to revisit Marino's statement that entrepreneurs should be careful not to transfer business management skills to their philanthropic endeavors? Questions that arise are: how do African entrepreneurs who transitioned to philanthropy compare to the above definitions? Who are these African entrepreneurs? Is there some evidence that African traditional philanthropists are transitioning to entrepreneurial philanthropy? What are their motivations, challenges and impact? What are the potential implications for the continent's economic growth? These questions and related discussions are explored below.

11.4   OVERVIEW OF THE CASE PROTAGONISTS

The *Forbes* top 40 African millionaires and billionaires include 12 from South Africa, 11 from Nigeria, 8 from Egypt, 5 from Morocco and fewer from other nations. Those who are identifiable as philanthropists include Aliko Dangote, Mike Adenuga, Jim Ovia and Folorunsho Alakija, of Nigeria; Naushad Merali of Kenya; Isabel dos Santos of Angola; and Stephen Saad, Patrice Motsepe, the Openheimer family and Allen Gray of South Africa. Others in the top 40 were not identified as noteworthy givers or philanthropists. *Forbes* researcher MfonObong Nsehe (2011) reported that many African millionaires are not free givers, but at the same time he noted that young African millionaires are stepping up to philanthropy now more than ever. The following ten entrepreneurs (details summarized in Table 11.2) were selected based on the listing from both the *Forbes* and the *Ventures Africa* lists of top philanthropists. The profiles and characteristics identified are based on published data available through the popular literature, press releases and Internet-based sources.

11.5   SELECT CASE STUDIES

11.5.1   Aliko Dangote – Nigeria

According to several articles and press, Alhaji Aliko Dangote was born in Kano City, Northern Nigeria on April 1, 1957. He completed his

Table 11.2   Profile of African entrepreneurs and philanthropists

Philanthropists/ entrepreneurs	Estimated philanthropy ($)	Estimated business net worth ($)	Name of foundation	Purpose of philanthropy	Year established
Aliko Dangote*	10 billion	52 billion	Denote Foundation	Health/ entrepreneurial	1992
Anthony Elumelu	200 million	NK	Tony Elumelu	Entrepreneurial	2010
Folorunsho Alakija	20 million	3.5 billion	Rose of Sharon	Motherless baby care	NK
Francois van Niekerk*	15 million	NK	Mergon	General charity	1990
Allen Gray	10.5 million	NK	Allen Gray Orbis	Entrepreneurship/ charity	1980
James Mwangi	NA	NK	NK	Micro credit investment	2004
Mo Ibrahim	5.1 billion	22 billion	Mo Ibrahim	Governance/ investment	2004
Ashish J. Thakkar	15.6 million	NK	MARA	General charity	1997
Mark Shuttleworth	10 million	NK	Shuttleworth		2001
Theophilus Y. Danjuma*	100 million	1 billion	TY Danjuma		1990

Notes: NK = not known; International = across countries in Africa.

Sources: Include *Oladoye (2012), Dolan (2012).

university education in Business Studies from the Al-Azhar University in Cairo, Egypt. Although Alhaji Dangote was born into a wealthy family, he was a self-made entrepreneur who started by purchasing and selling candy (sweets) while he was in primary school. Later at the age of 21, he received 500 000 naira (approximately US$3500 in current exchange) from his uncle to start what is known today as the Dangote Group of Companies. This conglomerate is a diversified organization with activities in manufacturing and service industries. Headquartered in Lagos, Nigeria, the organization has become a multinational with 18 subsidiaries in other African countries such as Benin, Cameroon, Ghana, South Africa and Zambia. The company is the largest manufacturer of cement in the continent. It is a major supplier of transportation and real estate. (See www. dangote-group.com for details of operations.)

Alhaji Dangote is the chief executive officer (CEO) of the company he founded in 1977. In 2012 the company employed more than 22 000,

Personal involvement in philanthropy	Scope/focus	Level of impact	National/ international influence/ focus	Types of philanthropy	Listed amongst top 10 African philanthropist/ givers
Yes/ Exec. Dir.	Multinational	NK	National & International	Traditional	Yes
Yes/ Exec. Dir.	Multinational	NK	International	Entrepreneurial	Yes
Yes/ Exec. Dir.	National	NK	National	Social	Yes
Yes/ Exec. Dir.	Multinational	NK	International	Social	Yes
Yes/ Exec. Dir.	National	NK	National	Social	Yes
Yes/ CEO	National	NK	National	Social	No
Yes/CEO	Multinational	NK	International	Social/ Entrepreneurial	Yes
CEO	Multinational	NK	International	Entrepreneurial	Yes
Yes/ Exec. Dir.	National	NK	National	Traditional	Yes
Yes/ Exec. Dir.		NK	International	Traditional	No

and recorded \$2.642 billion in revenues and \$1029 billion in profits. Dangote also serves as the executive director of the foundation named after him – Dangote Foundation. The foundation is responsible for all his philanthropic activities in several countries in and beyond the Nigerian boundaries.

Alhaji Dangote is ranked as the number one wealthiest African (Dolan, 2012; Dolan and de Morias, 2013) and is equally recognized for his philanthropy. He is credited with distributing over \$25 million in 2012 to various charities including the offer of grants to support small and medium-sized enterprises (SMEs). The donation of a \$15 million fund for loans to SMEs was followed by a \$2 million fellowship program designed to develop young African leaders.

Other philanthropic activities include 1 billion naira to one Nigerian university; a 500 million naira gift for business school program enhancement; and 230 million naira to Kogi State for activities such as micro loans to women in the human capital development initiative, and relief materials to victims of ethno-religious conflict.

Internationally, Dangote is credited with the donation of $2 million (2010) to the World Food Programme (WFP) for the relief of Pakistani flood victims. Alhaji Dangote sees this generosity as springing from African culture. His foundation has developed a strategic partnership with the Bill and Melinda Gates Foundation in the effort to eradicate polio in Nigeria.

Multiple articles in *Ventures* (www.ventures.africa.com) point to his philanthropic activities spanning from health care and poverty alleviation to new business support. He has been honored and cited as the Leading Employer in Nigeria and Grand Commander of Order of Niger (the second-highest national order given by the President). He is quoted as encouraging people to invest their money in Nigeria and Africa because, as he argues, it is the only way to develop the economy. (See www.dangotefoundations.org.)

11.5.2   Anthony (Tony) Elumelu – Nigeria

Several articles in *Ventures* (www.ventures.africa.com) speak of Tony Elumelu and his background. Tony Elumelu, as he is popularly known, was born in Jos, Northern Nigeria, on March 22, 1963. He received his first degree in economics from Ambrose Alli University, an MS from the University of Lagos, and is an alumnus of Harvard Business School's Advanced Management Program. Prior to founding his philanthropic organization, he acquired the then Standard Trust Bank in Nigeria which he turned into a top-five player in the country. In 2005 he led the largest merger in the banking sector in sub-Saharan Africa – with the United Bank for Africa (UBA). As a director of this bank, in five years he built the bank into a pan-African institution with over 7 million customers in 19 African nations.

In 2010, Tony Elumelu retired from UBA and founded HEIRs Holdings, a diversified business with foci on financial investment, energy, real estate, hospitality, agribusiness and health care sectors. In the same year he founded the Tony Elumelu Foundation (TEF). This is an African-based and funded philanthropic organization dedicated to the promotion of excellence in business leadership and entrepreneurship.

The foundation is located in Lagos, Nigeria and its major objective according to the founder is to 'spur African economy through promoting competitiveness and growth in the private sector' (www.tonyelumelufoundation.org). The foundation is positioned to operate as a twenty-first-century catalytic philanthropy, identified as a primary driver of 'Africapitalism', and committed to the economic transformation of Africa (Barboza, 2013).

Tony Elumelu's philosophy is to 'see Africans taking charge of the value adding sector of the economy and ensuring that those value-added processes happen in Africa, not through nationalization nor government policies (indigenization programs) but because there is a generation of private sector entrepreneurs with vision, the tools, and the opportunity to shape the destiny of the continent' (Barboza, 2013). He describes his concept of 'Africapitalism' as a rallying cry for empowering the private sector to drive Africa's economic and social growth, and not capitalism with an African twist. He subscribes to Michael Porter's concept of creating shared value (CSV), the concept that companies must take initiatives in bringing business and society together.

Elumelu's foundation is well established with a strong board. Led by a former Rockefeller Foundation Associate director, Dr Weiber Boer, the members include the Harvard Business School (HBS) professor, Michael Porter, as a founding patron. Other major figures include economist and former Pakistani Prime Minister Shaukat Aziz; Teresa Clarke, formerly of Goldman Sachs and CEO of Africa.com; and Dr Kusa Dias Diogo, Prime Minister of Mozambique, 2004–2010.

Major activities include investment in Mtanga Farms located in southern Tanzania (2012); establishment of an African markets internship program to mentor young entrepreneurs; the Blair Elumelu Fellowship Programme (BEFP), a three-year partnership between the Tony Blair (former British Prime Minister) Africa Governance Initiative and TEF for leadership development, and many others.

Elumelu has been hailed as a leading light in African philanthropy. He serves on several advisory boards including the US Agency for International Development (USAID). He was key driver in the formation of the National Competitiveness Council of Nigeria (NCCN) and serves as the co-chair of the Aspen Institute Dialogue series on Global Food Security. He is a member of the Bretton Woods Committee, a fellow of the Nigerian Leadership Initiative, and a trustee of the Infant Jesus Academy in Delta State, Nigeria. The number of annual grants from the foundation to start-ups which develop local-content applications to solve African challenges (social and economic) while providing sustainable returns has increased from 20 to 50 in 2013. He called these young entrepreneurs the 'Africapitalists' who will move Africa forward.

In March 2013, the Tony Elumelu Foundation hosted its founding patron Professor Michael Porter in Nigeria. Dr Porter also met and spoke with members of the recently inaugurated NCCN, which is chaired by the country's Minister of Trade and Investment, Olusegun Nganga. Porter spoke to entrepreneurs on how best to sustain market advantage. He further emphasized that, 'It is entrepreneurs who are going to change the developing world, not governments. The Nigeria50 is not about 50 companies, but a process of changing the status quo' (Amos, 2013). Mr Elumelu told reporters that, 'The Tony Elumelu Foundation has dedicated itself to the promotion of entrepreneurship, and the creation of an enabling environment for business leaders to reach their maximum potential and transform their communities. This is how economic prosperity for all will be achieved; this is what adds social value to Africa' (Ventures Africa, 2013).

11.5.3   Francois Van Niekerk – South Africa

South Africa is noted by *Forbes Magazine* as the second most giving nation in the world behind the United States of America. Mr Van Niekerk made the list as a philanthropist with an estimated donation of $170 million. He is noted by *Forbes* as one of the top five notable givers in Africa. As one of the 2012 '10 African Philanthropists who gave over $10m', Van Niekerk was credited with showing 'the spirit of modern philanthropy by giving away 70% of his equity in the company he founded, Mertech Group' (Oladoye, 2012). He was noted for taking the lead in South Africa with a stake value of $170 million given to the Mergon Foundation, a charitable trust he co-founded with his wife.

Core objectives of the Mergon Foundation include donations to the healthcare services for HIV/AIDs patients, provision for basic educational needs for pre-primary children, and recycling projects for South African youths in local districts. Van Niekerk also set out about R30 million annually to support social investment programs in South Africa, Namibia, Swaziland and the United Kingdom.

In 2010, a South African institute honored Van Niekerk with a special recognition for philanthropy and for his commitment to improving the lives of people for the past 31 years.

11.5.4   Allen Gray – South Africa

Allen Gray founded Allan Gray Limited in 1973 as a one-man trading company. In 2012 it was noted as the largest privately owned investment management firm in Southern Africa. Educated at Rhodes and Harvard (MBA), Gray has been described as the 'the most successful self-made South African business executive' (Makwela, 2012). He was listed in both the top five givers in Africa and the '10 African Philanthropists who gave over $10m' in 2012 (Oladoye, 2012). Oladoye (2012) described Mr Gray as one who is 'driven by a mission to promote prosperity through entrepreneurship' across South Africa. He has donated over R1 billion over a period of more than three decades to special programs, education and other causes. In 1979 he and his wife established the Allan and Gill Gray Charitable Trust, and in 2005 he founded the Allan Gray Orbis Foundation. Through these two philanthropic vehicles Gray is estimated to have contributed millions of dollars to social causes, especially in education, across South Africa. He set up the trust fund to assist university graduates to start their own businesses and support causes such as the World Wildlife Fund (now World Wide Fund for Nature), Cape Mental Health, and the adult literacy project Iziko lo Lwazi. The Foundation has contributed an estimated $150 million to cover full high school and university scholarships. The scholarships cover tuition, room and board in many top South African schools.

In 2011 Gray received a lifetime philanthropy award from the Inyatheto Institute (Philanthropy SA, n.d.) and in 2012 the University of Cape Town (UCT) honored him with an honorary Doctorate in Economic Science. UCT noted his 'visionary approach and belief that the encouragement of and support for entrepreneurship is crucial for the future of a prosperous South Africa' (Makwela, 2012). The awards were in recognition of his efforts and contributions to South African social change. In his acceptance remarks at UCT Gray himself noted, 'so little done, so much to do', as he shared the day with ten Candidate Allan Gray Fellows graduating from the university.

11.5.5   James Mwangi – Kenya, East Africa

Dr James Mwangi was born in Kenya at the time when the country was going through the throes of its transition from colonial governance to an independent nation. Mwangi's father died at the hands of the MauMau, leaving his mother to raise seven children in rural Kenya. His mother insisted on education for all her children, girls and boys. Mwangi completed preparation for certification as a Certified Public Accountant at the University of Nairobi. Beginning in 1993, Mwangi began the transformation of the Equity Building Society to become the leading microfinance bank in Africa, and then the well-respected, fully regulated and publically listed Equity Bank.

Mwangi undertook the transformation through multiple means: his own well-regarded emphasis on integrity, training the employees in customer service, encouraging them to buy shares in the revamping lender institution, putting emphasis on micro-lending, in 1997 extending the offer of ownership to customers, in 2000 obtaining support from the European Union to computerize the bank's transactions, and in 2004 transforming

Equity into a bank with multiple services and capabilities. Success followed success. The 2006 Equity Bank's listing on the Nairobi Stock Exchange (NSE) brought in additional needed capital for expansion and further computerization.

From a 1993 loss of Ksh 5 million, Equity went to a 2011 profit of Ksh 12 billion in 2011, achieved the status of holding over 40 percent of the Kenyan-based accounts, acquired the largest banking customer base in Africa, and provided a shareholder return since 2006 of 900 percent in stock value appreciation. Equity came to be the biggest majority-African-owned bank and the most profitable in East and Central Africa (Kwama, 2013; Rix, 2012; kcdnkenya.org, 2013). The USA-based Micro Capital has rated Equity Bank as the best microfinance bank in Africa and the third-best in the world in 2007 (www.zoominfo.com).

During this time of change James Mwangi served as Equity's director of finance and strategy for 12 years at Equity Bank, before becoming its managing director and chief executive officer in 2004 (Foundation Partnership, n.d.). Equity Bank has now become a case study for Strathmore Business School, Lagos Business School and Stanford Business School (www.foundation-partnership.org).

In 2007, Equity Bank received the Euromoney Award for Excellence as the best bank in Kenya. This award was given based upon the bank's achievements in lending to the retail sector, reaching out to the 'unbanked', and for pioneering efforts which bigger banks are now trying to emulate. Dr Mwangi, locally, serves on the technical team operationalizing Kenya Vision 2030. His business success was recognized with the African Banker of the Year Award in 2010 (Okafor, 2010) and his contributions to the country have been recognized by the Head of States Commendation (HSC) and Kenya's highest national award, Moran of the Burning Spear (MBS), a recognition few civilians have received.

Mwangi has received numerous other global and local awards. His recognition as an African social entrepreneur and intrapreneur include a seat on the UN Advisory Group on Inclusive Financial Systems (2006–present), his appointment (2007) as advisor to the United Nations Environmental Programme on Commercialization of Microfinance in Africa, and service on the eight-member global roundtable team that discussed the intervention of the Bill and Melinda Gates Foundation in microfinance. Other accolades include the 2007 Global Vision Award in Microfinance, alongside Nobel Peace Laureate Professor Mohammed Yunus, in recognition of microfinance as one of the concepts changing the world economy. He is on the membership of Clinton Global Initiative which brings together the world's most influential leaders to discuss its most pressing challenges. Dr Mwangi is highly educated, with a PhD in economics. In 2013 he received recognition for his achievements with the Ernst & Young World Entrepreneur of the Year Award.

11.5.6   Folorunsho Alakija – Nigeria

Mrs Alakija is a Nigerian female entrepreneur who started her business venture as a fashion designer. She is also a philanthropist worth over $600 million (2012). Recently, Venture Africa labeled her the richest black woman in the world (Atlanta Black Star, 2012). Her net worth has been variously estimated at $600 million to $2.6 billion (Dolan, 2013a; Wikipedia – Alakija, n.d.; Wilson, 2012). However, the estimates zoomed to $3.3 billion in 2012 when Nigeria's Supreme Court overturned earlier decisions in a feisty 12-year breach of contract suit Alakija brought against the Nigerian government. In 2000 the Nigerian government decreased her share in the $620 000 petroleum exploration venture to 50 percent and then 10 percent. The 2012 Supreme Court decision took her share from 10 percent to 60 percent, propelling her net worth into the top spot among women entrepreneurs throughout the world (Wilson, 2012).

Folorunsho Alakija was born in 1951, in Lagos, Nigeria. She attended the Muslim High School in Ogun State before travelling to Pitman Central College, London where she obtained a Diploma in Secretarial Studies. Mrs Alakija started as an administrative assistant in the 1970s but advanced quickly and ultimately became the first head of corporate affairs at IMB, Nigeria's International Merchant Bank (Ellis, 2012). She returned to school to study fashion at both the American College and the Central School of Fashion in London (Falode, 2011).

Along with raising four sons with her lawyer husband, Alakija has become popularly known as the queen of fashion design and a philanthropist. Her entrepreneurial ventures include The Supreme Stitches, a fashion label for upscale customers; FamFa Limited, an international joint venture with a Texaco subsidiary (Star Deep Water Petroleum); and Alakija Real Estate ventures.

Along with James Mwangi and other notable African philanthropists, Alakija has helped to found the African Philanthropy Forum, an associate organization of the Global Philanthropy Forum headquartered in San Francisco. Much of the Forum's mission is to help donors connect with programs that fit their interests, and with each other (Dolan, 2013b). Her own philanthropic interests are focused in the Rose of Sharon Foundation, an organization established to help widows and orphans by empowering them through scholarships and business grants (Wilson, 2012; Falode, 2011). The Rose of Sharon Foundation (ROSF) was founded in May 2008 and is based in Lagos State, Nigeria. The Foundation describes itself as a 'private, voluntary, non-profit, faith based, non-governmental . . . [that has the major mission of] . . . easing the burdens of existence for widows and orphans, which we do through our community network amongst others . . . [with] over 350 distinguished ladies and gentlemen drawn from various sectors of our society [pledging] . . . their support to our projects' (Rose of Sharon, n.d.). Alakija explained her focus on widows:

> We found out that widows are a stigma in this society . . . Once they lose their husbands, the society turns their backs on them, their in-laws begin to mistreat them, they become depressed, they don't know where to turn, they don't know where their next meal is coming from . . . We try our best to bring hope back into their lives . . . [and our organization has been able] to fend for 2751 widows and 963 widows' children, 66 orphans and actually 11 widows at university through the foundation.

The achievement of helping over 2700 widows with workshops that connect widows with each other, provision of monetary support, scholarships for their children and interest-free loans to start up small businesses is not insignificant (Soetan, 2012). Although, given the recent arrest of two aides, her philanthropic efforts are, like her entrepreneurial activities, not all plain sailing (Celebrity Talk Online, 2013).

11.5.7   Mo Ibrahim – Sudan

Mohamed (Mo) Ibrahim is a Sudanese with a global expertise in mobile communication (Wikipedia). He founded Mobile Systems International (MSI) in 1989, a technology consultancy and software business which he sold in 2000 for $900 million. In 1998, frustrated by Westerners' ignorance of the opportunities in the African market, he founded Celtel to build and operate mobile networks in Africa. The company operated in 16 African countries and was later (2005) sold to MTC Kuwait for $3.4 billion (*Jeune Afrique*, 2006; McBain, 2013).

Dr Mo Ibrahim holds a BSc in Electrical Engineering from the University of Alexandria, Egypt, an MSc in Electronics and Electrical Engineering from University of Bradford, and a PhD in Mobile Communications from the University of Birmingham. He has received several awards for his philanthropy and entrepreneurial activities including honorary doctorate awards in economics from University of London School of Oriental and African Studies (2007) and a Doctor of Laws Degree from University of Pennsylvania (2011). His net worth is estimated at $1.2 billion.

Dr Ibrahim is especially known for his Mo Ibrahim Foundation, which focuses on African leadership governance and transparency. The goals of the foundation, which is based in England, include: (1) provision of a framework with which citizens and governments can assess and measure progress in governance; (2) to recognize excellence in African leadership and provide practical ways for leaders to build positive legacies; and (3) to develop leadership and governance capacity in Africa. The foundation works to achieve these grand objectives through the following four bodies: the Mo Ibrahim Prize for Achievement in African Leadership, the Ibrahim Index of African Governance, the Ibrahim Discussion Forum, and the Capacity Building Program (www.moibrahimfoundation.org).

In 2004 Mo Ibrahim established the Mo Ibrahim Foundation as an African initiative to recognize achievement in African leadership and stimulate debate on good governance across sub-Saharan Africa (www. whartoncapetown08.com/bio-ibrahim-. . .). The foundation launched the Ibrahim Index of African Governance (IIAG) in collaboration with Kennedy School of Government, Harvard University. The Foundation also administers the Mo Ibrahim Prize. The prize awards an initial $5 million plus $200 000 per year for life. It is awarded to the democratically elected African leader who has delivered security, health, education, rights, rule of law and economic development to their constituents and who has democratically transferred power to a successor. The expectation is that the recipients will use the money to 'pursue their commitment to the African continent' after they step down from office. These criteria are based on Ibrahim's belief that 'good governance is critical'. Since inception, three former African presidents of African countries have won the prize: the first in 2007 was Joaquim Chissano of Mozambique; in 2008, Festus Mogae of Botswana; and in 2011, Pedro Pires of Cape Verde (*The Economist*, 2011; McGroarty, 2011).

There has been criticism of the Foundation's unwillingness to make the award more frequently, but in announcing no award would be given in 2013, Mo Ibrahim said, 'We set a very high standard, of course, and we are proud of our prize committee for being credible and tough . . . It's a prize for excellence, it's not a pension' (*Aljazeera America*, 2013). His overall purpose in establishing the award was to shift perceptions about African leadership. As he put it, 'The problem we have in Africa is an image problem. Everybody in Europe and the US, they know about our few corrupt leaders, even if they died 50 years ago' (McBain, 2013). He is hopeful that as Africa continues its economic growth and improvement, the political elite will take increasing responsibility to change the high poverty rate and governance difficulties. One observation is that he 'is setting a powerful personal example' (McBain, 2013), and that 'No one has done more to promote peace and good governance in a continent torn apart by corruption, poverty and violence' (*Time*, 2010). In addition to his interest in good government, Dr Ibrahim is becoming very active with youth development issues in Africa (Face2face Africa, 2011).

11.5.8   Ashish Thakkar – Uganda

Born in 1981, Ashish Thakkar is the youngest African entrepreneur in this sample (Wikipedia – Thakkar, n.d.). At 14 he and his family were refugees from the Rwandan genocide. He started his first company at age 15 by borrowing $6000 to sell computers to his classmates. A serial entrepreneur, Thakkar has grown his business interests into the Mara Group. The Mara Group is a conglomerate of companies with operations in 26 African countries that employs over 7000 people worldwide. Mara operates in multiple African countries and has operations in information technology (IT) services, business process outsourcing (BPO), multifaceted mobile-enabled online platforms, agriculture, real estate, hospitality, packaging and asset management (Nsehe, 2012).

However, the entrepreneur philanthropist has declared that the culmination of his business achievements has been instituting the Mara Foundation, the nonprofit social enterprise of the Mara Group. The foundation focuses on emerging African entrepreneurs, and works to create sustainable economic and business development opportunities for young business owners via its Mara Launchpad incubation centers and the Launchpad Fund (Wikipedia – Thakkar, n.d.).

In 2012, Thakkar launched a venture capital fund for young entrepreneurs – the Mara Launch Uganda Fund consisted of the Entrepreneur Launch Pad and the Launchpad incubation centers. The former program provides mentoring for young entrepreneurs. The Launch Pad centers are incubators for growing business, innovation and enterprise for the young businesses (TiEcon, n.d.; Imaralu, 2012). In launching the Fund, Ashish said, 'Funding has been the missing link, but with Mara Launch Uganda Fund now launched, we complete the ecosystem for supporting young entrepreneurs – after all, young people are our future' (Imaralu, 2012).

Ashish grew up in the United Kingdom and Uganda. He currently lives in Dubai and has been profiled by several publications and media including *Forbes, The Economist*, CNN and *Africa Business Journal*. Thakkar, who is a high school dropout, currently serves on the advisory panels to several heads of state in sub-Saharan Africa and is also a team member of the Commonwealth Business Council and the Common Market for Eastern and Southern Africa (COMESA). Mara Group (2010) was identified by the World Economic Forum as a 'Dynamic high-growth company with the potential to be a driving force for economic and social change' (www.mara-group.com). Ashish Thakkar is often quoted as using the phrase, 'The sky is not the limit' (Mugenyi, 2013), and when asked in an interview about his net worth, he claims he has not calculated that, and does not think it is important to dwell on finding out (Mugenyi, 2013).

11.5.9 Mark Shuttleworth – South Africa

Mark Shuttleworth is a South African entrepreneur with a net worth of over $500 million. He was the first African in space. He has a BSc in Finance and Information Systems from the University of Cape Town. As a student, he was involved in the installation of the first residential Internet connection in the university. Shuttleworth founded his first business, Thawte, in 1995. The company specialized in digital certificates and Internet security. He sold the business to VeriSign (Internet News, n.d.) in December 1999 for R3.5 billion (about US$ 575 million at that time). He founded the HBD Venture Capital (Here Be Dragons), a business incubator and venture capital provider. In March 2004, he formed Canonical Ltd, for the promotion and commercial support of free software projects, especially the Ubuntu operating system. He stepped down as the CEO of Canonical in 2010 to focus on product design, partnership and customers (Shuttleworth, n.d.).

The Shuttleworth Foundation, which was founded in 2001, is a nonprofit organization dedicated to social innovation and education and free and open source software projects in South Africa. In 2004, Shuttleworth returned to the free software world by funding the Ubuntu, a Linux distribution based in Debian (Akademy, 2006). This venture was followed in 2005 by the founding of the Ubuntu Foundation with an initial investment of $10 million. In this project, he is often referred to (with tongue in cheek) as 'Self-Appointed Benevolent Dictator For Life' (SABDFL) (CNET). He identified potential employees for the project from six months of the Debian mailing list archives, a list he took with him while traveling to Antarctica aboard the icebreaker *Kapitan Khlebnikov* in 2004. In 2005, he purchased a 65 percent interest in Limpi Linux.

Shuttleworth received an honorary degree from the Open University for his work on software design (http://www8.Open.ac.uk/students/.....2010). He gained worldwide fame in 2002 as the second self-funded space tourist and the first ever South African in space. His exploit was a source of African pride (*Finweek*, 2010). Shuttleworth paid approximately $20 million in addition to spending one year training and preparing in Star City, Russia.

11.5.10   Theophilus Y. Danjuma – Nigeria

General Theophilus Yakubu Danjuma GCON, FSS, psc (Rtd) is easily the most eclectic person among the protagonists in this study. He moved from a controversial military career and civil service to a business career and philanthropy. According to Wikipedia he was born (1938), in Tarkum, Taraba State (formerly Gongola) in the northern part of Nigeria. Tarkum was mainly a farming community where the farms were family owned and grew crops such as yam, rice, cassava and beniseed. Theophilous came from a highly respected family. His father was a farmer who also traded in metal parts for farming implements and tools.

Danjuma attended St Bartholomew's primary school prior to receiving his high school Certificate in 1958 from Benue Provincial Secondary School. In 1959, he enrolled in the Nigeria College of Arts, Science and Technology (now known as Ahmadu Bello University, Zaria) to study history on a Northern Nigeria Scholarship. In 1960, Danjuma left the university to enroll in the Nigerian Army.

Danjuma's military, political and multi-million-dollar business career is summarized below. He was a Nigerian Army Chief of Staff from 1975 to 1979; Minister of Defense under President Obansonjo, 2006; and the chairman of South Atlantic Petroleum (SAPETRO).

Military career

Danjuma's military career lasted from 1960 to 1979. He was commissioned as Second Lieutenant and Platoon Commander in the Congo in 1962. In 1963 he joined a UN peacekeeping force in Katanga Congo where he was promoted to Captain three years later. In 1966, Captain Danjuma was involved in the Nigerian counter-coup initiated by the 44th Battalion, Ibadan. On July 29, 1966, Danjuma arrested the military head of state, General Aguiyi-Ironsi, who was visiting the West as a tour of 'Meet the Nation'. The bullet-riddled bodies of the head of state and his host, Governor Fajuyi, were later found in a nearby forest. A year later, Danjuma was promoted to Lieutenant Colonel by the new military head of state, Yakubu Gowon (Akukwe, 2012).

In 1970 Danjuma attended an international court martial in Trinidad and Tobago as Nigeria's representative, where he was appointed president of the tribunal in a failed coup in that country. Following promotion to full Colonel in 1971, he spent the next two years with the responsibility of court-martialing army officers charged with corruption and indiscipline. He was promoted to Brigadier and General Officer Commanding in 1975, became the Chief of Army Staff in 1976 and retired from the Army in 1979 at the age of 41 (Barrett, 1979).

Business career

Following Danjuma's retirement at what seemed in society to be an early age, the comment was made that 'the road was obviously still long for him and [he] was speculating on what to do with the years ahead' (Barrett, 1979). However, Danjuma did not seem to think for long before he started the Nigerian America Line (NAL) in 1979. NAL began business by initially leasing a ship called *Hannatu* which traded between Lagos, Nigeria and Santos, Brazil under the bilateral trade agreement between Nigeria and South American markets. NAL activities grew with partnerships that started with Nigeria's National Supply Company (NNSC) bringing in government goods to companies such as DICON Salt (Nigeria), Iwopin Paper Mill, ANNAMCO (Mercedes) and Volkswagen Nigeria. NAL became a member of American West African Freight (AWAFC), Brazil Nigeria Freight Conference, and the Mediterranean Line (MEWAC). With the formation of the National Maritime Authority in 1987–1988, NAL was in a position to grow significantly. Indeed the company grew from 12 indigenous employees at its start in 1979 to over 250, including 12 expatriates, in 2009 (Akukwe, 2012).

NAL-COMET is headquartered in Lagos with offices in three other Nigerian seaport cities (Calabar, Warri and Port-Harcourt). In 2005 NAL-COMET acquired a roll-in-roll-out (RIRO) port in Lagos which made it the largest independent port operator in Africa. COMET Shipping Agencies Nigeria Ltd was established in 1984 to act as an agent for NAL. In 2009, COMET handled over 200 vessels at the four operating seaports.

South Atlantic Petroleum Limited (SAPETRO) (www.sapetro.com) is an oil exploration and production company that Danjuma founded in 1995. In 1998, the Ministry of Petroleum Resources awarded the oil prospecting license (OPL) to SAPETRO which partnered with Total Upstream Nigerian Ltd (TUPNI) and Brasoil Oil Services Company of Nigeria Ltd (Petrobras). The license permitted prospecting on the 1000 square miles OPL246. Between 2004 and 2009, SAPETRO grew into a multimillion oil company which divested part of its contractor rights to the China National Offshore Oil Corporation (CNOOC) in 2006.

TY Danjuma Foundation

The TY Danjuma Foundation was created in 2008 with the principal aim of 'providing durable advantages through implementation of development programs', a mission 'to enhance the quality of life of all Nigerians by supporting initiatives that improve access to health and educational opportunities', and a vision to 'build a Nigeria where all citizens have equal opportunities to realize their potentials' (http://www.tydanjumafoundation.org). In his explanation about the $100 million Danjuma put into his foundation and his reasons for establishing the foundation, Danjuma explained that it was 'because the Nigerian government, no matter how noble its intentions, cannot address these challenges on its own'. He also added, 'in all developed countries, the implementation of social projects is never the sole responsibility of the government; there are often strong collaborations with the private sector' (I made . . . oil block, 2010).

The Foundation operations rest on specific values including community involvement, government participation, accountability to beneficiaries, encouraging innovation and promotion of 'philanthropy rather than charity' in Nigeria (All Africa News, 2010). Its foci include community health care, quality education and income generation initiatives.

The foundation has a distinguished board of trustees and operates in partnership with non-governmental organizations (NGOs), and community-based groups to build institutional capacity that supports innovation and accountability to beneficiaries. It encourages partnerships with local, state and national agencies to enhance sustainability of projects. The foundation currently partners with over 50 NGOs in Nigeria with the support and cooperation of 36 state governors in the country. A special focus area and impact has been in Danjuma's home state of Taraba. Taraba has been historically identified as the nation's most impoverished state and its situation has been compounded by the absence of sufficient health services to provide care for its population. Taraba also has the highest number of cases of river blindness and other debilitating illnesses (All Africa News, 2010). Danjuma pledged a $5million grant (2010–2015) to the UN call for supporting women's and children's health – part of the Millennium Development Goals.

It is hard to determine General Danjuma's real net worth. However, *Forbes Magazine* lists him as one of the five notable African philanthropists having made over $100 million in philanthropic grants towards projects (Oladoye, 2012). He is also listed by *Forbes Magazine* as the 29th-richest African with a net worth of over $600 million.

11.6   PRELIMINARY FINDINGS AND CONCLUDING REMARKS

There are seven South Africans, two Nigerians and one Congolese in the *Venture Africa Magazine* listing of the top ten African philanthropists who have given over $10 million in 2012. This is not surprising, since a *Forbes Magazine* survey indicated that South Africans are the world's second-largest donors behind the United States. Additionally, William Gray HI, President and CEO of the United Negros College Fund (UNCF), indicated that Black philanthropy has increased (Oladoye, 2012). There is a new dawn of philanthropic atmosphere on the continent's soil, with more noteworthy givers compared to the prior years. This trend is in synch with the growth of African wealthy families and individuals. In 2010, *Forbes* recorded a total of 14 African billionaires, compared to the 42 recorded in 2012 (Nsehe, 2012).

This multiple case study demonstrates the different types of entrepreneurs among African entrepreneurs including classic, serial, social, lifestyle, intrapreneur and 'venture-preneurs'. There are also a growing number of young entrepreneurs in Africa including Ashish Thakkar of Uganda, Tony Elumelu of Nigeria, and Mark Shuttleworth of South Africa. In general, the entrepreneurs in Africa display characteristics similar to those found in the Western world. They are visionary, opportunity-seekers, risk-takers, business leaders and concerned about the bottom line. Most initiated the businesses for which they are noted, although there are aberrations such as Mwangi whose transformation of Equity Bank merited him the arguably ultimate commendation as Ernst & Young's Global Entrepreneur of the Year. There may be some African philanthropists who may be described as 'necessity' entrepreneurs rather than opportunity-seekers, but the entrepreneurs in this study were clearly opportunity-seeking.

General background information on the ten entrepreneurs studied show that over 70 percent have college education. Eighty-five percent are self-made and 30 percent started in business at the early age of 13–15 years. Their respective net worth ranges from $600 million to over $3 billion and they are generally engaged in diverse industries, including manufacturing, services, financial, investments and technology. Ninety percent have a registered foundation and 50 percent are actively involved in the management of philanthropy.

So what motivated this diverse group of entrepreneurs to evolve towards or integrate philanthropy in their business? What types of philanthropic activities are they attracted to or engaged in? What challenges do they face and what impact, if any, are they making? Most importantly, what are the potential implications for the African economy, and what is the future of the 'Africapitalism' or 'philanthro-capitalism', which Michael Porter endorsed and described as a model for private sectors' commitment to Africa's long-term development?

11.6.1 Evolution to Philanthropy: Motivation

As indicated earlier in the study, it is apparent that Africans give for various reasons. The reasons may be cultural or religious in nature. Certainly some are silent on their motives, at least in the public press, which makes it difficult to ascertain the motives for their philanthropy. This is another limitation of case study approaches, especially ones conducted in developing economies such as Africa where data and interview appointments are difficult to obtain. However, there are several documents (publications and foundations' websites) which present the vision, missions and objectives of several of the philanthropists. The culture of the well-to-do members of the family taking care of the less fortunate and the community certainly dominates the motives for traditional philanthropists such as Danjuma and Alakija.

In terms of religion, the 2005 report by Alterman and Hunter on the theory and practice of philanthropy in Muslim-majority communities identifies giving as an integral part of Muslim religious and social life. The commitment to giving is one of the Five Pillars of Islam and on average Muslims give 10 percent of their income to religious and/or secular charities. There are four types of Islamic giving or charities, three of which are law-based: *zakat*, the pillar of almsgiving (the obligatory 2.5 percent of general wealth); *sadaqa* (voluntary giving, both financial and non-monetary); *kaffara* (potential giving); and *khoms* (for Shi'a Muslims, this is the obligatory 20 percent of annual income). *Sadaqa* is the only type that is not required by law; however, this too is almost necessary because of the social pressure that surrounds giving. In a Muslim culture, giving is regarded as a unifying element of the community. It is not an act of piety but an obligation. Forty percent of African philanthropists in this study are of the Islamic faith, indicating that religious values play a significant role in the entrepreneurs' philanthropic motivations.

Other identifiable motives include interests in reducing poverty, improving health and providing educational opportunities, improving health by donating money to hospitals, and increasing intellectual capital by providing for educational scholarships. Mo Ibrahim, as something of an aberration, is interested in governance among African leaders as a way of building sustainable democratic governments and economic development.

The trend towards entrepreneurial philanthropy is seen among the younger philanthropists such as Tony Elumelu, Ashish Thakkar, Mark Shuttleworth and Allen Gray. These philanthropists have indicated in their vision and mission statements that the motivation to create a foundation includes the need to make a difference in the economic growth of Africa by creating grants and supporting aspiring young entrepreneurs. The Tony Elumelu Foundation is clearly 'focused on supporting entrepreneurs in Africa by enhancing the competitiveness of the private sector' (*Ventures Africa*, 2013). The foundation creates impact through business leadership and entrepreneurial development programs, impact investment, research and advocating policy. Thakkar, with a focus on youth entrepreneurial development, also spans across Africa (with a focus on Uganda) with grants and business development training for the youth.

11.6.2 Challenges and Impact

In this pilot study, the challenges articulated by the entrepreneurs and philanthropists through the documentation in their foundations include the issues of transparency among recipients and employees of the philanthropy, distribution and management of funds and the evaluation of needs, and the impact on the community. Many African philanthropists 'give while living'. A major dilemma is whether they should create a trust for the charity to continue after they have passed on. Another issue deciphered from this limited study is the issue of diversity; that is, the decision to focus on entrepreneurial philanthropy versus social issues such as health facilities, community development and water resources. Philanthropists like Tony Elumelu argue that investment in and development of the entrepreneurial community will eventually lead to community economic development and a better quality of life for all. In his proposed Africapitalism, he is convinced that the culture of the extended family system will eventually spread wealth among communities.

Another major challenge is that of scalability of projects as a way for effective and successful operations. However, this raises the challenge of measuring the value added by one act, and the impact to the community. Overall, it is clear that the real impact of African philanthropists is difficult to measure and this limited study makes drawing conclusions regarding impact especially difficult.

11.7 DISCUSSION AND FUTURE STUDIES

This study is an initial attempt to classify and understand the issues surrounding successful African entrepreneurs' evolution into philanthropy. Analysis of documented information provided some insight into the general characteristics, motives, challenges, diversity and scope of the operations. The cases studied show a mixture of charity and entrepreneurial philanthropic operations. Based on the reported information on the growing number of entrepreneurs evolving into philanthropic operations, the authors discovered that the older generation of successful entrepreneurs engages more in philanthropy that tends to enhance the quality of life for their community, including health care, water and education. However, the younger (40 and under) successful entrepreneurs, whose companies are generally growing faster than those of the older classic entrepreneurs, tend to focus on entrepreneurial philanthropy. These younger entrepreneurs tend to develop operations that support new venture creation and investment in the community. This group of young entrepreneurial philanthropists also engages in telecommunications and technology industries. Their business operations are diversified and are more global.

As is endemic with small sample case studies, this research has significant limitations. Yet the observations we have been able to make have major implications for the continent and national socio-economic development. The study generates many research questions, including the potential impact of the entrepreneurs on the economy of the continent, and the effective means of introducing and enhancing the entrepreneurial spirit and practices in the continent. Measuring the impact of entrepreneurship on the economic development of the continent is another noteworthy study. The question of how these entrepreneurs will serve as a catalyst for economic change and growth is another issue. Further, in keeping with the theme of this chapter, a study on what motivates successful entrepreneurs (classical, intrapreneurs, serial, lifestyle, social) to engage in philanthropy, especially entrepreneurial philanthropy, is yet another challenging area of study. Several researchers have referred to entrepreneurs as the engine that drives the economy (Fick, 2013; Maclean et al., 2010), while some have argued that entrepreneurship is the missing factor of production in the economic development of poor nations (Anyansi-Archibong, 2010), hence the need for classic entrepreneurs and entrepreneurial philanthropists in Africa's developing society.

There is a need to follow up this initial study with a more comprehensive study of how philanthropic ventures influence both societal and economic development. Further, a study of female entrepreneurs, their philanthropic organizations and the impact on society is worthy of study. The study of the basis for 'Africapitalism' and its potential for Africa's human capital development, economic growth and sustainability is a subject of interest for the academics.

REFERENCES

Acs, Zoltan (2006), 'How is entrepreneurship good for economic growth?', *Innovations*, Winter, 97–107.

Acs, Zoltan J. (2013), *Why Philanthropy Matters: How the Wealthy Give, and What It Means for Our Economic Well-Being*, Princeton, NJ: Princeton University Press.

Acs, Zoltan J. and Ronnie J. Phillips (2002), 'Entrepreneurship and philanthropy in American capitalism', *Small Business Economics*, 19(3), 189–209.

Akukwe, Obinna (2012), Danjuma's oil wells and murmuring of Nigerians, available at http://saharareporters.com/article/danjuma (accessed November 2013).

Aljazeera America (2013), No Mo Ibrahim Prize awarded, once again, October 14, http://america.aljazeera.com/articles/2013/10/14/no-mo-ibrahim-prizeawardedonceagain.html (accessed January 2014).

All Africa News (2010), TY Danjuma Foundation – inside Africa's biggest foundation, available at http://allafrica.com/stories/20100222118.4html (accessed December 2014).

Anyansi-Archibong, C. (2010), Entrepreneurship as the missing factor of production in the economic development of poor nations, *International Journal of Strategic Management (IJSM)*, 3(3–4), 7–20.

Atlanta Black Star (2012), Folarunsho Alakija dethrones Oprah as the richest Black woman, available at http://www.atlantablackstar.com/2012/.

Barboza, Steven (2013), Why African philanthropists seek 'Africapitalism', available at http://www.thisdaylive.com/articles/.

Barrett, L. (1979), *Danjuma, the Making of a General*, Enugu, Nigeria: Fourth Dimension.

Bekkers, René and Pamala Wiepking (2011), A literature review of empirical studies of philanthropy: Eight mechanisms that drive charitable giving, *Nonprofit and Voluntary Sector Quarterly*, 40(5), 924.

Celebrity Talk Online (2013), Aides of billionaire bizwoman, Folorunsho Alakija, arrested for fraud, January 16, available at http://www.youtube.com/watch?v=L6rs-FruymM (accessed January 2014).

Clark, Andrew (2010), US billionaires club together – to give away half their fortunes to good causes, *Guardian*, available at www.theguardian.com/news/technology/billgates.

De Lorenzo, Mauro and Apoorva Shah (2007), Entrepreneurial philanthropy in the developing world: A new face for America, a challenge to foreign aid, available at http://www.aei.org/article/foreignpolicy/regional/ (accessed December 2013).

Dilts, Jeffrey C. (2000), Volunteers assisting SMEs in Russia: The Citizens Democracy Corp, *Journal of Small Business Management*, 38(1), 108–114.

Dolan, Kerry A. (2012), Africa's 40 richest: 2012, *Forbes*, November 20, http://www.forbes.com/sites/kerryadolan/2012/11/20/africas-40-richest-2/ (accessed January 2014).

Dolan, Kerry A. (2013a), Number of African billionaires surges to 27, up two-thirds from 2012, *Forbes*, November 13, available at http://www.forbes.com/sites/kerryadolan/2013/11/13/number-of-african-billionaires-surges-to-27-up-two-thirds-from-2012/ (accessed January 2014).

Dolan, Kerry A. (2013b), African charitable giving gets a boost with newly launched African Philanthropy Forum, *Forbes.com*, April 18, p. 1.

Dolan, Kerry A. and R. Marques de Morias (2013), Daddy's girl: how an African 'princess' banked $3 billion in a country living on $2 a day, available at http://www.forbes.com/sites/kerryadolan/2013/08.

The Economist (2011), International: Mo money; Rewarding good governance, October 15, *The Economist*, 401(8755).

Eisenhardt, K.M. (1989), Building theories from case study research, *Academy of Management Review*, 14(4), 532–541.

Ellis, Jessica (2012), Nigerian billionaire takes on cause of 'mistreated widows', CNN, February 16, available at http://www.cnn.com/2012/02/16/world/africa/folorunso-alakija-philanthropist-nigeria/ (accessed January 2014).

Face2Face Africa (2011), Mo Ibrahim Foundation to host flagship events in honor of African youth, available at http://www.face2faceafrica.com/article/.

Falode, K. (2011), Fashion icon – Folarunsho Alakija at 60, available at http://www.thenationonline.net/2011/indes/php

Fick, David (2002), *Entrepreneurship in Africa: A Study Of Success*, www.amazon.com/books/dp/ ISBN: 156-7205-36 4.

Fick, David (2013), *African Entrepreneurship in the 21st Century: Their Stories of Success*, Ghana: EPP Books.

Fiduciary Trust of Canada (2008), *Perspectives*, 2(5), 11, available at http://www.fiduciary-trust.ca/ca/ftcc/en/pdf/newsroom/2008_spring_perspective.pdf

Finweek (2010), Magic moments, Ad Review Supplement, 56.

Glaser, B.G and A.L. Strauss (1967), *The Discovery of Grounded Theory: Strategies for Qualitative Research*, Chicago, IL: AVC.

Harvey, C., M. MacLean, J. Gordon and E. Shaw (2011), Andrew Carnegie and the foundations of contemporary entrepreneurial philanthropy, New Castle University Business School, et al., CAMH, Research Seminar, May 19.

Harvey, Charles, Mairi Maclean, Jillian Gordon and Eleanor Shaw (2011), Andrew Carnegie and the foundations of contemporary entrepreneurial philanthropy, *Business History*, 53(3), 425.

Howorth, Carole, Sue Tempest and Christine Coupland (2005), Rethinking entrepreneurship methodology and definitions of the entrepreneur, *Journal of Small Business and Enterprise Development*, 12(1), 24–40.

Imaralu, Douglas (2012), Ugandan billionnaire Ashish Thakkar launches venture capital fund for young entrepreneurs, available at www.maragroup.com/2010; http://www.ventures-africa.com/2012/07/ugandanbillionnaire (accessed September 2013).

Internet News (n.d.) Verizon buys South Africa's Thewte for $575 million, available at http://www.internetnews.com/bus-news/article.

Jeune Afrique (2006), Interview with Mo Ibrahim, founder and former chairman of Celtel, http://web.archive.org/ and http://celtel.com/mobile/en/our-company/leadership/mo-ibrahim.

kcdnkenya.org (2013), The story of James Mwangi – CEO Equity Bank, June 21, www.kcdnkenya.org, http://kcdnkomarockswatch.blogspot.com/2013/06/the-story-of-james-mwangi-ceo-equity.html (accessed January 2013).

Kwama, Kenneth (2013), Success story of Equity Bank CEO, James Mwangi, *Standard Digital*, December 4, available at http://www.standardmedia.co.ke/kenyaat50/article/2000099368/success-story-of-equity-bank-ceo-james-mwangi?pageNo=2 (accessed January 2014).

Lähdesmäki, Merja and Tuomo Takala (2012), Altruism in business – an empirical study of philanthropy in the small business context, *Social Responsibility Journal*, 8(3), 373–388.

Maclean, Mairi, Charles Harvey and Robert Cia (2010), Dominant corporate agents and the power elite in France and Britain, *Organization Studies*, 31(3), 327–348, available at http://www.sagepub.com/cleggstrategy/Mairi%20Maclea,%20Charles%20Harvey%20and%20Robert%20Chia.pdf (accessed January 2014).

Makwela, Mologadi (2012), UCT to honour Allan Gray, Fink Haysom and others, Politicsweb, February 12, available at http://www.politicsweb.co.za/politicsweb/view/politicsweb/en/page71654?oid=283103&sn=Detail&pid=71616 (accessed January 2012).

McBain, Sophie (2013), Fighting corruption with $5m in cash, *New Statesman*, 142 (5184), 15.

McGroarty, Patrick (2011), Cape Verde's former president wins leadership prize for a graceful exit, *Wall Street Journal – Eastern Edition*, 258(86), A11.

Morino, Mario (2007), Business entrepreneurs and philanthropy: Potentials and pitfalls, Key Note Speech – Legacy, National Philanthropic Trust Forum, September 28.

Mugenyi, Asaad (2013), For Ashish Thakkar, the sky is not the limit, available at http://www.theceomagazine.ug.com/interview/forashish-thakkar.

Nsehe, M. (2011), The philanthropy of Africa's 40 richest, Forbes, available at http://www.forbes.com/sites/mfonobong/.

Nsehe, Mfonobong (2012), Young, successful and African: Ashish J.Thakkar, CEO of Mara Group, June 18, http://www.forbes.com/sites/mfonobongnsehe/2012/06/18/young-successful-and-african-ashish-thakkar-ceo-of-mara-group/ (accessed January 2014).

Nsehe, M. (2013), The most generous philanthropists in Africa in 2012, http://www.forbes.com/sites/mfonobongnsehe/2013/01/20/the-most . . .

Okafor, Ogo (2010), Banking on success, *African Business*, 369 (November), 42–44.

Oladoye, Deji (2012), 10 African philanthropists who gave over $10m, May 18, available at http://www.ventures-africa.com/2012/05/10-african-philanthropists-who-gave-over-10m/ (accessed December 2013).

Olakitan, O. (1982) 'Conceptions of entrepreneurs', in Calvin Kent (ed.), *Encyclopedia of Entrepreneurship*, available at http://en.wikipedia.org/wikiindex/entrepreneur.

Rix, Craig (2012), The rise and rise of James Mwangi, *Kenya Yetu*, July 24, available at http://kenyayetu.net/the-rise-and-rise-of-james-mwangi/ (accessed January 2014).

Rose of Sharon Foundation (n.d.), available at http://roseofsharonfoundation.wordpress.com/ (accessed January 2014).

Schervish, P.G., M.A. O'Herlihy and J.J. Havens (2001), 'Agent-animated wealth and philanthropy: the dynamics of accumulation and allocation among high-tech donors', Boston, MA: Center on Wealth and Philanthropy, Boston College, available at http://www.bc.edu/content/dam/files/research_sites/cwp/pdf/hightech1.pdfß.

Schumpeter, J.A. (2012), *Capitalism, Socialism and Democracy*, Abingdon, UK and New York, USA: Routledge.

Shane, S. and S. Venkataraman (2000), 'The promise of entrepreneurship as a field of research', *Academy of Management Review*, 25(1), 217–226.

Shaw, Eleanor, Jillian Gordon, Charles Harvey and Mairi Maclean (2013), Exploring contemporary entrepreneurial philanthropy. *International Small Business Journal*, 31(5), 580.

Shuttleworth, Mark (n.d.), Here be dragons, available at http://www.markshuttleworth.com/biography (accessed December 2013).

Soetan, Folake (2012), Finance, fashion, philanthropy: Folorunsho Alakija, FAMFA Oil, August 2, available at http://www.ventures-africa.com/2012/08/finance-fashion-philanthropy-folorunsho-alakija-famfa-oil/ (accessed January 2013).

Taylor, Marilyn L. and Mikael Søndergaard (2014, forthcoming), *Designing and Implementing Case Study Research for Business and Management Students*, London, UK: Sage Publications.

TiEcon (n.d.) Ashish J. Thakkar, Founder, Mara Group Africa. TiEcon: The World's Largest Conference for Entrepreneurs, available at http://tiecon.org/speaker/ashish-thakkar (accessed January 2014).

Tilcsik, K. and C. Marquis (2013), Punctuated generosity: How mega events and national disasters affect corporate philanthropy in US communities, *Administrative Science Quarterly*, 58(1), 111–148, available at http://asq.sagepub.com/content/58/1/111 (accessed December 2013).

Time (2010), Person of the Year, *Time*, December 13, 0040781X, 176(24).

Tony Elumelu Foundation (2013), 'Tony Elumelu Foundation hosts foremost business expert Prof. Michael Porter', Entrepreneurs, Management and Players, available at http://Ventures-Africa.com/2013/03/tony-elumelu-foundation (accessed September 2013).

Ucbasaran, D., P. Westhead and M. Wright (2001), The focus of entrepreneurial research: Contextual and process issues', *Entrepreneurship Theory and Practice*, 25(4), 57–80.

Ventures Africa (2013), Tony Elumelu Foundation hosts foremost business expert Prof. Michael Porter, March 26, available at http://www.ventures-africa.com/2013/03/tony-elumelu-foundation-hosts-foremost-business-expert-prof-michael-porter/ (accessed January 2014).

Versi, Anver (2012), James Mwangi: A life stranger than fiction. *African Business–Le Magazine des Dirigeants Africains*, 389(August–September), 46–50.

Wikipedia – Danjuma (n.d.), Theophilus Yakubu Danjuma, available at http://en.wikipedia.org/wiki/theophilus-danjuma/ (accessed September 2013).

Wikipedia – Ibrahim (n.d.), Mo Ibrahim, available at http://en.wikipedia.org/wiki/mo-ibrahim (accessed August 2013).

Wikipedia – Thakkar (n.d.), Ashish J. Thakkar, available at http://en.wikipedia.org/wiki/Ashish_J._Thakkar (accessed December 2013).

Wilson, Julee (2012), Richest Black woman in the world, Folorunsho Alakija, was a major fashion designer in Africa, *Huffington Post*, December 5, available at http://www.huffingtonpost.com/2012/12/05/folorunsho-alakija-richest-black-woman-fashion-designer_n_2245703.html (accessed January 2014).

Yin, Robert (1994), *Case Study Research: Design and Methods*, Thousand Oaks, CA: SAGE Publications.

Yu, Xin and Susumu Ogawa (2012), What can we learn from user entrepreneurs? Systematic review, synthesis, and propositions, July, SSRN Working Paper Series.

12. Enabling, promoting and protecting the entrepreneur, philanthropist, entrepreneur-philanthropist, and the American way of life
*John Tyler**

12.1 INTRODUCTION

The United States' history of entrepreneurial achievement is remarkable. It has been a story of extraordinary innovations in products, services and even entire industries that have stimulated economic growth while simultaneously advancing human welfare generally and providing opportunities for individual comfort, convenience and fulfillment more specifically. A byproduct has been realization of unprecedented degrees of private wealth. That wealth has given rise to a distinctively US (hereafter: American) style of philanthropy and its own remarkable achievements in the irrevocable dedication of hundreds of billions of dollars of private resources to the broader interests of society and its charitable purposes.

Thus, entrepreneur and philanthropist often are connected, whether via a sequential continuum of earning the money earlier in life and devoting it to charitable purposes later, or through the more recent experience of the earning and dedicating happening at the same time, or even sometimes in concert as part of the same ventures.

None of this happens in a vacuum. It occurs in a context of principles and policies that favor both entrepreneurship and philanthropy. Some of them apply uniquely to each role – such as regulation of securities and financial markets that most directly affect the entrepreneur – while in other instances they may have materially shaped both roles, such as with tax policy. Some are new, such as the emerging hybrid business structures by which simultaneously pursuing distributable profits and the public good are accepted as matters of fiduciary duty. Others are hundreds of years old and are principled pronouncements such as are contained in our Declaration of Independence and Constitution.

Not all are in writing, nor are they necessarily unique to entrepreneurship or philanthropy. Instead, they include an amalgamation of principles, policies and behaviors that have allowed entrepreneurship and philanthropy freedom to flourish in practice. Among these are the spirit of self-reliance and responsibility for one's future, awareness of interconnectedness and degrees of mutual interdependence, and responsibility and respect for a distinctively private realm that chooses to intersect with and provide benefits to the public and broader society.

Too often, however, policy makers debate and decide the future of entrepreneurship and philanthropy and how they contribute to our community, national and societal prosperity without fully appreciating the principled and practical connections between entrepreneurship and philanthropy. Academics and researchers strive to illuminate the roles, contributions and vulnerabilities of entrepreneurs and philanthropists and the environments within which they operate, but too many do not account enough for the principles that shape entrepreneurial and philanthropic experiences and how they mutually serve our economic, political and social systems. Practitioners like the entrepreneurs and philanthropists themselves and those who work with and advise them (for example, boards of directors, senior leaders and managers, lawyers, accountants, and so on) frequently tend to take for granted their dependence on the stability and consistency of these principles and policies as they progress toward their endeavors' successes in every sense of that word.

Such gaps can have far-reaching consequences. This chapter seeks to begin closing those gaps by identifying some of the principles and policies that engage both entrepreneur and philanthropist. It also explores how these roles connect with each other and how they reinforce those very principles.

To begin, Section 12.2 proposes definitions of 'entrepreneur', 'philanthropist' and 'entrepreneur-philanthropist' for the purposes of this chapter. It then describes different approaches to philanthropy, and identifies points on that spectrum most relevant for this chapter. Section 12.3 explores certain characteristics that entrepreneurs and philanthropists share to varying degrees: opportunity recognition, risk taking, and dedicating financial, human and reputational capital toward a goal. There is even more substantial overlap between the entrepreneur and the entrepreneur-philanthropist who devotes not just money but also both entrepreneurial and philanthropic tendencies toward achieving charitable outcomes that benefit the public.

Section 12.4 explores how principles in the Declaration of Independence and the Preamble to our Constitution have fostered and protected both entrepreneurship and philanthropy and have contributed to connecting them to each other. This section also shows how the entrepreneur, philanthropist and entrepreneur-philanthropist exemplify and even fulfill those principles in action. While there is much to discuss from both documents, this chapter focuses on the Declaration's recognition of the unalienable right to pursue happiness and the Constitution's ambition of securing the blessings of liberty. Section 12.5 concludes.

12.2   CONTEXT FOR ENTREPRENEUR AND PHILANTHROPIST

The words 'entrepreneur' and 'philanthropist' and their connotations have so many definitions and nuanced applications that confusion can result unless speaker and listener, or writer and reader, have a common understanding of each. Potential for confusion is bad enough when each word is used separately, but it is exacerbated when the terms are linked such as in this chapter.

'Entrepreneur' can broadly mean anyone who takes risk to pursue an innovative approach to accomplish an objective or who has identified an opportunity or need and has begun pursuing it. Within this broad context, it does not matter whether the objective or opportunity relates to social goods, public benefit, economic gain, or some combination of the three. 'Entrepreneur' can more narrowly apply to anyone who starts a business whose purposes are gaining and ultimately distributing profits, whether or not the business grows or is intended to grow. Narrower still is the application of 'entrepreneur' only to those who successfully started and/or grew a business and generated wealth for themselves and/or others. Although this definition diminishes the relevance of risk, potential for failure and the benefits of luck, it is the definition that best links to opportunities for philanthropy because prosperity is inherent.

'Philanthropy' also has multiple definitions and connotations. In its broadest sense, the term literally means 'love of humanity', which makes a 'philanthropist' one who loves humanity. This definition interjects yet another ambiguous term – 'love' – but we do not need to go down that rabbit hole because the definition is too broad for our purposes. A narrower but still too broad definition of 'philanthropist' encompasses giving away resources in a way that presumably helps society and others without regard to accomplishing any specific charitable purposes other than divesting oneself of wealth. For example, insurance industry pioneer and real estate mogul John D. MacArthur somewhat famously declared that he made the money, and the board of his foundation would have to figure out what to do with it (MacArthur Foundation, 2014). Related to and maybe overlapping with Mr MacArthur's divestiture approach would be giving motivated mostly or exclusively to maximize tax savings, which may have more to do with directing funds away from government than with supporting charitable uses of the assets. Charities may still benefit from divestiture and tax avoidance, but neither is 'philanthropy' for the purposes of this chapter.

A still narrower and more common approach might be called 'donative' philanthropy in which decisions to dedicate personal assets to society's charitable purposes are intentional, including whether to contribute, which purposes to select, which organizations to support, how much to give, and when to give it.

Further along the continuum are those who are or have been both entrepreneur and philanthropist. As entrepreneurs, they started and/or grew companies, and they often invented and/or advanced innovations. In all instances, they generated resources – financial and otherwise – beyond their personal and family needs. As philanthropists, they intentionally pursued or are pursuing specific strategies and purposes intended for the benefit of society and the public good through activities that the law recognizes as 'charitable'.

Narrower still is the entrepreneur-philanthropist who affirmatively seeks to advance society and human welfare, often by using innovative approaches to investing resources – financial and otherwise. They often seek change in public policy and/or social conditions for the better as they and others conceive it. Their philanthropy is active, intentional, purposeful, strategic, multifaceted and outcome-oriented, rather than divestiture, tax avoidance or even donative philanthropy.

Examples of living entrepreneur-philanthropists might include Steve Case, Michael Dell, Larry Ellison, Chuck Feeney, Sam Gary, Bill Gates, Michael Milken, Tom Monaghan, Pierre Omidyar, Jeff Skoll, George Soros, Jim Stowers and Oprah Winfrey. An earlier generation might include Otto Bremer, William Hewlett, Ewing Kauffman, John Olin, David Packard and J. Howard Pew. Or consider the founding generation of modern American philanthropists who also started and/or grew companies: Andrew Carnegie, George Draper Dayton, George Eastman, Henry Ford, George Peabody, John D. Rockefeller, Julius Rosenwald, Leland Stanford and Madam C.J. Walker. As much credit as that founding generation deserves for their entrepreneurial and philanthropic spirit, they followed in the footsteps of people like Robert Brookings, Peter Cooper, Paul Cuffe and James Forten, Peter Faneuil, Ben Franklin, Stephen Girard, George Peabody and even Benjamin Thompson (Zinmeister, 2013a; Acs, 2013; Grimm, 2002).

Many if not all of the above entrepreneur-philanthropists also practice, or practiced, donative philanthropy, either as a precursor or complement to their more strategic efforts. Moreover, donative philanthropy and the entrepreneur-philanthropist have much in common, including in their contributions to society and expressions of American values. Both types of philanthropy also intersect with policy as one form of private engagement in the public sphere, which is a hallmark of civic engagement that is critical for preserving a democratic republic and to its flourishing.

Many of the contributions were made possible because of applicable principles and policies, and they simultaneously exemplified those same principles. For instance, philanthropic giving is as much an expression of the First Amendment's core freedoms of religion, speech, assembly and petition as it is protected by it. Robust philanthropic activity also benefits from respect for private property, self-determination and autonomous decision-making, which allow for the entrepreneur's accumulation of resources in the first place. At another level, those conditions are supported by what we recognize as the unalienable right to pursue happiness and the 'blessings of liberty', both of which protect the acquisition of wealth and the right to determine its disposition and contribute to completing a virtuous circle of giving back to the society that made the blessings possible in the first place.

Thus, donative philanthropy and the entrepreneur-philanthropist have much in common, but there are important differences that belie a one-size-fits-all approach to policy. For instance, tax treatment may be less relevant for the entrepreneur-philanthropist, particularly those with great wealth. In addition, the entrepreneur-philanthropist may be more inclined to rely on applicable principles and policies for both of their roles rather than only as prosperous entrepreneur. Their philanthropic endeavors also may be more likely to actively engage skill sets normally extolled in entrepreneurs. Policy that neglects or ignores these connections and differences has consequences; policies that affect philanthropy may also affect entrepreneurship and vice versa.

12.3   SIMILAR CHARACTERISTICS FOCUSED DIFFERENTLY

Entrepreneurs are somewhat famous for characteristics associated with recognizing opportunity, taking risk, and dedicating financial and human capital toward their objectives. US principles and policies have been receptive to permitting and even promoting the ability of people to develop and perfect these characteristics, which has resulted in new companies, new jobs, broader prosperity, improved quality of life and standards of living, and advances in human welfare.

Entrepreneur-philanthropists similarly recognize opportunities, take risks and dedicate capital toward benefiting society and solving or at least mitigating the effects of a variety of society's problems. Their efforts also have resulted in new companies, new jobs, improved quality of life and standards of living, and advances in human welfare. In some instances, these efforts have even created new wealth as innovations conceived in the charitable sector are matured in the for-profit market.

Arguably, then, the entrepreneur turned philanthropist does not really leave the former role behind but instead just changes focus on the opportunities being pursued and maybe even why they are pursuing them.

12.3.1 Opportunity Recognition

Entrepreneurs are frequently lauded for having recognized opportunities to introduce into the marketplace a new product, service or way of using or delivering a product or service. They might invent whole new ways of doing things, as Steve Jobs and Apple did with the computer interface and the iPod. They might anticipate market demand as Carnegie did with steel. They might create a brand new marketplace as Pierre Omidyar and Jeff Skoll did with eBay.

Entrepreneur-philanthropists do similarly. They might start a university from scratch, as Domino's Pizza founder Tom Monaghan is doing with Ave Marie University, and Leland Stanford and John D. Rockefeller did more than a century earlier. They might take an existing institution and give it renewed vitality, as Olivia (Mrs Russell) Sage did for Johns Hopkins University and as many others have done for other institutions. They might support research that gives rise to new industries, as the Guggenheims did for aviation and others have done for biomedical research, microbiology and nanotechnology. Their funding might support research that prevents, treats or cures disease. They might support critical analysis and corresponding research, as Robert Brookings and John Olin did in founding 'think tanks' that examine and understand the effects of various policies or possibilities on society. They might support replication and scale growth of efforts that contributed to their personal formation and well-being, as Carnegie did by making libraries broadly available to the public as his mentor, Colonel James Anderson, made books available to him and others in their youth (Zinmeister, 2013a; Acs, 2013; Grimm, 2002).

Entrepreneur-philanthropists might make connections previously unrealized. Some connections might be grand. Ewing Kauffman linked entrepreneurship with education, economic advancement for the individual and society, and defeating racism and discrimination. He also identified opportunities for philanthropy to actively and directly engage entrepreneurship toward those ends (Morgan, 1995: 335, 354–358). Some connections might be mundane but profound in their influence, such as the Dorr Foundation demonstrating the benefits of painted lines along the outer edge of roadways (Gaudiani, 2010: 138).

Entrepreneur-philanthropists might create innovative structures in order to most fully pursue their charitable interests broadly defined, as Pierre and Pam Omidyar and Dustin Moskovitz and Cari Tuna have done in their combinations of related private foundations, public charities and non-exempt investment funds. They might make philanthropy an essential part of their entrepreneurial venture, as Sergey Brin and Larry Page did in formalizing Google.org within Google, Inc. or as Paul Newman did with Newman's Own.

These are but a few of the many examples of opportunity recognition being applied to philanthropy. Whether in business or philanthropy, these possibilities are available in part because of the freedoms and respect for property, rule of law and self-determination that exist in the United States. Also contributing have been principles and policies that encourage and value the relative ease with which a person can pursue their ideas and attract others to them, oftentimes sharing the risks of loss and failure.

12.3.2   Risk Taking and Resources

Risk taking is frequently and rightly associated with entrepreneurship. The first thing that most often comes to mind is that money is at risk – their own and that of others who invest or provide credit. But money is not the only thing risked; time, energy, expertise and reputation – their own and others' – are also exposed. Furthermore, each of these risks has at least two dimensions: one direct and the other indirect. There is money, time, and so on that might be lost. There also are alternative opportunities that might have been pursued but for the choice to dedicate money, time, and so on to the selected venture.

Of course, risk and reward or outcome are inextricably intertwined in that the quality, quantity and likelihood of reward or outcome help to determine whether a venture or activity is worth pursuing. Often, the reward or outcome sought by the entrepreneur and what motivates them to take the above risks seems to be a combination of financial return, self-fulfillment and honor; having an effect on society as people use their product, service or app; and possibly even building a company that provides jobs and serves as a community asset.

Many efforts do not yield the intended results, or any positive result other than the intangible and sometimes invaluable benefits of lessons learned from experience. But many of those risks have generated wealth, livelihood, skills, dignity, pride, efficiency, effectiveness, better standards of living and improved health, welfare and environment – sometimes in the intended ways, but often in other ways as well. Regardless, taking those risks at a minimum affects individuals, families and communities, but the impact also can extend, and in many cases has extended more broadly to community, nation and internationally.

Our society rightly supports and encourages such risk taking and its effects as a reflection of our centuries-old culture of self-reliance, self-determination, innovation, aspiration, ambition and mutual dependence. Reflections of that support are seen in tax policy that allows deductions and provides credits for various activities; a Constitution that respects tangible and intangible property; laws and processes for enforcing contracts; bankruptcy protection that keeps failure from being a total barrier to future efforts; limitations on exclusivity of rights under patent and copyright laws that balance exploitation with innovation; and more. Thus, entrepreneurship has an opportunity to flourish.

This is very often the risk-taking context and experience that successful entrepreneurs bring with them into philanthropy. The categories of risk for the philanthropist are not very different, but the rewards and outcomes, and likelihood of being realized, are different, which is part of what distinguishes philanthropy generally from government and business. In many instances, and even though the methods, priorities and risk tolerances may differ, both entrepreneur and philanthropist (whether donative or entrepreneur-philanthropist) share a desire to contribute to and improve society, benefit the public and advance human welfare.

For instance, and like the entrepreneur, the philanthropist tends to put time, energy and expertise at risk in search of identifying and pursuing the desired outcome(s). Given that their family name is often connected to their activities – the Moskovitz–Tuna Good Ventures enterprise being an exception – and that they may be known for their business success, philanthropists also put reputations at risk. Lastly, they put their money at risk along with that of others who might join the crusade.

Regarding money, the philanthropist most often expects to get neither any money back nor a financial return on the funds provided. Normally, the entrepreneur is at least hoping for, if not expecting or demanding, their money back with a financial return. As others' money enters the respective ventures, the legal and fiduciary risks and responsibilities diverge. As the entrepreneur accepts others' money into the business, they now have legal obligations about how those funds can be used. They have fiduciary duties to target risk taking toward generating financial returns without regard to goals such as the social good, public benefit and advancing human welfare. The philanthropist who accepts others' money can remain focused on their original charitable purpose and may have legal and fiduciary responsibilities to do so.

Among other risks that affect both entrepreneur and philanthropist are opportunity costs. The philanthropist must make choices about the charitable mission, strategies, tactics, allocating resources, evaluation criteria and tools, and more. In other words, how will the philanthropist commit capital resources – financial and human? After all, money and time are no less renewable in philanthropy than they are in business. Decisions must be made, often from among equally desirable and worthy causes and recipients with similar risk–reward profiles. Those decisions affect the philanthropist, the recipient and those not selected for support. As such, and like the entrepreneur's business decisions, there are effects on end users, society, the public, living standards, life choices, opportunities and even human welfare.

Public policy recognizes that these risks are present for entrepreneur and philanthropist. Public policy also generally recognizes the relevance and value of private assessments of those risks and of private decision-making about whether and how to pursue or mitigate them and allocate resources. These principles and policies – whether for entrepreneur or philanthropist – frequently have many layers. They are often opportunistic in permitting individual expressions and pursuits. They are sometimes restrictive in leveling the playing field and trying to promote fairness for those who would take advantage of the opportunities they identify. Principles and policies establish boundaries for deterring government intervention or obstruction. They also execute on our three-sector system of how the business, governmental and charitable sectors complement each other, perform functions that the others cannot or should not perform, and keep the others in check.

These principles and policies operate on and function for entrepreneur and philanthropist in ways that are sometimes identical, other times similar, and still other times very different. Thus, there are times when policy changes intended to affect one will also affect the other, whether by design or accident.

12.4   DECLARING AND CONSTITUTING FOUNDATIONAL PRINCIPLES FOR POLICY

Arguably, America began as an extraordinary entrepreneurial experiment, at least to the extent that 'entrepreneurial' can describe civil society. Those who organized, led and fought in our Revolution rebelled against a particular form and practice of governing society because they recognized a need to demand and pursue something better for which they pledged everything, including life itself. The signers of the Declaration of Independence explicitly proclaimed: 'we mutually pledge to each other our lives, our Fortunes, & our sacred Honor'. There certainly was no pre-ordained, presumptively favorable outcome. In the course of events that followed, many found that they not only had pledged and risked everything, but they lost it; very few, if any, were unscathed.

Fortunately, the British were not victorious and the Founders had the chance to design and execute a civil society and government that would further the self-evident truths that they embraced, and to institute a new government on the principles that they deemed 'most likely to effect their Safety & Happiness'.

Their first attempt – the Articles of Confederation – failed in no small part because it did not sufficiently foster and actually inhibited economic self-determination and commercial growth for business, states and the confederation (Kurland and Lerner, 1987: 147–184, 186–187; The Federalist, No. 2, 11–13 in Wootton, 2003; Wills, 2001: 273). While a theoretically attractive structure, the realities of executing the Articles resulted in contracting being unpredictable, debt repayment being unreliable, and monetary policy being diffused and confused, among other problems. Thus, for entirely different reasons than those that motivated the Declaration and Revolution, but for reasons consistent with the principles then proclaimed, the people instituted a new government in 1789.

The second attempt – the Constitution – is as much ours as it was the Founders', maybe more so because it no longer affects them. While its longevity seems to indicate success, the nature of the document and its operational principles suggest an ongoing journey rather than a destination or single, assessable result. The Constitution did permit success in addressing many of the problems with the Articles: contracts became more reliable, extension of credit received better protection, monetary policy became unified as did intellectual property, defense, and certain other responsibilities and boundaries of government – all of which occurred within a principled context as decreed in the Declaration and the Constitution's Preamble.

That principled context has served and continues to serve many purposes, three of which have been the evolution of the entrepreneur, the emergence of the philanthropist and the interconnectedness of each to the other.

12.4.1   Entrepreneurship, Philanthropy and the Declaration of Independence – 'Pursuit of Happiness'

One essence of the American experiment and experience was stated in the introductory section of the Declaration of Independence in which the Founding Fathers boldly asserted:

> We hold these truths to be self-evident, that all men are created equal, that they are endowed by their Creator with certain unalienable Rights, that among these are life, liberty, and the pursuit of happiness. – That to secure these rights, Governments are instituted among Men, deriving their just Powers from the consent of the governed, – that whenever any Form of Government becomes destructive of these ends, it is the Right of the People to alter or abolish it, and to institute new Government, laying its foundation on such principles and organizing its powers in such form, as to them shall seem most likely to effect their Safety and Happiness.

'Happiness' appears twice in this historic, original approach to organizing a people in society: once as part of the litany of 'unalienable rights' and again as an objective for government as instituted and organized by the 'People'.

The Declaration was not the only one of our nation's founding documents to emphasize the importance of protecting and ensuring the ability to pursue happiness as a fundamental right. The Virginia Declaration of Rights in 1776, which its subsequent 1786 bill of rights reiterated (Ely, 2008a: 697), the bill of rights and preamble to the 1780 Massachusetts constitution and the early constitutions of Pennsylvania, Vermont, Maryland, North Carolina, South Carolina and New Hampshire, all similarly recognized this (Rahe, 2005: 3; Ely, 2008a: 697–698; Ely, 2008b: 30). In ratifying the Constitution, Virginia specifically listed natural rights of persons and included 'pursuing and obtaining happiness and safety' (St George Tucker, 1999 [1803]: 112).

The notion of 'happiness' was not merely some abstract, esoteric concept, nor was its objective extending fleeting feelings of joy or satisfaction. 'Happiness' was understood both more broadly and directly as connecting to the economy and individual welfare. As a leading thinker of the Revolutionary time, Pelatiah Webster wrote in the first of several *Essays on Free Trade*: 'Freedom of trade, or unrestrained liberty of the subject to hold or dispose of his property as he pleases, is absolutely necessary to the prosperity of every community and to the happiness of all individuals who compose it' (Grampp, 1965: 130).

Thus, and as part of our nation's genetic disposition and primary responsibilities of government, 'happiness' – or more particularly and better stated, 'the pursuit of happiness' – is a fundamental principle against which policy and activities should be consistently evaluated. Entrepreneurship and philanthropy in America both have deep links to the 'pursuit of happiness'. Both are derived from opportunities made available because principles associated with 'pursuit of happiness' allow them to take root and thrive. In addition, both exemplify its fulfillment in that entrepreneurial and philanthropic experiences can be distinctive realizations of happiness pursued. Finally for our purposes, entrepreneurship and philanthropy are complementary points along the continuum of happiness, whether pursued by or for the individual or society.

'Pursuit of Happiness' and entrepreneurship

At its most basic level, the 'happiness' proclaimed in the Declaration can be linked to security in material possessions and property currently held. Thus, along with life and liberty, the 'unalienable rights' individually and collectively recognize inherent limits on government (including on its ability to divest property from a person) and a corresponding duty of government to prevent the unauthorized taking of property already possessed. Such a conception of 'happiness' is consistent with British understandings of property and its enshrinement in a class structure that inhibited class mobility. But the concept of 'pursuit of happiness' goes at least two steps further and incorporates a third step not connected to material or real property at all. Those extensions are part of what makes the Declaration's proclamation both a threshold and a barometer for policies regarding entrepreneurship.

By declaring 'pursuit of happiness' – not 'happiness' itself – as one of three listed unalienable rights, the Declaration recognizes security in the right to acquire additional property, which is also entitled to protection from and by government. In many ways, this phrasing and certain principles that underlie it acknowledge and give legitimacy to personal ambition to 'acquire property as fast as he can' and realize rewards from individual and collective pursuits, including those of the entrepreneur (Lincoln, 1992b [1860]: 144). Thus does the Declaration enshrine opportunity to move from one socio-economic class into another (Gaudiani, 2003: 6, 135), which Abraham Lincoln characterized as:

> allow[ing] the humblest man an equal chance to get rich with everybody else. When one starts poor, as most do in the race of life, free society is such that he knows he can better his condition; he knows that there is no fixed condition of labor, for his whole life. (Lincoln, 1992b [1860]: 144)

If anyone understood this, it was Abraham Lincoln. One Lincoln historian summarized his philosophy as 'the right to rise' (Von Drehle, 2012).

Such mobility is part of what distinguished American conceptions of property from those of Britain. It also helped to motivate entrepreneurial activity and inspire the 'American dream' and its realizations.

The third property-related aspect of the Declaration's phrasing, after possession and acquisition, is the right and ability to dispose of property according to the owner's preferences. For entrepreneurship, that can mean undertaking the risk of loss, whether through one's own efforts or by investing in another, and regardless of whether the choice is smart and thoughtful or ridiculous and wasteful. That risk is part of what makes downward socio-economic mobility the corollary to the right to rise. The right to choose for oneself how to dispose of property, including by dedicating it to charitable purposes, also helps protect against multi-generational concentrations of wealth that tend toward aristocracy and against a democratic republic.

The 'pursuit of happiness' also transcends material possessions and real property. 'Happiness', both now and at the time of our founding, also encompasses personal fulfillment, knowledge, industry and progress (Pollack, 2001: 773–774). As such, 'pursuit of happiness' acknowledges an unalienable right to opportunities to develop talent, explore potential, innovate, create and otherwise progress as one may elect, and accept the consequences (McDowell, 2010: 318). In making choices and exerting the requisite effort, we can make personal progress and thus pursue happiness for ourselves, which also connects to and enables Lincoln's 'right to rise'. Thomas Jefferson saw how the 'opportunity to pursue [one's] own happiness' could 'unleash new opportunities for self-development' (Yarbrough, 1989: 73), which can contribute to happiness more broadly.

Extending the concept from individual to society, George Washington in his first annual address recognized a connection between individual knowledge and public happiness: '[t]here is nothing which can better deserve your patronage, than the promotion of science and literature. Knowledge is, in every country, the surest basis of public happiness' (Washington, 1997 [1790]: 750). Intellectual property statutes in Massachusetts, New Hampshire and Rhode Island from the 1780s similarly encapsulated connections between improving knowledge and 'advancing human happiness' and their mutual dependence on discrete efforts of individual people pursuing 'various arts and sciences' (Pollack, 2001: 784; Walterscheid, 1994: 22). Jefferson also saw the link between personal progress and benefits to society when he wrote in 1780: 'No other sure foundation can be devised for the preservation of freedom and happiness' than 'the diffusion of knowledge among the people' (Meacham, 2012: 469).

James Madison posited an even grander conception for 'pursuit of happiness'. Madison suggested that there may be a responsibility to affirmatively act toward those ends, particularly among the 'class of literati' – those who had financial security and therefore the luxury of time and resources to contemplate the public good of society – to be 'cultivators of the human mind – manufacturers of useful knowledge – the agents of the commerce of ideas and the teachers of the arts of life and the means of happiness' (Kramer, 2004: 112; Kramer, 2006: 730–731).

Of course, individual 'pursuit of happiness' also has limitations because the individual exists in, benefits from and contributes to community, society and nation (Siegan, 2006: 62, citing Hume; Gaudiani, 2003: 142–143). As such, there are responsibilities, boundaries and presumptive limits in one's pursuit of happiness, including on infringing the rights of others or sacrificing the public good (Urofsky and Finkelman, 2002: 48; Gaudiani, 2003: 155). Thus does 'pursuit of happiness' encompass and transcend both material and real property and the individual.

Among such pursuits can be starting and growing businesses, hiring people, and facilitating opportunities for them to develop talent, explore potential, progress in knowledge, and so on, and pursue happiness. By extension, the entrepreneur and their team advance society; at a minimum because their efforts can influence economic growth and prosperity, but also because they can further society's knowledge and progress in using that knowledge to advance human welfare and in creating new opportunities. In these ways, the individual's pursuit of happiness directly influences the happiness of community, society and nation.

Explicit connections between the unalienable right to pursue happiness and entrepreneurship and the policy implications for them include property and non-property characteristics, and they simultaneously engage individual and society. Regarding property, they secure protections for property already possessed and for the ability to develop and use talents and ingenuity to acquire and ultimately dispose of more property – inherently entrepreneurial pursuits. Those efforts, however, also can contribute to society's economic growth and well-being. They also can permit, provide and even depend on opportunities for others to develop and use their talents and ingenuity who, then, likewise expand their property and rights to dispose of it as they so choose.

Of course, no one is guaranteed equal happiness or even happiness itself (Rahe, 2005: 6). Moreover, not every person is equal in talent, potential or interest, which means that not everyone's opportunities for or types of happiness are the same (Rahe, 2005: 7; Pocock, 2003: 68; St George Tucker, 1999 [1803]: 163, citing Montesquieu; Lincoln, 1992a [1857]: 398; Madison, 1999 [1787]: 161). But all are blessed with talent, potential and interests that they have obligations to develop and use (Pocock, 2003: 373). They should have the stability and growth of a free society that recognizes that 'pursuit of happiness' as an unalienable right must exist to mobilize the talents, potential and interests of all citizens, as uneven or unequal as they may be (Pocock, 2003: 94; Gaudiani, 2003: 31).

Far from being a detriment or something to be overcome, divergence of talent, potential and interests is often the genesis for identifying opportunities to create and/or advance new products, services, processes or approaches. When the right and opportunity to develop talents, potential and interests are combined with others doing the same – whether in cooperation or in competition with each other – the result can be entrepreneurial endeavors and their resulting contributions to self and society, including happiness pursued and even freedom preserved.

Although not guaranteeing happiness or equal distribution of talent or material possessions, the Declaration does pronounce a conviction that all are created equal in having been endowed with unalienable rights from which we extrapolate equal entitlement to impartial applications of the rule of law, expectations for objective treatment and consideration from government, and opportunity for an environment in which to cultivate talents, potential and interests and to pursue progress (Pocock, 2003: 469; Gaudiani, 2003: 109).

Sadly, that equality is limited by the reality of being implemented in a context of human frailty. Society and human welfare have suffered and continue to suffer as a result of not permitting our nation's full complement of diverse talents and interests the chance to most fully explore potential, recognize new opportunities, and contribute to the pursuit of happiness for self and society. Rectifying those deficiencies in and shortcomings of human nature is one application of philanthropy, whether donative or as practiced by the entrepreneur-philanthropist.

'Pursuit of Happiness' and philanthropy

Like the relationship between pursuing happiness and entrepreneurship, the link with philanthropy also has dimensions of property, non-property, self and others or society. Philanthropy in its most basic financial sense occurs when a person irrevocably devotes property to charitable purposes, which is one way of disposing of property and a fundamental expression of the triune character of property in a free society; that is, being secure in its holding, acquisition and disposition. In other words, our government and society more broadly do not and cannot mandate how a person disposes of their property – at least not without due process of law and just compensation. Although government's power to tax can force a person to relinquish property to government, our governments cannot constitutionally force person A to give property to person B. Government and society can and do provide various incentives – like tax-favored treatment and recognition

– to encourage certain dispositions, including toward philanthropy; but the actual decision to dispose of property and its execution remain personal.

A critical non-property component to philanthropy and pursuit of happiness is the extent to which making decisions for the explicit benefit of others and society more broadly engages experiences of earthly happiness as Aristotle and many others over the millennia have envisioned it (Aristotle, 2004 [1883]; Gaudiani, 2003: 143). In the 1600s an English philosopher wrote that promoting the well-being of our fellow human beings is essential to understanding the 'pursuit of happiness' (Cumberland, 2005 [1727]: 523–525). Scottish Enlightenment philosopher and influencer of our Founding Fathers, Adam Ferguson, wrote about happiness deriving from being devoted to the 'good of mankind', from doing kindness for others as bestowing happiness on the actor rather than on the beneficiary of the action, and from ensuring that others can experience the happiness of giving to others and devotion to the good of mankind (Ferguson, 1996 [1767]: 56). Enlightenment leader John Hutcheson believed similarly: 'The surest way to promote . . . private happiness [is] to do publicly useful actions . . . The general happiness is the supreme end of all political union' (Gaudiani, 2003: 143). In his treatise on the Declaration of Independence, Garry Wills characterizes Jefferson's immortal phrasing as constituting both the basic drive of the individual and 'the only means given for transcending the self' (Wills, 2002: 247).

Noted philanthropists similarly have expressed the connection between happiness and serving others. Madam C.J. Walker, a renowned entrepreneur and philanthropist from the late nineteenth and early twentieth century, disclaimed an objective for her life as 'simply to make money for myself or to spend it on myself'. Instead, what made her happy was using part of her wealth 'in trying to help others' (Grimm, 2002: 330). Booker T. Washington pronounced similarly that 'those who are happiest are those who do the most for others' (Grimm, 2002: 333). Ewing Kauffman noted similarly his wish that he had begun his earnest philanthropic efforts sooner because of how much joy he found in giving to and for others (Morgan, 1995: 319). Oilman and philanthropist Jim Calaway recently declared: 'Making a lot of money and spending it on yourself is not a lot of fun . . . What is a lot of fun is to live modestly so that you can give to the common good. That's where happiness really lies' (Zinmeister, 2013b).

In addition to bringing personal happiness and fulfillment, an other-centric orientation toward happiness as practiced through philanthropy can provide opportunities for people to develop their talents and position themselves to advance their potential. They then contribute to their own progress and efforts to pursue happiness, which ultimately further benefits society (Pocock, 2003: 94; Gaudiani, 2003: 188).

This happens through traditional philanthropy – whether divestiture, tax avoidance or donative – such as contributions to serving basic human needs. It also happens through donations to educational, arts and cultural institutions that advance knowledge and progress. The effect is particularly profound for the entrepreneur-philanthropist whose pursuit of happiness through philanthropy occurs both in the giving itself and in the focus of talent and energy on seeing society and human welfare progress over time, as its problems hopefully are better understood and solutions more readily identified and made available.

More than merely being an opportunity to give or engage, Madison believed that democratic republics depend on those who have provided for their physical needs and experienced material success to fulfill a responsibility to contribute to the education, edification and enlightenment of 'public sentiment sufficient for demands of self-government' (Kramer, 2006: 731). This might be construed as advocating for philanthropy broadly and, more specifically, for philanthropic support for civic engagement as action for the benefit of others and society as a whole.

Philanthropy contributes to the happiness of a democratic republic in another critical way. One danger to self-government is obscene wealth tightly concentrated over generations when there is widespread generational poverty combined with loss of hope in the 'right to rise' and prospects for socio-economic mobility (Acs, 2013: 91–96, 119; Brooks, 2008: 140–141). This threat has at least two dimensions that philanthropy helps address, by protecting against 'idle wealth' and by providing mechanisms for the recirculation of wealth in ways that provide opportunity (Acs, 2013: 151–152, 185).

One dimension is that concentrations of wealth in such circumstances can lead to broadly held perceptions that prosperity is only available by means that are either arbitrary or based on favoritism or connectedness instead of merit and fairness of opportunity. Those perceptions can undermine belief in prospects for rising oneself or for one's children. That can breed mistrust in our legal, political, economic, social and other systems that contribute to actual or perceived disparity, thereby threatening the democratic republic (Brooks, 2008: 137–138).

Philanthropy helps address this threat by contributing to opportunities for people to rise, preparing people to take advantage of those opportunities, and contributing meaningfully to generally accepted notions of advancing human welfare. In advancing 'generally accepted' notions of human welfare, however, philanthropy must avoid pandering to the masses or perceived popular opinion for the sake of such pandering. Doing so can undermine philanthropy and its responsibilities to society by sacrificing its quintessential ability to support ideas and initiatives that may not be well known or even well received, such as philanthropic support for civil rights movements when unpopular and even dangerous. Philanthropy likewise must protect against support for 'generally accepted' efforts that hurt society, such as the eugenics movement (Schambra, 2012).

Another problem with the combination of obscene wealth, generational poverty and lost hope is the tendency that people from Machiavelli to Jefferson recognized of luxury to corrupt its citizenry by undermining the values, mental and physical toughness, manners and practices of virtue that are essential for society – a democratic republic in particular – to survive and defend itself from external threats (Yarbrough, 1989: 75; Pocock, 2003: 430, 493). The threat is 'corruption, vice and luxury' resulting over time in 'the decline of public liberty, the termination of social happiness and the final subjugation of our country' (Wortman, 1796: 30).

Philanthropy helps address this threat through the donor's decision to physically and legally separate dedicated assets from use by the donor and their family for their own personal consumption and comfort. In conjunction with other policies, then, philanthropy stimulates voluntary disaggregation of wealth and the dilution of social, economic and political power that can often accompany wealth. Compare the wealth and power of the current generations of the Rockefeller, Guggenheim and Kennedy families with the wealth and power that existed in their founding patriarchs John D. Rockefeller, Meyer Guggenheim and Joseph P. Kennedy.

In addition, by more affirmatively requiring that the assets be used for society's charitable purposes as specified by the donor, philanthropic assets also benefit society more directly. Dedication of assets through philanthropy dilutes the concentration of wealth and mandates an other-centric perspective, thereby advancing civic virtue and opportunities for others to pursue happiness. And it accomplishes these purposes without denigrating 'pursuit of happiness' and while respecting that 'blessings of liberty' helped make the pursuit and its achievement possible.

12.4.2   Entrepreneurship, Philanthropy and the Constitution of the United States of America – 'Blessings of Liberty'

In order to organize a government based on the principles proclaimed in the Declaration and to rectify the failed effort of the Articles, the Founders drafted and the people instituted a Constitution for purposes expressly declared in its Preamble:

> We the people of the United States, in order to form a more perfect union, establish justice, insure domestic tranquility, provide for the common defense, promote the general welfare and secure the blessings of liberty to ourselves and

our posterity, do ordain and establish this Constitution for the United States of America.

Thus does the Preamble declare the responsibilities and purposes of the federal government (Sandefur, 2012: 323; Webster, 2003 [1787]: 127), its principal ends and designs (Brutus, 2003 [1788]: 88), and its boundaries (Sandefur, 2012: 322–323).

While the Declaration enshrines a right to pursue happiness as a right to journey towards an end, the Preamble envisions security not of liberty for its own sake but for the 'blessings of liberty'; that is, the objects or ends that liberty serves – that which liberty makes possible. Also, the objective is not merely for ourselves but also for 'our posterity', which necessarily requires consideration beyond present circumstances and imposes a responsibility to consider some level of 'other' at least to the extent that 'other' means future generations.

For the entrepreneur, the 'blessings of liberty' might mean security for the contexts in which they operate. It embraces the rule of law that provides degrees of stability and predictability of circumstance, enforcement and protection for the fruits of their efforts; freedom to develop talent, interests and relationships that allow for chances to experiment, innovate and recognize and pursue opportunities; and respect for self-determination and the ability to choose which risks to take (or not) and to what degree with the resources (financial and otherwise) available to them (Siegan, 2006: 109, 120). There is no promise of individual wealth, bounty or prosperity, but there should be individual hope and confidence in its potential along with the capacity for prosperity for society more broadly.

For the successful entrepreneur who becomes a philanthropist, the 'blessings of liberty' might encompass the distinct right and ability to choose whether and how to dispose of the wealth and resources made possible by the 'blessings of liberty'. By recognizing that those blessings contributed to their material success, there might even be some recognition of an internalized responsibility to contribute to preserving and propagating those same blessings or the liberty that underlies it for distinct groups of others or society more broadly. Among the most noble ways of fulfilling that responsibility would be to help 'inform [the people's] discretion', as they are the safest 'depository of the ultimate powers of the society' (Kramer, 2004: 108, quoting Madison). The sense of responsibility might also (or instead) be directed toward preparing people or society to exploit their opportunities and potential, including by helping them overcome circumstances that might inhibit or prevent their efforts.

For the entrepreneur-philanthropist, the 'blessings of liberty' can have additional meanings that tend toward the common good or even the 'happiness' of society and its people. In that case, the sense of responsibility for the entrepreneur-philanthropist involves devoting their own talents, interests, resources and relationships – in addition to money – to experimenting with, identifying and pursuing opportunities to achieve the desired change, possibilities and rewards, without regard to or undue emphasis on financial returns or maybe even monetary costs.

There are less grandiose, arguably more practical ways to approach the 'blessings of liberty' in which the attention is on tangible, quantifiable 'blessings'; that is, money or material possessions as the objective or ends of liberty. Those approaches tend to inspire movements that seek distribution of those 'blessings' according to measurable notions of equality (Rakove, 1996: 314; Siegan, 1989: 102). As money and possessions can be counted, they can then be divided and distributed; whereas rule of law, opportunity, talent and the other previously discussed 'blessings' are not amenable to formulations, division or redistribution.

Such a quantitative approach is fraught with a number of problems. At a basic level, a variety of difficult decisions must be made, and they must be made in ways that are and are perceived to be consistent with the relevant principles, policies and delegated authority, at the risk of threatening those very principles, policies and authority.

Among the decisions about intrinsic quantified 'blessings' and the temptations toward redistribution are who should receive the redistributed 'blessings'. Should they be those most in need? Is 'need' defined as ability to meet a relative quality of life, or does it refer to those people truly at the bottom of Maslow's hierarchy who lack basic food, clothing and shelter? Or maybe recipient status should be based on rewarding voters for their support?

Decisions also must be made about how much should be received. Should shares be equal? Should everyone be guaranteed a certain base level of funding through which they either meet their basic needs or achieve a pre-determined relative standard of living? Or perhaps the share should be determined not from the perspective of what the recipients receive, but the portion of 'blessings' that should be taken away in order to ensure that no one is 'too rich', however that then gets defined.

Then there are decisions to be made about who gets to make the decisions. Is it government? If so, at which level: federal, state or local? And which branch: legislative, executive or judicial? Or, is it the private sector, such as currently happens with philanthropy?

Additionally, inherent in quantifying 'blessings' as monetary or materialistic ends that can be redistributed is the unavoidable problem that doing so necessarily involves taking money and/or possessions away from some person(s) or group. That taking renders already acquired tangible property insecure, especially if done without due process and just compensation as required by the Fifth and Fourteenth Amendments. Among other consequences, insecure property alienates the right to pursue happiness by acquiring and disposing of property, and undermines confidence in economic, political and social systems. Diminished confidence weakens hope, and it is hope that contributes to ambition being constructive and creative for the individual, society and human welfare.

Policies that treat financial riches and material possessions as the ends of 'blessings of liberty' can also endanger philanthropy and the charitable sector as fewer decisions are made privately by individuals, and as taking care of society and others in it is seen less as the responsibility of all (including the wealthy) and more that of government.

Consequently, a choice must be made in how policies treat security for the 'blessings of liberty'. One option is for policy makers and the public to whom they are accountable to ignore the concept altogether, whether as an objective for our government or a fundamental purpose of American society. Under that option, the definition does not matter. However, its prominent place in our Constitution suggests that as a bad alternative, which leaves the quantitative and qualitative approaches discussed above.

The quantitative, redistributive approach is inconsistent with and substantially defeats the qualitative application. It also deadens other essential American principles and institutions. Although it is an option, it has extensive consequences – some tangible, others not; some immediate, others longer term; some that might alleviate certain difficulties, while destroying means for overcoming others. The potential impact is far-reaching and should be thoughtfully and thoroughly understood, as the benefits of short-term comfort for some risk long-term harm for many, including some who may have benefited from the short-term comfort.

The qualitative approach to the 'blessings of liberty' is less likely to interfere with the ability to possess, acquire or dispose of money or possessions; should facilitate that potential for more people; and is more consistent with other principles on which our nation was founded and has thrived. But for the qualitative approach to work, the policies derived from it must not permit success only for a few. Policies must allow the many to pursue and realize prospects for economic mobility and hope for the future. And the approach must reflect the inherent sense of responsibility that looks beyond oneself to others and the broader society that has been part of the American experience since before colonial times.

The choices made about and the policies implemented pursuant to securing the 'blessings of liberty' must help ensure that entrepreneurship and philanthropy continue to instill confidence, grow hope and nurture productive ambition consistent with American principles and advancement of individual, social and human welfare.

12.5   CONCLUSION

There is substantial overlap in the principles and policies that shape the environment in which both entrepreneurship and philanthropy thrive in the United States. Among these are the unambiguously declared right to pursue happiness and commitment to securing the 'blessings of liberty'. Both of these principles risk being disregarded as too ethereal or merely aspirational, but too many entrepreneurial and philanthropic experiences evidence the real-world applications of those principles, their contributions and benefits for individuals, communities and society more broadly.

Entrepreneurs and philanthropists are not just bystanders passively shaped by the contexts that these principles nurture. They also actively express these principles in practice. Their experiences both are affected by and help give definition to these principles, including through:

- protections of the ability to acquire property;
- ambition that is allowed to risk failure and success in the 'right to rise';
- respect for private decision-making to dispose of their property as they choose, even by dedicating it to charitable purposes that serve society; and
- responsibility to maximize the opportunities made available to them and that they make available for others, whether as entrepreneur, philanthropist or both.

Therefore, as policy makers evaluate various bills, laws, practices and regulations that might affect entrepreneurship and philanthropy in the United States, they better fulfill their responsibilities to the public they serve if they remember that their actions have consequences not just for entrepreneurs and philanthropists but also for bedrock principles that gave birth to our nation, remain relevant today and are intended to serve posterity. As academics and researchers seek to better understand entrepreneurship and philanthropy and to enhance the performance and contributions of both, society is advanced by their continued mindfulness of the forest in which the trees they study flourish. As entrepreneurs, philanthropists and those who work with them identify opportunities, take risks and make the multifaceted decisions that balance complex factors and effects, they and society benefit when they maximize their efforts but remain attentive to the contexts that make their experience possible.

America and the world have benefited from our nation's approach to entrepreneurship and philanthropy, and the US entrepreneur and philanthropist have benefited from opportunities that America and the world have made available.

NOTE

*   The author is grateful for various contributions to this chapter from David Back, Kim Dennis, Claire Gaudiani, Lori Kettner, Tony Luppino, Adam Meyerson, David Renz, Sue Santa, Bill Schambra, Carl Schramm, Dane Stangler and Bob Strom. Among their contributions were reviewing drafts or engaging in discussions that helped inform and sharpen some of the chapter's concepts. Dane was particularly helpful in both respects. None, however, are responsible for this chapter's mistakes or shortcomings.

REFERENCES

Acs, Zoltan (2013), *Why Philanthropy Matters: How the Wealthy Give and What It Means for Our Economic Well-Being*, Princeton, NJ: Princeton University Press.

Aristotle (2004 [1883]), *Nichomachean Ethics*, transl. F.H. Peters, New York: Barnes & Noble.

Brooks, Arthur C. (2008), *Gross National Happiness: Why Happiness Matters for America – and How We Can Get More of It*, New York: Basic Books.

Brutus (2003 [1788]), 'Letters from Brutus #12 February 7 and 14, 1788', in David Wootton (ed.), *The Essential Federalist and Anti-Federalist Papers*, Indianapolis, IN: Hackett Publishing, pp. 86–92.

Cumberland, Richard (2005 [1727]), *A Treatise on the Laws of Nature*, trans. John Maxwell (1727), ed. John Parkin (2005), Indianapolis, IN: Liberty Fund.

Ely, James W. Jr (2008a), 'Economic liberties and the original meaning of the Constitution', *San Diego Law Review*, 45, 673–708.

Ely, James W. Jr (2008b), *The Guardian of Every Other Right: A Constitutional History of Property Rights*, 3rd edn, Oxford: Oxford University Press.

Ferguson, Adam (1996 [1767]), *An Essay on the History of Civil Society*, ed. Fania Oz-Salzberger, New York: Cambridge University Press.

Gaudiani, Claire (2003), *The Greater Good: How Philanthropy Drives the American Economy and Can Save Capitalism*, New York: Henry Holt & Company.

Gaudiani, Claire (2010), *Generosity Unbound: How American Philanthropy Can Strengthen the Economy and Expand the Middle Class*, West Chester, PA: Broadway Publications.

Grampp, William D. (1965), *Economic Liberalism: Vol. 1 The Beginnings*, New York: Random House.

Grimm, Robert T., Jr (ed.) (2002), *Notable American Philanthropists: Biographies of Giving and Volunteering*, Westport, CT: Greenwood Press.

Kramer, Larry D. (2004), *The People Themselves: Popular Constitutionalism and Judicial Review*, New York: Oxford University Press.

Kramer, Larry D. (2006), 'The interest of the man: James Madison, popular Constitutionalism and the theory of deliberative democracy', *Valparaiso Law Review*, 41, 697–754.

Kurland, Phillip B. and Ralph Lerner (eds) (1987), *The Founders' Constitution: Volume 1 – Major Themes*, Indianapolis, IN: Liberty Fund.

Lincoln, Abraham (1992a [1857]), 'Speech on Dred Scott Decision, June 26, 1857', in Don E. Fehrenbacher (ed.), *Abraham Lincoln: Speeches and Writings, 1832–1858*, New York: Library of America, pp. 390–403.

Lincoln, Abraham (1992b [1860]), 'Speech at New Haven, Connecticut, March 6, 1860', in Don E. Fehrenbacher (ed.), *Abraham Lincoln: Speeches and Writings, 1859 – 1865*, New York: Library of America, pp. 132–150.

MacArthur Foundation (2014), John D. and Catherine T. MacArthur Foundation, 'About us – our history', available at http://www.macfound.org/about/our-history/ (accessed January 2, 2014).

Madison, James (1999 [1787]), 'The Federalist No. 10', in Jack N. Rakove (ed.), *Writings*, New York: Library of America, pp. 160–167.

McDowell, Gary L. (2010), *The Language of Law and the Foundations of American Constitutionalism*, New York: Cambridge University Press.

Meacham, Jon (2012), *Thomas Jefferson: The Art of Power*, New York: Random House.

Morgan, Anne H. (1995), *Prescription for Success: The Life and Values of Ewing Marion Kauffman*, Kansas City, MO: Andrews McMeel Publishers.

Pocock, J.G.A. (2003), *The Machiavellian Moment: Florentine Political Thought and the Atlantic Republican Tradition*, Princeton, NJ: Princeton University Press.

Pollack, Malla (2001), 'What is Congress supposed to promote? Defining "Progress" in Article I, Section 8, Clause 8 of the United States Constitution, or Introducing the Progress Clause', *Nebraska Law Review*, 80, 754–810.

Rahe, Paul A. (2005), 'The political needs of a toolmaking animal: Madison, Hamilton, Locke and the question of property', in Ellen Frankel Paul, Fred D. Miller Jr and Jeffrey Paul (eds), *Natural Liberalism from Locke to Nozick*, Cambridge: Cambridge University Press, pp. 1–26.

Rakove, Jack N. (1996), *Original Meanings: Politics and Ideas in the Making of the Constitution*, New York: Alfred A. Knopf.

Sandefur, Timothy (2012), 'In defense of substantive due process, or the promise of lawful rule', *Harvard Journal of Law and Public Policy*, 35, 283–350.

Schambra, William A. (2012), 'Philanthropy's arrogance and insularity on eugenics offer cautionary tale', *Chronicle of Philanthropy*, December 2, available at http://philanthropy.com/article/Philanthropy-s-Arrogance-and/136028/ (accessed January 3, 2014).

Siegan, Bernard H. (1989), 'One people as to commercial objects', in Ellen Frankel Paul and Howard Dickman (eds), *Liberty, Property, & the Foundations of the American Constitution*, Albany, NY: SUNY Press, pp. 101–120.

Siegan, Bernard H. (2006), *Economic Liberties and the Constitution*, 2nd edn, New Brunswick, NJ: Transaction Publishers.

St George Tucker, H. (1999 [1803]), *View of the Constitution of the United States and Selected Writings*, Indianapolis, IN: Liberty Fund.

Urofsky, Melvin I. and Paul Finkelman (2002), *A March of Liberty: A Constitutional History of the United States, Vol. 1: From the Founding to 1890*, Oxford: Oxford University Press.

Von Drehle, David (2012), 'The Emancipation Proclamation and the "Right to Rise"', *Wall Street Journal*, December 28, http://online.wsj.com/news/articles/SB10001424127887323476304578197613213918112 (accessed December 21, 2013).

Walterscheid, Edward C. (1994), 'To promote the progress of science and useful arts: the background and origin of the intellectual property clause of the United States Constitution', *Journal of Intellectual Property Law* 2 1.

Washington, George (1997 [1790]), 'First annual message to Congress', in John Rhodehamel (ed.), *Writings*, New York: Library of America, pp. 748–51.

Webster, Noah (2003 [1787]), 'An examination into the leading principles of the Federal Constitution, October 17, 1787', in David Wootton (ed.), *The Essential Federalist and Anti-Federalist Papers*, Indianapolis, IN: Hackett Publishing.

Wills, Gary (2001), *Explaining America: The Federalist*, New York: Penguin Books.

Wills, Gary (2002), *Inventing America: Jefferson's Declaration of Independence*, New York: Mariner Books.

Wootton, David (ed.) (2003), *The Essential Federalist and Anti-Federalist Papers*, Indianapolis, IN: Hackett Publishing.

Wortman, Tunis (1796), 'An oration on the influence of social institution upon human morals and happiness delivered before the Tammany Society at their anniversary on the twelfth of May, 1796', New York: C.C. Van Alen & Co.

Yarbrough, Jean (1989), 'Jefferson and property rights', in Ellen Frankel Paul and Howard Dickman (eds), *Liberty, Property, and the Foundations of the American Constitution*, Albany, NY: SUNY Press, pp. 65–84.

Zinmeister, Karl (ed.) (2013a), 'American History's Greatest Philanthropists', *Philanthropy Magazine*, Winter, 8–29.

Zinmeister, Karl (2013b), 'DoNation', *Philanthropy Magazine*, Summer, http://www.philanthropyroundtable.org/topic/donor_intent/donation (accessed December 27, 2013).

PART IV

TWO ENTREPRENEURS – TWO TRANSITION PATTERNS

In our final chapter, Chapter 13, editors Taylor, Strom and Renz along with their colleagues Coates and Holman compare the experiences of two entrepreneur-philanthropists. Mr 'K' or Ewing Marion Kauffman was born in 1917 and initiated his company in the post-World War II period in the pharmaceutical industry. He did not enter actively into philanthropy until the 1980s, when surging wealth from his company and the transition to a professional management team, enabled his doing so. In contrast Mr 'M', Mario Morino, was born post-World War II, initiated his company in the 1970s in the computer software industry, sold his firm while in his forties, and became very active in his philanthropic efforts. The authors offer an evolutionary model that captures some of the dimensions of the entrepreneurs' experiences. The emphasis is on the learning process in both the for-profit entrepreneurial realm and the not-for-profit or philanthropic realm.

The case study series on each of these two successful entrepreneurs in their companies and in their philanthropies that resulted in this chapter initiated the project that led to this volume. These insights combined with those proffered by the authors of the foregoing chapters provide, we believe, a rich foundation for future investigation. It was not the intent of the volume to be a definitive portrayal of the dynamics of the for-profit entrepreneurs' engagement in philanthropy. Rather it is the offering of varying perspectives to both celebrate the contributions of these individuals as they strive to create wealth, intellectual capital and jobs in both realms, and to urge expansion of our systematic investigation of this phenomenon.

13. Exploring the transitions from entrepreneur to philanthropist – learning from Mr 'K' and Mr 'M'

Marilyn L. Taylor, Theresa T. Coates,
Robert J. Strom, David O. Renz and
Rhonda Holman

13.1 INTRODUCTION

Entrepreneurs make significant contributions to our society. The contributions through the companies they initiate and run are highly visible. Many entrepreneurs also give generously towards the social issues with which our communities wrestle, for example, issues in education and homelessness. The current press has highlighted numerous philanthropic contributions by entrepreneurs as they account for more than half of the philanthropic giving in the world and thus have significant impact on how their societies approach social issues (Acs and Phillips, 2002).

In spite of the impact, however, little academic management research has examined the entrepreneurs' experiences in their transitions to philanthropic activities or sought to understand the motivation, logic or vision which elicited such behavior. Systematic study of entrepreneurs as philanthropists is critical to understanding their impact on the myriad social issues that confront society. The aim of this research is to explore the issues that may be significant in the emergence of philanthropic behavior in entrepreneurs. Given the striking successes of many entrepreneurs in the 1990s and on into the early twenty-first century, the study of entrepreneurs' transition to philanthropy is most timely.

Using a grounded theory approach, this chapter identifies factors that relate to the entrepreneurs' origins, success in their companies, their philanthropic activities and their transitions. The research involves two case studies which examine the experiences of two well-known entrepreneur-philanthropists in the US, Ewing Marion Kauffman, founder of Marion Laboratories and the Kauffman Foundation, and Mario Morino, founder of Legent Corporation and the Morino Institute. These two men made strong commitments to address social issues through their philanthropic activities, in particular through the development and work of their foundations.

The philanthropic foci of the two entrepreneurs are parallel – encouraging development of youth and other entrepreneurs. Initial field work focused mainly on the two entrepreneurs' philanthropic activities. However, as with all exploratory research, issues emerged that went far beyond the initial focus. These additional issues are both fascinating and rich for study. One set of issues concerns the factors that have an impact on the entrepreneurs' interest in philanthropy and focus their concerns on selected social issues. Another set of issues revolves around the choices about how they carry out their philanthropic activities.

Before engaging in the exploratory process, it is vital to establish an understanding of the literature which exists at the intersection of entrepreneurship and philanthropy. The literature examining entrepreneurs as philanthropists remains scant although, as noted, the popular press often lauds entrepreneurs' involvement in philanthropic activities. Three distinct streams emerge in the limited literature. First, there is a stream that examines the entrepreneurs' historical practice of philanthropy and its economic impact. The second stream considers the characteristics of different types of philanthropy in today's society. Finally, there is a stream of work that focuses on advising would-be philanthropists in their financial planning and strategies.

13.2   ENTREPRENEURS' PRACTICE OF PHILANTHROPY

Multiple authors note that successful US entrepreneurs and businessmen have had a tradition of philanthropy (Boschee, 1995; Acs, 1999). Acs and Dana (2001) trace the history of philanthropy among US (hereafter: American) entrepreneurs. They document that successful wealthy entrepreneurs over the last 150 years have provided a great deal of money for charitable acts and social programs. The art of philanthropy during the nineteenth century was influenced by George Peabody. Lauded as an inscrutably honest business success, Peabody innovated the idea of charitable endowments and influenced others such as Johns Hopkins who lent his name and wealth to the three institutions (university, medical school and hospital) that bear his name (Acs, 1999). Other well-known successful entrepreneur-philanthropists who used their great wealth to make significant social differences included Andrew Carnegie, John D. Rockefeller, Henry Ford and J. Paul Getty (Boschee, 1995). These entrepreneurs sponsored the arts and education by setting up foundations and giving endowments to universities.

The rise of the nouveau riche and development of a capitalistic society has been criticized, most notably by Karl Marx (1906). Acs and Dana (2001) note, 'Perhaps the greatest criticism of market economies is their unequal distribution of income and wealth that flows from the very nature of the system' (p. 63). However, these researchers also note that American entrepreneurs not only concentrate wealth in their pursuit of success, but also 'reconstitute' it as part of their social contract with American society. The entrepreneurs live, after all, in a nation that rewards the wealthy with generous tax write-offs for their donations of monies and other gifts to charitable causes. There is the argument that American philanthropists tend to sponsor wealth creation (that is, entrepreneurship) and thus utilize their wealth to form the basis of economic growth or to ease social concerns. This social contract dates from the Puritans who came to the US with the Calvinist notion that Christians are stewards of their wealth. Economic data demonstrate a negative relationship between the involvement of the government sector and economic growth. In contrast, the data suggest a positive relationship between reconstitution of wealth and economic growth in the long run (Delany, 2000). Acs and Karlsson (2002) thus argue, 'American philanthropists – especially those who have made their own fortunes – create foundations that, in turn, contribute to greater and more widespread economic prosperity through knowledge creation' (p. 132).

13.3   CHARACTERISTICS OF THE NEW AND OLD PHILANTHROPISTS

Research identifies the similarities as well as the differences between the philanthropy of the Gilded Age of the late 1800s and modern-day eras (Acs and Dana, 2001; McGee, 2004). During the latter part of the 1800s there was an enormous concentration of new wealth due to the industrial revolution. A fraying of the social fabric occurred as opportunities abounded and the middle class grew significantly. This milieu gave rise to a number of wealthy entrepreneurs who gave generously to social causes.

Beginning in the 1990s, similar wealth concentration and concerns over social consequences were evident. For example, as much as $4 trillion of new wealth was created in the stock market in a three-year period in the late 1990s (Acs and Dana, 2001). Even with the recent stock market declines, the extent of the nouveau rich is stunning. Multiple observations have been made which suggest that the end of the twentieth century was another Gilded Age of wealth concentration and philanthropic giving. First, real wealth increased by over $40 billion from the 1980s through the 1990s. Entrepreneurs account for over 80 percent of the richest people in America (Byrne et al., 2002). In contrast, in 1950, 80 percent of the richest people in America had inherited their money. According to the Foundation Center the number of grant-making foundations went from 56000 in 2000 to 81777 in 2011 (Blackwood et al., 2012). The Foundation Center reported that the top 50 donors had invested a 'dizzying' $65 billion in various social causes.

In the past, major gifts were generally bequests associated with wills and thus the death of the benefactor. In today's world gifts are far more frequently made by the living and account for a significant increase in the number of foundations (*The Economist*, 2004). In 2013, according to figures by Giving USA, Americans donated $316.23 billion to charitable causes. Just over three-quarters of this amount came from living individuals ($228.93 billion). The rest came from foundations ($45.74 billion), bequests ($23.41 billion) and companies ($18.15 billion). The non-profit sector of the economy accounts for 8 percent of US gross domestic product (GDP), a figure that has more than doubled since 1960. This sector employs nearly 9.2 percent of the American workforce – more than federal and state governments combined (Blackwood et al., 2012).

The current wealth base of entrepreneurs provides opportunity for today's nouveau riche to shape America and the world just as profoundly as Carnegie and Peabody shaped the nineteenth and into the early twentieth century. Numerous popular publications have identified the differences between the old guard among wealthy and the more recently minted wealthy. Most notably, the nouveau riche have been younger – in their fifties, forties and even in their thirties with potentially 20 or more years of high activity remaining. Their entrepreneurial experiences have contributed to defining how they approach their philanthropic activities.

The result of this increasing wealth creation in America and in parts of Europe has been a more directed and a more engaged philanthropy. The new guard has wanted to ensure their money is properly used and they also want to be involved in its expenditure. Indeed, Bill Gates has argued that one must work just as hard at giving one's money as one does to make it. Many of this new breed of entrepreneurs have been referred to as 'social entrepreneurs'. They invest the time personally to vet the projects that are proposed to them directly rather than have foundations to do it. This new breed has been seen as wanting to solve specific problems in a specific way rather than just earmarking money for some general benevolent purpose. They have focused on performance and tried to make the projects self-sustaining so that recipients did not keep coming back for more funds. Rosabeth Moss Kanter of Harvard Business School is quoted as characterizing the attitude of the new givers thus: 'We fixed American business; now we need to fix charity' (*The Economist*, 1998). Research in the area of philanthropy in the last two decades has used a number of new terms which designate the new philanthropists, including venture philanthropists, engaged grant-makers, social entrepreneurs and investors (Dees, 1998; Letts et al., 1997).

Wagner (2002) delineated the current philanthropic activity into either 'transactive philanthropy' or 'investment philanthropy'. Transactive philanthropy is essentially the traditional philanthropy, that is, focused on giving wealth and support through charitable donations. It is charity in its purest form with emphasis on the 'right thing to do'. The major criticisms of transactive philanthropy have included non-support of innovation, lack of building non-profit capacity or infrastructure, and failure to demand tangible results. Modern philanthropists have criticized traditional foundations for investing in program innovation rather than organizational infrastructure and capacity building (Dees, 1998).

In contrast, investment philanthropy (also referred to as venture philanthropy) encourages the involvement of philanthropists who are funding the activity (Fellers, 2001). Investment philanthropy fosters an entrepreneurial spirit focused on solving social problems. Investment philanthropists provide counsel along with cash. The process is charitable giving with a venture bent. The investment philanthropists tend to be entrepreneurs in their thirties and forties who, even as they have turned their attention from business to good works, cling to phrases like 'leverage', 'network' and 'exit strategy'. These new givers see no reason why they cannot apply the concepts responsible for their business success to reshaping philanthropy into more efficient, more effective undertakings (Porter and Kramer, 1999; McGee, 2004). Table 13.1 summarizes the characteristics of investment philanthropists, their investment orientation and anticipated outcomes.

Investment philanthropy has many supporters. Kosminsky (1997) states, 'Of all the institutions involved in charity, business is perhaps best positioned to offer the advice and expertise needed to revitalize needy communities at the grassroots. By partnering with entrepreneurial, community-based organizations that are acting as "laboratories of the streets", business can help catalyse "bottom-up" solutions to social problems' (p. 29). The philanthropist and the non-profit initiate a strategic partnership into which the philanthropist brings not only funds and expertise, but also networks, plans for growth, quantified assessment, investment (broadly in the organization or narrowly in a specific project) and hands-on participation.

However, venture philanthropy also has its critics, who ask, among other questions, whether the new philanthropy will be able to make significant differences compared to the old (Carlson, 2000). These opponents of

Table 13.1 Investment philanthropists

Characteristics of new philanthropists – compared to traditional philanthropists	Investment orientation	Outcomes
Want involvement in decision-making; don't just write a check	More ambitious: tackling giant issues including issues such as redoing the American educational system or curing cancer	Foster entrepreneurial spirit
Younger, under 40; don't wait until death to distribute their wealth	More strategic: donors take systematic approaches drawn from their business success, including carefully laid plans to get at causes, not just symptoms	Provide counsel along with cash
Focus their attention on one organization or issue rather than multiple	More global; operate beyond national borders	Ensure accountability measures
Avoid established organizations, seeking new initiatives rather than donating to established initiatives	Demand for greater results: 'The new philanthropists attach a lot of strings. Recipients are often required to meet milestone goals, to invite foundation members onto their boards, and to produce measurable results – or risk losing their funding' (Byrne et al., 2002: 83)	Push for innovative programs

Invest in infrastructure and capacity building, not just programmatic innovation or continuity	More involvement by donors	Non-profit organizational changes
Encourage others to be actively involved rather than giving passively	Venture philanthropy	Expanded funding sources
Have high expectations as they have often changed the course of business within their industry and expect the same results through their philanthropy	Greater insistence on results and accountability	Focus on results
Not concerned with charity per se; emphases on seeing near-term results and making differences rather than establishing long-term memorial in their memory	Accountability is crucial	Changes in nonprofits over the last decades with greater emphasis on measurement of outcomes (i.e., outputs), than on effort (i.e., inputs)
Argue that there are no tax advantages from giving after death, so might as well give now	Giving now, rather than later	Greater funds availability with potential for greater knowledge on the part of the philanthropist

Sources: Byrne et al. (2002), Carlson (2000), *The Economist* (2004), Greenfeld (2000), McGee (2004), Morse (2001), Streisand (2001).

the new mode of philanthropy argue that a return-on-investment mentality cannot be translated into social goods that improve lives and advance society. They argue that social issues are intangible and are difficult to quantify with a bottom-line focus. Further, non-profit managers question the hands-on approach of new philanthropists and their usefulness, given that they have little or no prior non-profit experience (Carlson, 2000). However, Hero (2001) argued that the movement was too new to draw conclusions.

13.4   FINANCIAL ADVICE FOR THE PHILANTHROPIST

The act of philanthropy requires a great deal of financial planning (Reis, 1999; Delaney, 2000; Passy, 2003). Both traditional and investment philanthropists draw on advice from the personal financial investment community. The work that is in this area is primarily focused on providing financial planners with guidance in understanding the needs of the entrepreneur. Financial advice for the potential philanthropist includes considering the choice of non-profit structures and setting up foundations and trusts. These writers argue that it takes very careful planning to make financial gifts that are conditional and have accountability measures. Karoff and Marble (1998) suggest that financial planners must understand that the philanthropists look at themselves as venture capitalists supporting risky new programs or organizations in their donor strategies. They note that others view their primary role in their philanthropic 'giving' as being change agents who seek to advance ideas that influence public policy or institutional change through philanthropic giving. However, some donors see themselves primarily as stewards of charitable resources, often supporting established organizations or programs. Other writers in this area go beyond financial implications. For example, Delaney (2000) highlights potential downfalls in acquiring entrepreneurial wealth. He notes that successful entrepreneurs may experience familial difficulties, lost or damaged friendships, or loss of direction. Advisors to successful entrepreneurs must be sensitive to these issues.

Within the entrepreneurship domain, the body of literature on philanthropy is limited. Most of the observations come from business periodicals and the popular press. Some insight is provided in the family business literature (Bork, 1996; Kaye, 1998; Sonnenfeld, 1998; Sonnenfeld and Spence, 1989), the financial planning literature (Kosminsky, 1997; Reis, 1999, 2000), and the work of Acs with its economic bent (Acs and Dana, 2001; Acs and Phillips, 2002). The area begs more exploration and research. This current project is exploratory in nature and reports on the experiences of two successful entrepreneurs who transitioned into philanthropic activities.

13.5 METHODOLOGY

Case study research is especially appropriate for exploratory research where the focus is on: (1) documenting a phenomenon within its organizational context; (2) exploring the boundaries of a phenomenon; and (3) integrating information from multiple sources (Glasser and Strauss, 1967; Eisenhardt, 1989; Yin, 2009; Savin-Baden and Major, 2013). Grounded theory means sifting through information and making connections from those pieces of information in the context of the situation. It is the first step in theory building (Glasser and Strauss, 1967; Yin, 2009).

The research underlying this work is qualitative and longitudinal as the data gathering took place over three decades. The research team, at various stages, consisted of four academics, three foundation officers and a consultant. The entrepreneurs for this study were chosen for three reasons. First, they had developed highly successful firms and were considered among the new guard of philanthropists. Second, the research team wanted to have intensive longitudinal information about each entrepreneur, his company and his philanthropic activities, both from extensive public records as well as from direct access to the entrepreneur, executives from the firm and representatives from the non-profit organization that the entrepreneur established (that is, his foundation). Third, the team wanted diversity in the industry, the entrepreneurs' firms and their ages.

The first entrepreneur was Ewing Marion Kauffman, founder of the pharmaceutical firm Marion Laboratories, and later the Ewing Marion Kauffman Foundation. Mr Kauffman was chosen because of the foundation's significant impact on entrepreneurship as well as the extensive information available to the researchers on the man, his company and his foundation.

The second entrepreneur was Mario Morino, founder of the highly successful software company Legent and later the Morino Foundation. Mario Morino was chosen because of his reputation for his accomplishments and his emphasis on encouraging 'new entrepreneurs', that is, those who have become wealthy from their activities with computer or computer-related companies.

Both men established foundations that bore their names. The overviews of their companies and philanthropic activities are detailed in the next two sections.

Interviews and internal documents from the archives of four organizations provided data for the cases: Marion Laboratories, the Ewing Marion Kauffman Foundation, Legent Corporation, and the Morino Foundation. For each entrepreneur the researchers undertook an extensive search of newspaper, magazine, trade periodical and book publications. The initial research focused on the entrepreneurs' philanthropic activities. However, during the research process it became apparent that other themes and patterns about the entrepreneurs' lives were becoming relevant to their engagement in philanthropy. The researchers tracked the entrepreneur, his family origin, the firm's development and its top management, the philanthropic activities which the entrepreneur participated in or developed, and the social context. Performances of the firm and the philanthropic activities were assessed using data either from the corporations' yearend financial reports filed with the Securities and Exchange Commission or from the non-profit organizations' annual or periodic reports. Interviews with the entrepreneurs, firm executives, philanthropic associates, and the foundations' employees provided additional, and often rich, insights.

For reliability of observations, some people were interviewed multiple times. In the case of the Kauffman series, some primary executives were interviewed multiple times over two decades to confirm early observations and opinions from other interviewees, as suggested by Eisenhardt (1989) and Yin (2009). Multiple interviews of the same individuals over time provide validation of the information. Using data from multiple interviewees reduces the risk of undue influence that a single individual interview may have on the case study, brings a richer portrait of the case, and provides better data for analysis (Eisenhardt, 1989; Yin, 2009; Miles and Huberman, 1994). The organizations made internal documents available. In the case of Kauffman, the lead researcher's accumulation of documentation began in the early 1980s. In contrast, the data gathering for the Morino series occurred over a three-year period. The data from the interviews, internal documents and public sources developed the context, historical references and insights.

Using the information, the researchers developed two historical case study series about each entrepreneur. The case studies in each series focused on the entrepreneur and his firm, and then on the entrepreneur's philanthropy. Each case study averaged about 30 pages in length and helped to condense the data. This step follows the pattern employed to structure qualitative data as suggested by Miller (2003). The data analysis involved finding commonalities among significant events noted by the interviewees. These common factors and key events were then linked as suggested by Miles and Huberman (1994), who recommend, 'connecting relevant data segments with each other, forming clusters, or networks of information' (p. 44). Time-ordered matrices were developed. The matrices documented the transition and factors involved in the entrepreneurs' lives (see Table 13.2). In addition, the interviewees were asked to review the case studies that drew on their insights. Such corroboration from the people interviewed is appropriate to confirm the findings and gain feedback during the course of the validation process as suggested by Guba (1981) and Miles and Huberman (1994). The outcomes of this exploratory research are presented in the following section.

13.6 OVERVIEW OF THE CASE STUDIES

The two case study series have many parallels: wildly successful companies overlapping with the building of significant philanthropic commitment. The subsection immediately below presents a brief overview followed by summaries of Ewing Marion Kauffman's early life, entrepreneurial venture and his philanthropic activities. The second subsection parallels the same dimensions of Mario Morino's experiences. Each subsection also summarizes the entrepreneur's leave-taking from his foundation.

13.6.1 Ewing Marion Kauffman

Overview

Ewing Marion Kauffman grew up with few resources. He developed a very successful company, Marion Laboratories, from 1950 through the late 1980s. During the first two decades of the company's activities, Mr Kauffman was not involved in philanthropic activities. During the last decade he was not only deeply involved in his foundation's activities and projects, but he also encouraged other executives around him to establish their own foundations or initiate community activities. Finally, Mr Kauffman had to plan for the future of the foundation after his death.

Mr Kauffman's early years

Born in 1917, Ewing Marion Kauffman spent most of his early years in central Kansas City. He was the son of a divorced couple who remained an integral part of his life. He lived with his mother who ran a boarding house. He was able to experience two years of college and served in the Navy during World War II. He was very good at cards and accumulated sizeable winnings during his time of service. Post-discharge he became a sales person for a pharmaceutical company. After the company owner cut his territory and commission percentage, he decided to open his own company, and he vowed never to treat his employees in the same way.

Table 13.2   *Ewing Marion Kauffman and Mario Morino as entrepreneurs and philanthropists – comparing characteristics, issues and dynamics*

	Ewing Marion Kauffman	Mario Morino
I. Influences in early years		
Childhood poverty	Yes	Yes
Mother's influence	High (including): – Educational background – Worked to earn family living	High (including): – Hospitality: caring for people – Worked to help earn family living
	Self-esteem: mother built	Self-esteem: from teachers
Father's influence	Skills building (e.g., math)	Values (e.g., resilience and flexibility)
Parental marriage	Not clear: parents divorced. Took care of mother in later years Also close to father	Not clear: parents remained together Took care of parents in later years
Siblings' influence	Not clear	Brother's example of caring for a 'bum' communicated belief that everyone has value
Navy service	Opportunity for exhibiting skills and judgment Playing cards with other sailors won him a large stake that helped initiate the program	Navy utilized and enhanced the computer skills Worked in off hours on jobs that led to the formation of Morino Associates as the early company was called
Religion	Denied as a major driver (but) influence by well-known local Presbyterian minister, Rev. Meneilly	Never talked about role of religion Went to parochial schools (did not appear to be a positive experience)
Community:		
Grew up in	Kansas City	Cleveland, but spent most of his adult years in the DC region

Table 13.2   (continued)

	Ewing Marion Kauffman	Mario Morino
Relationship in community	Developed an appreciation and sense of gratitude for the community	Most philanthropic activities carried out in DC. Not clear what will happen in Cleveland where he has now moved
Acceptance by community	Appears to have been rocky at the beginning but shifted after: (1) the company went public; and (2) he purchased the franchise and developed the Royals baseball team	Significant acceptance after the Potomac Knowledgeway project Not clear prior to that time
Marriage	Married relatively young. Widowed about age 44 Remarried about age 46	First married – age not known. Remarried in early 40s. Married to Dana who has strong values about family
Children	Two (adopted) children from first marriage. Stepdaughter from second marriage appeared to have some influence (Julia Irene Merrel McBride) with regard to philanthropic activities	Three children in his 40s. At conclusion of research was in his 50s. Moved back to original hometown of Cleveland primarily so that his children could grow up in an environment rich with personal and family relationships

II. Personal abilities and values

	Ewing Marion Kauffman	Mario Morino
Time period of formation	1950s: Post WWII favorable business environment	Mid-1970s: Computer technology and industry developing
Influence of mentors	Had a role model/mentors, but started the business on his own	Started with a mentor (Wetzel) High energy to address opportunities (e.g., Mario's Marauders)
Skills	Salesmanship and financial acumen Mentoring	IT and customer intimacy Mentoring
Values	Strongly supportive of: – Self-sufficiency – Education	Explicit re values: – Customer intimacy

Table 13.2   (continued)

	Ewing Marion Kauffman	Mario Morino
	– Sharing of wealth (e.g., with employees and community)	– Take care of your people (extended family) – Education

III. Development of the firm

1950s	Company founded in 1950 Company grew significantly during the 1950s	N/A
1960s	Stock flying high in the late 1960s; founder uses high value to acquire companies.	N/A
1970s	Encountered significant difficulty; at one time there was concern about the company's viability	Founded in the 1970s. Went public; used stock to acquire other firms which extended the product line and enlarged the customer base
1980s	High growth in revenues ($100M at the beginning of decade and over $1B at the end); even higher growth in profits based on phenomenal success with two drugs In 1989 merged with Merrell-Dow, a subsidiary of Dow Chemical Most senior executives left the merged company at the time of the merger or shortly thereafter	Continued mergers with various companies. Merger in the late 1980s with a company of comparable size resulted in difficulties trying to merge both firms
1990s	N/A	Founder took a board role and reduced activities within the company Acquired by Computer Associates International in 1995
Product/time period	Product: pharmaceuticals. Growth occurred in the 1950s (internal), in 1960s after IPO (via acquisitions), and in 1980s (internal)	Product: software/service. Internal growth in 1970s and early 1980s; acquisitions after IPO

Table 13.2 (continued)

	Ewing Marion Kauffman	Mario Morino
Reason for going public	So that employees nearing retirement would be able to cash out Company stock held widely among company employees	Founder, board, and investors had stock. Wanted public stock in order to attract talent to the company Not clear how widely stock was held among employees
Role with company	Reduced role with company to major stockholder and senior advisor Younger executives encouraged involvement: (1) as visionary; (2) motivational for employees; and (3) PR for firm with external constituencies	Moved off the board during Discovery Process, then rejoined before decision to be acquired
Personal characteristics and the company	High energy – sleep requirement low Relinquished CEO role and moved to Chairman of Board about 1985	High energy – sleep requirement low Became co-CEO after 1980s merger Moved to board in early 1990s; remained active in management for several years and then reduced role in company
Sales/ separation from the company	From late 1960s to mid-1970s hired a cadre of younger managers (Lyons, Holder, Herman, McGraw, and others) who had capacity to grow; gave a significant responsibility, and decision-making authority to them	Merged with a comparably sized company – apparently struggled for dominance; moved to board and then took on operational/strategic role of a subsidiary to rescue it; board member at the time of merger
IV. Philanthropic issues		
Initial foundation purpose	Donated money to the Foundation for tax purposes and then dispersed it as requests were approved	Established private foundation to begin carrying out philanthropic activities
Original visions	Initial vision for the Foundation was not at all clear	Initial vision for the Foundation was not clear

Table 13.2   (continued)

	Ewing Marion Kauffman	Mario Morino
Evolving vision(s)	Benefit youth Use Marion Labs' research skills to pursue measurement of results	Benefit disadvantaged youth Use technical/computer skills in pursuit of vision
	Benefit entrepreneurship (influenced by junior executives who were very appreciative of his business success)	Benefit entrepreneurship (evolved from pursuit of world extensively during Discovery Process to create vision (e.g., Sister Kit Collins)
	Sought out successful models for social change.	Same
	Entrepreneurship focus came late and included training for mentors and entrepreneurs	Entrepreneurship focus came midstream and occurred because invited to participate in a movement to energize the region economically
Structure	Private foundation and Charitable Remainder Trust: – Trust was established to retain the funds until Foundation needed or until death of founder – Never envisioned a public charity	Private Foundation and Public Institute: – Foundation remained private – Intent in founding the Institute as a public charity was to attract new monies to activities
Operating vs. grants foundation	Envisioned bringing skills learned at Marion to the social issues addressed Voracious reader, reading influenced his choices. Grant-making emerged, apparently with influence from others (new Foundation president and experienced philanthropists who joined the board, contracted as consultants, or became employees)	Envisioned bringing skills learned at Legent (and beyond) to the social issues addressed Relied heavily on verbal communication with issue leaders (i.e., Discovery Process) Grant-making emerged, but was coupled with direct intervention and coaching

Table 13.2 (continued)

	Ewing Marion Kauffman	Mario Morino
	During 1990s grant-making was highly linked with Foundation's internal operations and skills (e.g., communications, publicity, evaluation)	
V. Foundation board		
At founding:		Trusted friends.
Board evolution	Enlarged with known entrepreneurs and local business people Later added professional philanthropists (e.g., Nelson Gardner, etc.) Involvement of other professional philanthropists and other successful entrepreneurs	Same
Approach to addressing social issues	Our business expertise can make a difference	Same
VI. Awakenings		
Earliest programs (and initiating influences)	CPR Now! (Company initiated as PR and outreach to community) STAR (Royals players' involvement with drugs)	Economic development (location in DC, nation's capitol, and requested to make a speech regarding intersection of computers/Internet and economic development)
First major youth programs and effect	Project Choice created to assist high school students with schooling after graduation; realized that 'just' offering the carrot of education to disadvantaged youth was not enough	Project to increase computer/Internet capacity of four inner DC community organizations led to realization that the issues were even more extensive than originally thought

Table 13.2   (continued)

	Ewing Marion Kauffman	Mario Morino
Public policy expertise/ impact	Later experiences with President George Bush's commission/task force led to realization of the difficulty of influencing public policy	Was embedded in DC and saw the extensive social difficulties. It was suggested by others that location was advantage because national policy makers could see the 'experiments' the Foundation/Institute was undertaking
Understanding of non-profits	Skepticism regarding non-profit's success in dealing with social issues to date Never admitted ignorance publicly; others indicated how up the learning curve he had come	Similar.
Expertise sought	Read widely and drew on expertise; was always in the process of learning	Similarly, drew on expertise; was always in process of learning; wrote extensively
Sought professional help	Especially to structure the Foundation and the Board Early on relied on Marion executives and those brought to the table Later hired professional non-profit managers to undertake programs (e.g., Jerry Kitzi and Siobhan Nicolau)	Sought vision of professionals in the not-for-profit world extensively during Discovery Process to create vision (e.g., Sister Kit Collins)
Influences on board and foundation/ institute direction(s)	Explicitly acknowledged that being poor when young but getting education and mentoring made a difference	Similar
	No similar experience	Alzheimer's experience with father led to interest in 'FreeNet' – developed vision of the Internet to address social issues

Table 13.2   (continued)

Ewing Marion Kauffman	Mario Morino
Purchased the Royals (analogy: acquired other 'sons'; the highly visible role of owning the Royals, i.e., Kansas City's baseball team and the players' arrests for drug activity led to focus on issues in the community)	Married, and children (ultimately three) began to arrive and occupy his interest/ time
Wife played a strong role in direction of company and the direction of Foundation	Wife played a strong role in early direction of Foundation
Stepdaughter becomes confidant	Children too young for roles as professional colleagues to arise; but leaving a legacy for his children
Worked with schools on Star and Project Choice programs	Wanted to adopt a school and link it with Net, but found the bureaucracy too intractable
Adopted alma mater (Westport H.S., an inner city school) for Project Choice	Adopted brother's university alma mater for early scholarship program to benefit the disadvantaged
Activities are project-based and each has a life-cycle	Similar
Evolving and growing respect for the non-profit world's leaders	Same
Project Choice was established early and led to discovery that 'just' offering the carrot (i.e., four years higher education) to disadvantaged youth was not sufficient. Rather, required family system support as well as support of the schools (e.g., tutoring and Saturday school); worked with city social services	Came to the DC-based youth intervention project with four inner city community organizations with high level of expectations. Found had to expand support system (e.g., lack of desk/office space, training of staff members)

Table 13.2 (continued)

	Ewing Marion Kauffman	Mario Morino
Evolving foundation interests/ activities	Foundation gave away money until after Royals cocaine incident Developed STAR program for youth (interplay with company) Develop program #2 (Project Choice) for youth, then program #3 (Project Early), then program #4 (Project Essential)	Youth Development programs initiated with a pilot with four DC-based community organizations. Was 'intimately involved' with implementation. Migrated the codified knowledge to the Internet in YouthLearn and also initiated a fund to provide follow through and migrate program to a self-sustaining basis
Issues of operating vs. grants-making foundation – how resolved?	Moved back and forth with influence of various individuals	Is still early evolution and not clear which way will evolve. After moving to Cleveland made grants available as risk funds to enable other organizations to take over the work of ongoing projects (e.g., YouthLearn)
	Trust was established to absorb funds transferred before death and to receive funds from estate	Foundation supports the Institute which establishes and runs programs as a 501(c) (3). (Not clear whether Morino has considered setting up a charitable remainder trust)
Hostility from the non-profit world?	Yes: resentment existed because the Foundation initiated its own programs internally when there were programs already in existence to address the issue, and the established programs had leaders and staff with experience	Incurred some resentment. However, all four community-based organizations when offered the opportunity took grants and involvement rather than 'just' funds

Table 13.2   (continued)

	Ewing Marion Kauffman	Mario Morino
Leave-taking from philanthropy	Death of founder, i.e., leave-taking (research did not track beyond the death of the Founder)	Geographical move of founder, i.e., leave-taking (research did not track the post-move period)
How resolved	Foundation fully funded from the Charitable Remainder Trust Foundation board executives and staff in place, i.e., organization has structural maturity	Foundation remains private to benefit the Institute Institute seeks funds from broadened set of sources
Fundamental differences re the foundation	Foundation increasingly became professionalized	Not at all clear what would ultimately evolve. Would Foundation begin benefiting Cleveland, in addition to DC area?

Note: * Mr K repeatedly pointed out that Joyce Hall, founder of Hallmark, had been a mentor and role model for him.

The company – Marion Laboratories

Mr Kauffman started Marion Laboratories in his garage in 1950. The firm grew significantly in its first decade and a half. Mr Kauffman shared stock ownership with many of the employees. He took the firm public in 1965 to provide liquidity for a number of employees who were approaching retirement age. The firm's stock was a 'high flier' and Mr Kauffman was able to acquire several firms by exchanging stock on a favorable basis. By the mid-1970s the firm was moderately diversified into health care and agricultural chemicals.

However in 1976 Marion Laboratories encountered its first financial difficulties. The performance stumble led to a subsequent divestiture program. The freed cash flow was used to fund the introduction of two drugs into the US market – Cardizem and Carafate. During the 1980s these two drugs enjoyed significant success. Their success propelled the firm from approximately $100 million in revenues in 1980 to nearly $1.2 billion in 1989 with even more explosive growth in earnings. In mid-1989, after much deliberation, the Marion Laboratories executives accepted an offer from Dow Chemical Company to merge their company with Dow's pharmaceutical subsidiary, Merrell-Dow. The new firm was Marion-Merrell-Dow.

Foundation activities

The 1980s growth was managed successfully by a set of talented executives that Mr Kauffman had attracted to the firm beginning in the late 1960s and early 1970s. One of these men in particular urged Mr Kauffman to systematically plan his foundation's activities. The foundation's legal structure had been established in the mid-1960s as a vehicle to channel money into Mr Kauffman's initially modest charitable gifts. Approaches from the not-for-profit community increased as Mr Kauffman's visibility in the community rose, beginning after the company went public in the 1960s, and continuing in the 1970s because of his ownership of the Kansas City Royals baseball team, and in the 1980s because of the firm's phenomenal growth and success.

During the 1960s and 1970s Mr Kauffman contributed funds on occasion to various programs. One program to which he donated helped disenfranchised families with utility bills. When approached for a donation in the second year of the program, he refused to contribute because, he explained, the program had not assisted the disenfranchised families in bettering their situations. It had been, in essence, simply a give-away program. This incident especially solidified Mr Kauffman's philosophy of using his resources to enable disenfranchised individuals to improve their capabilities and move toward greater self-sufficiency. During the 1970s and the early 1980s Marion Laboratories initiated several activities directly sponsored by the firm. One, CPR Now!, was initially established as part of the company's outreach and public relations. Mr Kauffman found that participants' testimonies about saving lives gave him a great deal of satisfaction.

When three Royals players were implicated in cocaine dealings in the early 1980s, Mr Kauffman began to read widely regarding the drug problem in the United States. He was dismayed to learn the young age at which drug habits often begin. His concern led to the formation of the STAR program, a successful drug use prevention program for junior higher and high school students.

Mr Kauffman's extensive reading about youth also sensitized him to the high dropout rate among inner city high school-aged youth. He hired staff to consider the issue and subsequently chose Westport High School, his own alma mater located in the inner city, in which to initiate the Project Choice program. Project Choice focused on motivating youth to finish high school in four years by going to school every day, staying out of legal trouble, and avoiding drugs and pregnancies. Successful participants were offered support to pursue up to four years of post-high school education. During the first year of the program, it became clear that the offer of funding for higher education alone was not sufficient to ensure Westport High School students finished four years of high school on a timely basis. Ultimately the program included such services as Saturday school, tutoring, social support, taxi service for parents to attend evening meets for families that had transportation difficulties, funds for drug rehabilitation participation, and relaxation of the no-pregnancy requirement. In short, Mr Kauffman found it took changing the support system for the young people in order to assist them to complete high school and move into post-secondary learning opportunities. Although not without its difficulties, the program was deemed successful at Westport High School and subsequently migrated to other inner city high schools in the area.

One of the emerging issues from Project Choice was that intervention was needed at younger ages. This observation led to the establishment of Project Essential and Project Early programs. Both programs were targeted at younger children.

Later in the 1980s Mr Kauffman's became interested in establishing a program to encourage entrepreneurship in the United States. This interest was encouraged by executives who had worked with him in Marion Laboratories. Investigation led to establishing the Center for Entrepreneurial Leadership within the Foundation. The ongoing youth-focused activities came to be known as Youth Development. Both sets of activities remained within the Foundation. During the late 1980s Mr Kauffman also established a Charitable Remainder Trust as a means for channeling a significant proportion of his personal wealth to the Foundation to assure its continuity after his death.

Leave-taking
In 1993, just four years after the merger of Marion Laboratories with Dow Chemical's pharmaceutical division, Mr Kauffman died of bone cancer. Indomitable almost to the end, he remained keenly interested and involved in the Foundation's activities. After his death, the Foundation's board and senior executives had to decide what changes to make in the foundation's strategic directions and operations.

13.6.2 Mario Morino: Legent Corporation and the Morino Foundation and Institute

Overview
In the case of Mario Morino we see the development of a successful company from the mid-1970s through the mid-1990s. During the first

decade and a half of this period, Mr Marino's focus was on establishing and growing the company. As his involvement in the firm lessened, he immersed himself in considering the social issues that his talents and resources could affect. Further, he encouraged other entrepreneurs to become involved with both their resources and talents. Finally, moving his family from Washington, DC to his original hometown of Cleveland entailed leave-taking from at least part of his Washington, DC-based philanthropic activities.

Growing-up years

Mr Morino grew up in the urban Cleveland area in a warm Italian family. One of his most vivid memories was his mother's hospitality to the disenfranchised. He often found himself moving out of his bed to accommodate one of his mother's invited guests. Another significant experience was his older brother's care and consideration for an individual whom others termed 'a bum'. In addition to these experiences of his family reaching out to the more unfortunate, Morino also appreciated the encouragement he received from teachers all throughout his formal education, including the early part of a doctoral program he did not complete.

Mr Morino's service in the Navy led to significant experience with computers and moonlighting in his off hours to help businesses. The skills he learned in the military and the clients he served while moonlighting chiefly in the Washington, DC area led to the establishment of his service and software company, Morino Associates, in the mid-1970s.

The company – Legent

Morino Associates grew internally until it went public in the mid-1980s. A series of acquisitions and mergers followed. Morino Associates' major merger with Duquesne in the late 1980s brought two comparably sized companies together to form Legent. The two chief executive officers (CEOs) found living in the same 'house' difficult and the company brought in an experienced executive from a larger, more established firm as the chairman and CEO of Legent as the combined company was named. Mr Morino moved to a board position, but remained actively involved in the firm until 1992. In 1994 he rejoined the Legent board, remaining in that role until Computer Associates acquired the firm in 1995.

The Foundation and Institute

The initial board for the Morino Foundation included trusted friends. The Foundation was set up in 1992. In 1993–1994 Mr Morino and a close friend undertook a 'Discovery Process' which involved a year and a half of interviewing various individuals across the country regarding social issues and how those issues were currently being addressed. The two interviewed as many as 700 people to provide input into ideas or foci Mr Morino might undertake. A major theme the Morino Foundation developed was the use of for addressing social problems.

In the wake of the Discovery Process, Mr Morino made donations to several colleges for scholarships targeted at disenfranchised students. Subsequently he established the Morino Institute as a public charity, the purpose of which was to seek resources from multiple sources and to carry out programs. The expectation was to set up a 'Knowledge Center' that would enable individuals to communicate and learn in such a way as to address social issues.

As the Discovery Process came to a close, Mr Morino became involved with the Potomac Knowledgeway. The Knowledgeway was a major effort to develop the 'new economy' in the northern Virginia and DC areas. Area leaders credit Mr Morino as being the catalyst in developing the vision and inspiration for bringing together the knowledge and technologies embedded in area firms to think in terms of the larger picture. Many of the organizations involved in the Knowledgeway were government departments or organizations that were government funded. The initiative was credited with providing the impetus to rejuvenate the area's depressed economy.

The Knowledgeway initiative gave rise to Netpreneur, an organization that the Morino Institute funded. Netpreneur used the Internet in various ways. For example, the organization targeted new entrepreneurs to exchange information and seek help via Internet-based communications, such as help from venture capitalists. In addition, Netpreneur also used the Internet for marketing its meetings. The meetings featured experts on topics of interest and importance to entrepreneurs. The successful Netpreneur series was targeted especially at those in the 'new economy', that is, the economic activities occurring at the intersection of computers and Internet technologies.

While the Potomac Knowledgeway effort was ongoing, the Foundation gave a grant to a Connecticut-based organization. The grant was in the form of matching funds for a Department of Commerce grant aimed at integrating the Internet and related information technologies into the lives of people in low-income communities. Subsequently, Mr Morino initiated the Youth Development Project (YDP) with pilot projects in four DC-based community organizations. YDP activities were managed through the Institute and focused on developing the capacities of the community organizations to facilitate learning experiences among inner-city youth through the use of computers and the Internet. The YDP grants had significant strings attached; Institute personnel, including Mr Morino, were deeply involved with the organizations in the development and implementation of the programs. In a broad sense these four programs aimed at reducing the 'digital divide' by combining Mr Morino's skills and knowledge of the computer and Internet world with his entrepreneurship and executive skills, along with the talents of others who understood youth learning processes and not-for-profit management.

During the process, those involved codified the evolving knowledge base and migrated it to YouthLearn, an online resource for youth leaders. As the YDF pilot programs came to a close, Mr Morino established Venture Philanthropy Partners (VPP), an effort that raised $30 million. The initial purpose of VPP was to provide grants made on a competitive basis to community organizations within the greater DC area for programs that aimed to increase computer and Internet skills among inner-city youth.

13.7   FINDINGS

In inductive studies, it is often difficult to distinguish data collection from theory building as the data gathering and refining is an iterative process in which the completion of interviews and validation of the information in the case studies is compared to each case (Eisenhardt, 1989; Miles and Huberman, 1994). What has emerged from analysis of these two sets of longitudinal and qualitative data is a model shown in Figure 13.1. The model depicts the factors that appear to contribute to the development of the entrepreneur into a philanthropist.

The study reveals interesting similarities and issues between what appear to be two very different people. They were born in different time periods – Mr Kauffman was born in the early part of the twentieth century and Mr Morino later in the 1940s. The underlying technology bases and industries of their companies were dissimilar. Nonetheless, common characteristics, themes and issues arose in their development as entrepreneurs and philanthropists. In particular we see two patterns occur. First, we see similarities in the contexts and behaviors of the two men. Second, we observe a similar process for how these entrepreneurs began to engage in philanthropic behavior.

13.7.1   Similarities in the Two Case Studies

The intensive cross-case analysis identified five themes which are relevant to the transition or emergence of the entrepreneur into the philanthropic arena. Table 13.2 summarizes the results of within- and cross-case analysis. Among the observed similarities were early experiences, personal

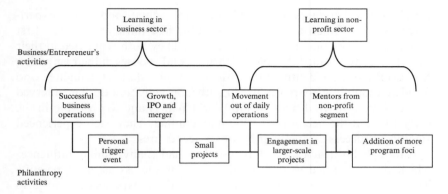

Figure 13.1   Entrepreneur to philanthropist – process of transition

abilities, the process of moving from entrepreneur to philanthropist, and the learning process. In addition, there were differences that need to be considered between the two examples.

Theme 1 – early experiences

The data analysis showed some commonalities in the early experiences of the entrepreneurs. Early experiences are comprised of the situations before the start of their respective entrepreneurial efforts and the people who influenced the entrepreneur-philanthropists. In the two case study series we see successful entrepreneurs who grew up in relatively poor financial circumstances in the Midwest and who were grateful for the support given to them from various people and institutions they designated as key in their lives. Section I in Table 13.2 details the influences in their early lives.

The mothers of both men were important influences. They gave significant credit to their mothers for their examples. Mr Morino's mother took care of individuals in her community and served as a significant role model for him. In Mr Kauffman's case his respect for his mother's education level, as well as the impact of his own education, led to an interest in sharing that experience for others.

Their fathers had less of an impact, but both men credited their fathers for developing their skills. Mr Kauffman explained how his father had drilled him in math. Mr Morino's father encouraged him to be flexible and have fair values. In addition, they noted the influence of other institutions. For example, Mr Kauffman talked about the Boy Scouts, while Mr Morino indicated that his formal schooling promoted his sense of self-esteem.

Success came early to both entrepreneurs: in Mr Kauffman's sales activities at other firms and in Mr Morino's school and sports experiences. Mr Kauffman and Mr Morino also had difficulty in their first marriages as they pursued business success. They both remarried in their early forties and valued the roles of their second spouses in their activities. Mr Kauffman also identified the influence of his adult stepdaughter who acted as a sounding board for his philanthropic activities. Both men served in the Navy: Mr Kauffman during World War II and Mr Morino in the early 1970s at the height of the Vietnam conflict. They each experienced significant success during their Navy service tenures.

Although born at different times, they had many similar influences which they identified as contributing to their success as entrepreneurs. The data also provide some evidence that these experiences may also factor into how they chose to diminish their activity level in their respective firms and began to actively participate in philanthropy. For example, Mr Morino told the story of his older brother responding to the plight of an injured 'bum', and how this experience was an epiphany for him that everyone has value. Living up to his brother's image was very important, and it influenced his resolve to help people. Such situations and personal influences appeared to drive the development of these two men's deeply internalized values. They suggest a factor associated with the development of the societal contract of reconstituting wealth that Acs and Karlsson (2002) describe: that is, that self-made men attempt to give back to society by creating foundations for prosperity. Mr Kauffman certainly encouraged other entrepreneurs and executives who sought his counsel to consider giving back. Mr Morino engendered a give-back philosophy in the outreach to help entrepreneurs in Netpreneur. Especially in Venture Philanthropy Partners he challenged other successful entrepreneurs in his network to participate and fund activities in which the fund would invest.

Theme 2 – personal abilities

These men have a number of traits and skills which provide a basis for their engagement in philanthropy and their philanthropic mode. In particular we note their entrepreneurial successes, personal values, energy levels, social embeddedness, crafting of a vision, and their willingness and ability to mentor in their companies and beyond.

The entrepreneurs in these two cases had significant success very early with their firms. They initiated their companies in industries that were early in the growth stage and that had tremendous return potential in the time periods in which they founded them; Mr Kauffman in pharmaceuticals in the post-World War II period and Mr Morino in the computer field in the late 1970s. Both entrepreneurs had innovative business models for creating value. Mr Kauffman was innovative in how he approached the process of marketing pharmaceuticals to doctors. Mr Morino was innovative in his approach to interacting with his customers who wanted to utilize his software and services. The analysis suggests that early success in business encouraged the entrepreneurs to develop a mindset that they could use their business knowledge and skills to develop solutions to society's problems.

The data substantiates that both entrepreneurs had a paternalistic approach to mentoring people. For example, Mr Kauffman found great satisfaction in mentoring the set of younger executives whom he drew together in the late 1960s and into the 1970s. He coached them as they worked alongside him to bring the firm to the significant success it enjoyed in the 1980s. Mr Kauffman put a great deal of emphasis on the value driven by Marion Laboratories' employees, whom he referred to as 'Associates'. For example, he said, 'We owe them [the Associates] a great deal.' Similarly Mr Morino viewed his company like a large Italian family network, akin to the extended family he experienced as a child. Mr Morino, much like Mr Kauffman, held that employees were indeed the drivers of value in their firms.

As seen in Section II of Table 13.2, these men have very explicit values about taking care of people, sharing in the results and helping people achieve. Both men also expressed a value sentiment about the external entities which interacted with their firms. Mr Kauffman believed that supplier partnerships should be win–win relationships and that it was the responsibility of Marion Laboratories to support its partners. In Morino Associates, customer relationships and satisfaction were critical, so much so that Mr Morino stationed employees inside the clients' offices to ensure that satisfaction. These observations suggest that the entrepreneurs sought to have control over their firms' external relationships in such a manner that was mutually beneficial to both parties in the relationship.

Social embeddedness within their local societies was also important for these entrepreneurs' engagement in philanthropy. Kansas City, where Mr Kauffman lived, had a rather small, exclusive society which was closed to him for a number of years. The elite appeared more open to him after his firm went public and even more so after his 1969 purchase of the Major League franchise and establishment of the Royals baseball team. He subsequently became a very prominent figure in the region and beyond. Similarly, Mr Morino worked in the Washington, DC area and became more embedded in the local society after participating in an economic revitalization effort. The research suggests that after the two entrepreneurs became more socially embedded, their involvement in philanthropy increased.

The analysis highlights a number of important factors which led to the entrepreneurs' early efforts to take a hands-on approach to working in the social arena. First, they both experienced early business successes without major setbacks, which may have led them to expect to be able to solve social problems with business-oriented logic. They have a history of success *and* they expect to duplicate that success in another 'market'. Second, their hands-on orientation in their for-profit endeavors can be tied to the way in which they enact their philanthropy, that is, by putting their own time and effort into developing and overseeing the programs. Third, their value for development of people increases their commitment to investing not only their financial resources but also their time into their philanthropic efforts. Finally, there seems to be an important relationship with their integration into the social network that paved their way into initiating philanthropic programs.

Theme 3 – exit from the daily operations of the company

Mr Kauffman and Mr Morino labored for a decade or more to drive the growth and wealth bases in their firms. During that time neither made much investment of self or wealth into philanthropic activities. Mr Morino began to establish an active agenda with his Foundation and Institute at age 40, unlike Mr Kauffman who was in his sixties. Mr Kauffman became more active in his foundation after his company merged with Merrell-Dow. In the case of Mr Morino, the company merged with another to become Legent and came to be headed by an outside CEO shortly after the merger. Consequently Mr Morino's personal involvement in the firm lessened. The data suggest that entrepreneurs' decreasing involvement in daily operations at their firms correlates with increasing involvement in their foundation activities. This relationship indicates that the transition to philanthropy is employed as a personal exit strategy from the firm.

Figure 13.1 depicts the process of the entrepreneur's decision to engage in philanthropic behavior that emerged from the case analyses process. The data suggest the presence of some key elements that influence philanthropic behavior, which are anchored in the entrepreneur's early experiences, personal abilities and exit strategies from daily business operations. The cases suggest that the nature and intensity of the entrepreneur's philanthropic interests evolve. Both of these men focused on growing their respective companies in the first two decades of their companies. As Mr Kauffman put it, in the early stages of his company he was making a contribution to the community through the jobs he provided, and after the initial public offering (IPO) in the wealth bases his company generated for stock owners. Mr Morino, likewise, did not become involved in philanthropic activities until the early 1990s, more than a decade and a half after he started his firm. The analysis suggests these three issues interact:

the degree of involvement in driving company growth, the development of wealth bases (their own and that of employees and stockholders), and the freeing up of personal time from the company as it approaches a more mature stage in its evolution.

Among the issues that are important to understanding the entrepreneur as a philanthropist are the entrepreneur's early life and values; his evolving philanthropic interests; the learning curve that accompanies entrance to the not-for-profit arena; and the need for the non-profit community to understand, value and accommodate the entrepreneur. The interplay among these issues, and the stages of the journey from entrepreneur to philanthropist, are summarized in Figure 13.1.

Theme 4 – philanthropic issues
These two men brought the skills they had initially developed and applied in their companies to their philanthropic activities. Mr Kauffman brought his renowned salesmanship and staunch personal values. In addition, he brought his acquired skills of program and data evaluation in order to ensure that the resources being invested in the philanthropic programs paid off. In Mr Morino's case we see programs like Netpreneur and Youth Development which drew on previous aspects of his background. Netpreneur facilitated the exchange of information between entrepreneurs and venture capitalists. Youth Development Program's efforts to assist people in learning about the Internet and computers utilized Mr Morino's computer knowledge and skills, especially his insights into the power of the Internet.

In their choices of social problems in which to invest, both men heavily emphasized the needs of youth. They had been poor when they were young and experienced great pleasure in giving another generation of youth a 'leg up'. In creating their programs, they acted again as true entrepreneurs. They largely went their own way, sometimes finding partners with which to create exciting new programs. Section III of Table 13.2 outlines each entrepreneur's earliest programs and philanthropic issues. The specific issues the two men championed emerged from their experiences, and may be seen at one level as opportunistic. Mr Kauffman, impelled by his humiliation that Royals players were using drugs, resolved to do something about the nation's drug issue. The result was the activities that became the highly regarded STAR program. Through the Project Choice program he moved to motivate inner city youth with the college education opportunity he had dreamed about when he was young. The lessons learned from the Project Choice program led to the vision to intervene earlier, and the establishment of the Project Early and Project Essential programs for younger children. Others, notably the Marion executives whom Mr Kauffman had mentored, encouraged him to pursue another interest: an emphasis on entrepreneurship. They urged that he impart the skills with which he founded the company and the enduring values which underlay the Marion Laboratories culture.

In a similar vein, Mr Morino initiated programs that addressed the needs of entrepreneurs and youth. He utilized this same grand plan in a bold venture to assist inner city kids and community center staff to become computer and Internet literate. Mr Morino eschewed the formal school systems as too bureaucratic, too resistant to change and new ideas, and too slow to act to be effective partners in addressing youth issues. He chose instead to work with four selected community organizations. The entrepreneurial encouragement originated with a need that presented itself in the region. The Northern Virginia and DC region was floundering economically in the mid-1990s. Mr Morino came as an individual with a much-needed vision. His vision focused on coupling the significant wealth of knowledge and skills spawned by the vast government network in the DC area with the computer and new Internet-related technologies. The analysis shows that the life experiences of the entrepreneurs fed directly into how they engaged in philanthropy and their choice of target programs.

Theme 5 – learning curve in the non-profit arena

Beyond weaving together the resources and abilities of their distinct firms, these two entrepreneurs experienced a definite learning curve as they entered the non-profit domain. Although neither talked explicitly about their initial lack of understanding, it is clear that their respect for not-for-profit leaders increased as they became more immersed within philanthropic activities. Initially both entrepreneurs assumed that their approaches which had been so successful in business would significantly contribute to solving the social ills and improve outcomes in the non-profit realm. In the data, the non-profit leaders observed and expressed frustration with the entrepreneurs' naiveté regarding the complexity of the social problems that they were intent on solving.

The entrepreneurs' talents were effective in the for-profit world. But, applying talent in the non-profit world required a learning process. For example, Mr Kauffman developed the Project Choice program to help underprivileged youth finish high school, and attend post-secondary programs if they maintained a C average along with several other requirements. After the program began, it became apparent that the students would not be able to achieve the objectives without additional support programs. During implementation of Project Choice, Kauffman Foundation personnel became deeply involved with the high school on activities not originally envisioned. These included testing for drugs, counseling students, meeting with parents and organizing supplementary educational activities.

The entrepreneurs learned that developing social programs had significant differences as compared to developing a business. In both cases, the non-profit leaders indicated that the entrepreneurs had learned and adapted to the non-profit sector. Further, the data revealed that the entrepreneur's learning had come from multiple sources. Mr Kauffman relied heavily on his voracious reading as well as on individuals with extensive philanthropy experience. Mr Morino drew especially from a vast array of people who were willing to share their knowledge. He was methodical in gaining information from a variety of sources. He stated, as noted earlier, that he had spoken with over 700 people before he began to develop his philanthropy programs. This process was designed to help him identify social issues and understand what was going on with regard to selected social issues. Both men opened their foundations' boards and activities to input from leaders in the non-profit community.

At the same time the non-profit community had to develop an understanding and value for the entrepreneur, and also adapt. Just as the entrepreneur has a learning curve in the not-for-profit community, we observed not-for-profit community leaders learning to understand and respect the entrepreneurial leaders. The non-profit community had to accommodate the entrepreneurs' skills and approaches. In the case of the Morino Institute, Mr Morino explicitly offered $75,000 for development of computer-based outreach to kids, or $75,000 *and* involvement of Morino Institute employees. All four recipient organizations chose the second alternative, that is, the involvement option. During the next 18 months, Mr Morino met regularly with these community organizations' leaders. In addition, there were training programs, often early in the morning – a schedule which necessitated additional hours of commitment and rescheduling of work days by community organization employees.

In this study, both of these successful entrepreneurs were intent on bringing the skills and knowledge that had driven their respective for-profit successes to help solve the broader social issues. Indeed, they did bring tremendous enthusiasm, energy and resources – their own as well as those of others. However, their individual involvement – particularly in the case of Mr Morino – made significant differences in the impetus for change as well as in the entrepreneurs' own lives. Section III of Table 13.2 gives examples of each entrepreneur's interaction with the non-profit community.

13.7.2   Differences in the Two Case Studies

Besides the entrepreneurs' ages and the context or time period within which they developed their businesses, a number of other differences exist between the two cases. The first difference is when in the process the foundations were started. The Kauffman Foundation was started very early for tax shelter purposes. It was left essentially as a shell for many years before Mr Kauffman began creating non-profit programs. Mr Morino created the Morino Foundation and Institute when he began to give actively. The second difference is that Mr Kauffman dabbled in social programs inside his company. For example, his company created a program called CPR Now! which trained employees to earn cardiopulmonary resuscitation (CPR) certification. The results of the CPR Now! program provided an epiphany for him when an employee described saving a neighbor's life as a result of having taken this program. Mr Kauffman discovered how much pleasure he experienced as he learned about this result of the program. Mr Kauffman continued with these programs in the company and with the Royals baseball team. In addition, he encouraged other baseball team owners to initiate similar programs.

In contrast, Mr Morino was much more methodical in the process he used to decide on what social issues could use his skills, where his interests lay and what he would participate in. Both men began giving to non-profits through their foundations in a traditional manner (for example, endowment to colleges, money for heating programs). However, Mr Kauffman was not satisfied with the end result of his charitable investments. He felt that the process was simply a hand-out that did not encourage nor assist the recipients to improve their circumstances. Thus, his programs responded to his dissatisfaction. On the other hand, Mr Morino continued traditional giving, but added the investment philanthropy aspect.

Another difference is apparent in how they initially funded their major activities. Mr Kauffman provided most of the funding for the philanthropic programs in which he was involved. Mr Morino, in contrast, sought financial resources from a number of individuals. The final difference is that Mr Kauffman exited the foundation at his death. Mr Morino at age 50 moved his domicile to another region and began to exit from some of the DC-based activities funded by the foundation which bears his name.

13.8   DISCUSSION

The rise in the creation of wealth through entrepreneurship coupled with the increasing number of wealthy entrepreneurs has given rise to increasing participation in a new type of philanthropy: investment philanthropy. This chapter attempts to investigate why wealth-creating entrepreneurs engage in philanthropy and begins to identify the factors which influence this behavior. The cross-case analysis identifies a number of common patterns that have a bearing on entrepreneurs' choices. A number of insights emerge from the analysis. The first is that there may be some factors which influence the choice of how an entrepreneur transitions out of their organization and begins to engage in philanthropic behavior. In the analysis the themes command equal attention and suggest no single established theoretical framework which can explain the evolution of the entrepreneur's transitions into philanthropic activities.

Grounded theory often provides research directions and more focused questions (Yin, 2009). This research identifies a number of important issues. The first issue is understanding how entrepreneurs become interested in philanthropy. This research observed how family and other early influences have an impact on the entrepreneur's choices regarding the for-profit activities as well as the activities in the not-for-profit world. These influences include both constraints and impelling factors. The entrepreneur's social interactions within the community where they have established the business also affect the decision to engage in philanthropy. Entrepreneurs' personal values have an impact on the choice of activities. The data also point to a learning curve issue for the entrepreneur as he begins to work in the non-profit world. This discovery fits with the realization that these entrepreneurs experienced a transition process as they let go of their firms and evolved as philanthropists. In both instances these transitions overlapped. The transitions and influences on the decision to engage in philanthropy can be mapped into a process, as depicted in Figure 13.1.

This chapter is a first step in an attempt to understand the issues surrounding entrepreneurs who move into the non-profit sector. The qualitative data allowed the researchers to identify specific factors that influenced the directions of the two entrepreneurs' philanthropic activities. These observations provide some evidence of how entrepreneurs develop their philanthropic behaviors. In developing their philanthropic activities, both men mixed professional non-profit managers and successful business people rather than relying solely on professional non-profit managers. The men established operating, rather than grant-making foundations. Thus, they are appropriately termed investment philanthropists and as investment philanthropists they encouraged assessment as well as program innovation.

13.9   LIMITATIONS OF THE RESEARCH

The research has significant limitations. First it is hampered by its reliance on a limited sample of two. Granted, the two-case series provides a source of data that is 'thick description' (Miles and Huberman, 1994; Shamaz, 2006; Savin-Baden and Major, 2013) and offers rich insights into multiple issues. The significant similarities between the experiences of the two entrepreneur-philanthropists in this study suggest that we are likely to find similarities with other successful entrepreneurs who have undertaken the challenges of addressing social issues. However, the limited sample size requires caution in generalizing. Second, the choice of the two was dependent on multiple considerations including the approval for intensive access. There is, of course, potential bias in the study of these two. At the same time, a great deal of effort went into collecting information from multiple sources in order to increase reliability and decrease subjectivity.

13.10   ADDITIONAL RESEARCH QUESTIONS

This exploratory research generates a number of interesting and challenging paths for future investigation, including questions such as:

1. How deficient are entrepreneurs in their understanding of the not-for-profit world as they initiate their philanthropic activities?
2. What are the most effective ways for entrepreneurs to learn about the not-for-profit community?
3. What are best practices in the not-for-profit world for incorporating successful entrepreneurs?
4. What personal processes do the entrepreneurs experience in leaving their for-profit and later their non-profit activities?
5. What are the best structures for entrepreneurs to use for their philanthropic activities at various stages in their lives, companies and the evolution of their interests?

This chapter suggests a transition process that requires a parallel shift in the thinking and behavior of the entrepreneur. However, more extensive research is needed to generalize the process. A major conclusion is that for both of the entrepreneurs, their exit from their companies and entry into the not-for-profit or philanthropic world comprises a process with major influences and influencers. A skeletal outline of the stages and influences is captured in Figure 13.1.

These processes have nodes with accompanying 'leverage points' for intervention. The processes can be anticipated, planned for and rehearsed – if the entrepreneur is willing and the mentor skilled. The example of Mr Kauffman, in particular, indicates that appropriate management of relationships can make significant differences in the transition away from the firm into philanthropic activities. Those relationships include the entrepreneur/owner/founder to executive reports and the executive reports to the entrepreneur/owner/founder. Both sets must be considered.

With regard to the philanthropic world, the examples of Mr Kauffman and Mr Morino indicate that successful entrepreneurs can and do bring more than their financial resources to the table. But the process of their becoming involved in broader social issues is not without its difficulties. For example, the initial projects of experiments they undertake may be more costly than anticipated, and perhaps than they need be. The modes the two entrepreneurs in this study used to seek out information, their openness to learning, and the willingness of the not-for-profit community to embrace them, suggest issues that can be managed. In short, the models established by Mr Kauffman and Mr Morino provide insights for entrepreneurs and those who work with them with regard to successful transitions from for-profit to not-for-profit activities.

The examination of these two entrepreneurs' transition to philanthropy indicates that they brought their entrepreneurial skills to the social problems and issues they adopted. They found they had to adapt the formidable skill sets, energy levels and sheer intellectual talents that had driven their success as entrepreneurs. Both approached the social venture venue as a series of projects. They wanted to initiate experiments on the leading edge, with the expectation that there would be 'followers' that would move in behind them to make investments where their first-mover efforts had demonstrated advantages in their approaches to addressing social issues.

REFERENCES

Acs, Zoltan J. (1999), 'The new American evolution', in Zoltan J. Acs (ed.), *Are Small Firms Important*, Boston, MA: Kluwer.

Acs, Zoltan J. and Leon Paul Dana (2001), 'Contrasting two models of wealth redistribution', *Small Business Economics*, 16 (2), 63–72.

Acs, Zoltan J. and Charlie Karlsson (2002), 'Introduction to institutions, entrepreneurship and firm growth: from Sweden to the OECD', *Small Business Economics*, 19 (3), 132 – 165.

Acs, Zoltan J. and Ronnie Phillips (1999), *Entrepreneurship and Philanthropy in the New Gilded Age*, Baltimore, MD: University of Baltimore Press.

Acs, Zoltan J. and Ronnie J. Phillips (2002), 'Entrepreneurship and philanthropy in American capitalism', *Small Business Economics*, 19(3), 189–209.

Blackwood, Amy, Katie L. Roeger and Sarah L. Pettijohn (2012), *The Nonprofit Almanac, 2012*, Washington, DC: Urban Institute Press, available at http://www.urban.org/UploadedPDF/412674-The-Nonprofit-Sector-in-Brief.pdf.

Bork, D. (1996), *Working with Family Businesses: A Guide for Professionals*, San Francisco, CA: Jossey-Bass.

Boschee, Jerr (1995), 'Social entrepreneurship', *Across the Board*, 32(3), 20–24.

Byrne, John A., Julia Cosgrove, Brian Hindo and Adam Dayan (2002), 'The new face of philanthropy: today's donors are more ambitious, get more involved, and demand results', *Business Week*, 3810, 82–86.

Carlson, N. (2000), 'Enlightened investment or excessive intrusion?', *Grantsmanship Center Magazine*, Fall, 21–23.

Dees, J. G. (1998), 'The meaning of "social entrepreneurship"', available at http://www.caseatduke.org/documents/dees_sedef.pdf (accessed April 7, 2008).

Delaney, Dennis R. (2000), 'Client strategies – venture philanthropists: when it comes to charitable contributions, many newly wealthy give more yet expect more from organizations they benefit', *Financial Planning*, June 1, pp. 1–8.

The Economist (1998), 'The gospel of wealth', May 30, available at http://www.economist.com/node/130414.

The Economist (2004), 'Special Report: Doing well and doing good – Philanthropy', 372(8386), 57–59.

Eisenhardt, K. (1989), 'Building theories from case study research', *Academy of Management Review*, 14(4), 532–550.

Fellers, Charles R. (2001), 'Charitable giving with a venture bent', *Venture Capital Journal*, July 1, pp. 1–8.

Glasser, B. and A. Strauss (1967), *The Discovery of Grounded Theory: Strategies for Qualitative Research*, Chicago, IL: Aldine Publishing Company.

Greenfeld, K.T. (2000), 'A new way of giving', *Time Magazine*, July 24, pp. 49–51.

Guba, E.G. (1981), 'Criteria for assessing the trustworthiness of naturalistic inquiries', *Educational Communication and Technology Journal*, 29, 75–92.

Hero, P. deCourcy (2001), 'Giving back the Silicon Valley way: Emerging patterns of a new philanthropy', *New Directions for Philanthropic Renaissance: Understanding Donor Dynamics: The Organizational Side of Charitable Giving*, 32 (Summer): 47–58.

Karoff, H. Peter and Melinda Marble (1998), 'Strategic philanthropy: the concept of the investor/donor', *Trusts & Estates*, 137(7), 3–10.

Kaye, K. (1998), 'Happy landings: the opportunity to fly again', *Family Business Review*, 11(3), 275–280.

Kosminsky, Jay (1997), 'Venture philanthropy a new model for corporate giving', *Fund Raising Management*, 28(6), 28–31.

Letts, Christine, William Dyer and Allen Grossman (1997), 'Virtuous capital: What foundations can learn from venture capitalists', *Harvard Business Review*, March–April, 2–7.

Marx, Karl (1906), *Capital: A Critique of Political Economy, Vol. I. The Process of Capitalist Production*, Chicago, IL: Charles H. Kerr & Co.

McGee, Suzanne (2004), 'Creative giving', *Barron's*, 84(48), 21–25.

Miles, B. and A.M. Huberman (1994), *Qualitative Data Analysis: A Sourcebook of New Methods*, Thousand Oaks, CA: Sage.

Miller, Danny (2003), 'An asymmetry-based view of advantage: towards an attainable sustainability', *Strategic Management Journal*, 24(10), 961–976.

Morse, Jodie (2001), 'Innovators: Charity without the checks', *Time*, 158(20), 80–82.

Passy, Charles (2003), 'Tricks of trade: a philanthropist's giving', *Wall Street Journal* (Eastern edition), August 6, p. D1.

Porter, Michael E. and Mark R. Kramer (1999), 'Philanthropy's new agenda: Creating value', *Harvard Business Review*, November–December, 121–130.

Reis, George R. (1999), 'US philanthropy boosted by high-tech billions', *Fund Raising Management*, 30(6), 3.

Reis, George R. (2000), 'New report examines impact of new economy on philanthropy', *Fund Raising Management*, 31(7), 3.

Savin-Baden, M. and C. Major (2013), *Qualitative Research: The Essential Guide to Theory and Practice*, London: Routledge.

Sonnenfeld, J.A. (1998), *The Hero's Farewell*, New York: Oxford University Press.

Sonnenfeld, J.A. and P.L. Spence (1989), 'The parting patriarch of a family firm', *Family Business Review*, 2(4), 355–375.

Streisand, Betsy (2001), 'The new philanthropy', *US News and World Report*, available at http://www.usnews.com/usnews/issue/010601l/biztech/philanthropy.htm.

Wagner, Lilya (2002), 'The "new" donor: creation or evolution?', *International Journal of Nonprofit and Voluntary Sector Marketing*, 7(4), 343–353.

Yin, R. (2009), *Case Study Research and Design*, 4th edn, Thousand Oaks, CA: Sage Publications.

Index